INUYASHA

VOL. 50

Shonen Sunday Edition

STORY AND ART BY

RUMIKO TAKAHASHI

CONTENTS

Long ago, in the "Warring States" era of Japan's Muromachi period, dog-like half demon Inuyasha attempted to steal the Shikon Jewel—or "Jewel of Four Souls"—from a village. The village priestess, Kikyo, put a stop to his thievery with an enchanted arrow. Pinned to a tree, Inuyasha fell into a deep sleep, while mortally wounded Kikyo took the jewel with her into her funeral pyre. Years passed...

In the present day, Kagome, a Japanese high school girl, is pulled down into a well and transported into the past. There she discovers trapped Inuyasha—and frees him.

When the Shikon Jewel mysteriously reappears, demons attack. In the ensuing battle, the jewel *shatters*!

Now Inuyasha is bound to Kagome with a powerful spell, and the grudging companions must battle to reclaim the shattered shards of the Shikon Jewel to keep them out of evil hands...

LAST VOLUME When Inuyasha defeats Kanna, his sword is restored. Naraku then deploys Kanna as a living grenade! Before she explodes, she reveals that a spark of purity survives inside the Shikon Jewel.

Two bone-hunting demons try to steal Sango's boomerang, Hiraikotsu. The weapon is ruined and Sango is left in critical condition. A demon sage advises her to hop into a demon-infested urn to fight for her life! Sango obeys and is ejected from the urn with a restored Hiraikotsu.

Then, a mysterious, eyeless boy approaches Sesshomaru claiming to know a secret

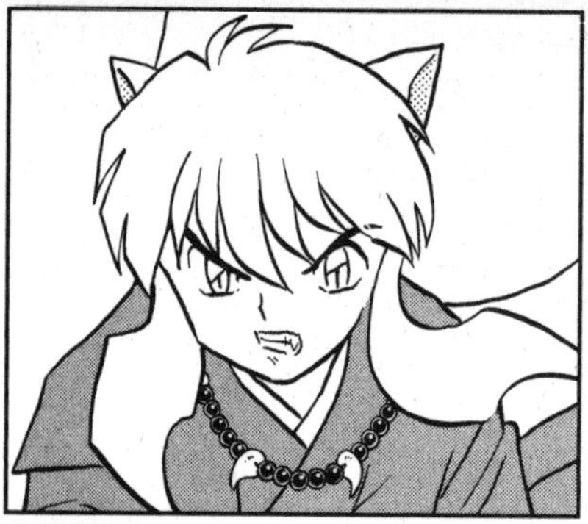

INUYASHA
Half-demon hybrid, son of a human mother and demon father. His necklace is enchanted, allowing Kagome to control him with a word.

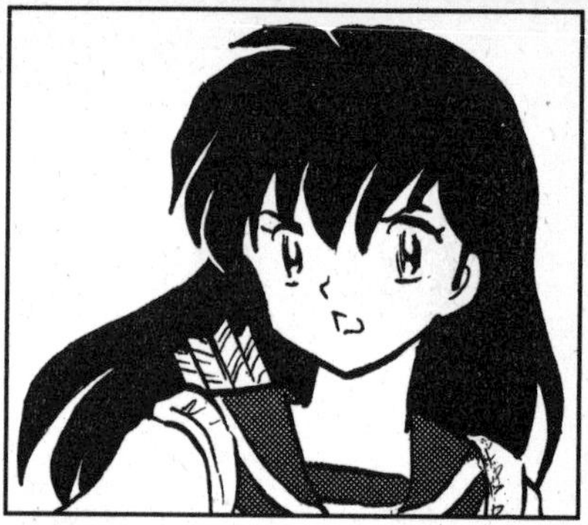

KAGOME
Modern-day Japanese schoolgirl who can travel back and forth between the past and present through an enchanted well.

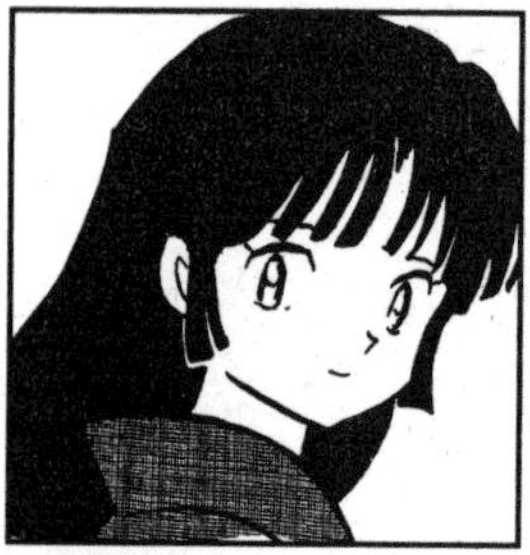

SANGO
A demon slayer from the village where the Shikon Jewel originated.

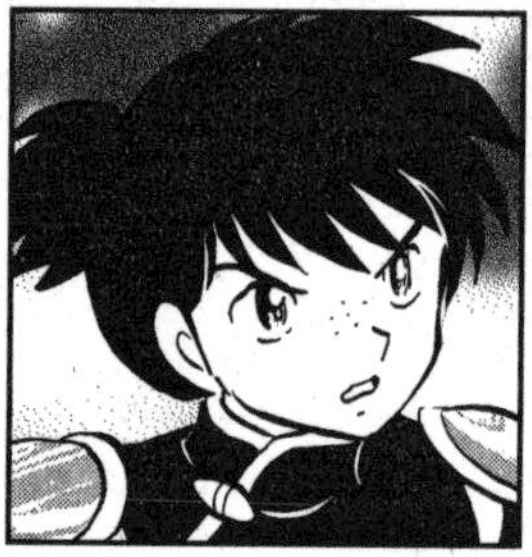

KOHAKU
Naraku controlled Kohaku and used him as a puppet. Kohaku is trying to redeem himself by helping Kikyo and Sesshomaru.

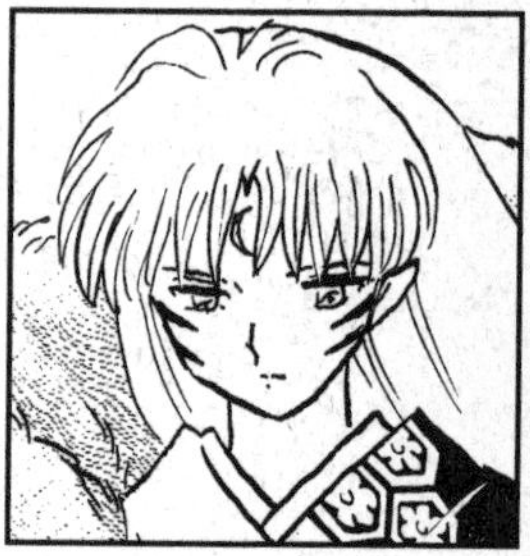

SESSHOMARU
Inuyasha's completely demon half brother. Sesshomaru covets the sword left to Inuyasha by their demon father.

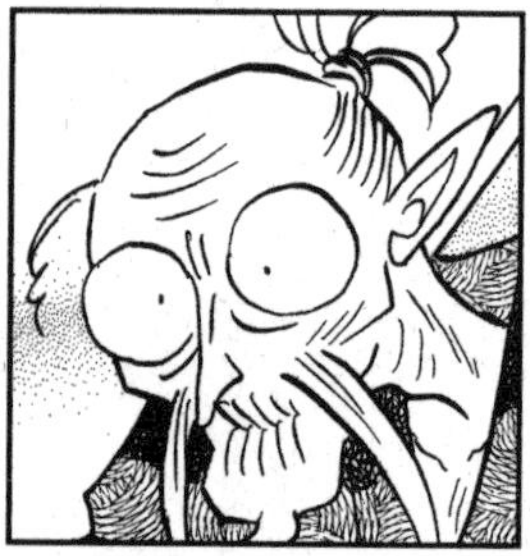

TOTOSAI
The fire-breathing old blacksmith who forged Inuyasha's blade Tetsusaiga and Sesshomaru's blade Tenseiga.

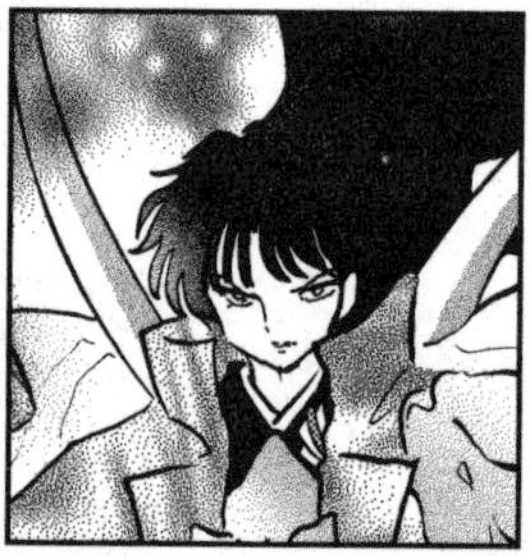

NARAKU
Enigmatic demon mastermind behind the miseries of nearly everyone in the story. He has the power to create multiple incarnations of himself from his body.

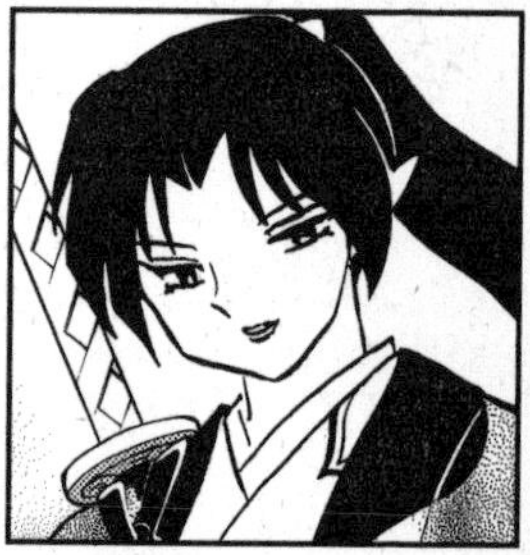

BYAKUYA
A powerful sorcerer and master of illusions created by Naraku.

SCROLL 1

A COMPLETE MEIDO

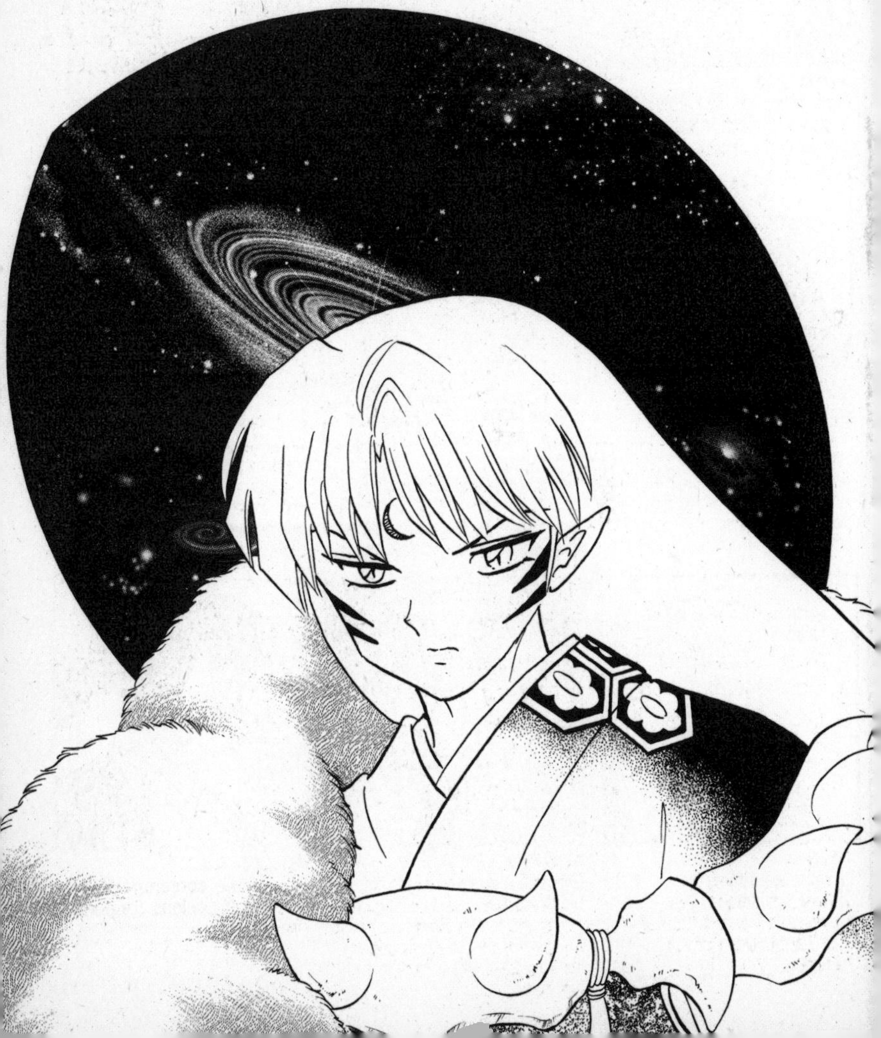

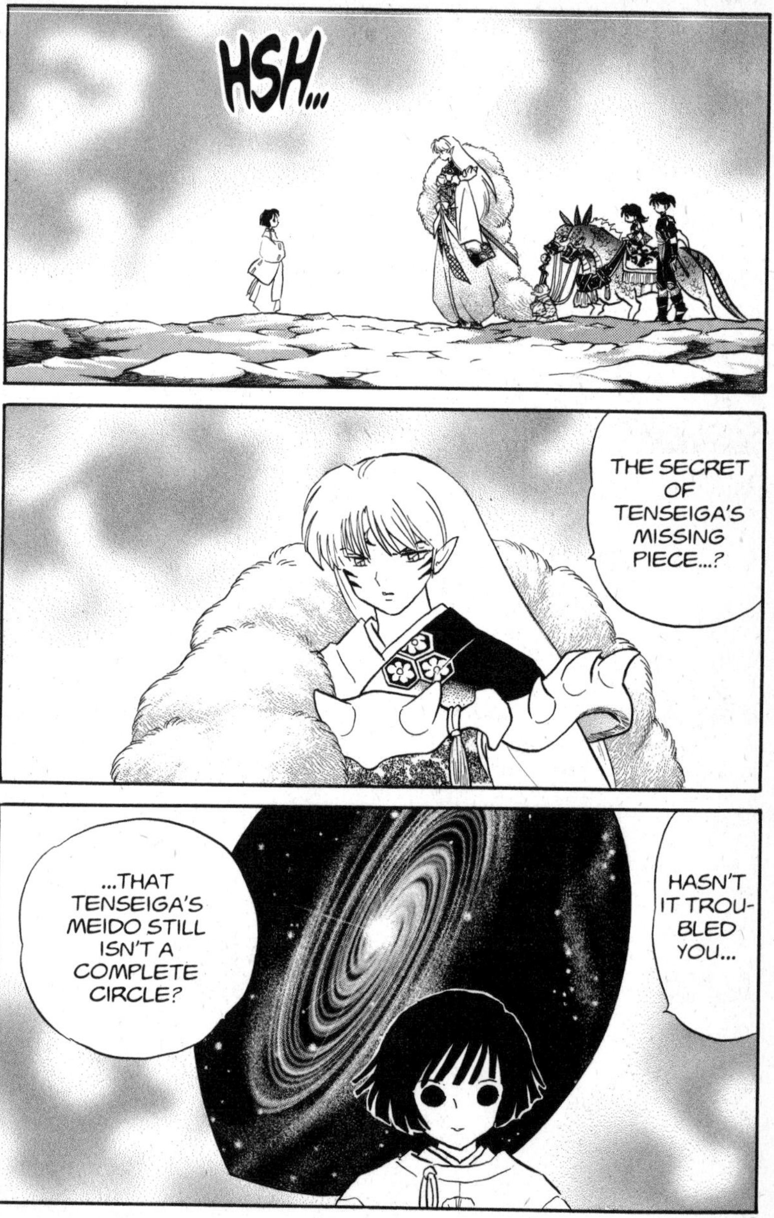
HSH...
THE SECRET OF TENSEIGA'S MISSING PIECE...?
HASN'T IT TROUBLED YOU...
...THAT TENSEIGA'S MEIDO STILL ISN'T A COMPLETE CIRCLE?

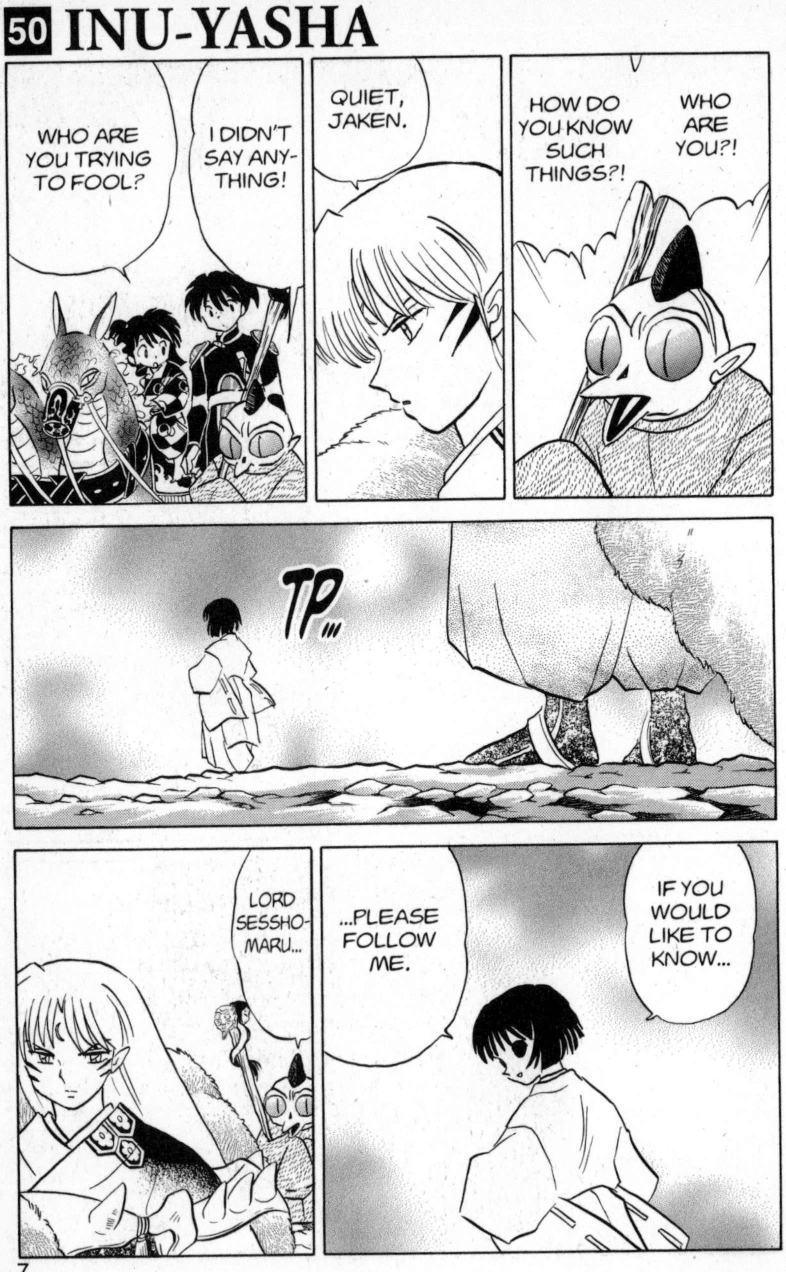
WHO ARE YOU?!
HOW DO YOU KNOW SUCH THINGS?!
QUIET, JAKEN.
I DIDN'T SAY ANY-THING!
WHO ARE YOU TRYING TO FOOL?
TP...
IF YOU WOULD LIKE TO KNOW...
...PLEASE FOLLOW ME.
LORD SESSHO-MARU...

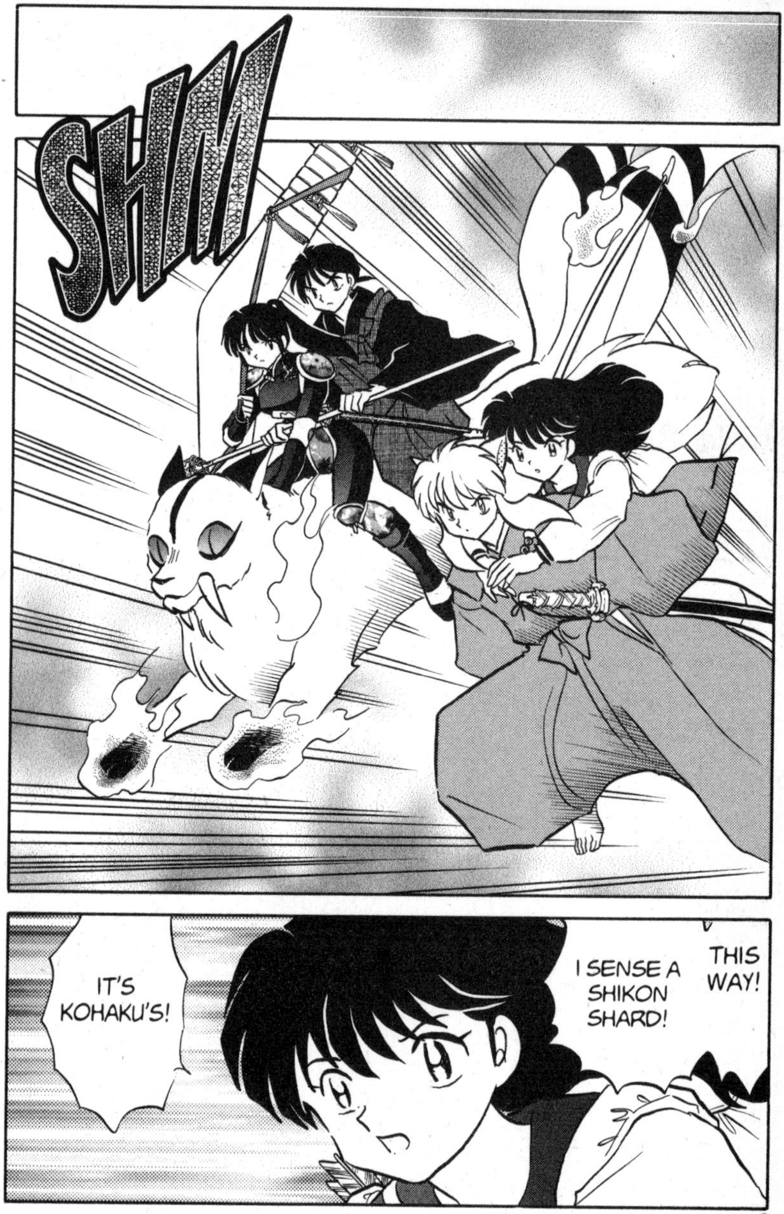
SHIN
THIS WAY!
I SENSE A SHIKON SHARD!
IT'S KOHAKU'S!

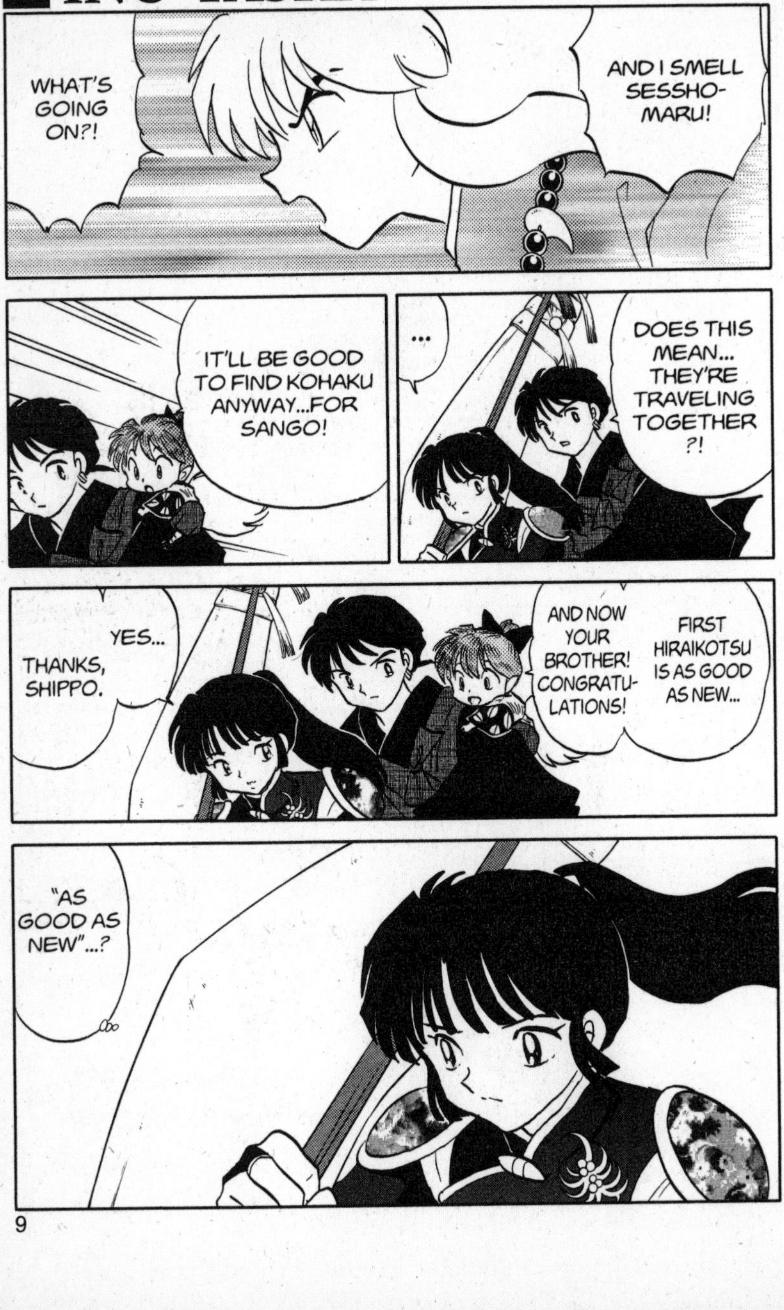
AND I SMELL SESSHOMARU!
WHAT'S GOING ON?!
DOES THIS MEAN... THEY'RE TRAVELING TOGETHER?!
...
IT'LL BE GOOD TO FIND KOHAKU ANYWAY...FOR SANGO!
FIRST HIRAIKOTSU IS AS GOOD AS NEW...
AND NOW YOUR BROTHER! CONGRATULATIONS!
YES...
THANKS, SHIPPO.
"AS GOOD AS NEW"...?

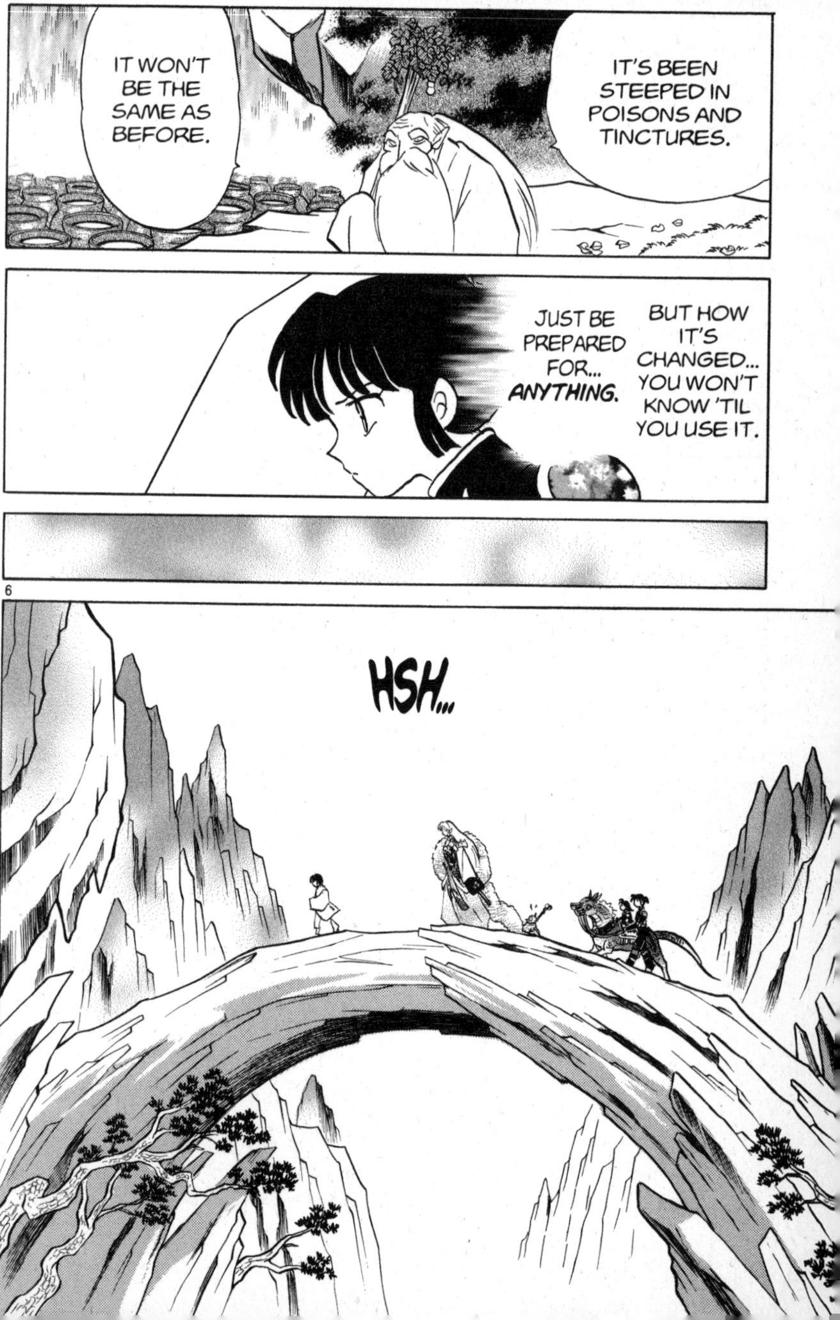
IT'S BEEN STEEPED IN POISONS AND TINCTURES.
IT WON'T BE THE SAME AS BEFORE.
BUT HOW IT'S CHANGED... YOU WON'T KNOW 'TIL YOU USE IT.
JUST BE PREPARED FOR... ANYTHING.
HSH...

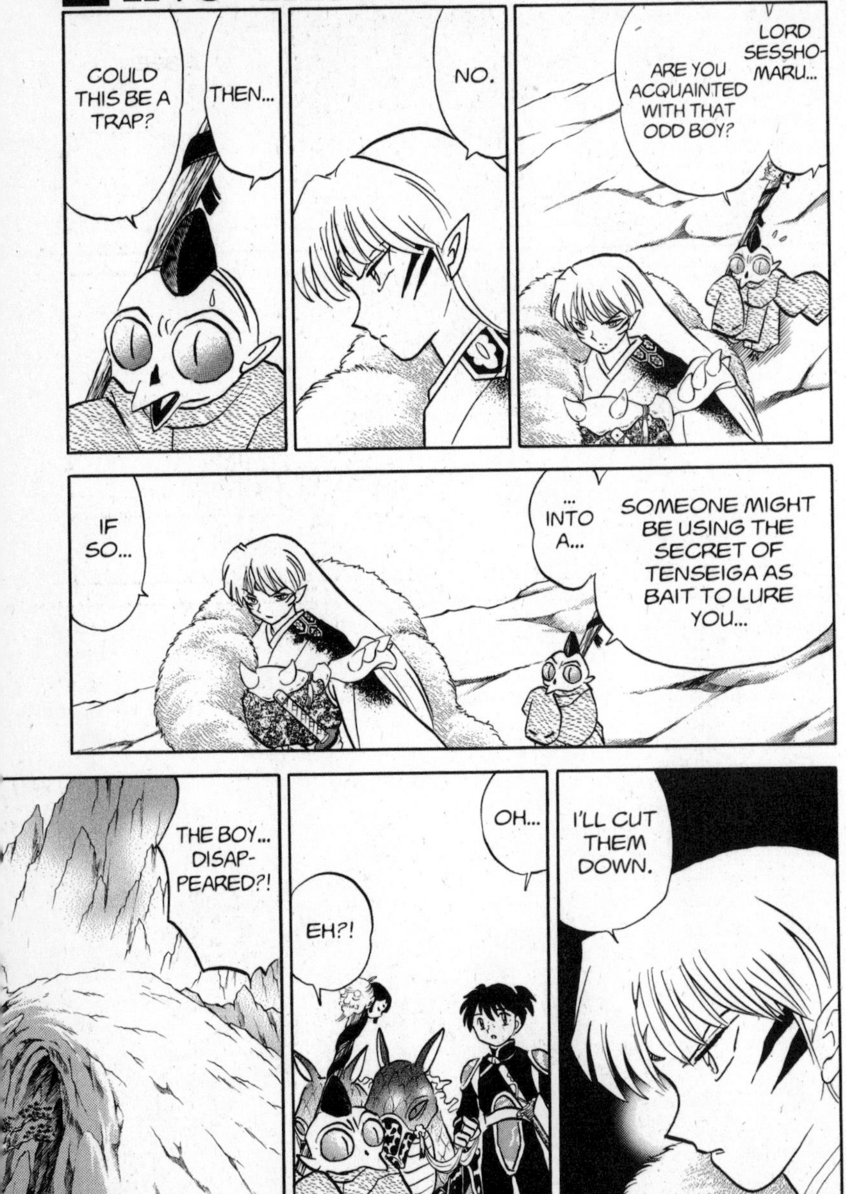
LORD SESSHO-MARU...
ARE YOU ACQUAINTED WITH THAT ODD BOY?
NO.
THEN...
COULD THIS BE A TRAP?
SOMEONE MIGHT BE USING THE SECRET OF TENSEIGA AS BAIT TO LURE YOU...
... INTO A...
IF SO...
I'LL CUT THEM DOWN.
OH...
EH?!
THE BOY... DISAP-PEARED?!

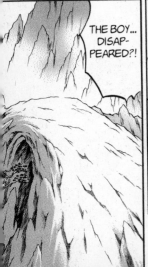

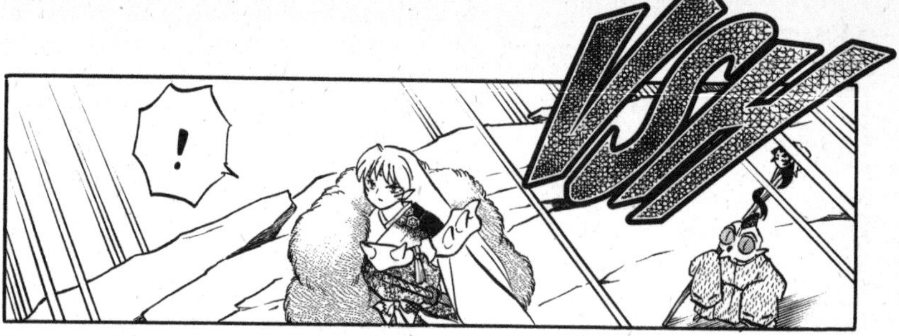
VSH
!
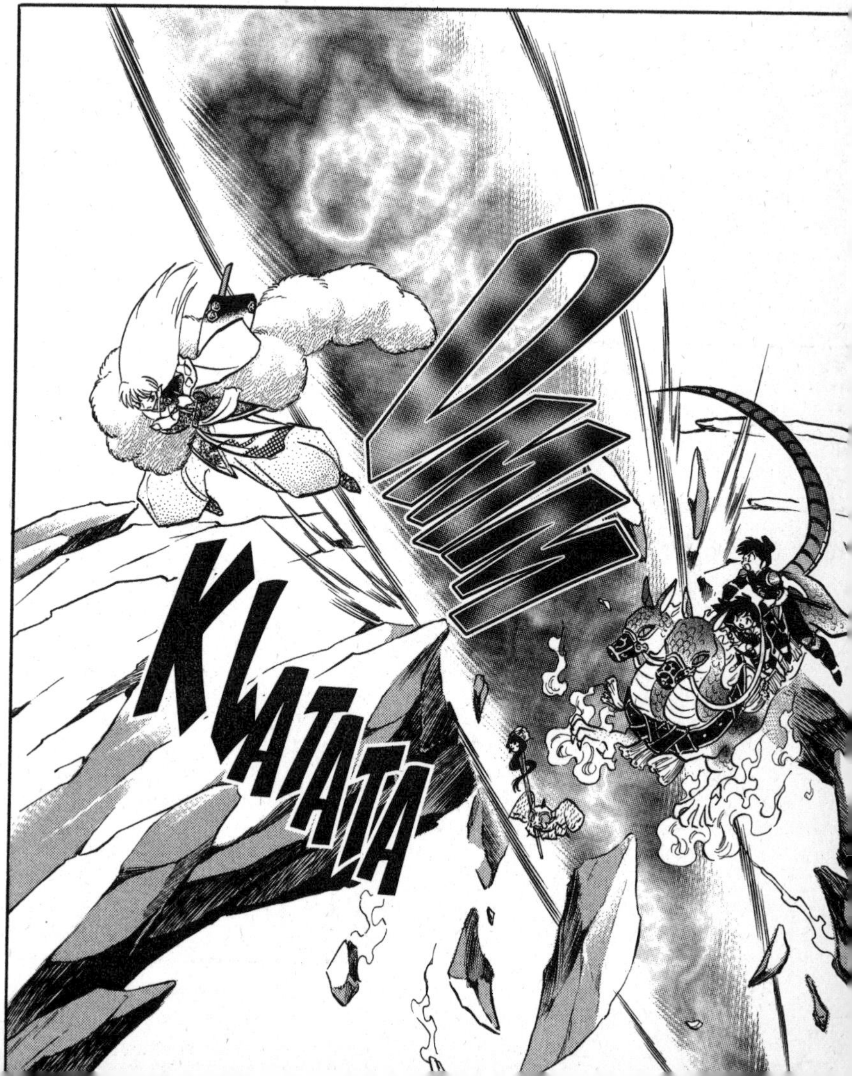
KWATATA

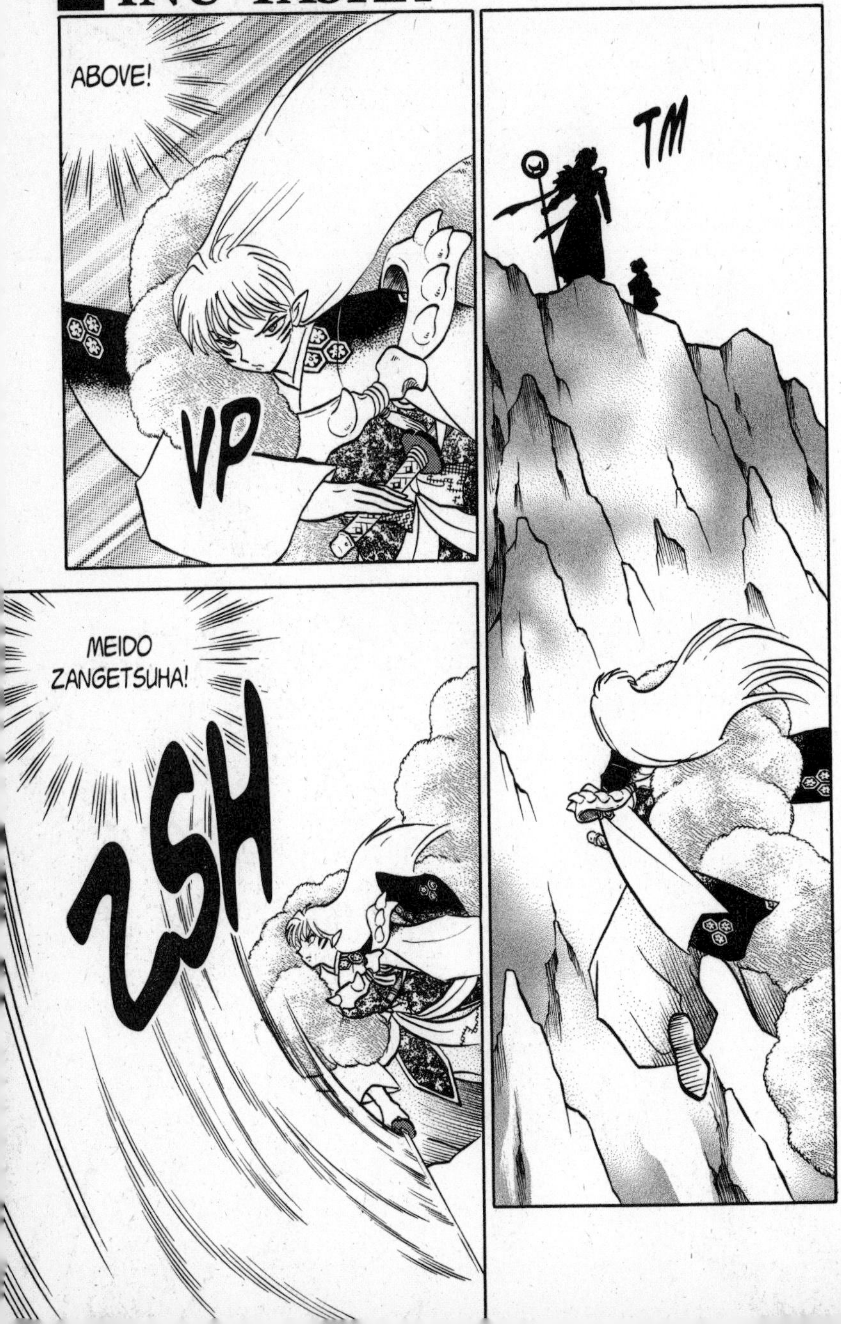
TM
ABOVE!
VP
MEIDO ZANGETSUHA!
ZSH

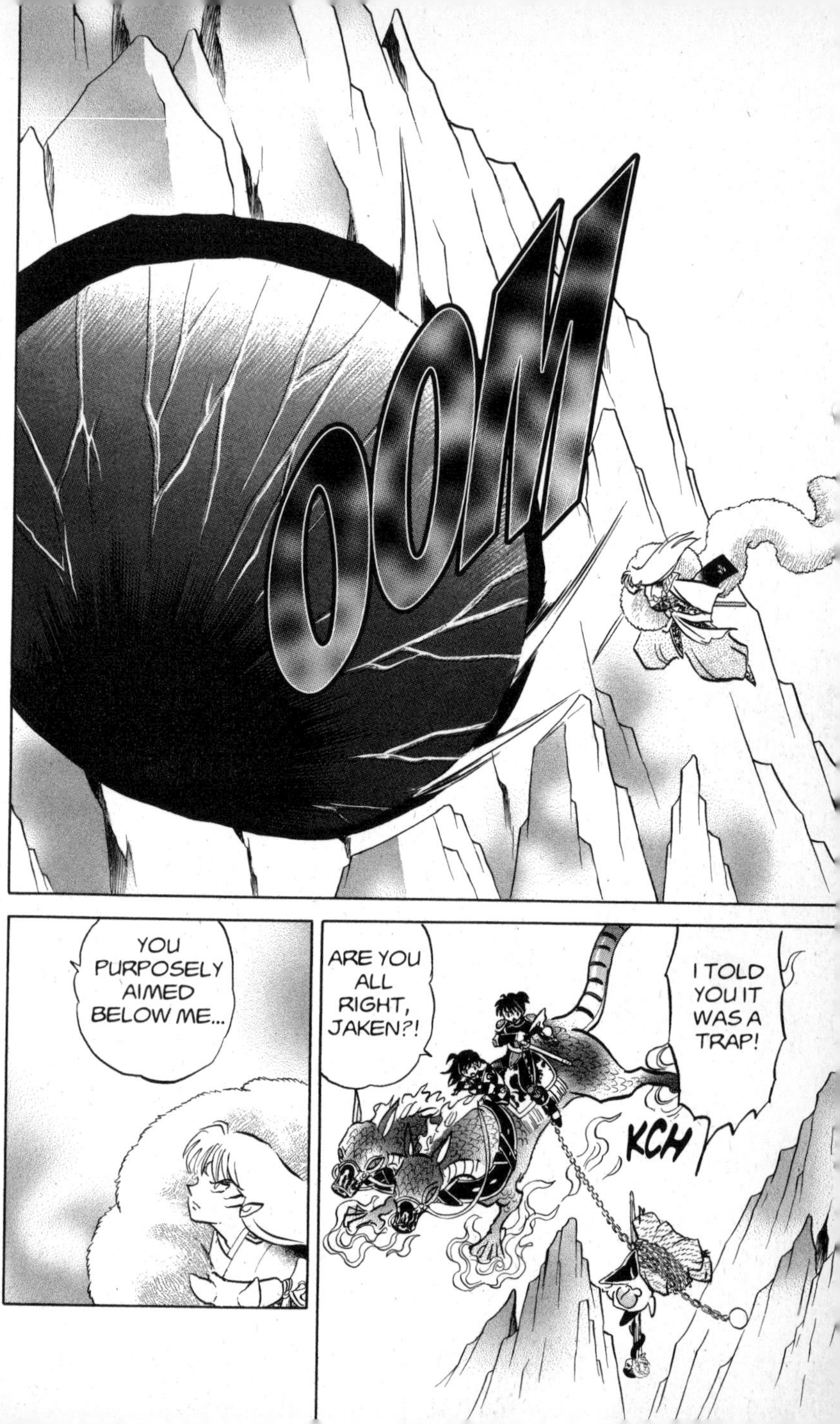
OOM
I TOLD YOU IT WAS A TRAP!
ARE YOU ALL RIGHT, JAKEN?!
KCH
YOU PURPOSELY AIMED BELOW ME...

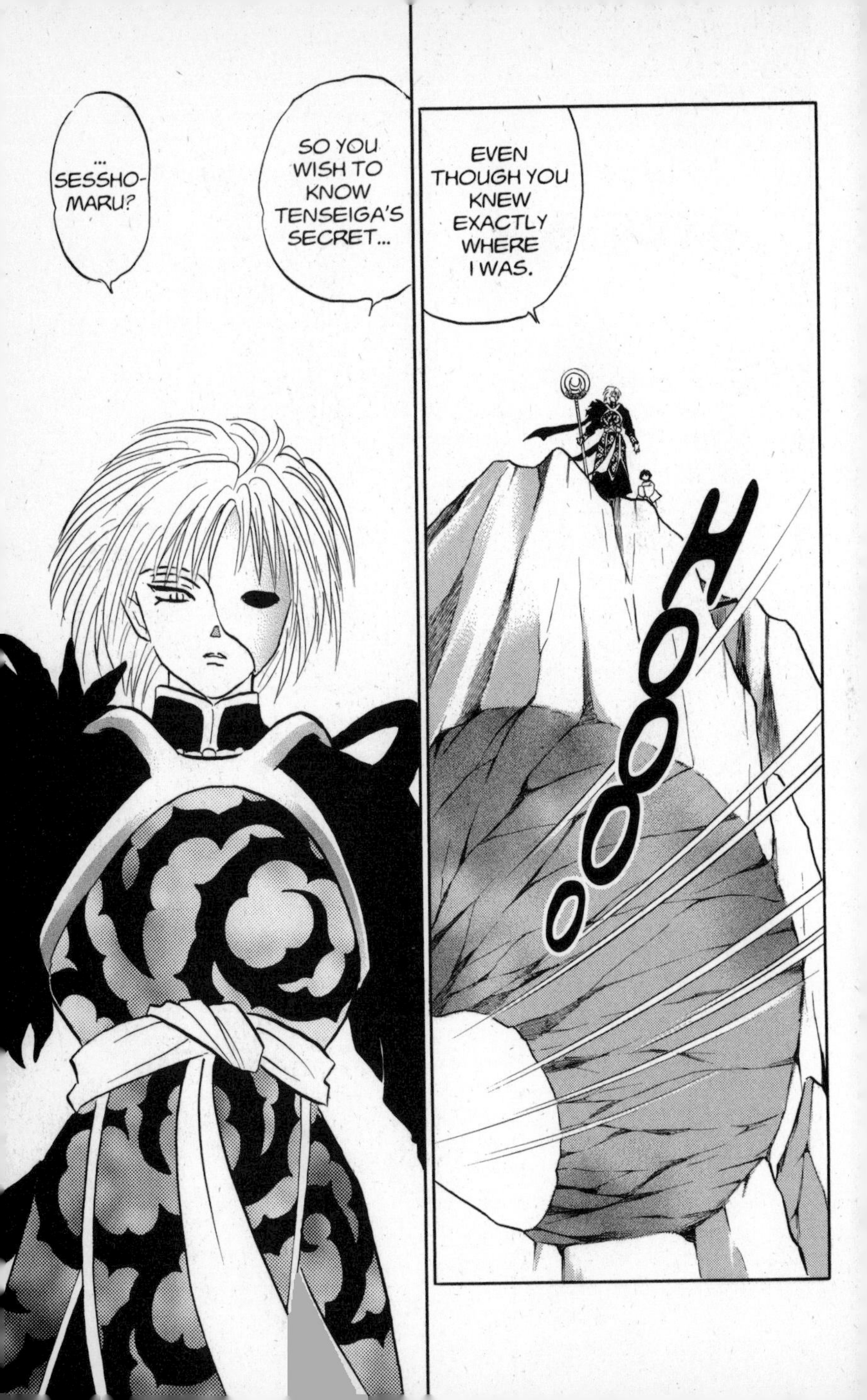
EVEN THOUGH YOU KNEW EXACTLY WHERE I WAS.
HOOOOO
SO YOU WISH TO KNOW TENSEIGA'S SECRET...
...SESSHO-MARU?

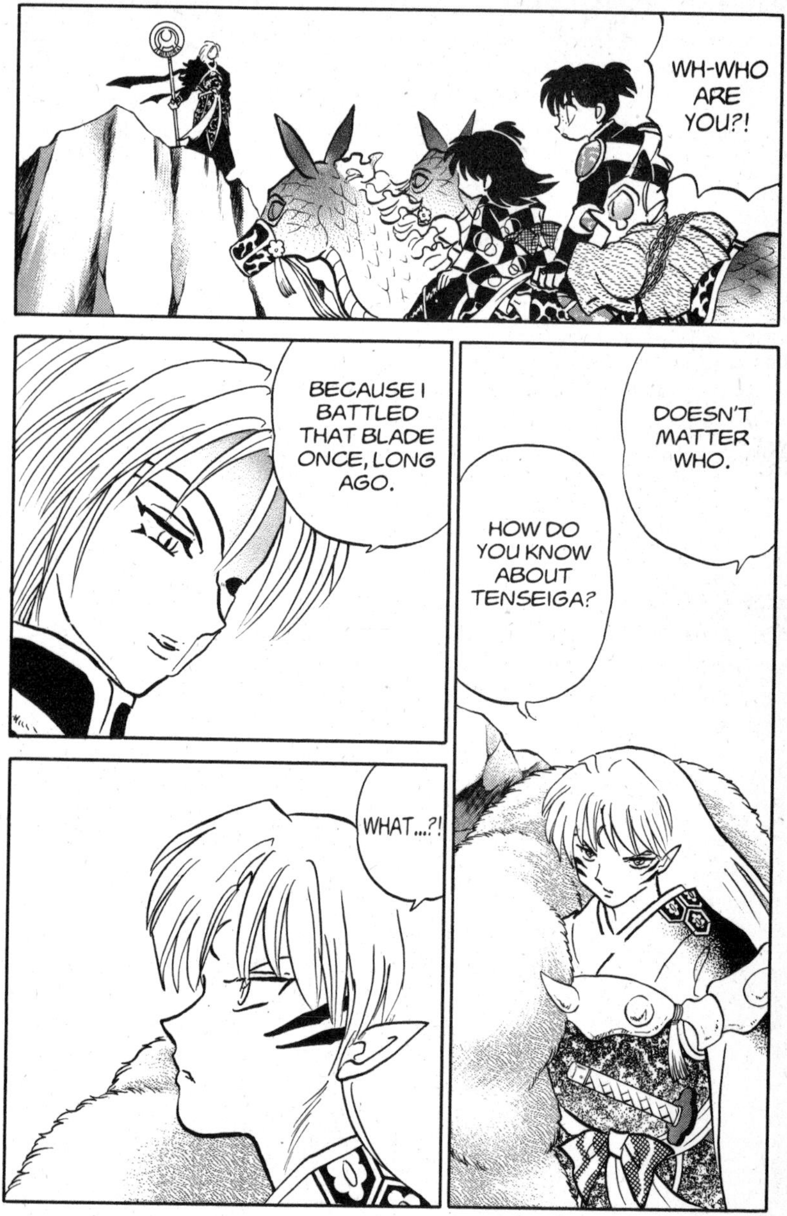
WH-WHO ARE YOU?!
DOESN'T MATTER WHO.
HOW DO YOU KNOW ABOUT TENSEIGA?
BECAUSE I BATTLED THAT BLADE ONCE, LONG AGO.
WHAT...?!

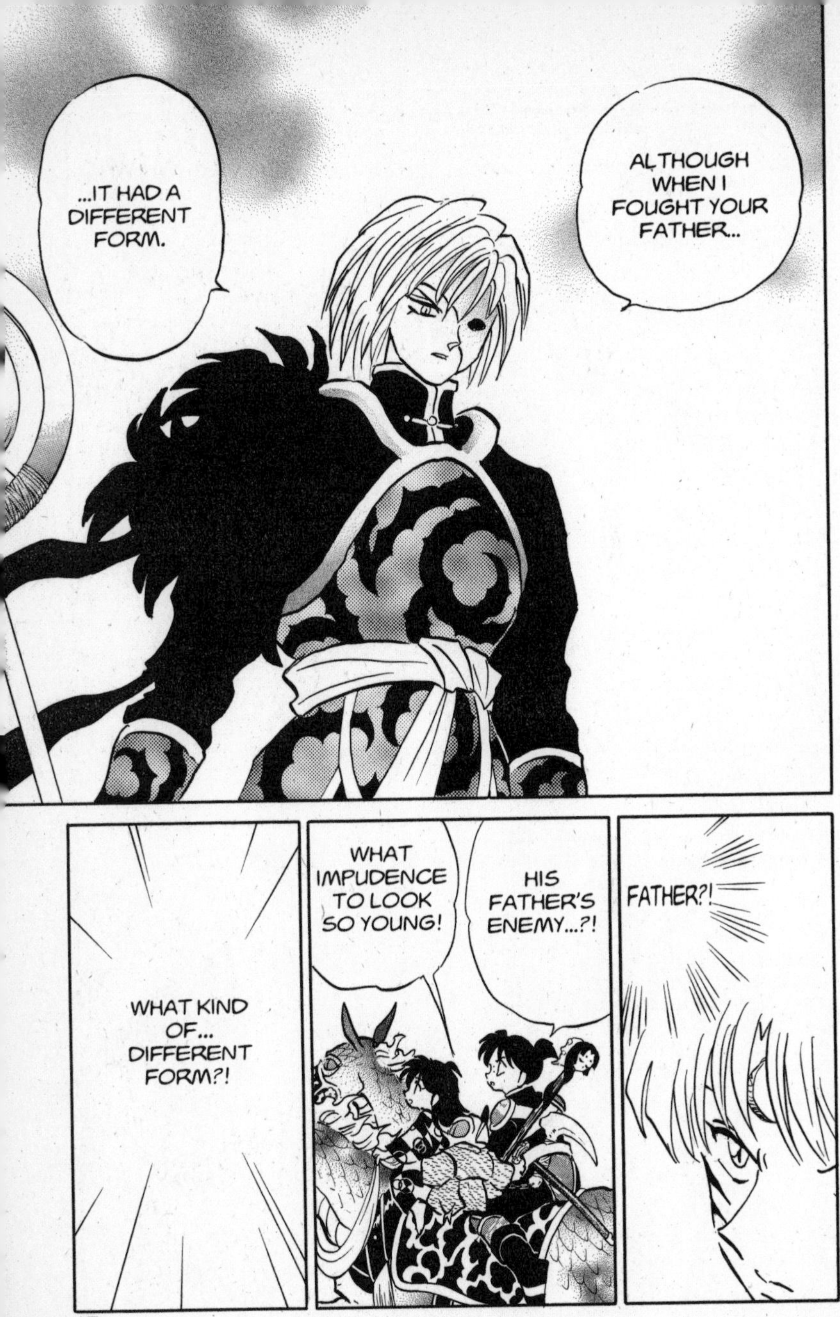
ALTHOUGH WHEN I FOUGHT YOUR FATHER...
...IT HAD A DIFFERENT FORM.
FATHER?!
HIS FATHER'S ENEMY...?!
WHAT IMPUDENCE TO LOOK SO YOUNG!
WHAT KIND OF... DIFFERENT FORM?!

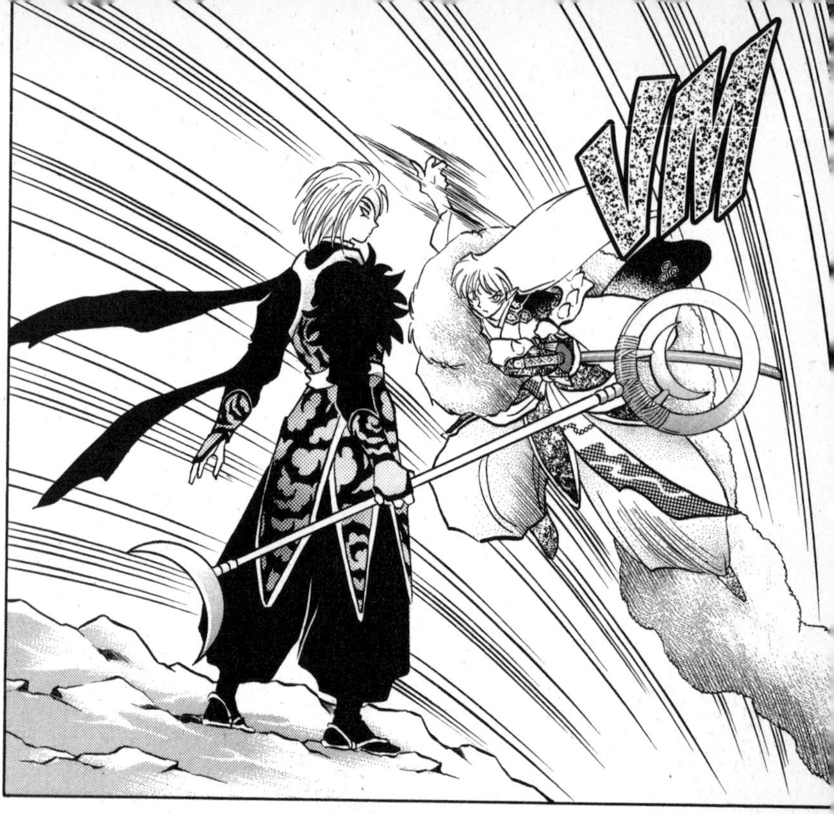
VM

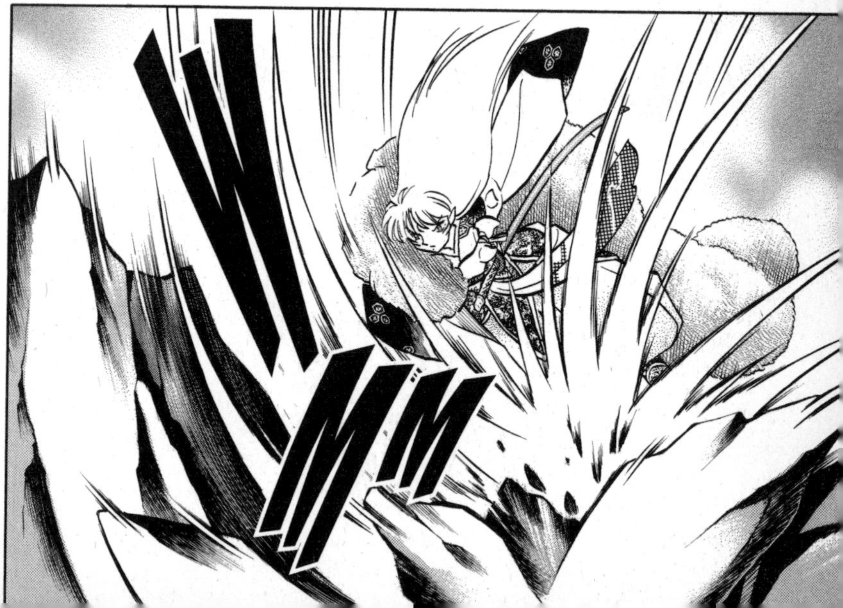
WMM

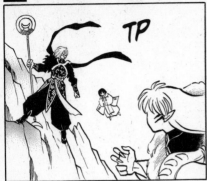

KBOOM
TP
HOPING TO DEFEAT ME...
...WITHOUT WIELDING YOUR BLADE?
NEVER MOCK SHISHINKI!
VSH

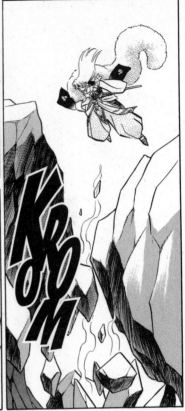

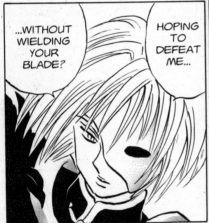

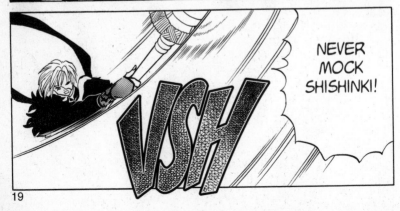

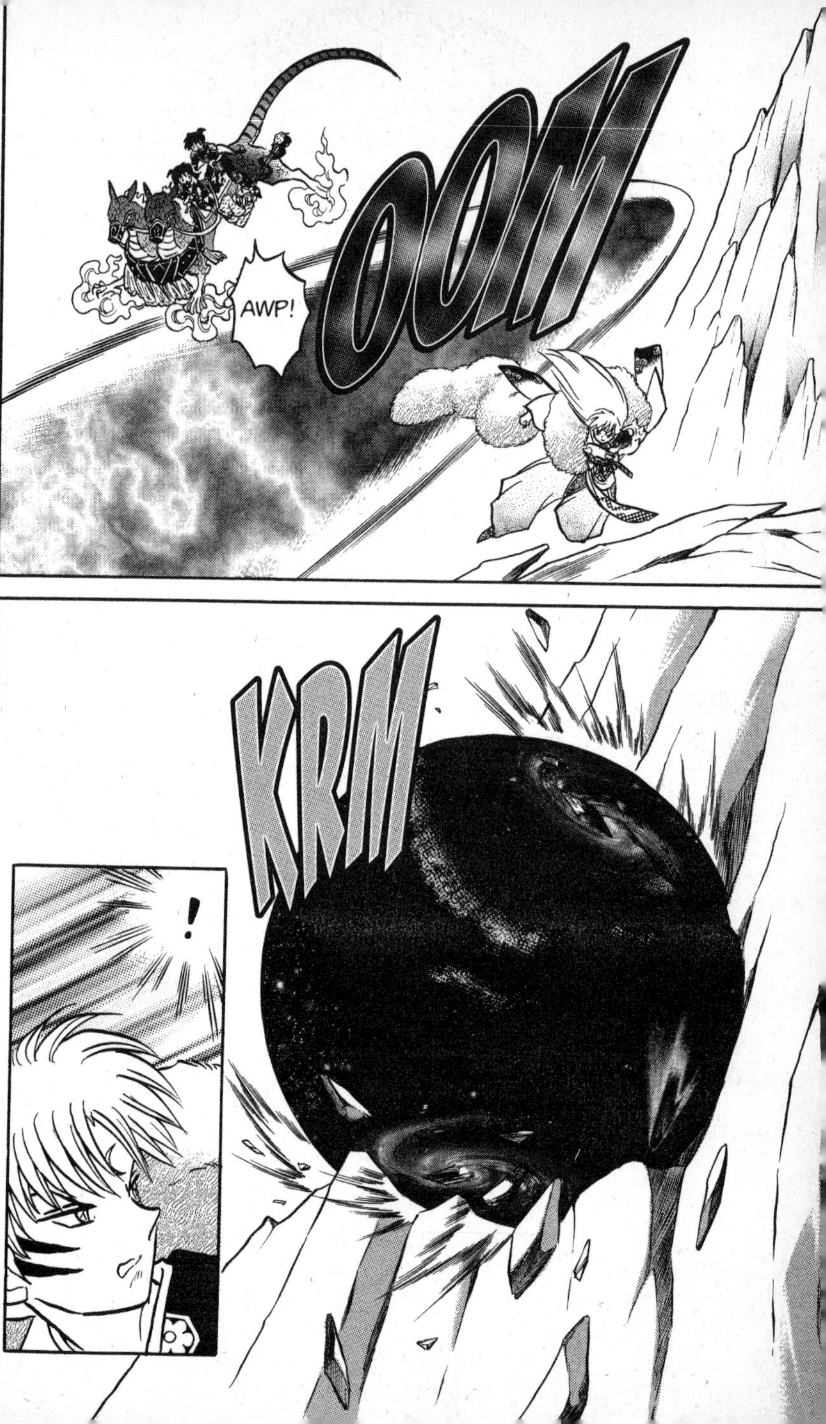
OOM
AWP!
KRM
!

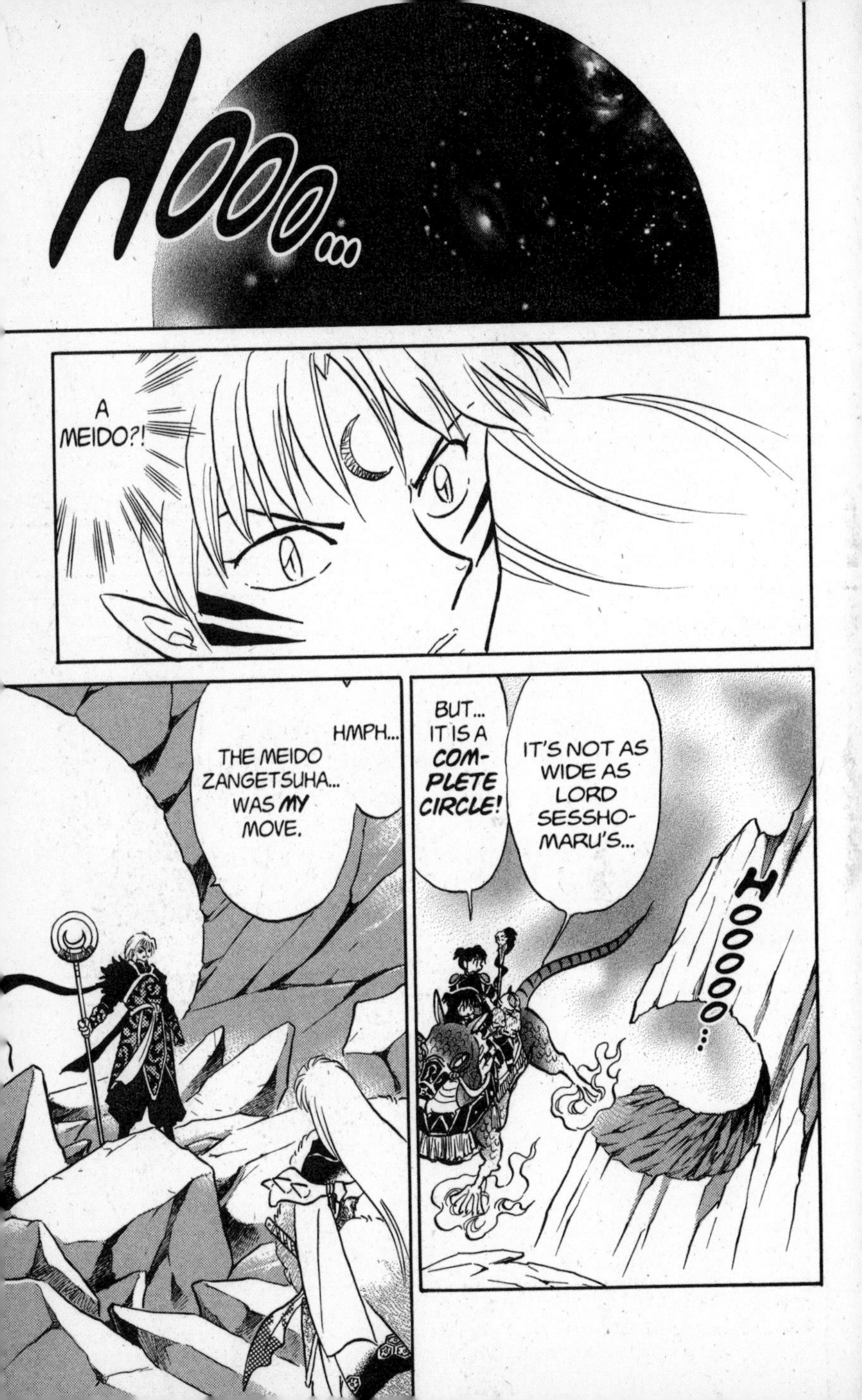
HOOOO...
A MEIDO?!
IT'S NOT AS WIDE AS LORD SESSHO-MARU'S...
BUT... IT IS A COMPLETE CIRCLE!
HOOOOOO...
HMPH...
THE MEIDO ZANGETSUHA... WAS MY MOVE.

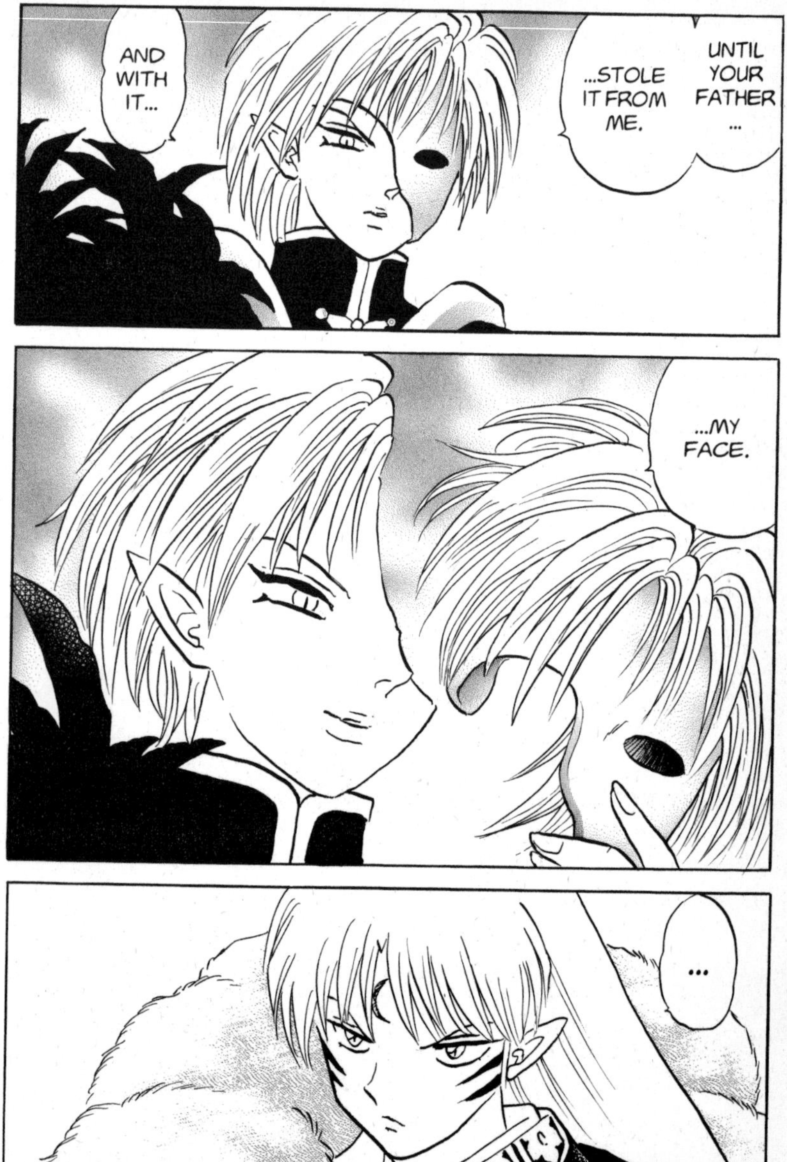
UNTIL YOUR FATHER ...
...STOLE IT FROM ME.
AND WITH IT...
...MY FACE.
...

SCROLL 2

TENSEIGA'S SECRET

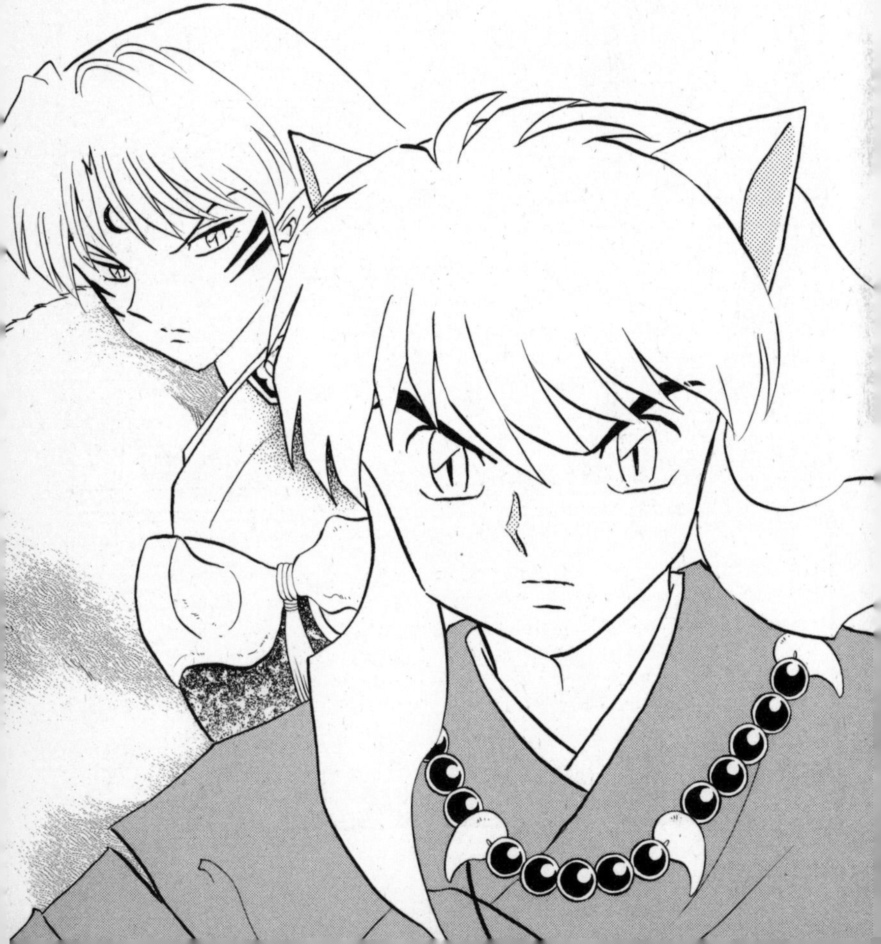

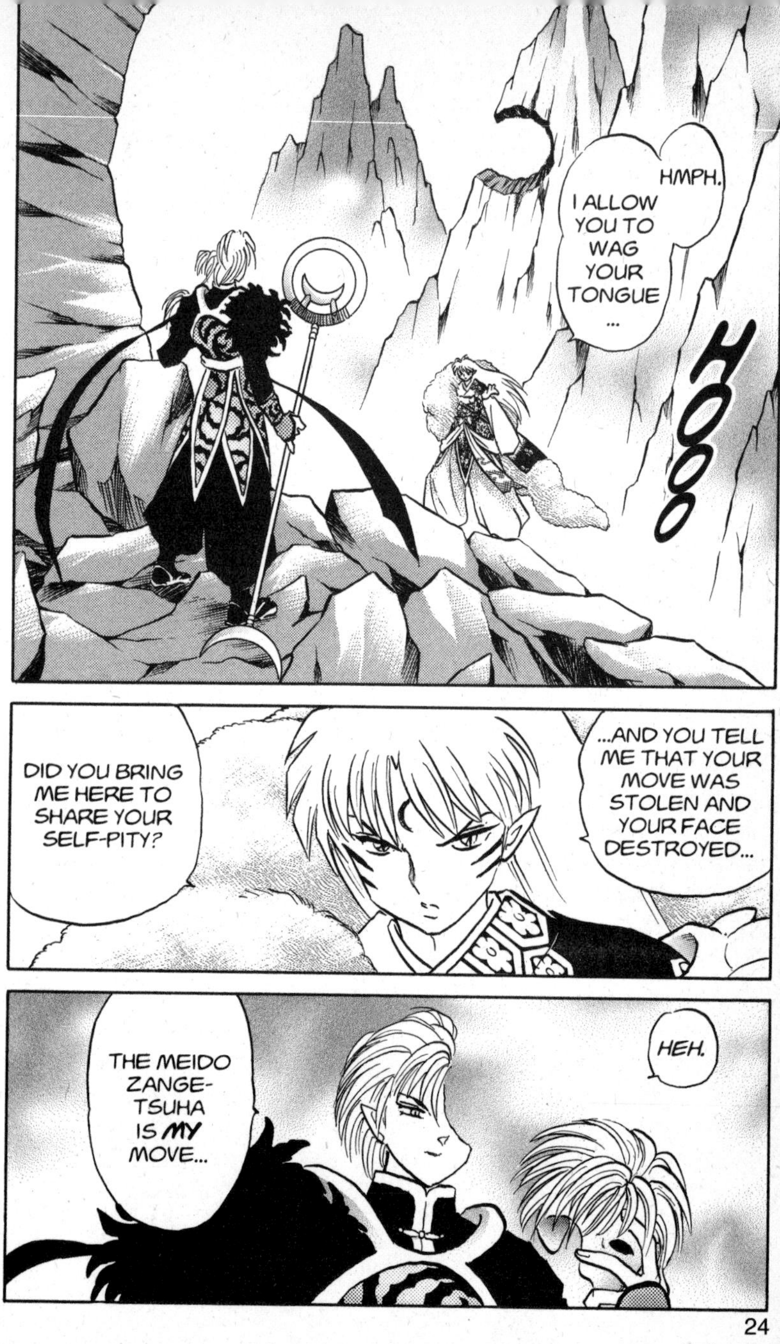
HMPH. I ALLOW YOU TO WAG YOUR TONGUE ...
HOOOO
...AND YOU TELL ME THAT YOUR MOVE WAS STOLEN AND YOUR FACE DESTROYED...
DID YOU BRING ME HERE TO SHARE YOUR SELF-PITY?
HEH.
THE MEIDO ZANGE-TSUHA IS MY MOVE...

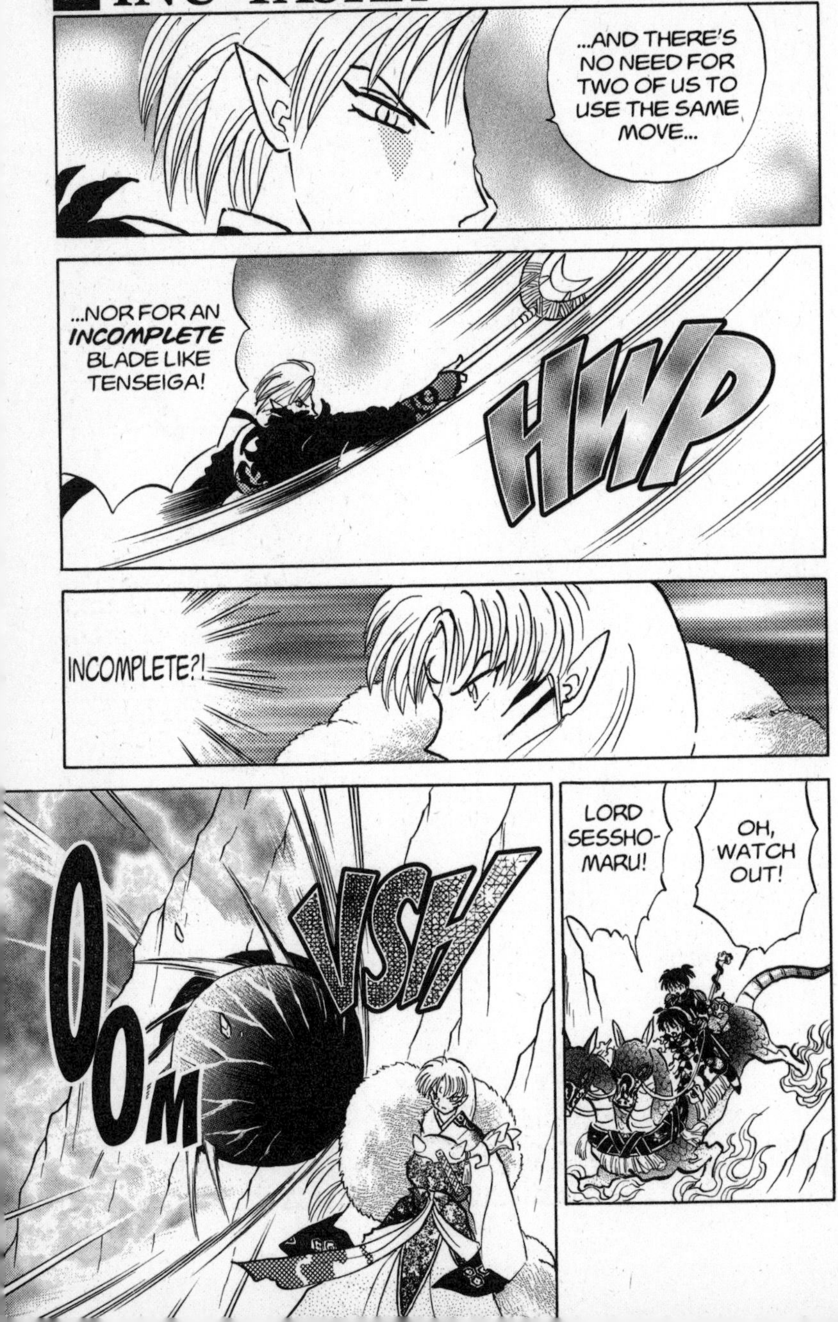
...AND THERE'S NO NEED FOR TWO OF US TO USE THE SAME MOVE...
...NOR FOR AN *INCOMPLETE* BLADE LIKE TENSEIGA!
HWP
INCOMPLETE?!
OH, WATCH OUT!
LORD SESSHO-MARU!
VSH
OOOM

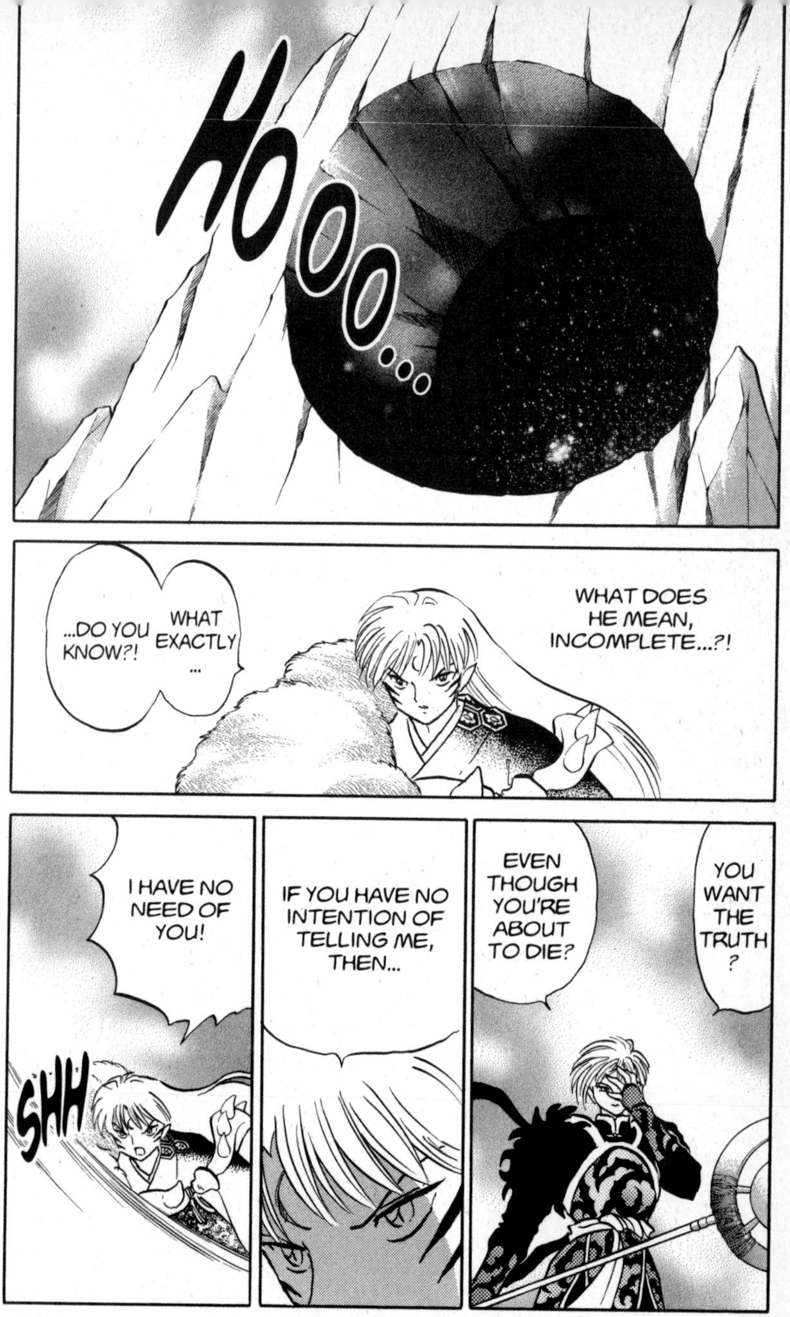
HOOOO...
WHAT DOES HE MEAN, INCOMPLETE...?!
WHAT EXACTLY ... ...DO YOU KNOW?!
YOU WANT THE TRUTH?
EVEN THOUGH YOU'RE ABOUT TO DIE?
IF YOU HAVE NO INTENTION OF TELLING ME, THEN...
I HAVE NO NEED OF YOU!
SHH

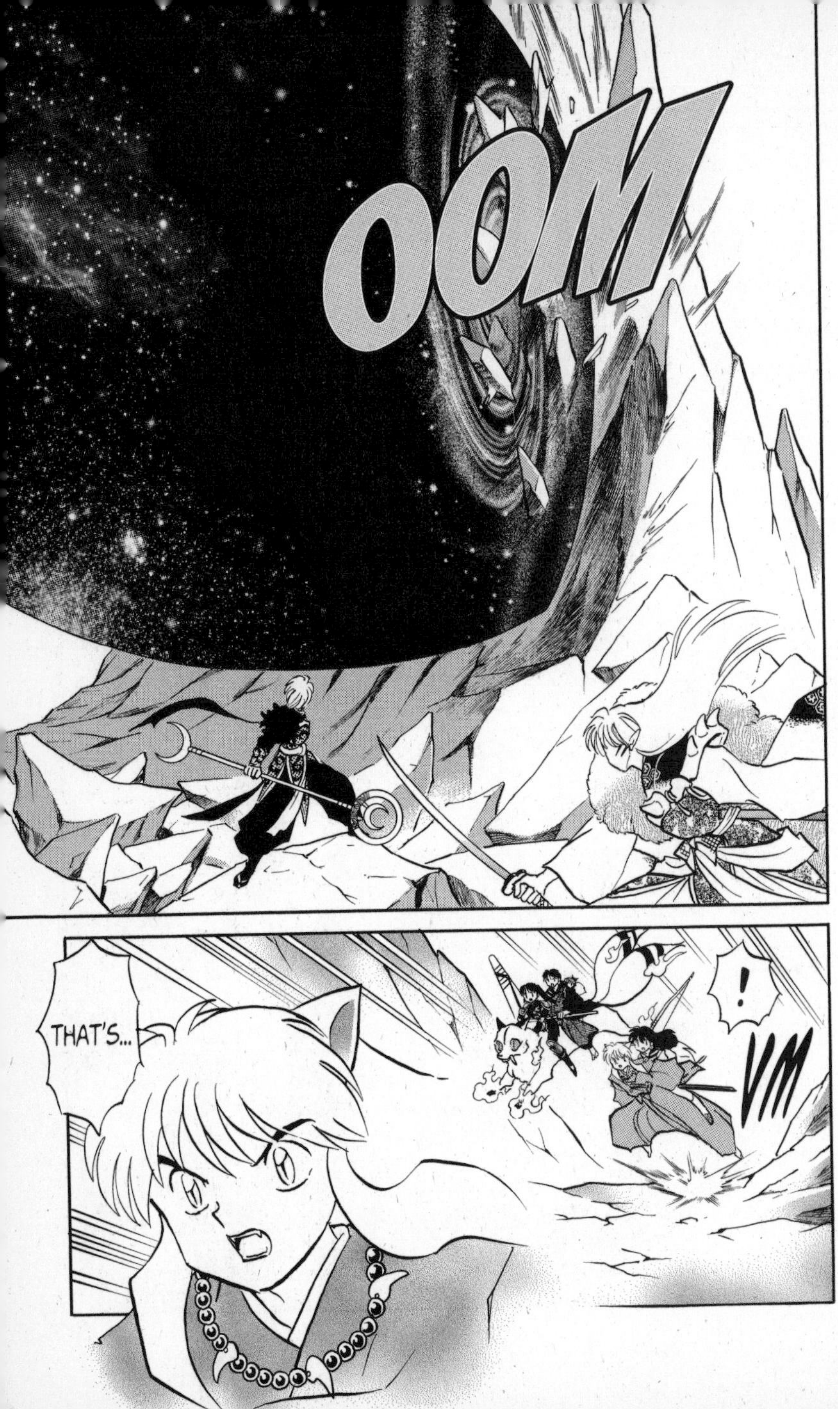
OOM
!
VM
THAT'S...

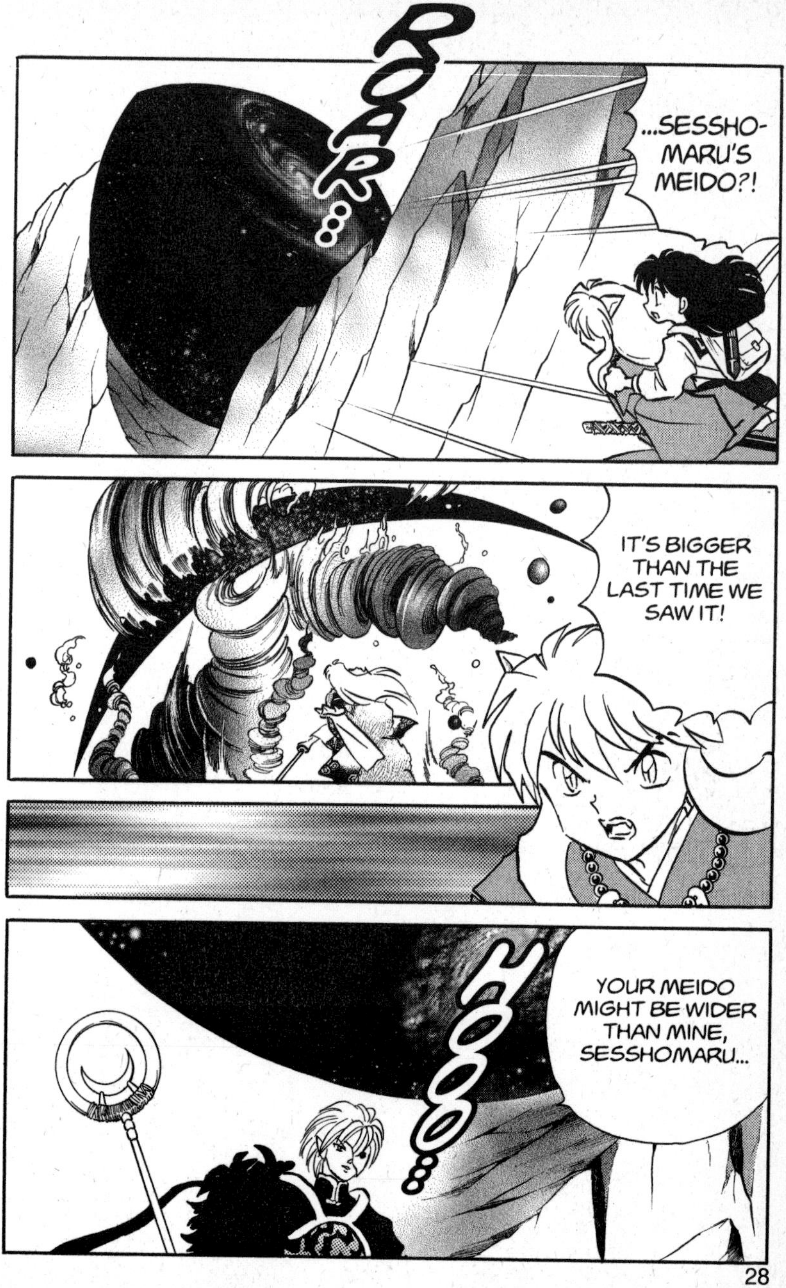
...SESSHO-MARU'S MEIDO?!
ROAR...
IT'S BIGGER THAN THE LAST TIME WE SAW IT!
YOUR MEIDO MIGHT BE WIDER THAN MINE, SESSHOMARU...
HOOOO...

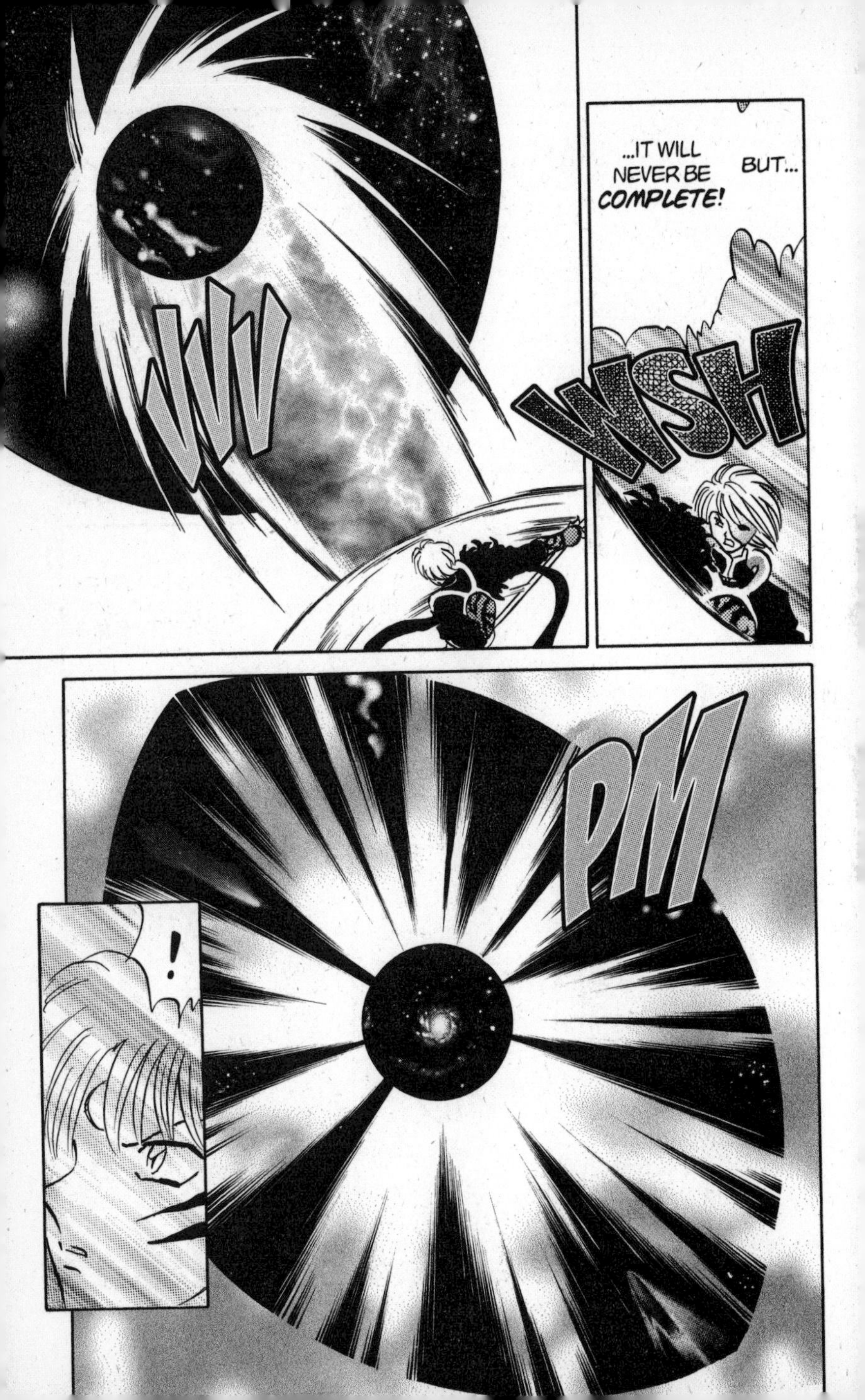
BUT...
...IT WILL NEVER BE COMPLETE!
WSH
JWW
PM
!

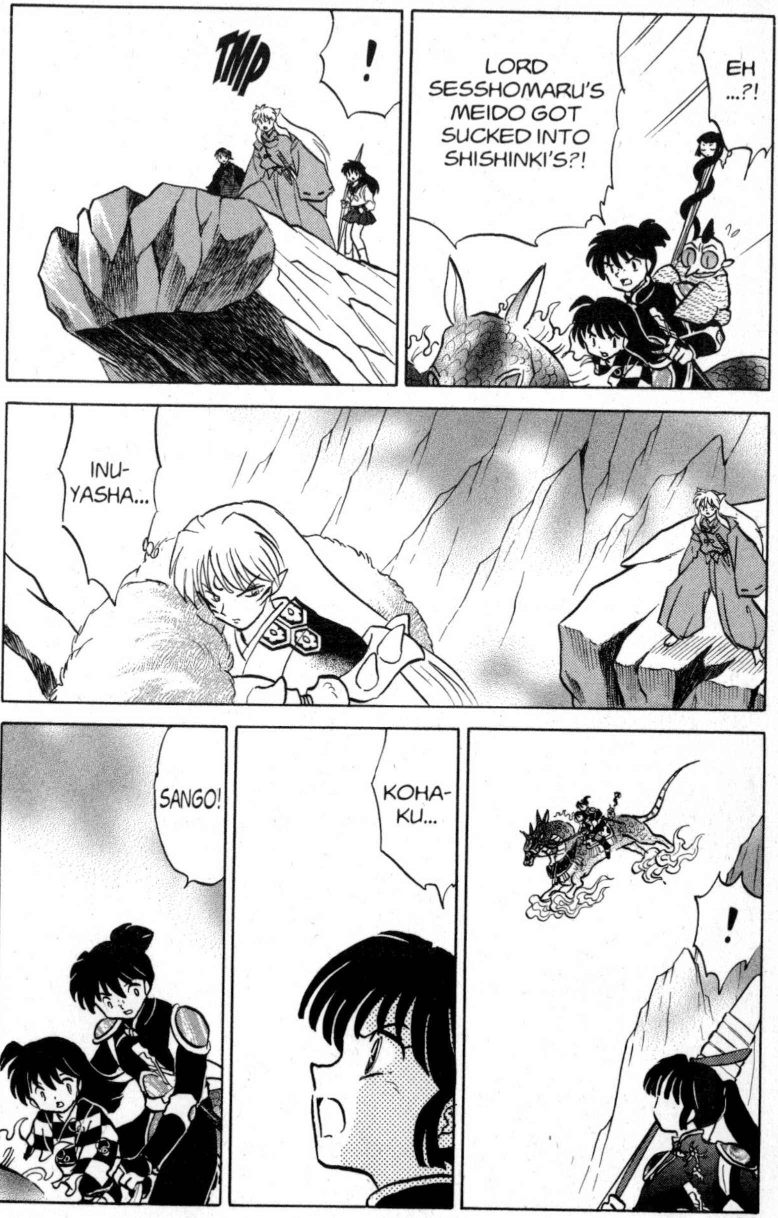
EH ...?!
LORD SESSHOMARU'S MEIDO GOT SUCKED INTO SHISHINKI'S?!
!
TMP
INU-YASHA...
!
KOHA-KU...
SANGO!

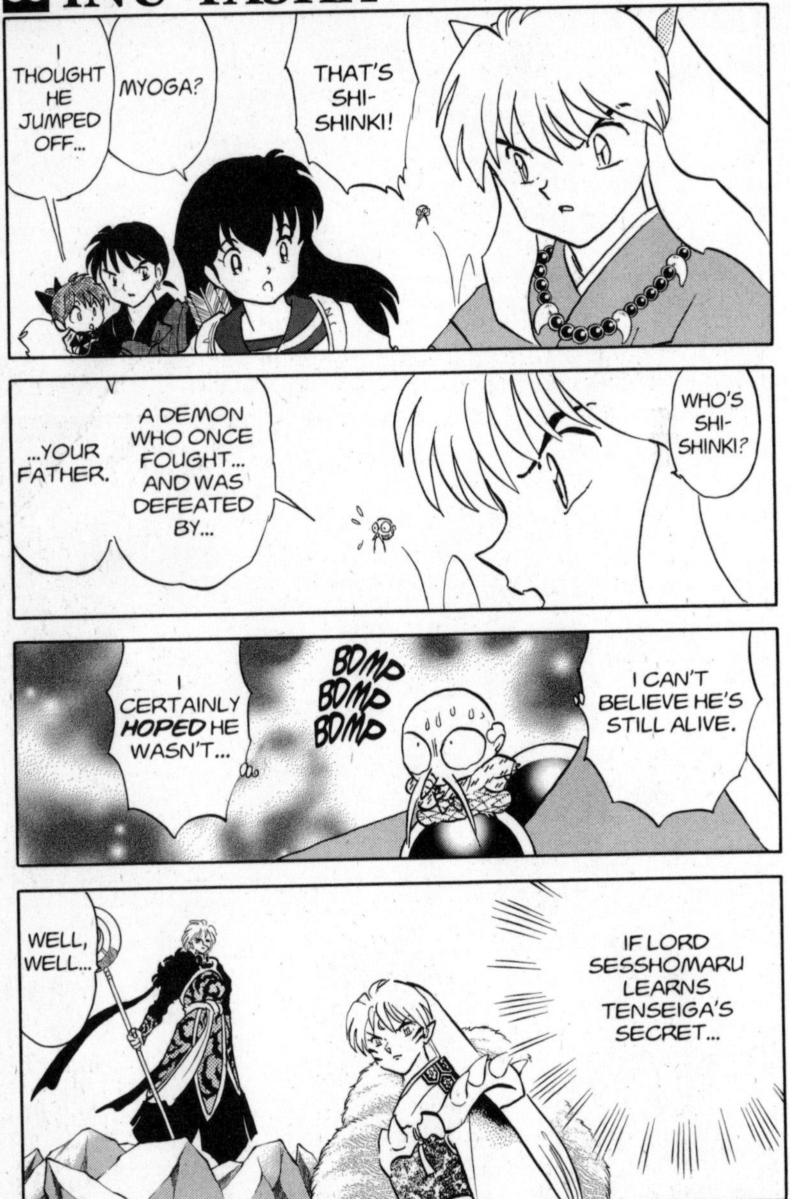
THAT'S SHI-SHINKI!
MYOGA?
I THOUGHT HE JUMPED OFF...
WHO'S SHI-SHINKI?
A DEMON WHO ONCE FOUGHT... AND WAS DEFEATED BY...
...YOUR FATHER.
I CAN'T BELIEVE HE'S STILL ALIVE.
BDMP BDMP BDMP
I CERTAINLY *HOPED* HE WASN'T...
IF LORD SESSHOMARU LEARNS TENSEIGA'S SECRET...
WELL, WELL...

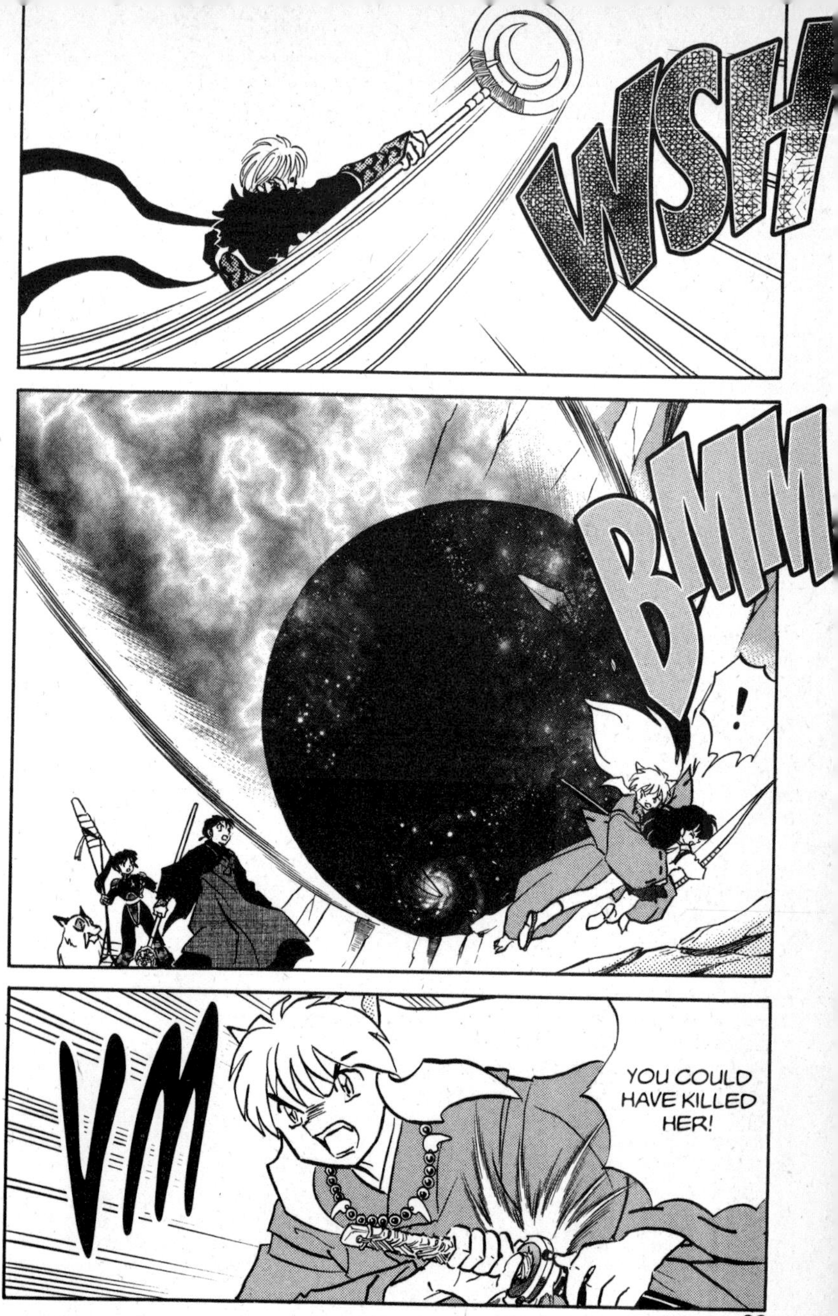
WSH
BMM
!
VM
YOU COULD HAVE KILLED HER!

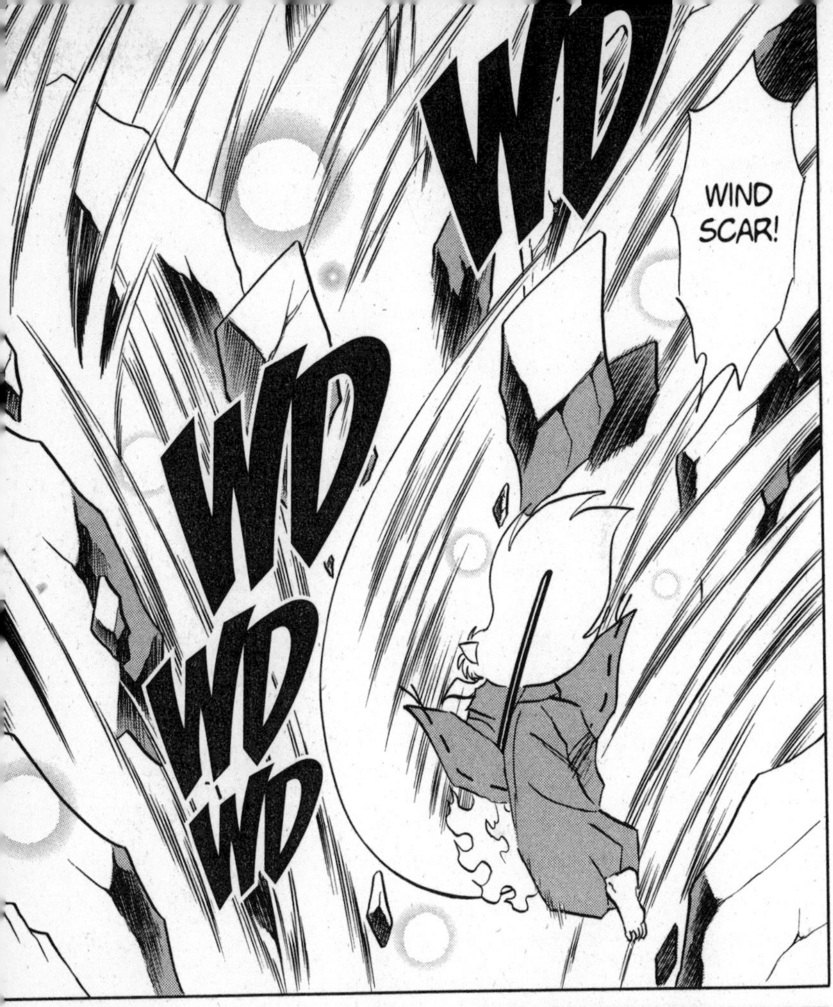
WIND SCAR!
WD
WD
WD
WD
WD

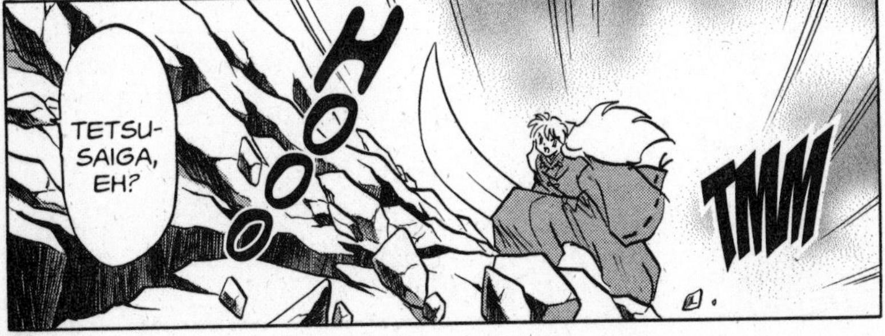
TMM
HOOOO
TETSU-SAIGA, EH?

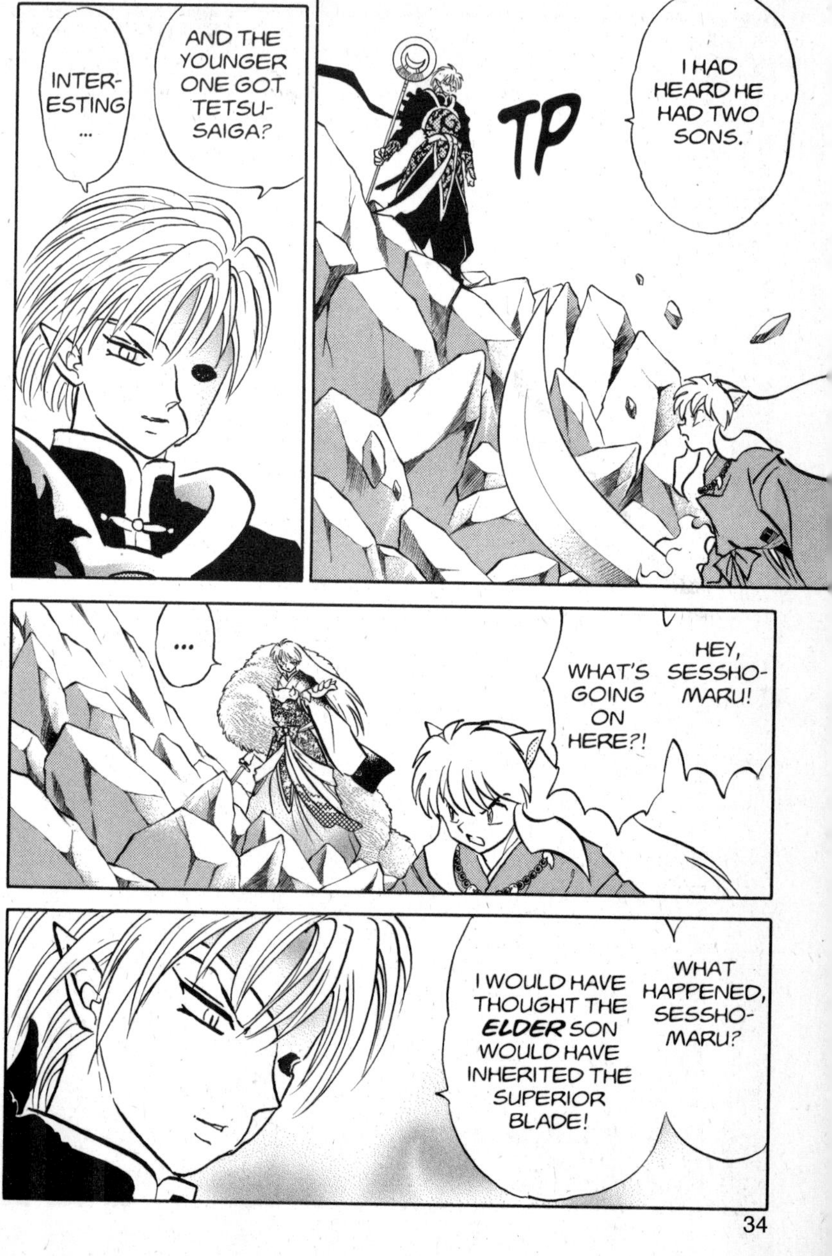
I HAD HEARD HE HAD TWO SONS.
TP
AND THE YOUNGER ONE GOT TETSU-SAIGA?
INTER-ESTING ...
HEY, SESSHO-MARU!
WHAT'S GOING ON HERE?!
...
WHAT HAPPENED, SESSHO-MARU?
I WOULD HAVE THOUGHT THE ELDER SON WOULD HAVE INHERITED THE SUPERIOR BLADE!

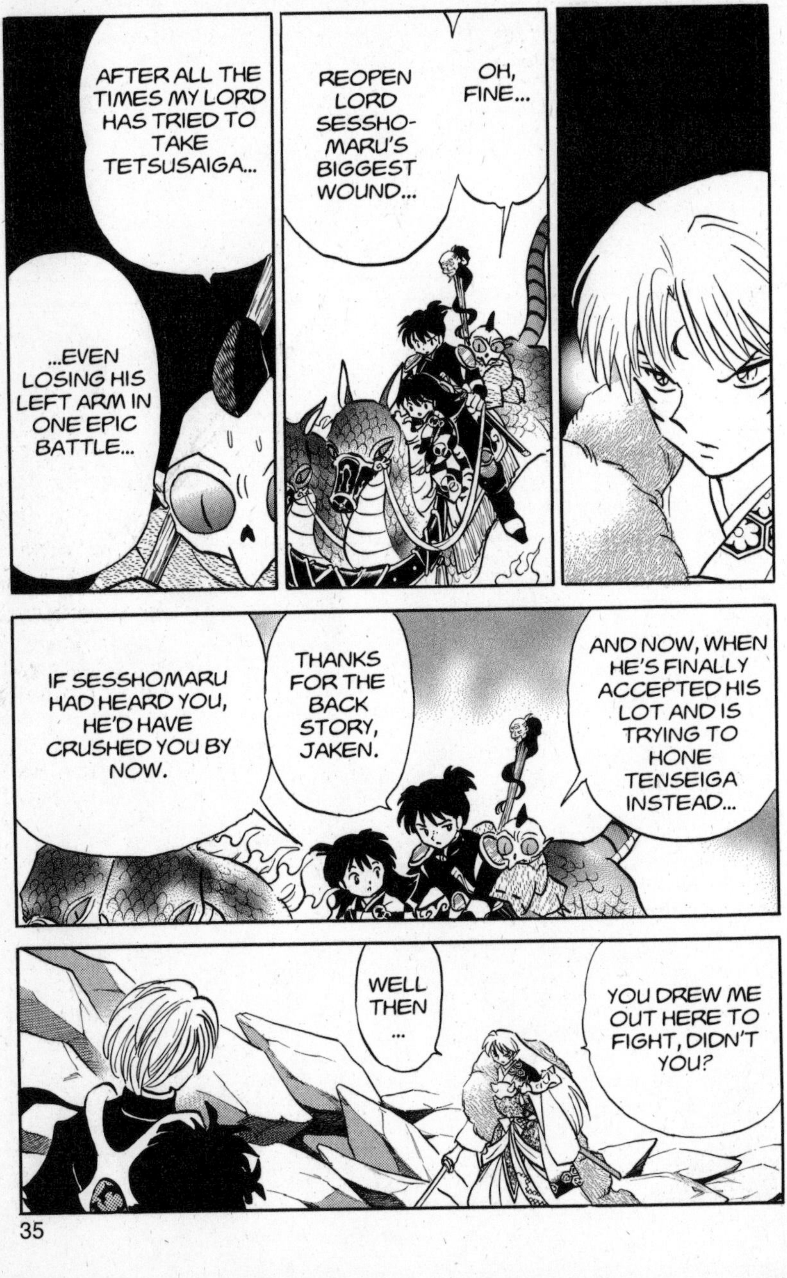
OH, FINE...
REOPEN LORD SESSHO-MARU'S BIGGEST WOUND...
AFTER ALL THE TIMES MY LORD HAS TRIED TO TAKE TETSUSAIGA...
...EVEN LOSING HIS LEFT ARM IN ONE EPIC BATTLE...
AND NOW, WHEN HE'S FINALLY ACCEPTED HIS LOT AND IS TRYING TO HONE TENSEIGA INSTEAD...
THANKS FOR THE BACK STORY, JAKEN.
IF SESSHOMARU HAD HEARD YOU, HE'D HAVE CRUSHED YOU BY NOW.
YOU DREW ME OUT HERE TO FIGHT, DIDN'T YOU?
WELL THEN ...

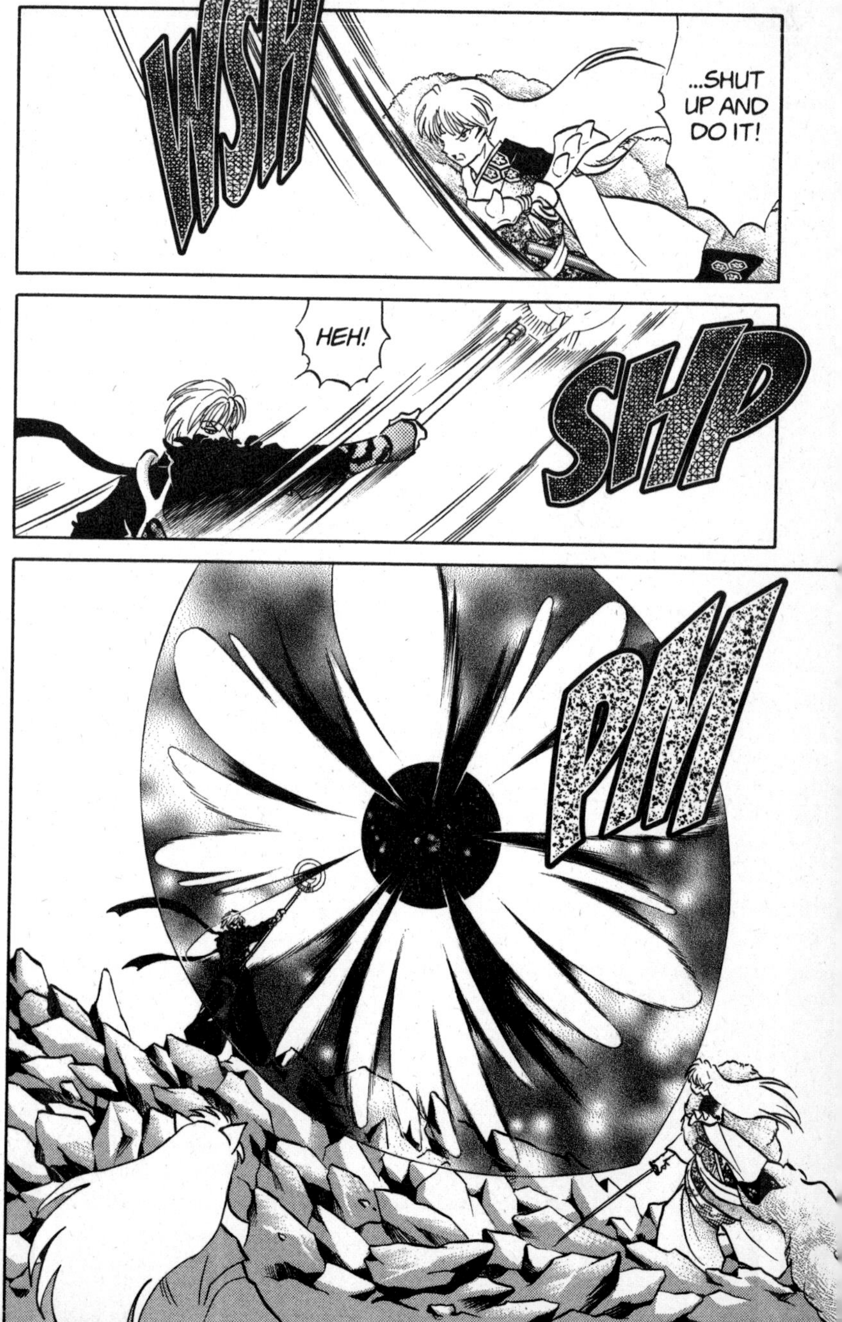
...SHUT UP AND DO IT!
WSH
SHP
HEH!
PM

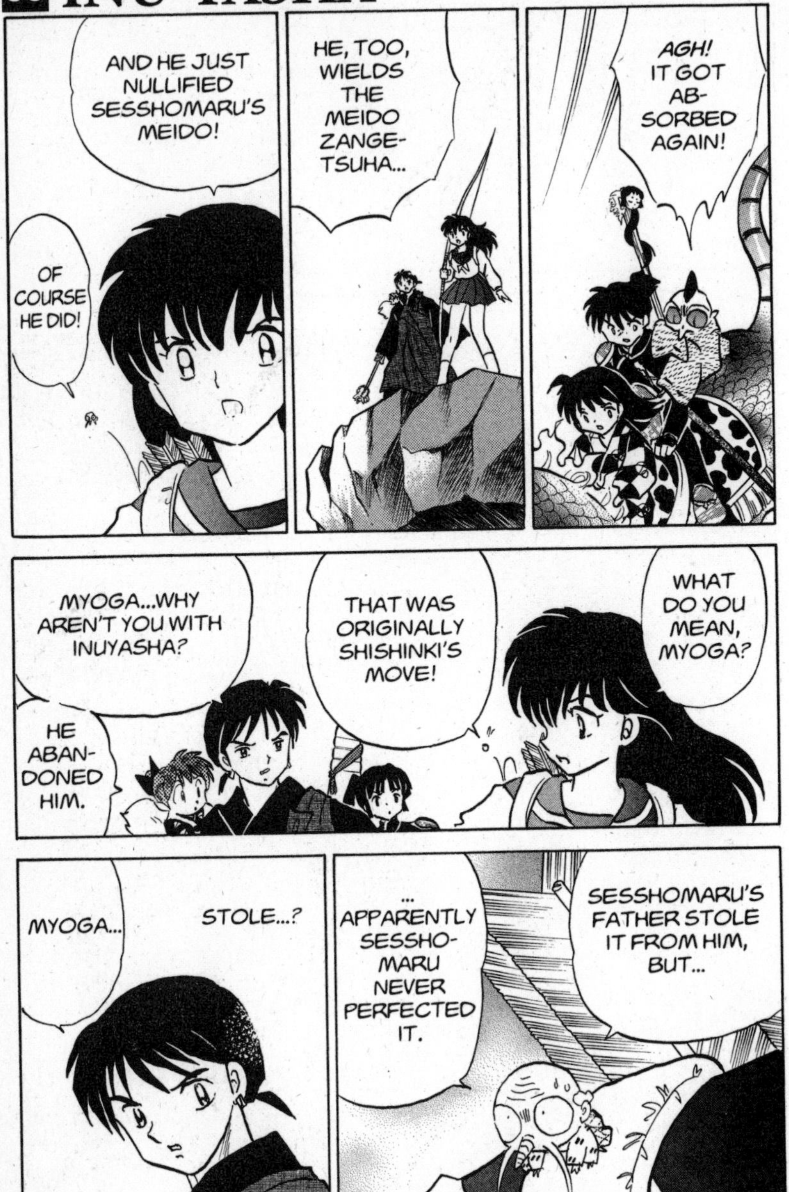
AGH! IT GOT AB-SORBED AGAIN!
HE, TOO, WIELDS THE MEIDO ZANGE-TSUHA...
AND HE JUST NULLIFIED SESSHOMARU'S MEIDO!
OF COURSE HE DID!
WHAT DO YOU MEAN, MYOGA?
THAT WAS ORIGINALLY SHISHINKI'S MOVE!
MYOGA...WHY AREN'T YOU WITH INUYASHA?
HE ABAN-DONED HIM.
SESSHOMARU'S FATHER STOLE IT FROM HIM, BUT...
... APPARENTLY SESSHO-MARU NEVER PERFECTED IT.
STOLE...?
MYOGA...

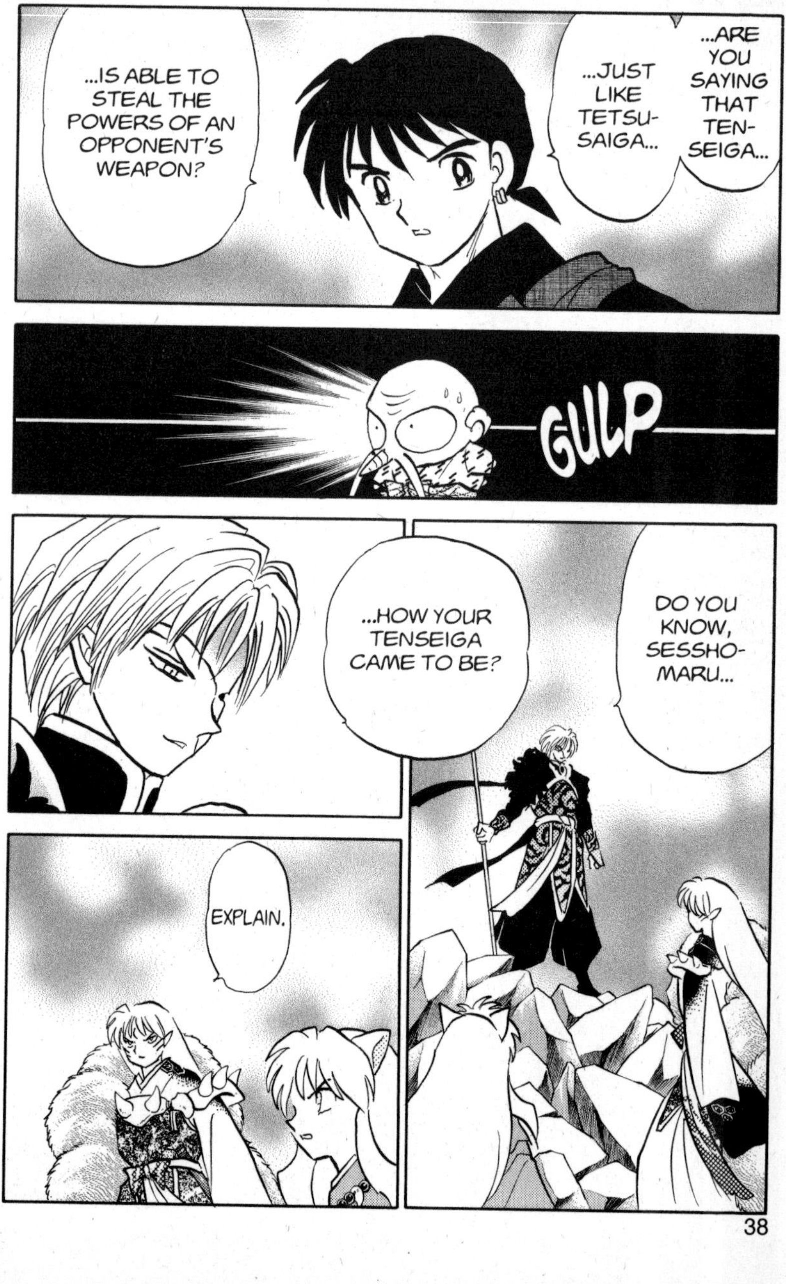
...ARE YOU SAYING THAT TEN-SEIGA...
...JUST LIKE TETSU-SAIGA...
...IS ABLE TO STEAL THE POWERS OF AN OPPONENT'S WEAPON?
GULP
DO YOU KNOW, SESSHO-MARU...
...HOW YOUR TENSEIGA CAME TO BE?
EXPLAIN.

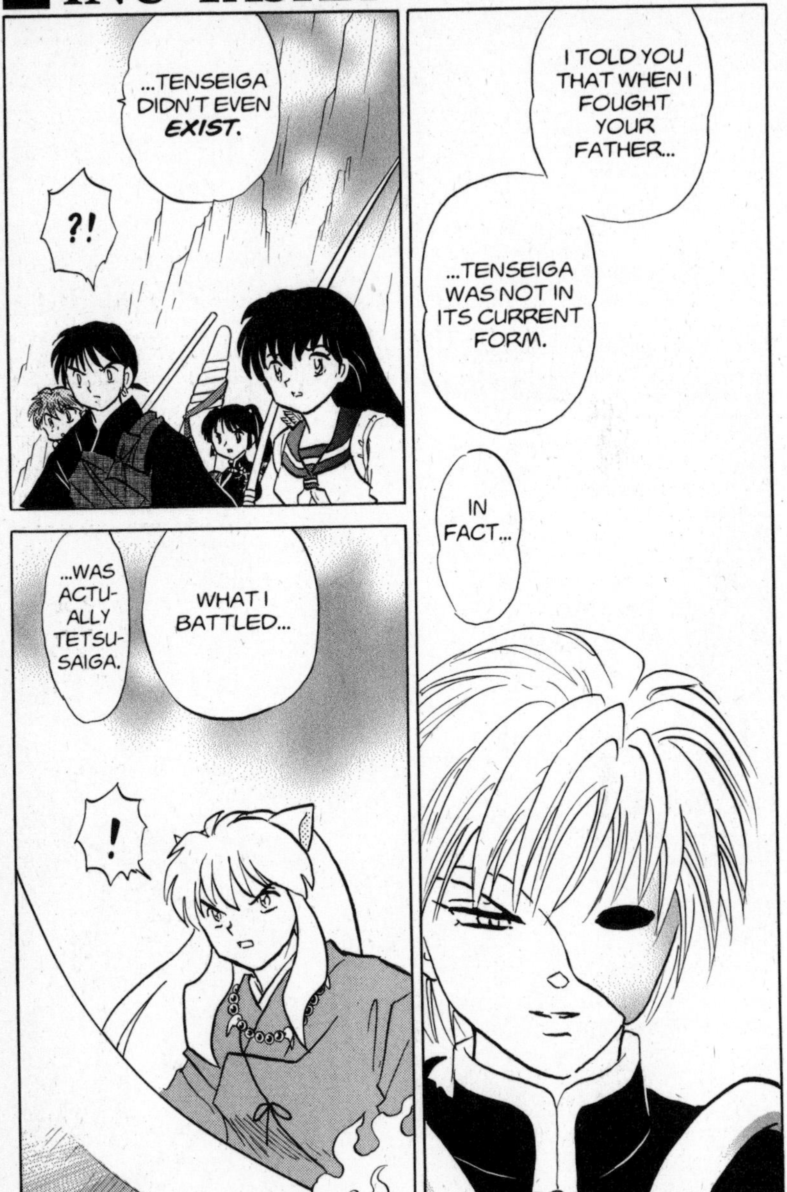
I TOLD YOU THAT WHEN I FOUGHT YOUR FATHER...
...TENSEIGA WAS NOT IN ITS CURRENT FORM.
IN FACT...
...TENSEIGA DIDN'T EVEN *EXIST*.
?!
WHAT I BATTLED...
...WAS ACTU-ALLY TETSU-SAIGA.
!

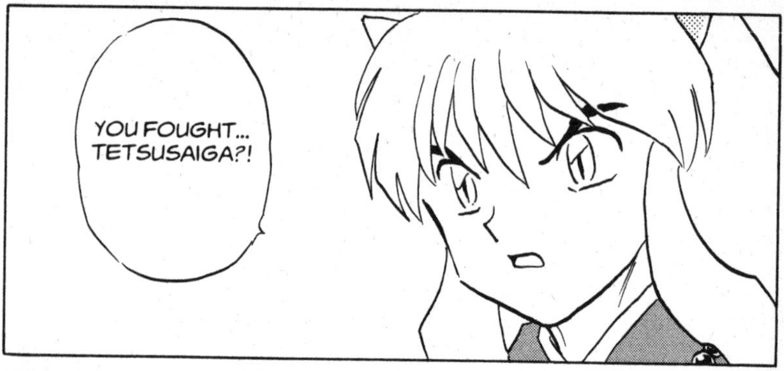
YOU FOUGHT... TETSUSAIGA?!

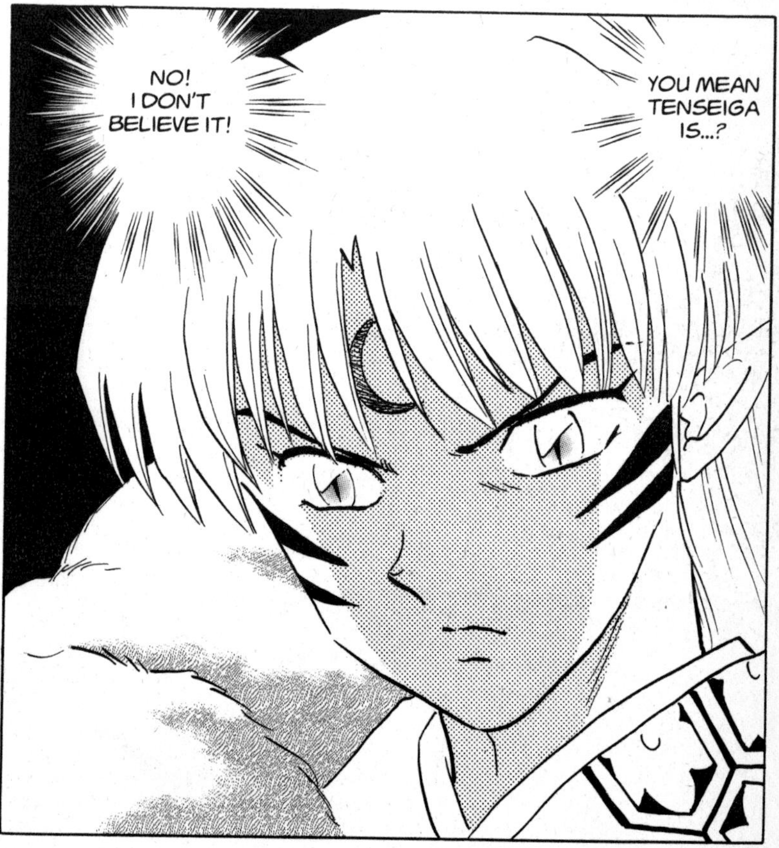
YOU MEAN TENSEIGA IS...?
NO! I DON'T BELIEVE IT!

SCROLL 3

TETSUSAIGA AND TENSEIGA

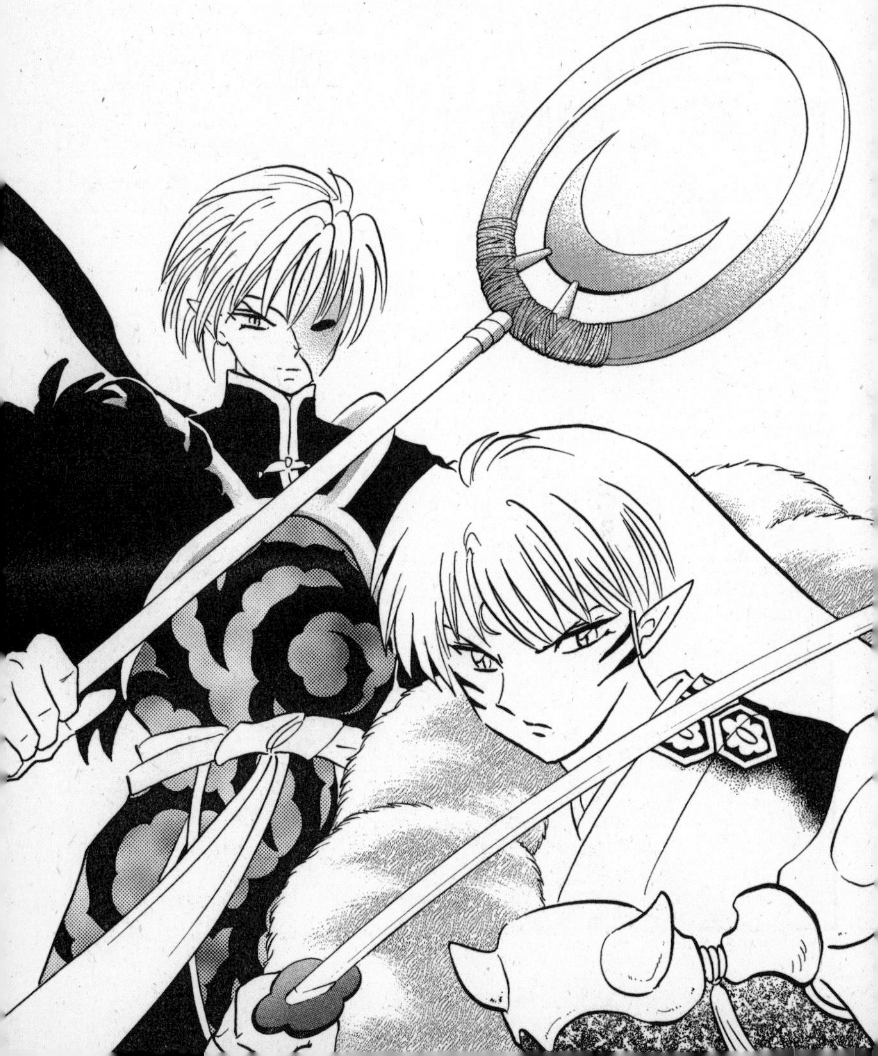

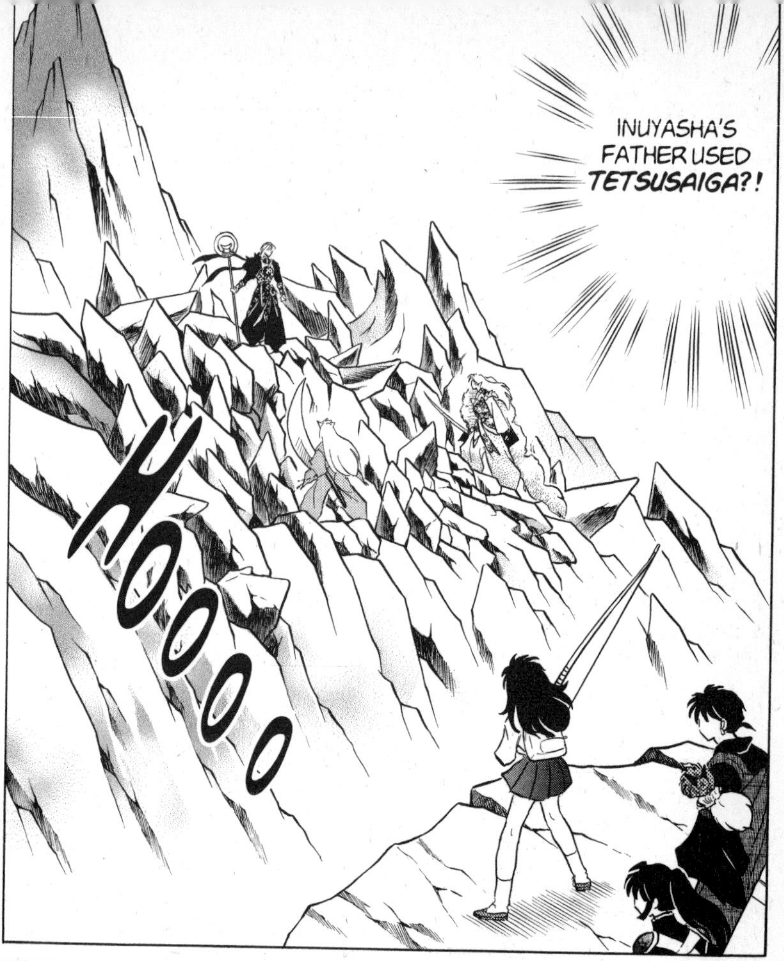
INUYASHA'S FATHER USED **TETSUSAIGA?!**
HOOOOO

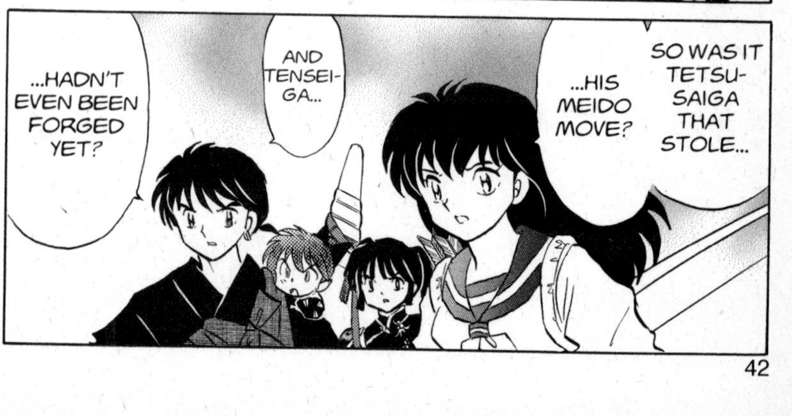
SO WAS IT TETSU-SAIGA THAT STOLE...
...HIS MEIDO MOVE?
AND TENSEI-GA...
...HADN'T EVEN BEEN FORGED YET?

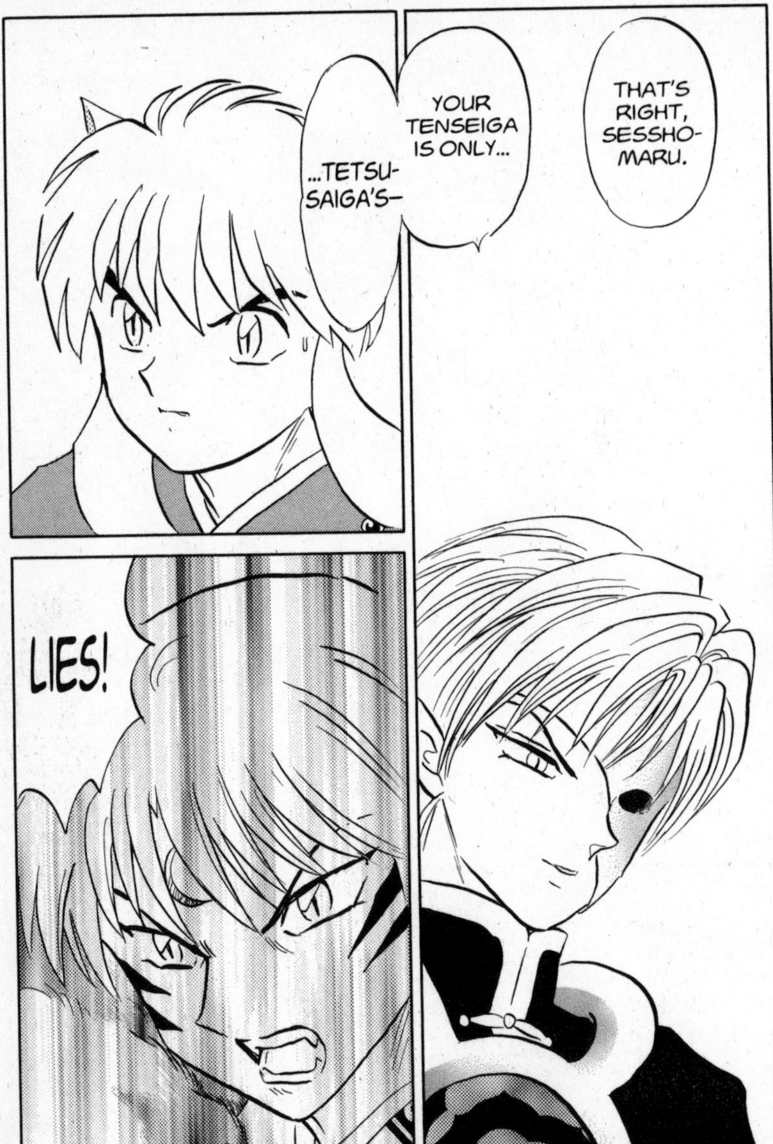
THAT'S RIGHT, SESSHO-MARU.
YOUR TENSEIGA IS ONLY...
...TETSU-SAIGA'S—
LIES!

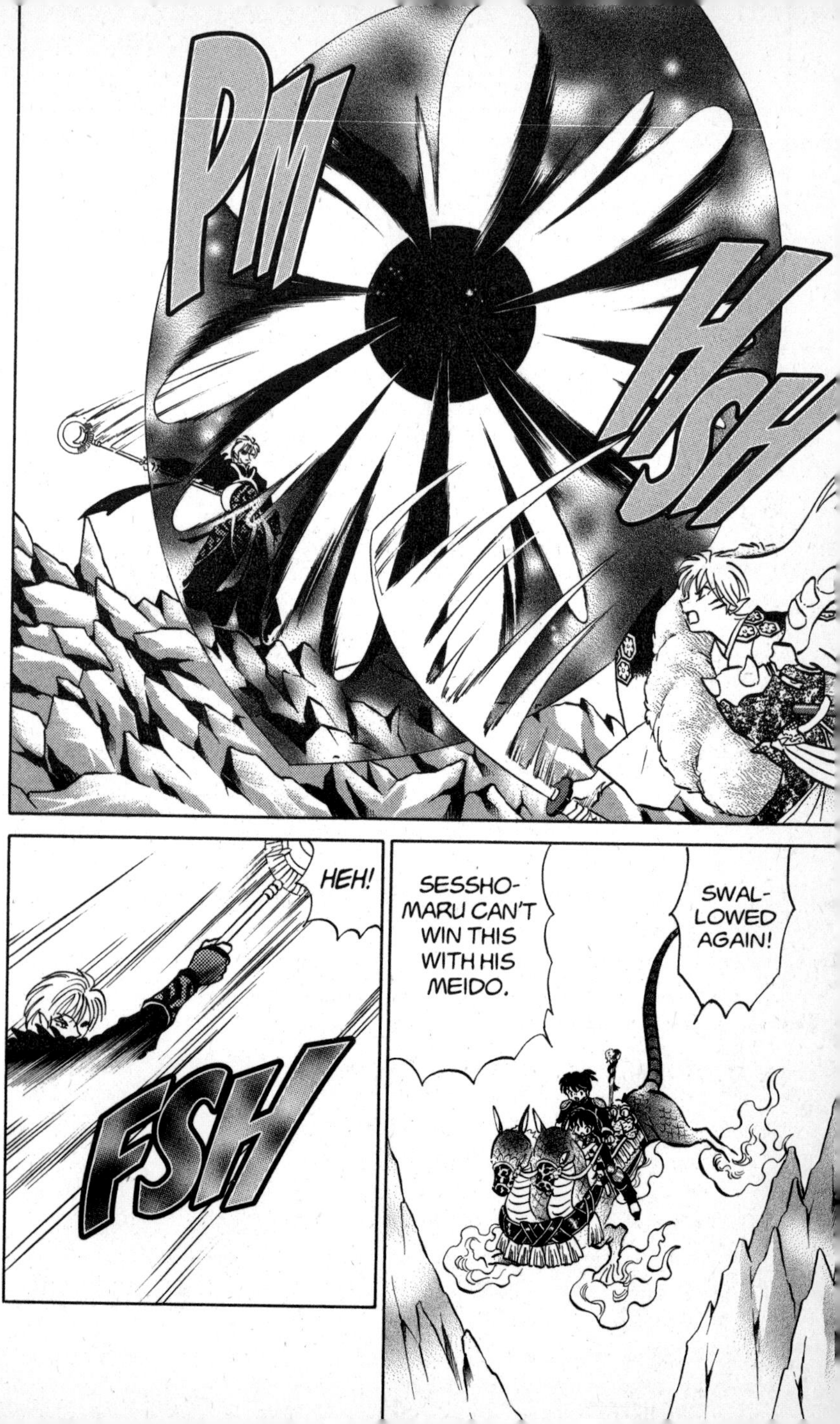

PM
HSH
SWAL-
LOWED
AGAIN!
SESSHO-
MARU CAN'T
WIN THIS
WITH HIS
MEIDO.
HEH!
FSH

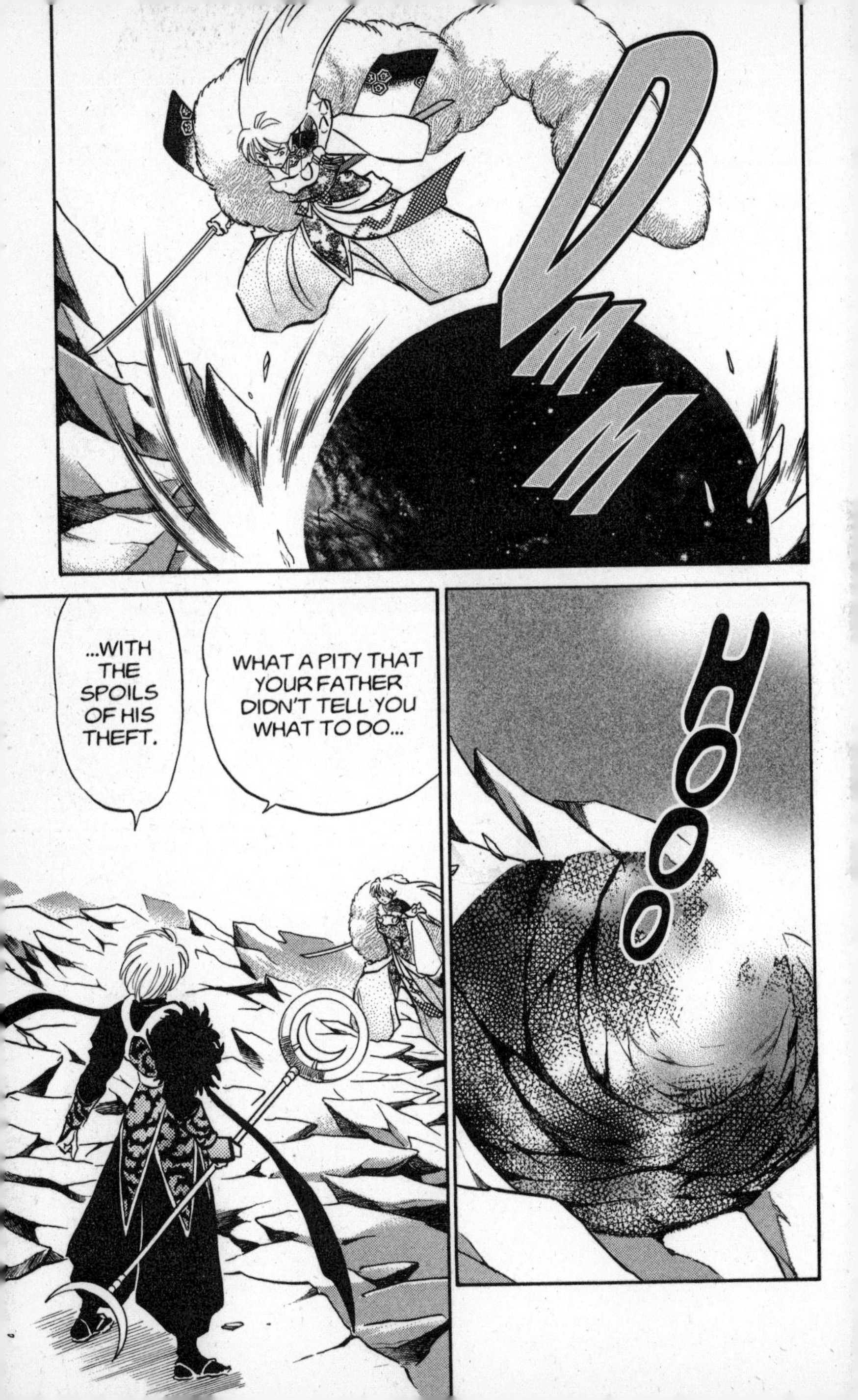
DOMM
HOOOO
WHAT A PITY THAT YOUR FATHER DIDN'T TELL YOU WHAT TO DO...
...WITH THE SPOILS OF HIS THEFT.

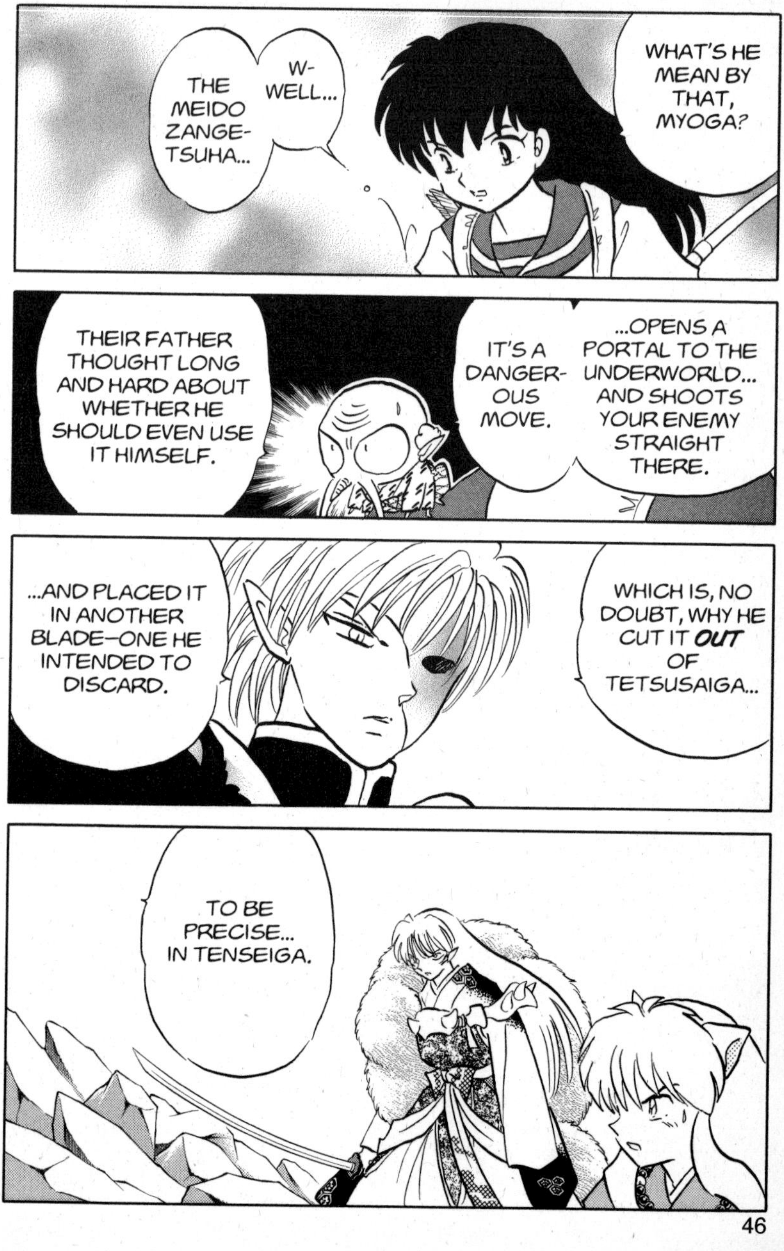
WHAT'S HE MEAN BY THAT, MYOGA?
W- WELL...
THE MEIDO ZANGE-TSUHA...
...OPENS A PORTAL TO THE UNDERWORLD... AND SHOOTS YOUR ENEMY STRAIGHT THERE.
IT'S A DANGER-OUS MOVE.
THEIR FATHER THOUGHT LONG AND HARD ABOUT WHETHER HE SHOULD EVEN USE IT HIMSELF.
WHICH IS, NO DOUBT, WHY HE CUT IT ***OUT*** OF TETSUSAIGA...
...AND PLACED IT IN ANOTHER BLADE—ONE HE INTENDED TO DISCARD.
TO BE PRECISE... IN TENSEIGA.

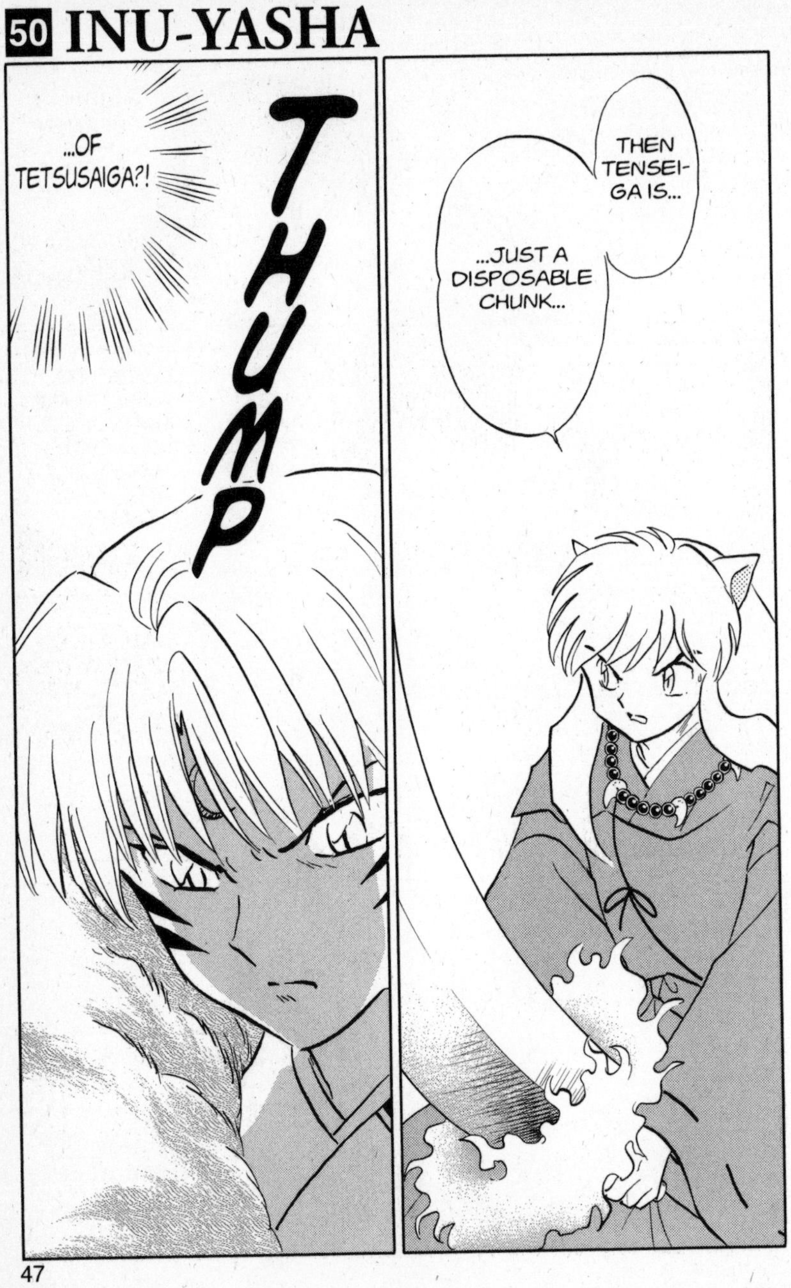
THEN TENSEI-GA IS...
...JUST A DISPOSABLE CHUNK...
...OF TETSUSAIGA?!
THUMP

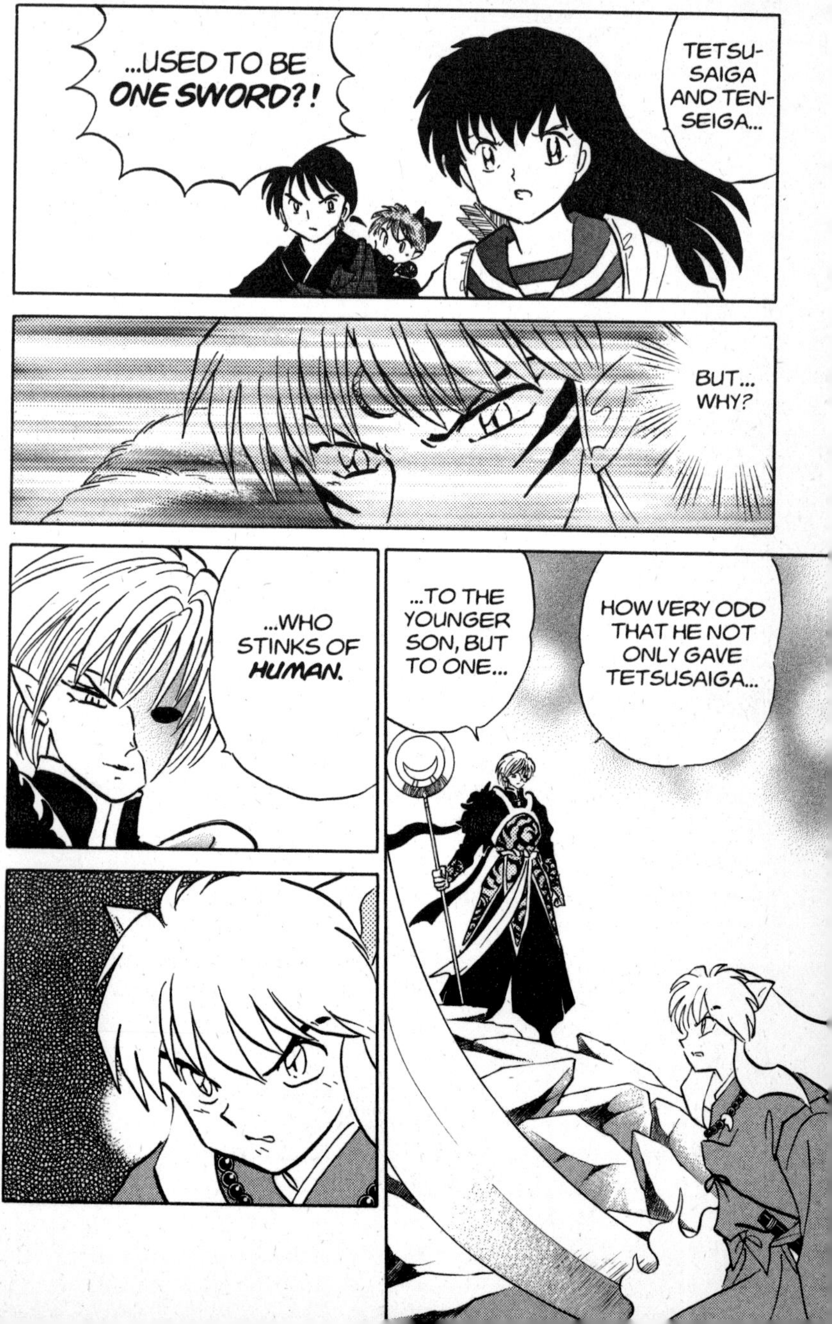
TETSU-SAIGA AND TEN-SEIGA...
...USED TO BE **ONE SWORD?!**
BUT... WHY?
HOW VERY ODD THAT HE NOT ONLY GAVE TETSUSAIGA...
...TO THE YOUNGER SON, BUT TO ONE...
...WHO STINKS OF **HUMAN.**

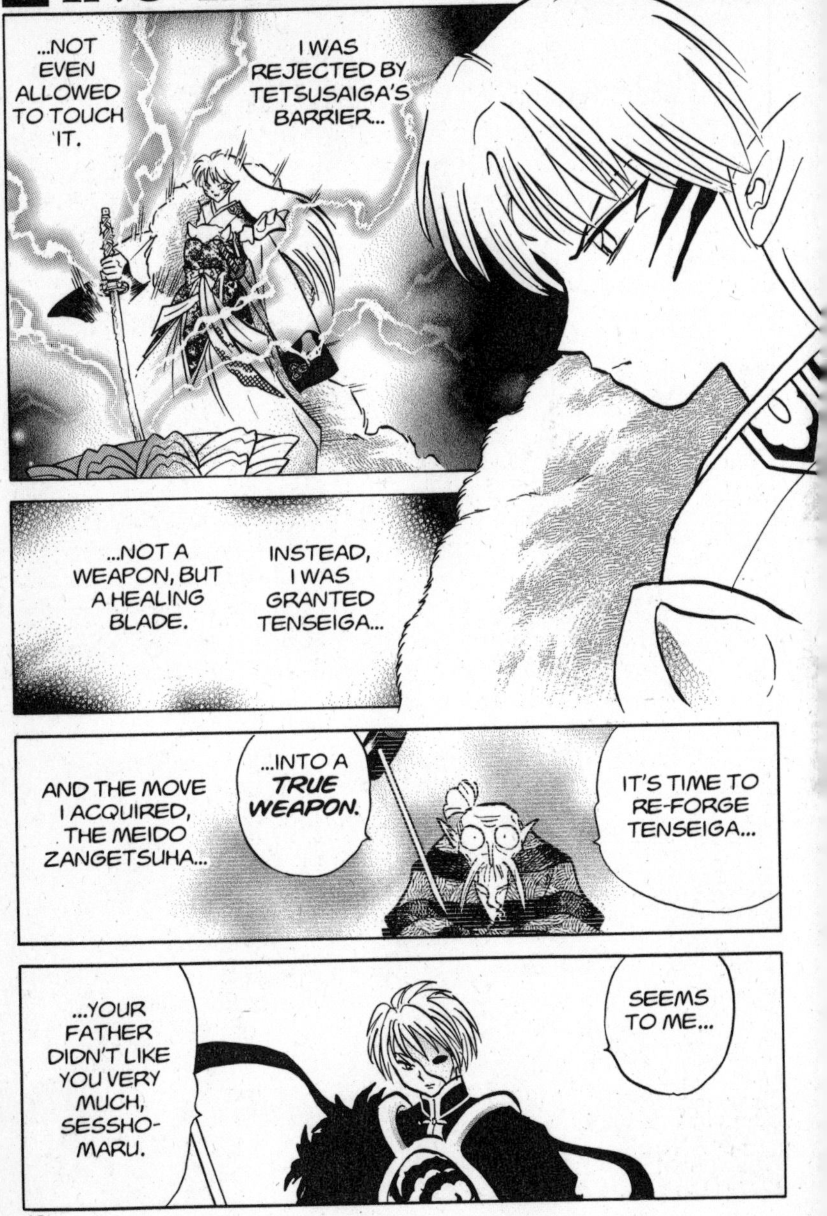
I WAS REJECTED BY TETSUSAIGA'S BARRIER...
...NOT EVEN ALLOWED TO TOUCH IT.
INSTEAD, I WAS GRANTED TENSEIGA...
...NOT A WEAPON, BUT A HEALING BLADE.
IT'S TIME TO RE-FORGE TENSEIGA...
...INTO A ***TRUE WEAPON.***
AND THE MOVE I ACQUIRED, THE MEIDO ZANGETSUHA...
SEEMS TO ME...
...YOUR FATHER DIDN'T LIKE YOU VERY MUCH, SESSHOMARU.

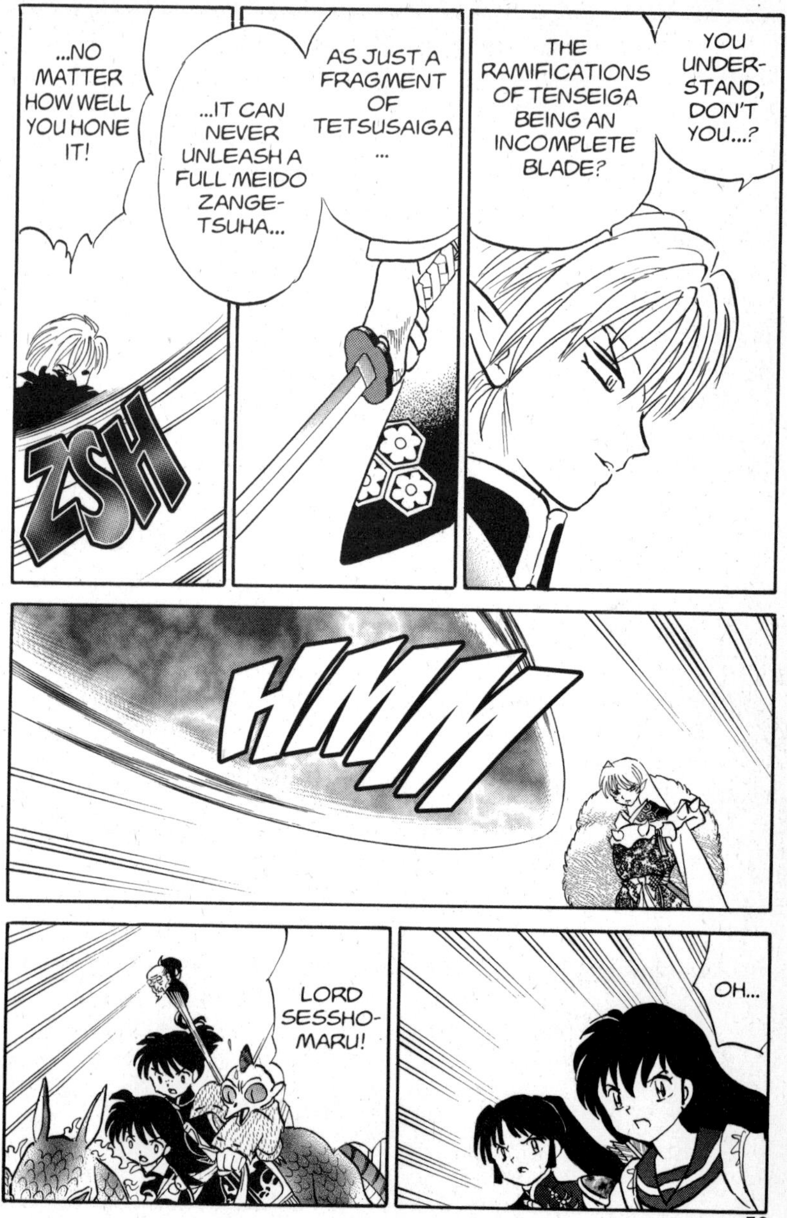

YOU UNDER-STAND, DON'T YOU...?
THE RAMIFICATIONS OF TENSEIGA BEING AN INCOMPLETE BLADE?
AS JUST A FRAGMENT OF TETSUSAIGA ...
...IT CAN NEVER UNLEASH A FULL MEIDO ZANGE-TSUHA...
...NO MATTER HOW WELL YOU HONE IT!
ZSH
HMM
OH...
LORD SESSHO-MARU!

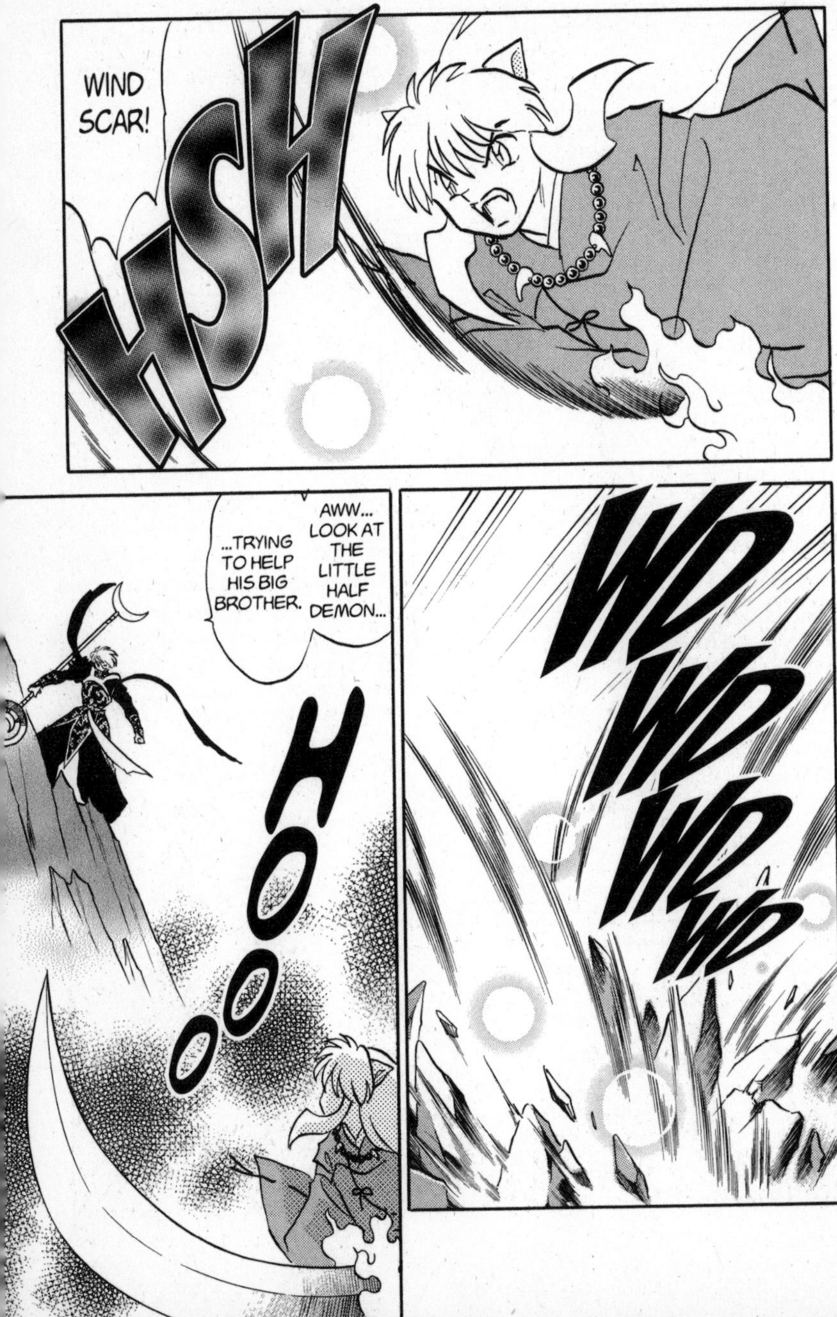
WIND SCAR!
HSH
WO WO WO WO WO
AWW... LOOK AT THE LITTLE HALF DEMON...
...TRYING TO HELP HIS BIG BROTHER.
HOOOO

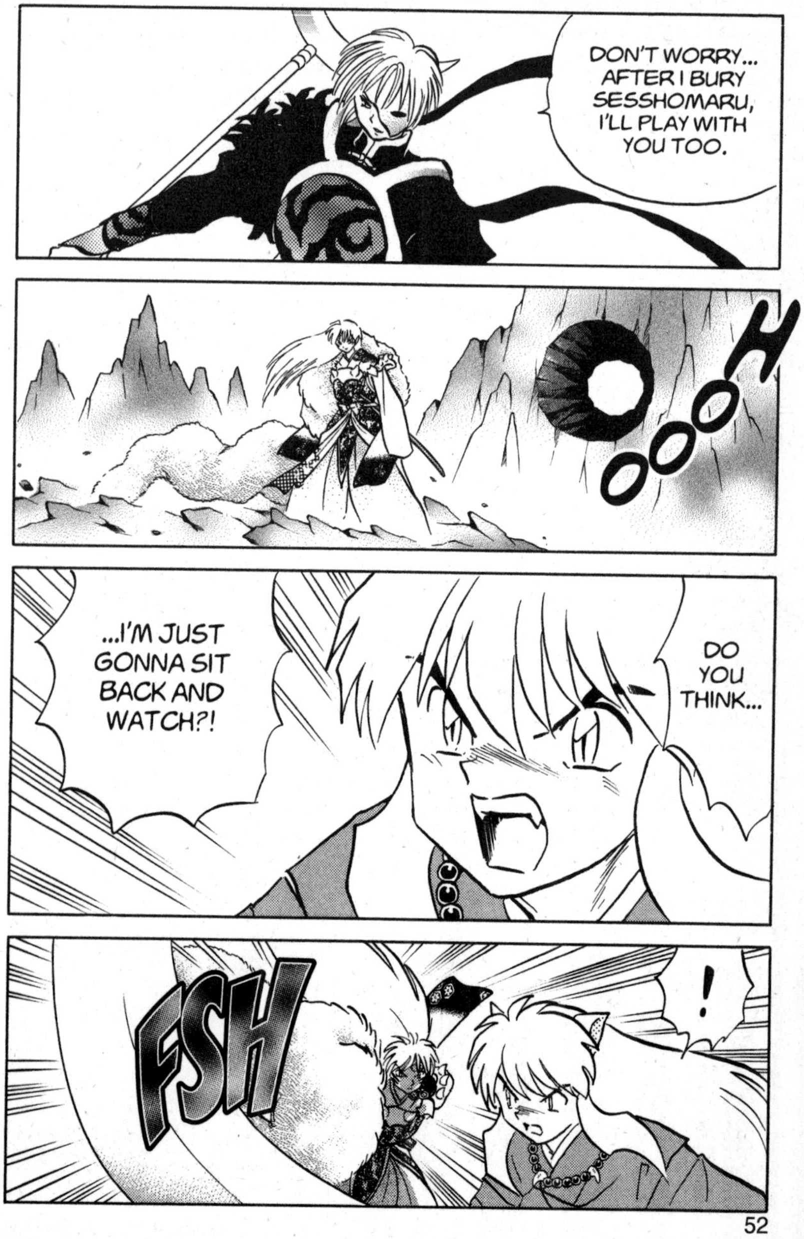

DON'T WORRY... AFTER I BURY SESSHOMARU, I'LL PLAY WITH YOU TOO.
OOOOH
DO YOU THINK...
...I'M JUST GONNA SIT BACK AND WATCH?!
!
FSH

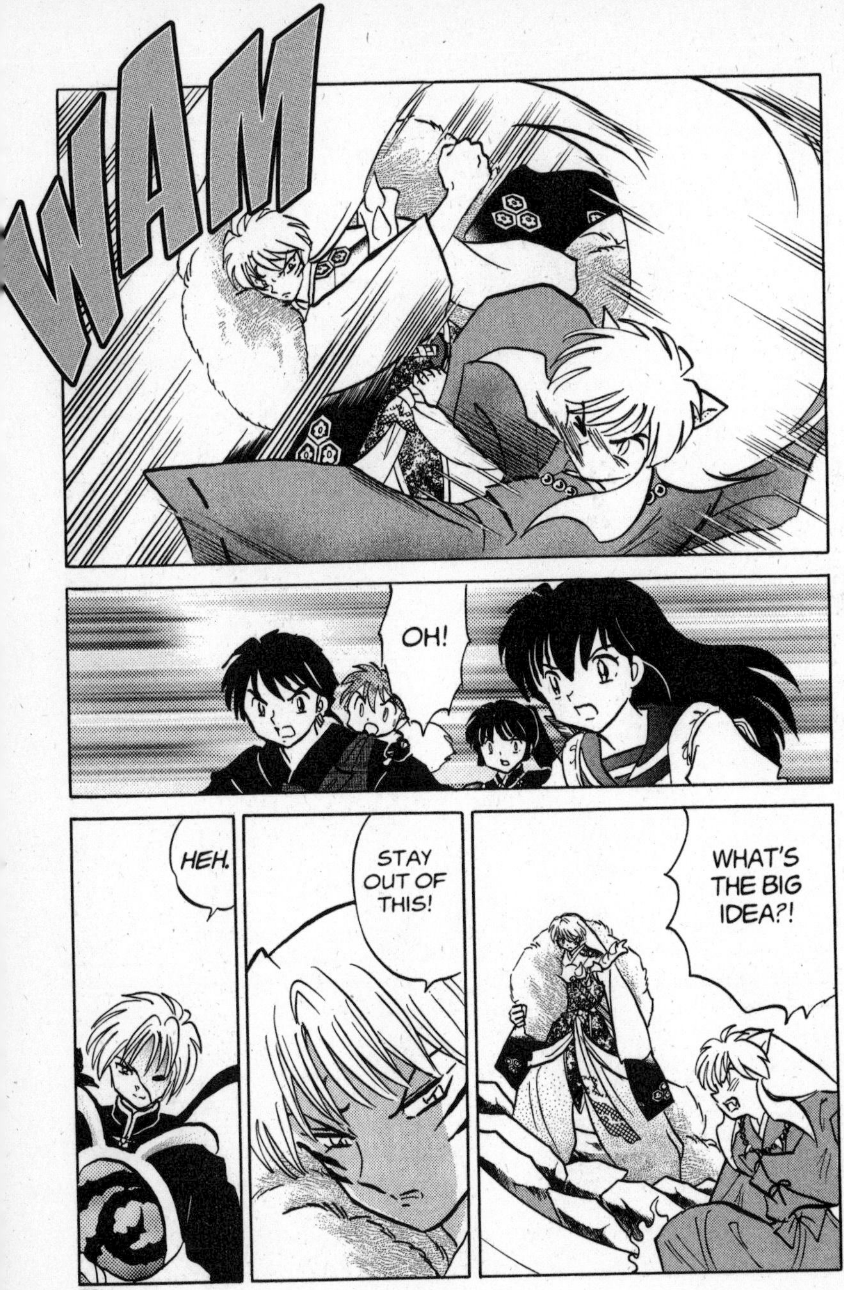

WAM
OH!
WHAT'S THE BIG IDEA?!
STAY OUT OF THIS!
HEH.

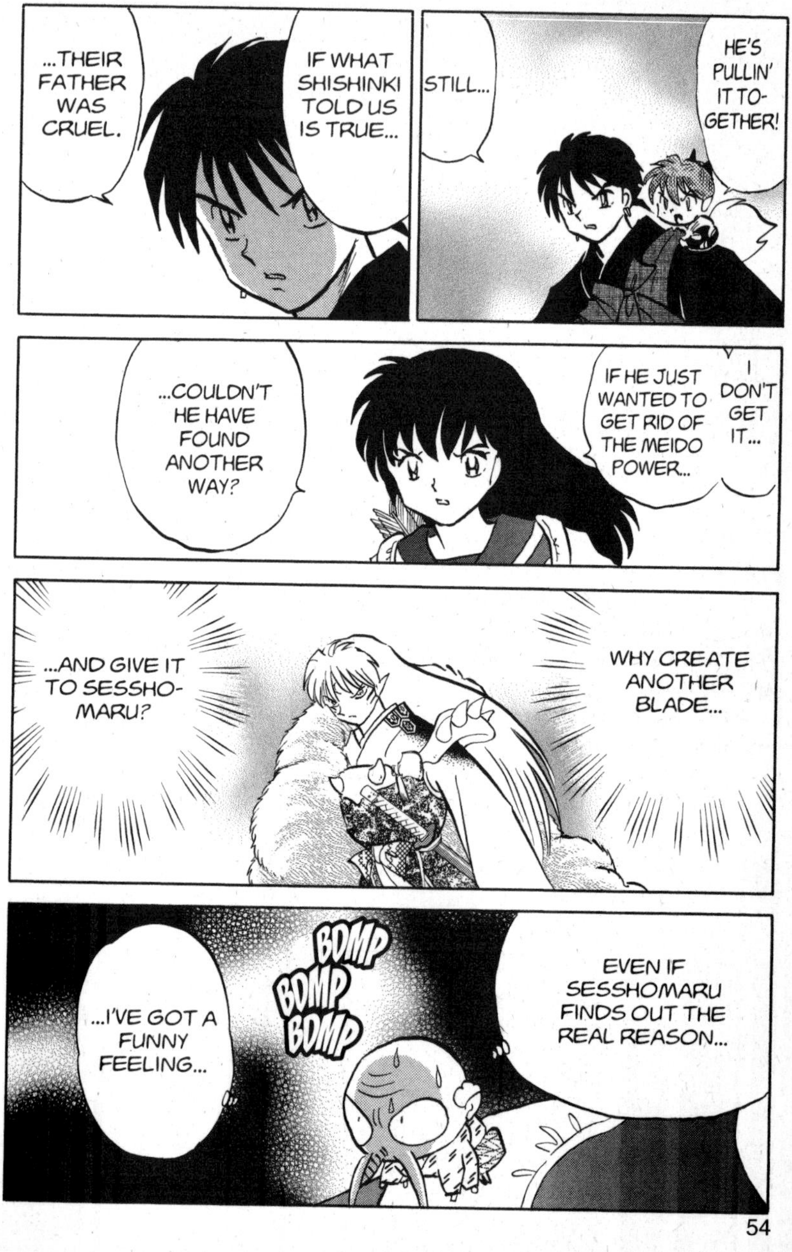
HE'S PULLIN' IT TO-GETHER!
STILL...
IF WHAT SHISHINKI TOLD US IS TRUE...
...THEIR FATHER WAS CRUEL.
I DON'T GET IT...
IF HE JUST WANTED TO GET RID OF THE MEIDO POWER...
...COULDN'T HE HAVE FOUND ANOTHER WAY?
WHY CREATE ANOTHER BLADE...
...AND GIVE IT TO SESSHOMARU?
EVEN IF SESSHOMARU FINDS OUT THE REAL REASON...
BDMP BDMP BDMP
...I'VE GOT A FUNNY FEELING...

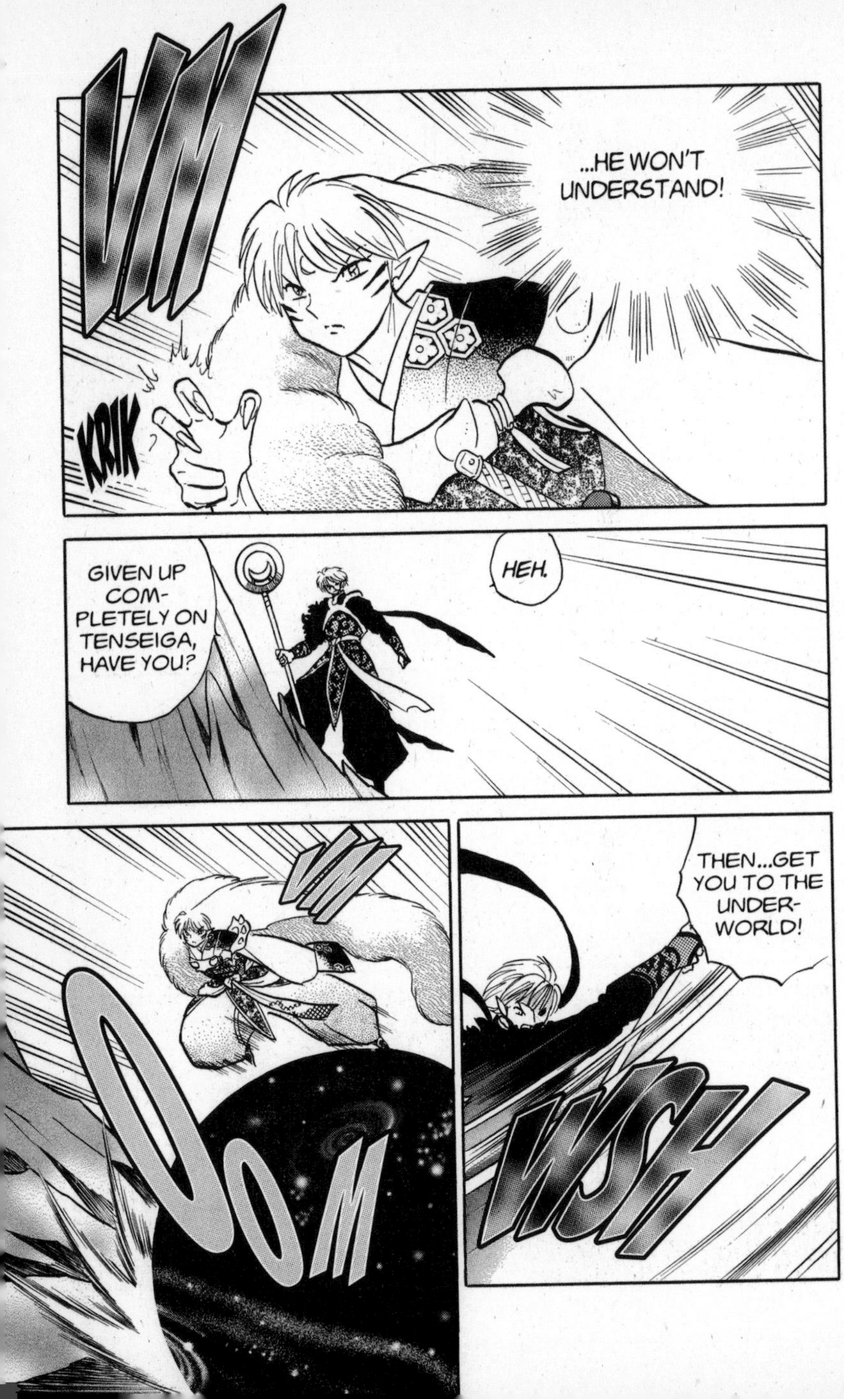
VIIN
...HE WON'T UNDERSTAND!
KRIK
HEH.
GIVEN UP COM-PLETELY ON TENSEIGA, HAVE YOU?
THEN...GET YOU TO THE UNDER-WORLD!
WSH
VIN
ZOOM

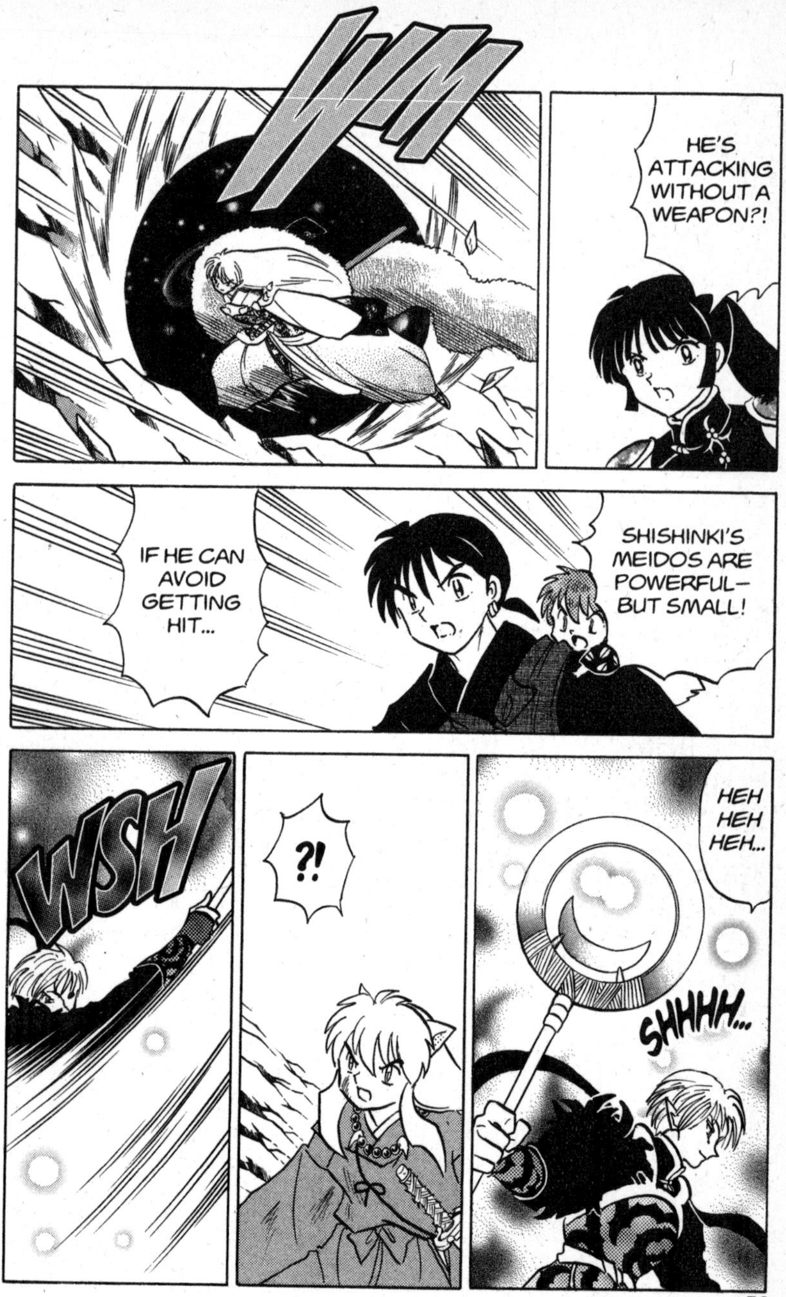
HE'S ATTACKING WITHOUT A WEAPON?!
WM
SHISHINKI'S MEIDOS ARE POWERFUL– BUT SMALL!
IF HE CAN AVOID GETTING HIT...
HEH HEH HEH...
SHHHH...
?!
WSH

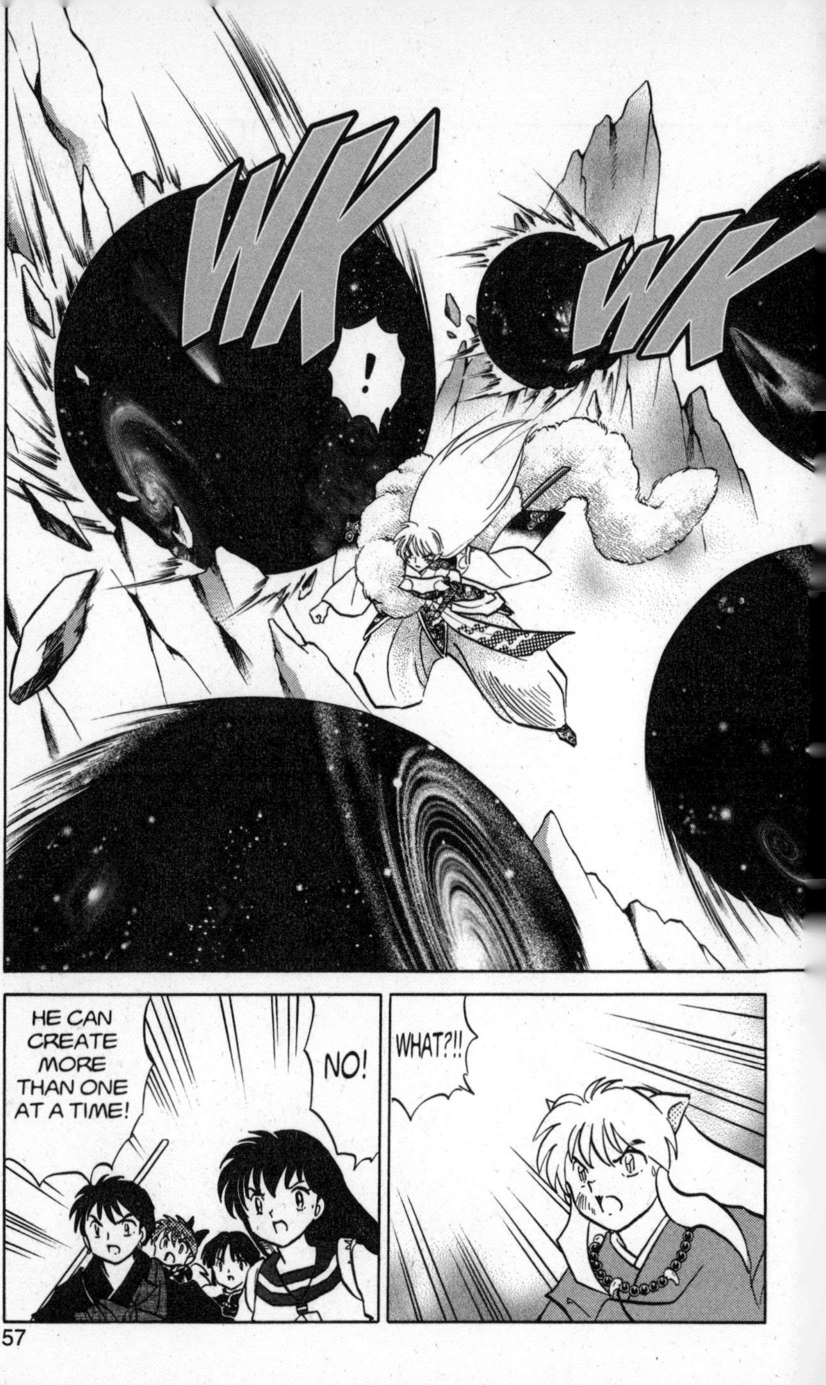
WK
WK
!
WHAT?!!
NO!
HE CAN CREATE MORE THAN ONE AT A TIME!

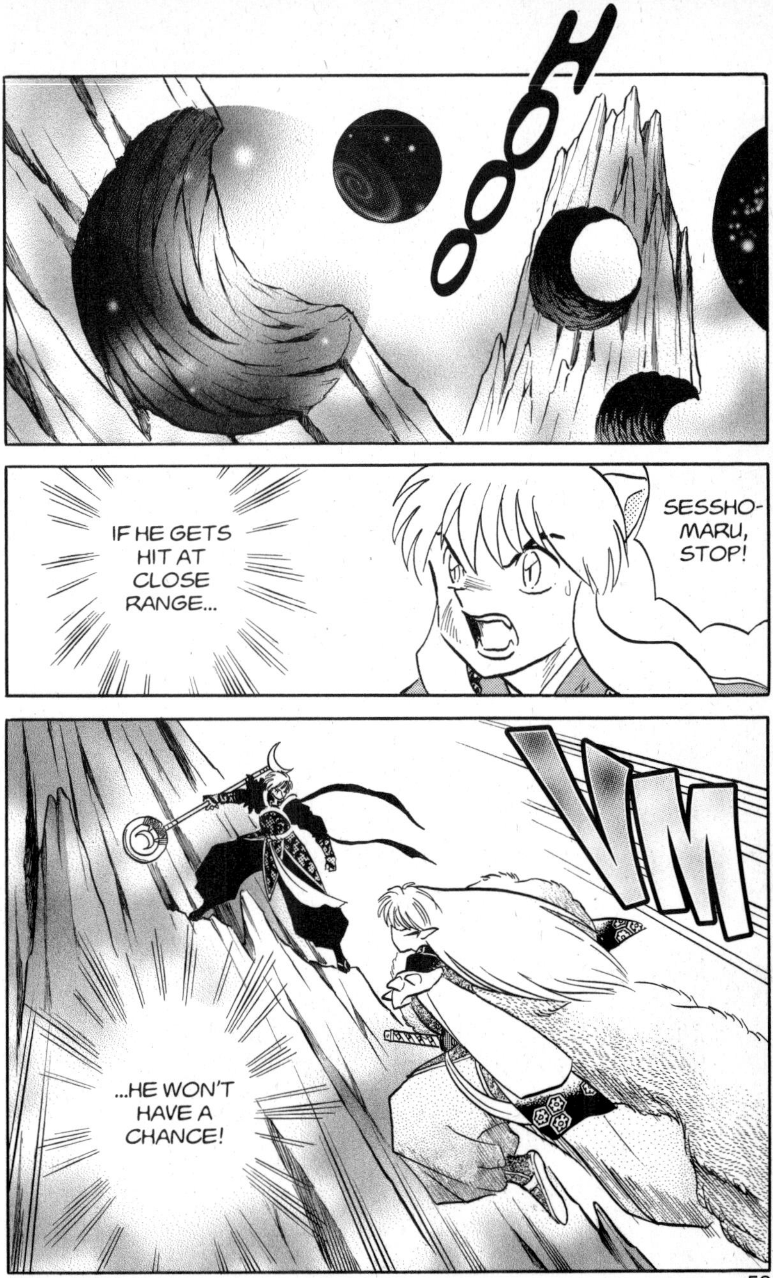
OOOH
SESSHO-
MARU,
STOP!
IF HE GETS
HIT AT
CLOSE
RANGE...
VMM
...HE WON'T
HAVE A
CHANCE!

SCROLL 4

A FATHER'S TRUE INTENTION

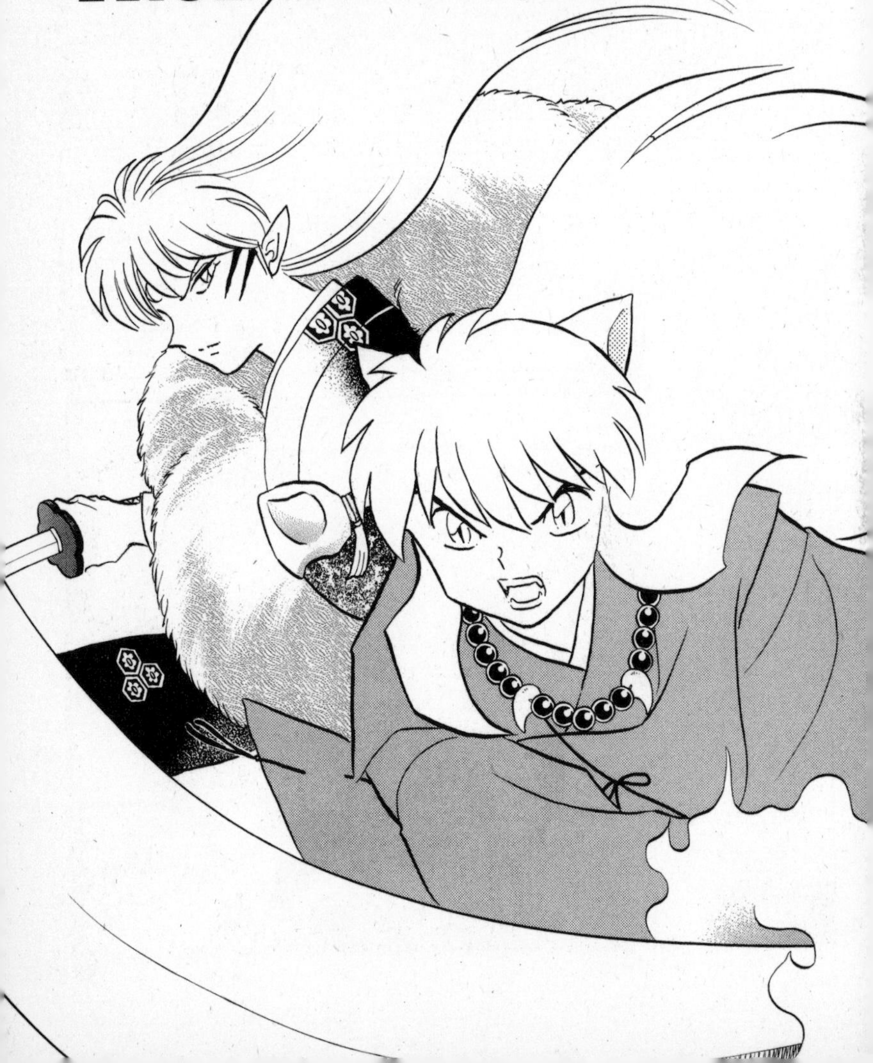

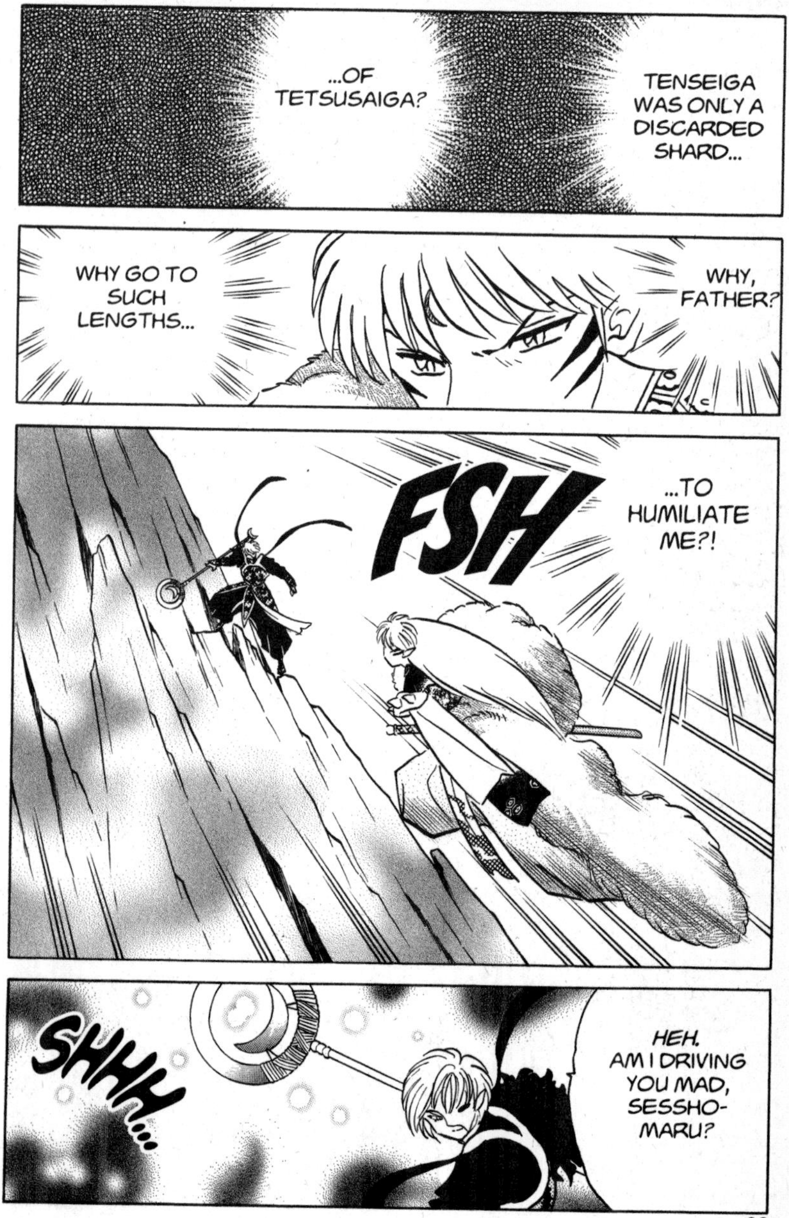
TENSEIGA WAS ONLY A DISCARDED SHARD...
...OF TETSUSAIGA?
WHY, FATHER?
WHY GO TO SUCH LENGTHS...
...TO HUMILIATE ME?!
FSH
HEH. AM I DRIVING YOU MAD, SESSHO-MARU?
SHHH...

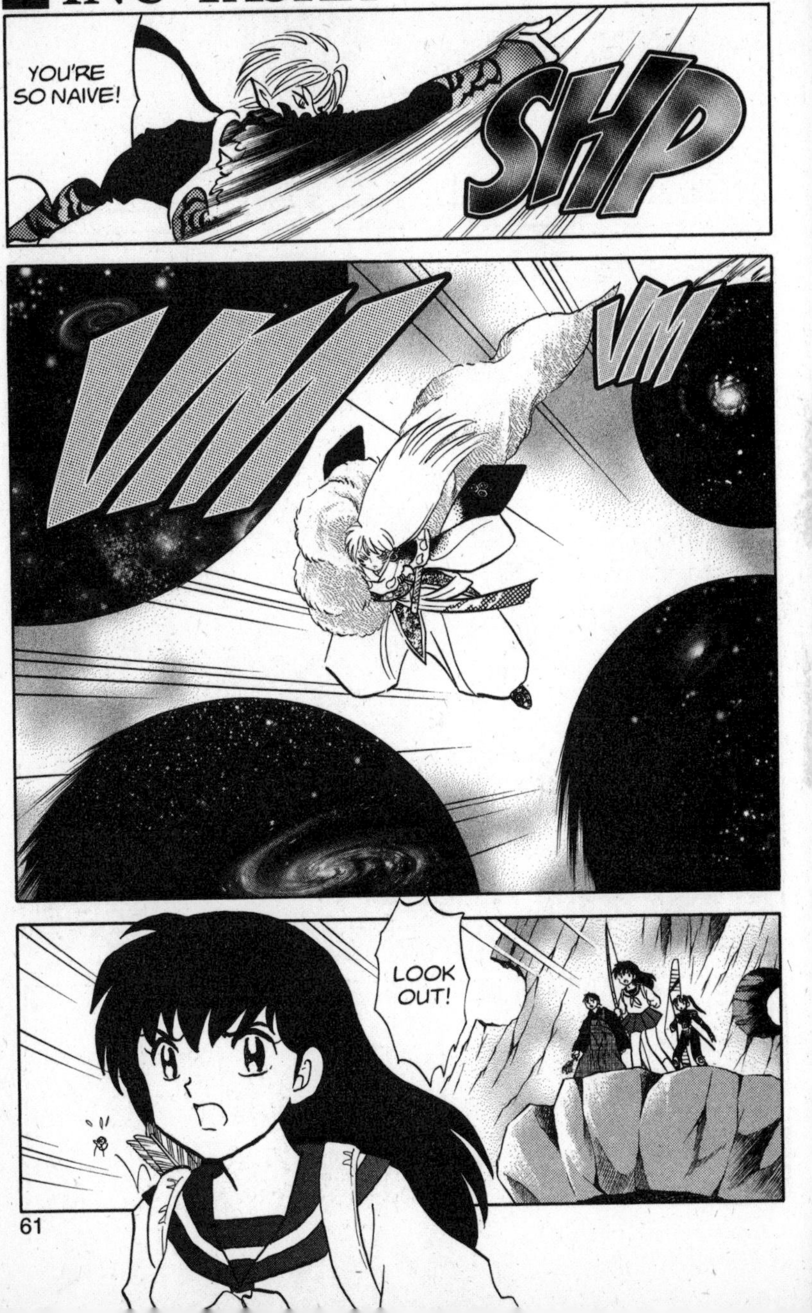
YOU'RE SO NAIVE!
SHP
VM
VM
LOOK OUT!

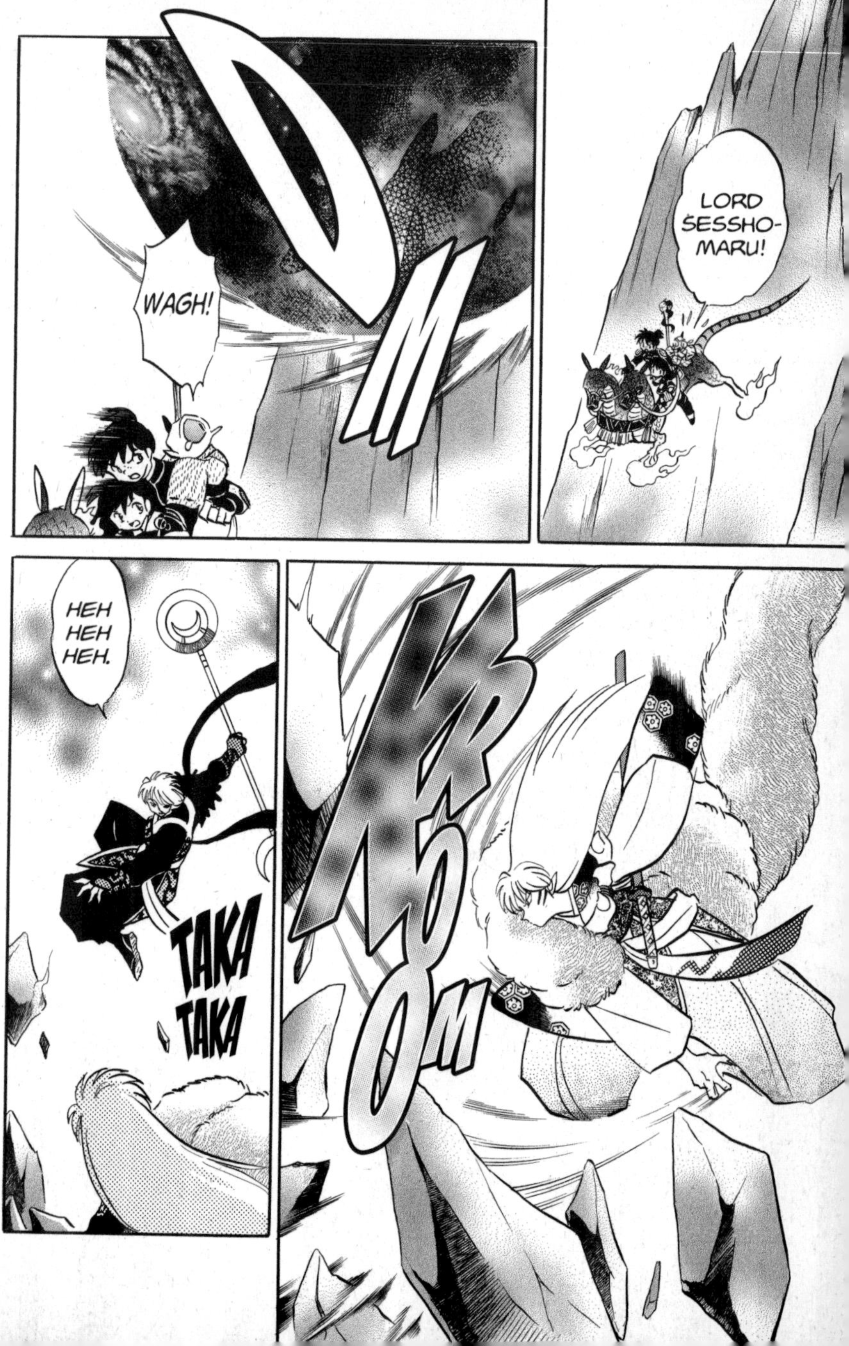
LORD SESSHO-MARU!
WAGH!
HEH HEH HEH.
TAKA TAKA

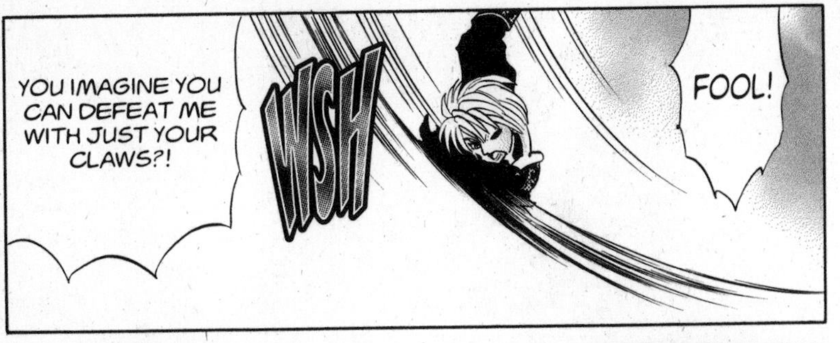
FOOL!
WSH
YOU IMAGINE YOU CAN DEFEAT ME WITH JUST YOUR CLAWS?!

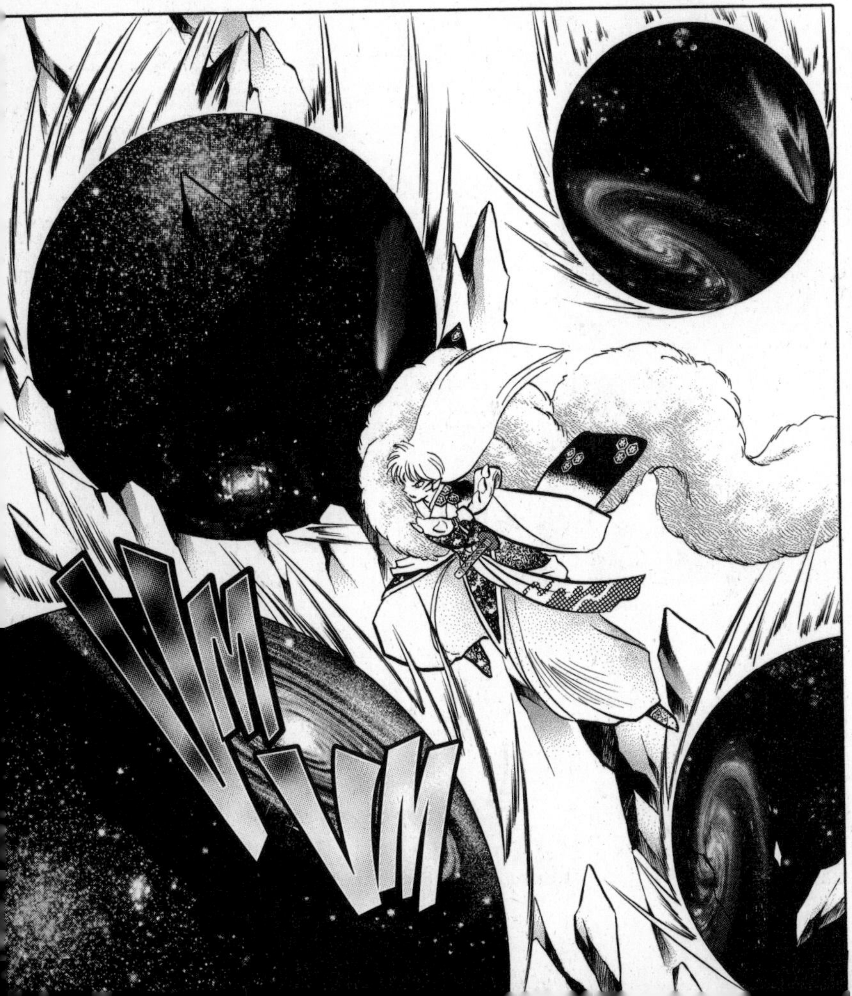
VVM VVM

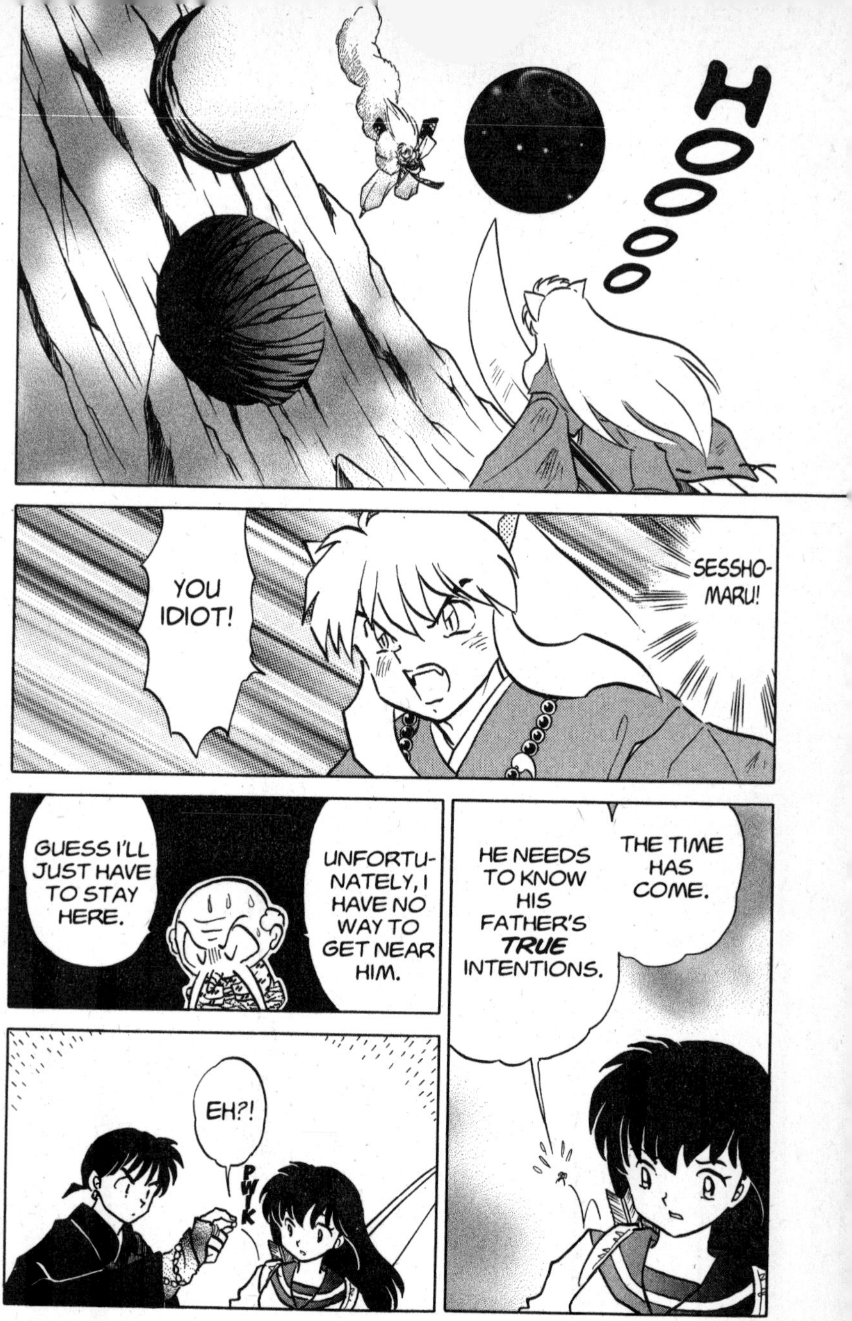
HOOOOO
SESSHO-MARU!
YOU IDIOT!
THE TIME HAS COME.
HE NEEDS TO KNOW HIS FATHER'S **TRUE** INTENTIONS.
UNFORTU-NATELY, I HAVE NO WAY TO GET NEAR HIM.
GUESS I'LL JUST HAVE TO STAY HERE.
EH?!
PWIK

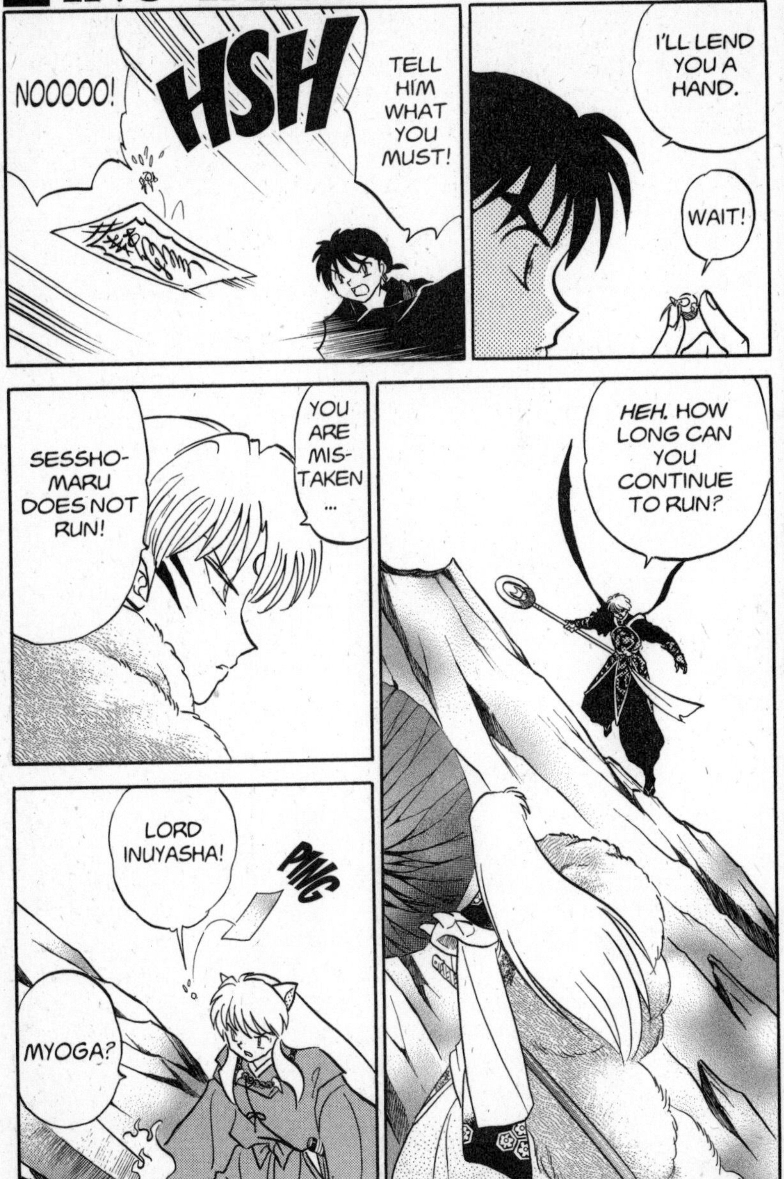
I'LL LEND YOU A HAND.
WAIT!
TELL HIM WHAT YOU MUST!
HSH
NOOOOO!
HEH. HOW LONG CAN YOU CONTINUE TO RUN?
YOU ARE MIS-TAKEN ...
SESSHO-MARU DOES NOT RUN!
LORD INUYASHA!
PING
MYOGA?

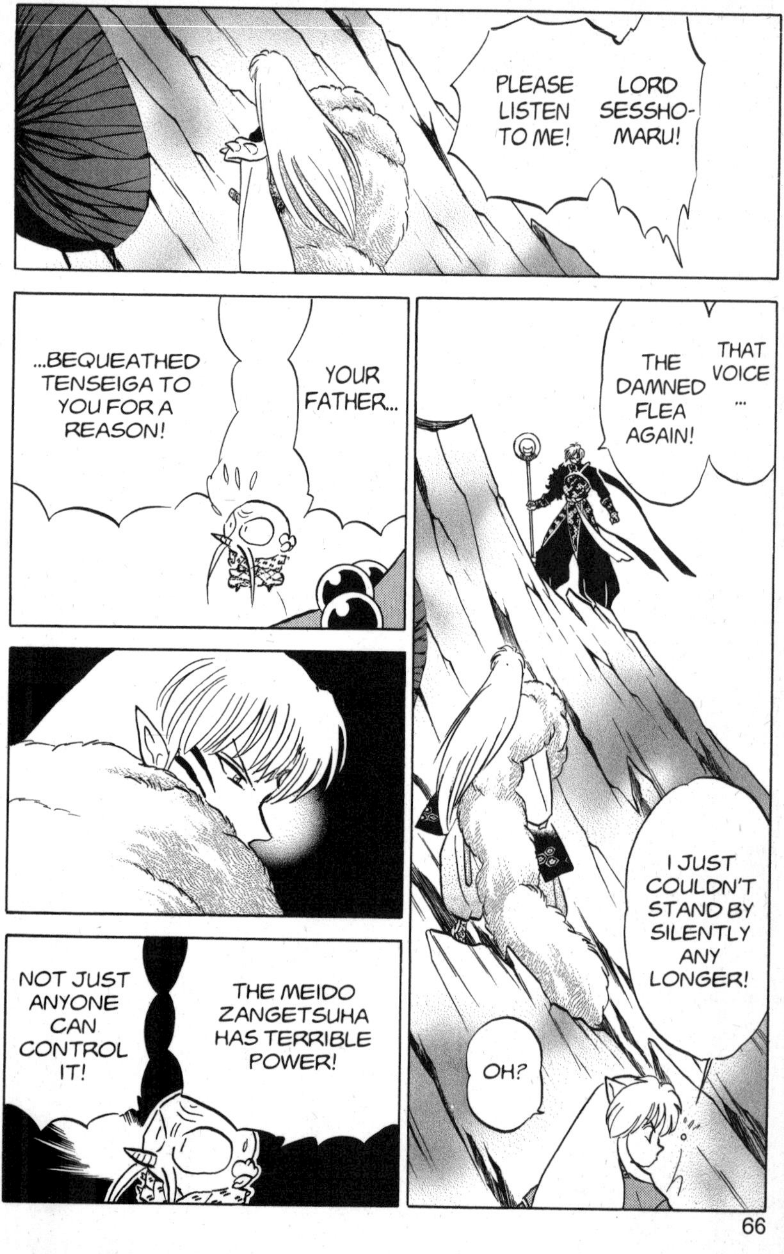
LORD SESSHO-MARU!
PLEASE LISTEN TO ME!
THAT VOICE ...
THE DAMNED FLEA AGAIN!
I JUST COULDN'T STAND BY SILENTLY ANY LONGER!
OH?
YOUR FATHER...
...BEQUEATHED TENSEIGA TO YOU FOR A REASON!
THE MEIDO ZANGETSUHA HAS TERRIBLE POWER!
NOT JUST ANYONE CAN CONTROL IT!

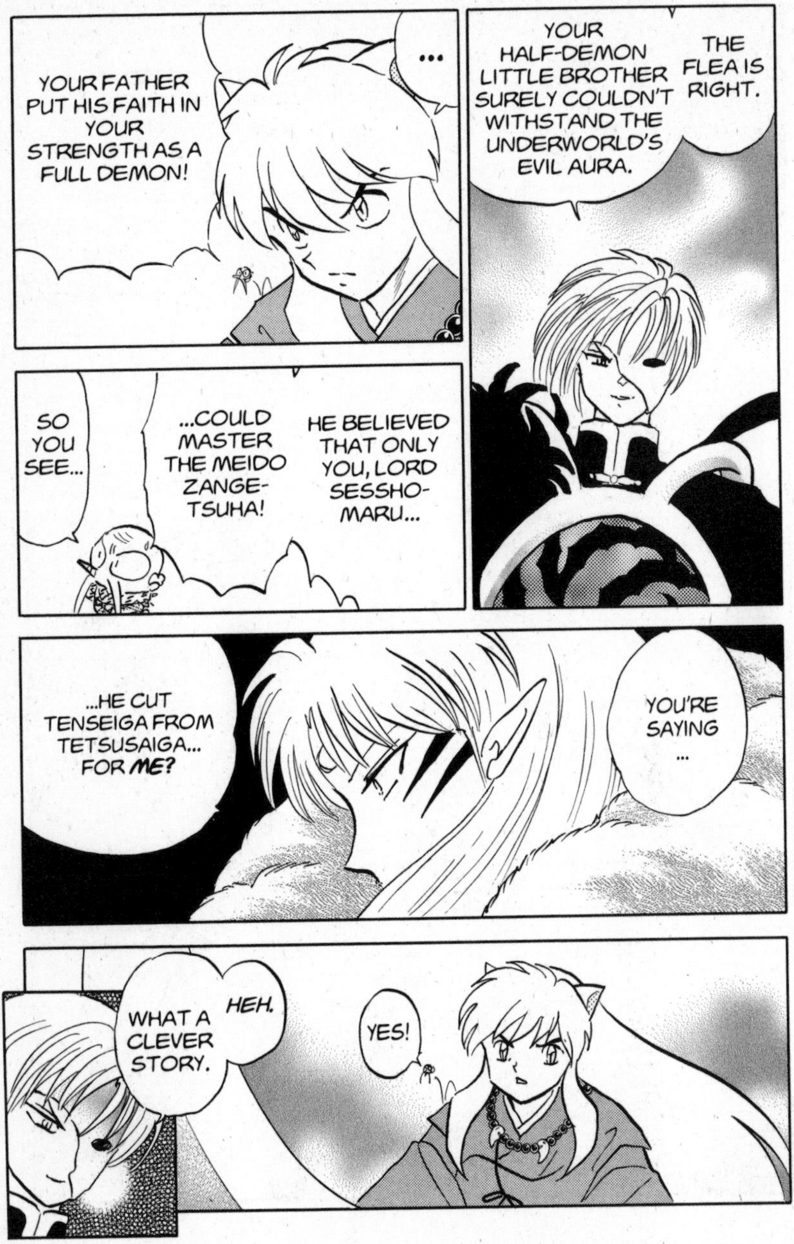
THE FLEA IS RIGHT.
YOUR HALF-DEMON LITTLE BROTHER SURELY COULDN'T WITHSTAND THE UNDERWORLD'S EVIL AURA.
...
YOUR FATHER PUT HIS FAITH IN YOUR STRENGTH AS A FULL DEMON!
HE BELIEVED THAT ONLY YOU, LORD SESSHO-MARU...
...COULD MASTER THE MEIDO ZANGE-TSUHA!
SO YOU SEE...
YOU'RE SAYING ...
...HE CUT TENSEIGA FROM TETSUSAIGA... FOR *ME*?
YES!
HEH.
WHAT A CLEVER STORY.

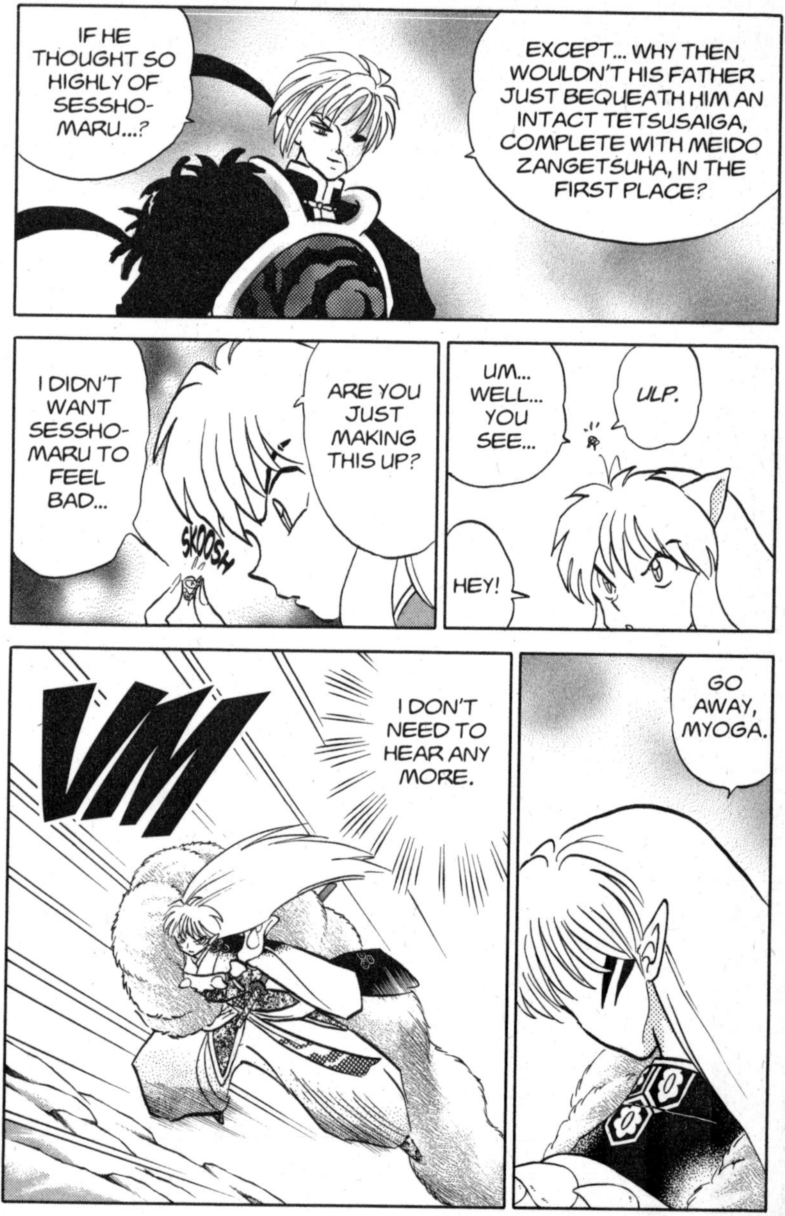
EXCEPT... WHY THEN WOULDN'T HIS FATHER JUST BEQUEATH HIM AN INTACT TETSUSAIGA, COMPLETE WITH MEIDO ZANGETSUHA, IN THE FIRST PLACE?
IF HE THOUGHT SO HIGHLY OF SESSHO-MARU...?
ULP.
UM... WELL... YOU SEE...
HEY!
ARE YOU JUST MAKING THIS UP?
I DIDN'T WANT SESSHO-MARU TO FEEL BAD...
SKOOSH
GO AWAY, MYOGA.
I DON'T NEED TO HEAR ANY MORE.
VM

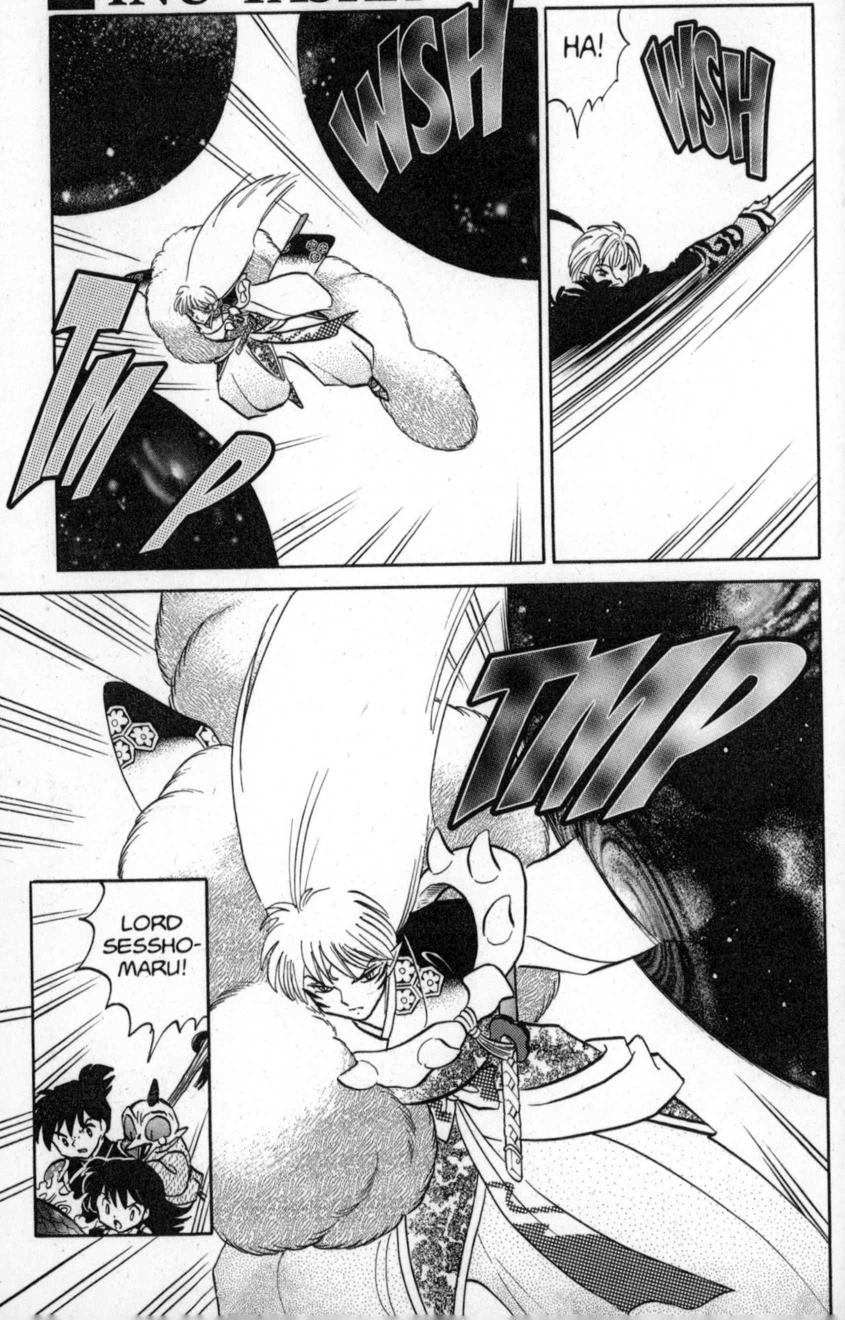
HA!
WSH
WSH
TMP
TMP
LORD SESSHOMARU!

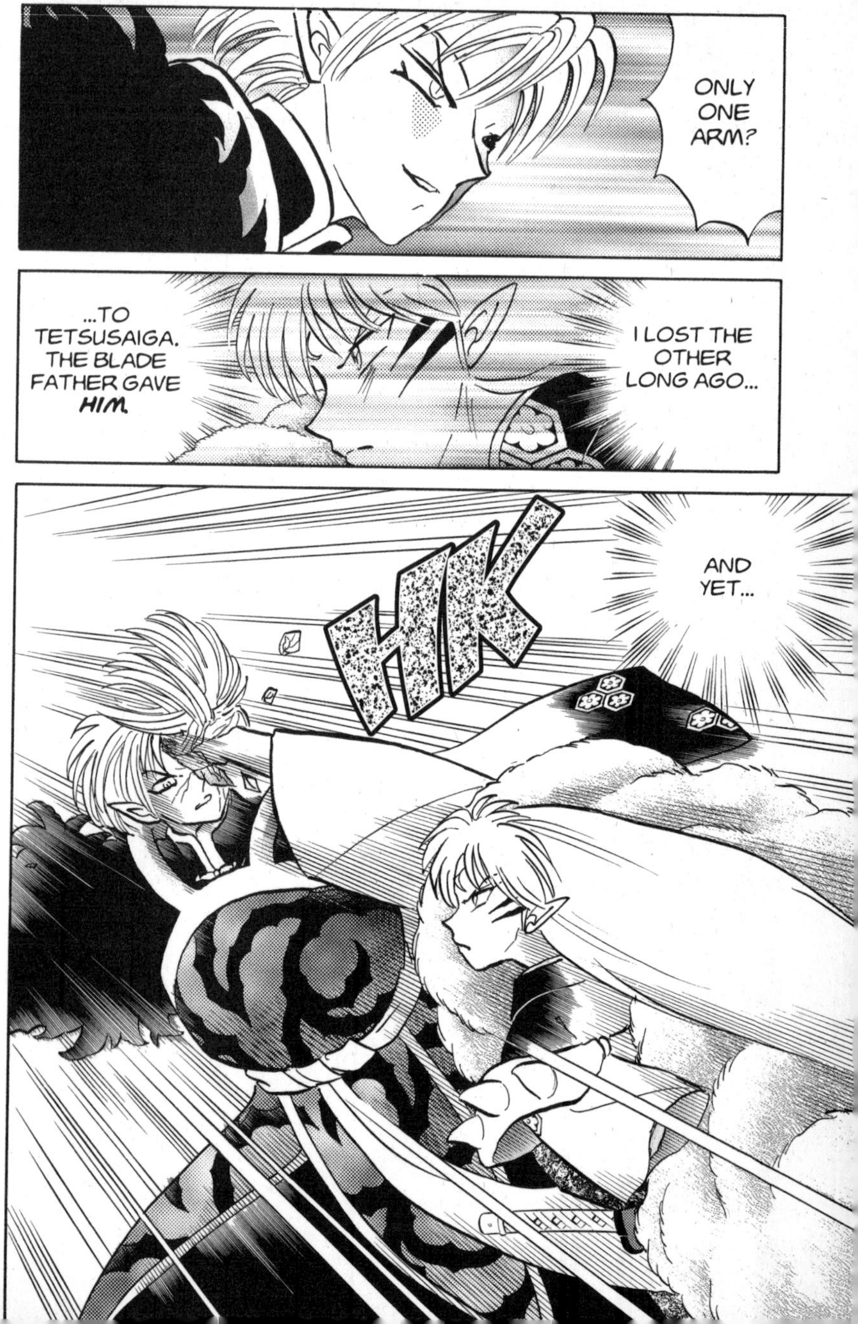
ONLY ONE ARM?
I LOST THE OTHER LONG AGO...
...TO TETSUSAIGA. THE BLADE FATHER GAVE *HIM*.
AND YET...
HIK

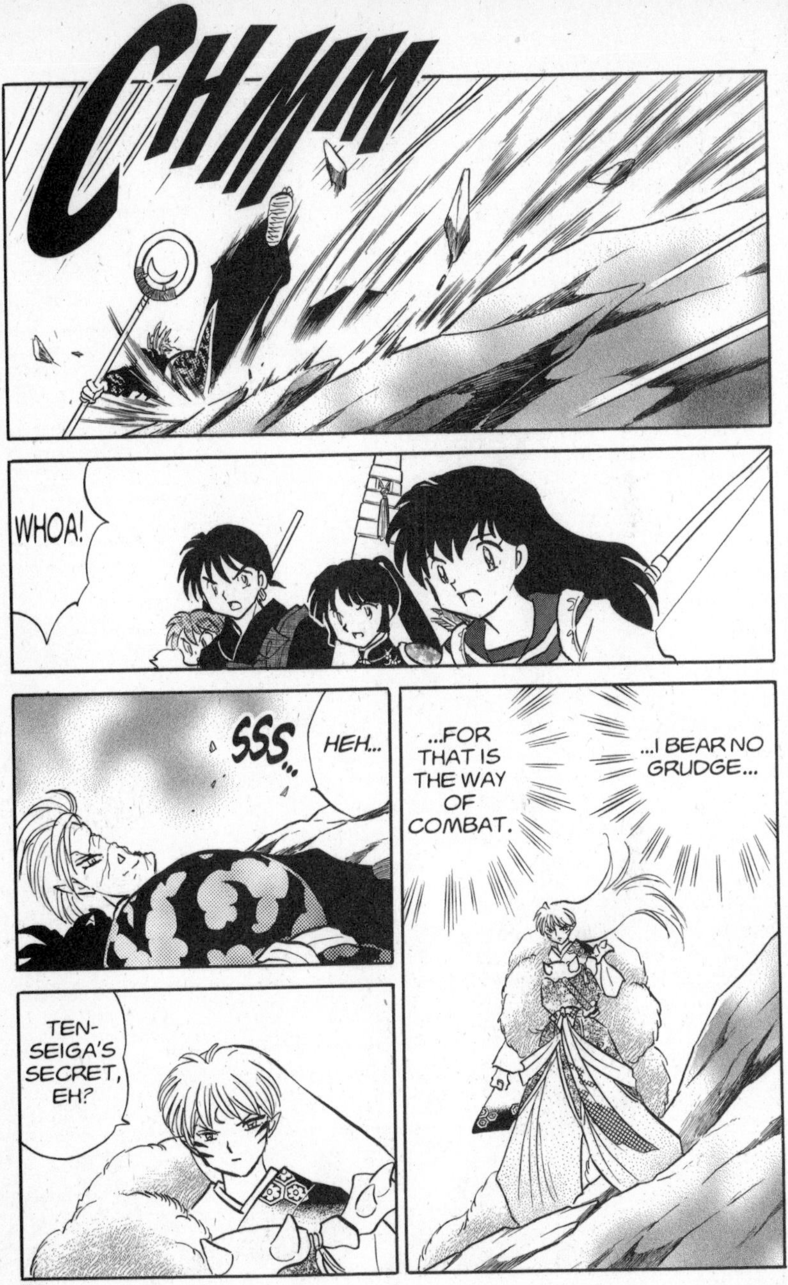
CHMM
WHOA!
...I BEAR NO GRUDGE...
...FOR THAT IS THE WAY OF COMBAT.
HEH...
SSS...
TEN-SEIGA'S SECRET, EH?

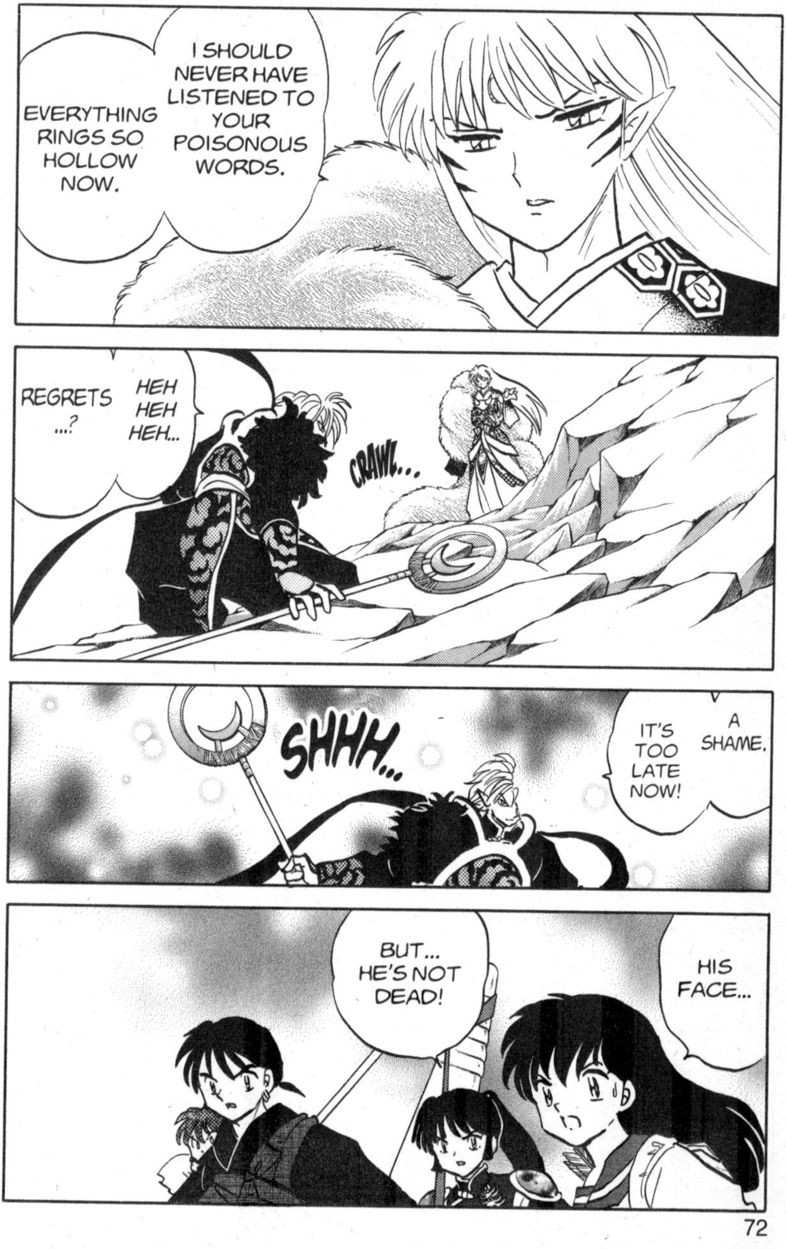
I SHOULD NEVER HAVE LISTENED TO YOUR POISONOUS WORDS.
EVERYTHING RINGS SO HOLLOW NOW.
HEH HEH HEH...
REGRETS ...?
CRAWL...
A SHAME.
IT'S TOO LATE NOW!
SHHH...
HIS FACE...
BUT... HE'S NOT DEAD!

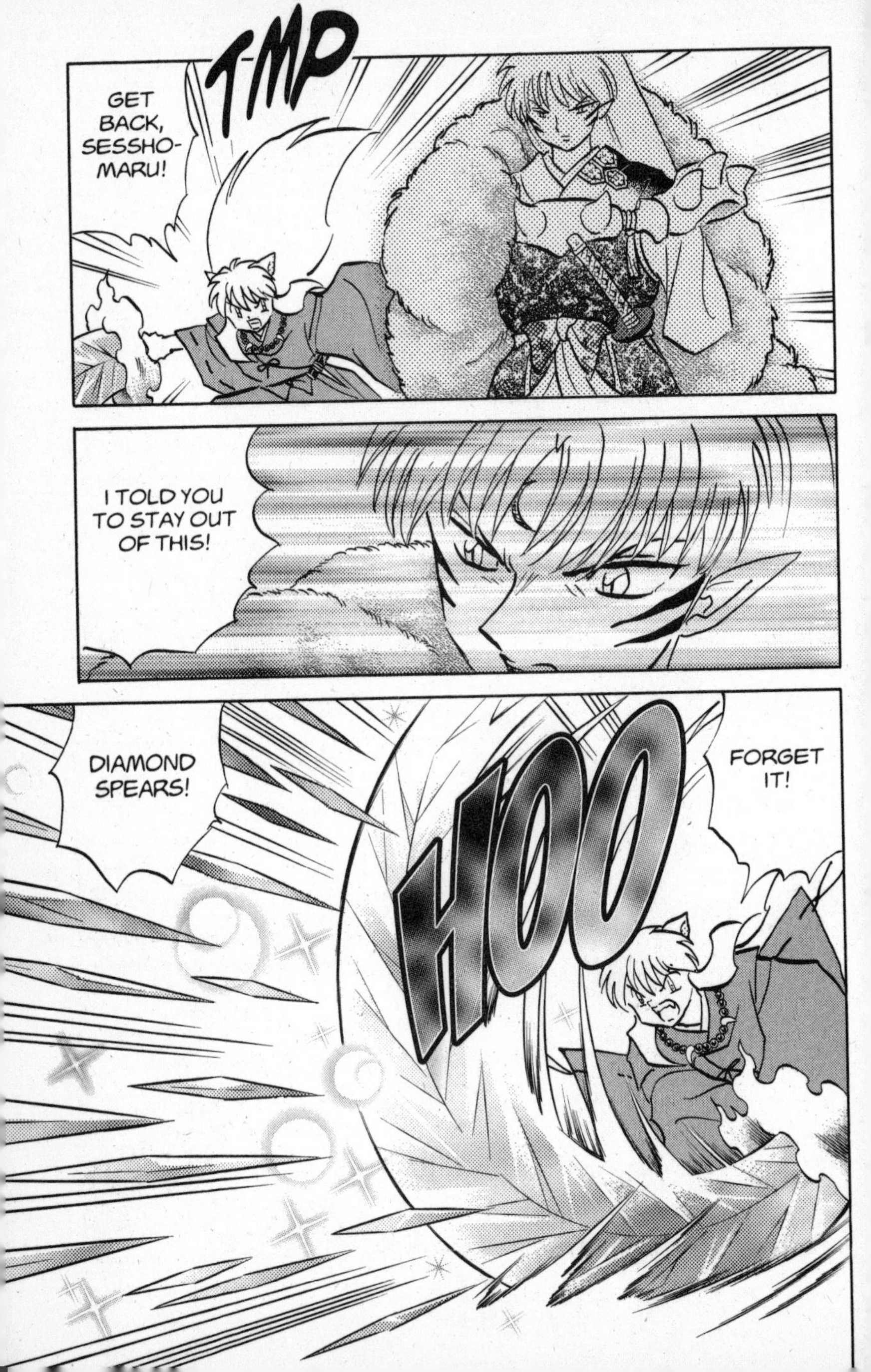
TMP
GET BACK, SESSHOMARU!
I TOLD YOU TO STAY OUT OF THIS!
FORGET IT!
HOO
DIAMOND SPEARS!

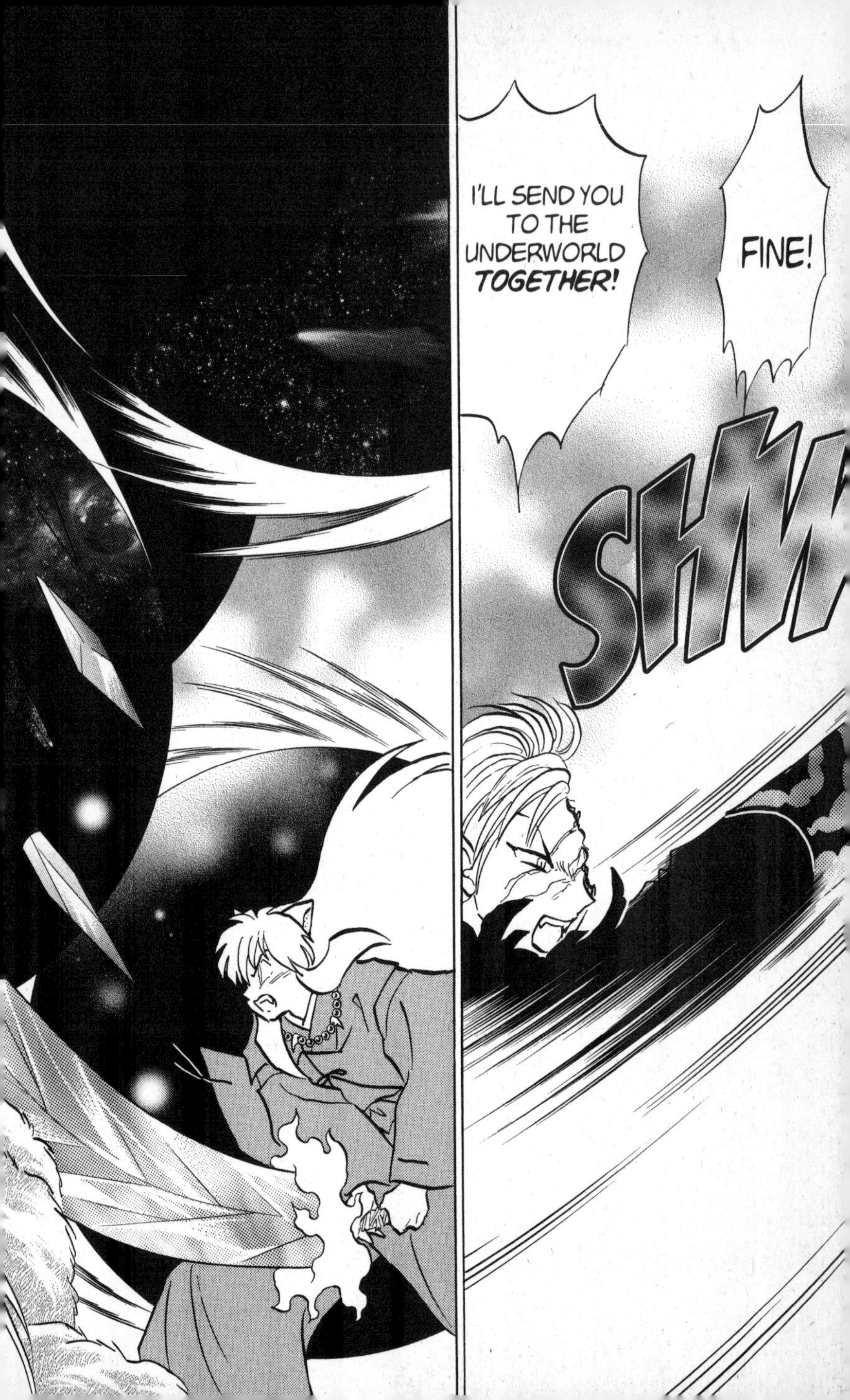
FINE!
I'LL SEND YOU TO THE UNDERWORLD *TOGETHER!*
SHW

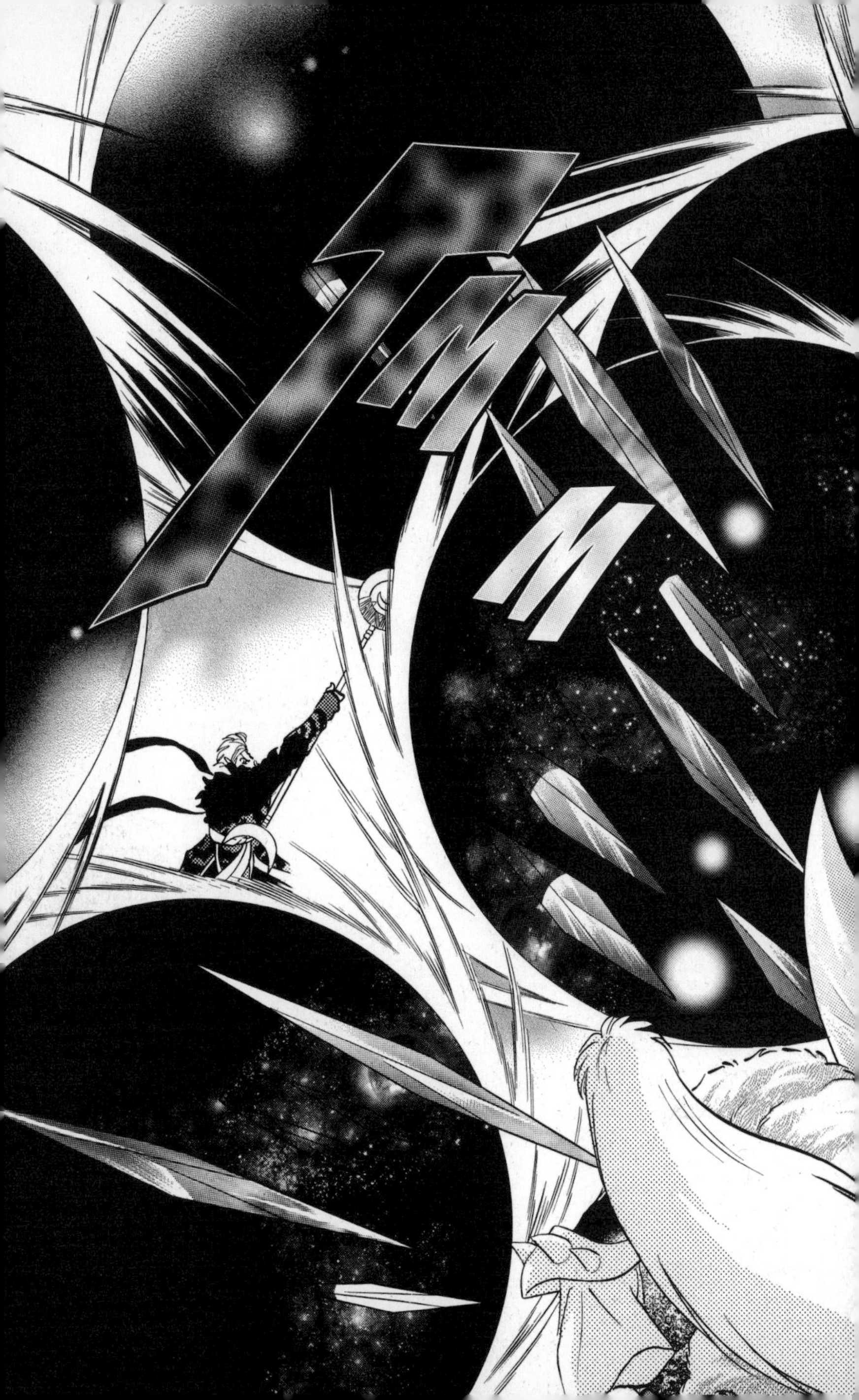

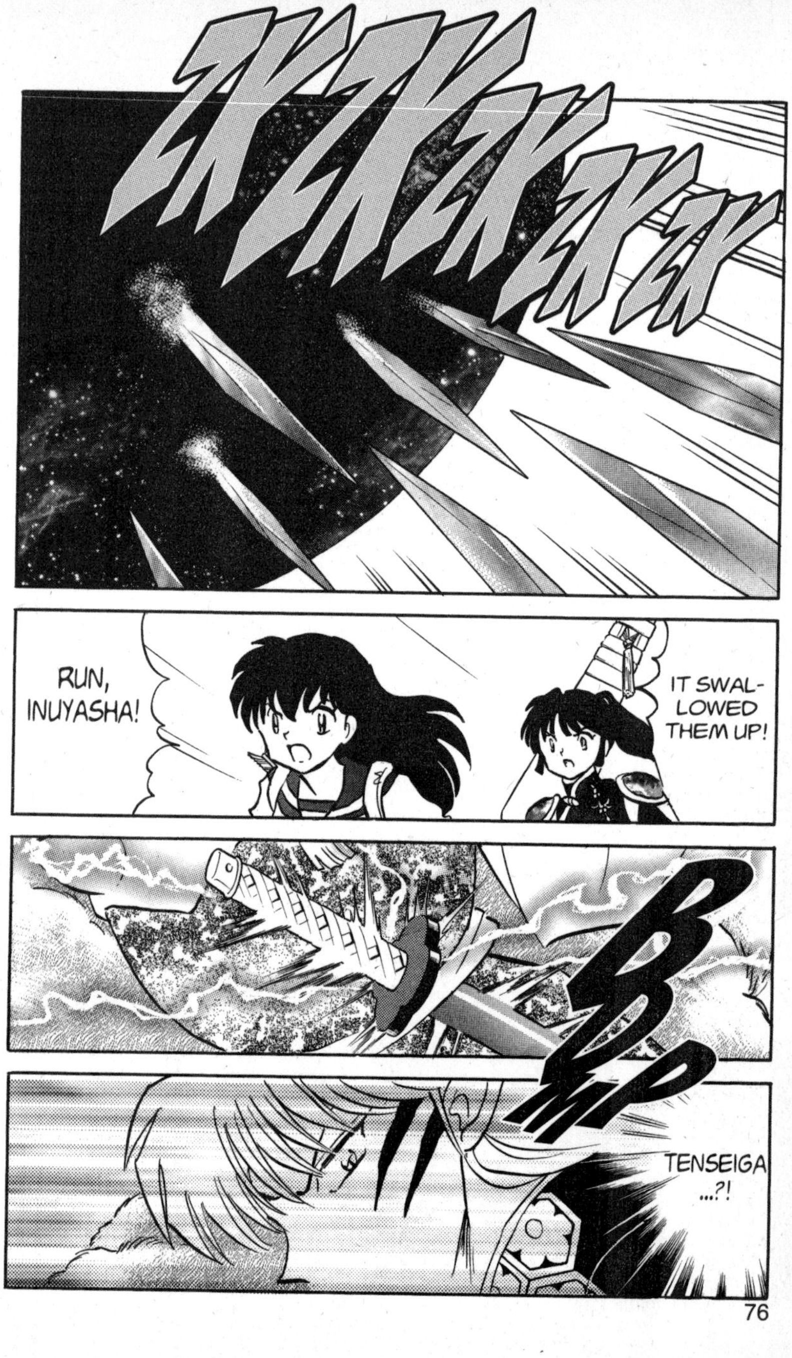
IT SWAL-
LOWED
THEM UP!
RUN,
INUYASHA!
TENSEIGA
...?!

SCROLL 5

RESONANCE

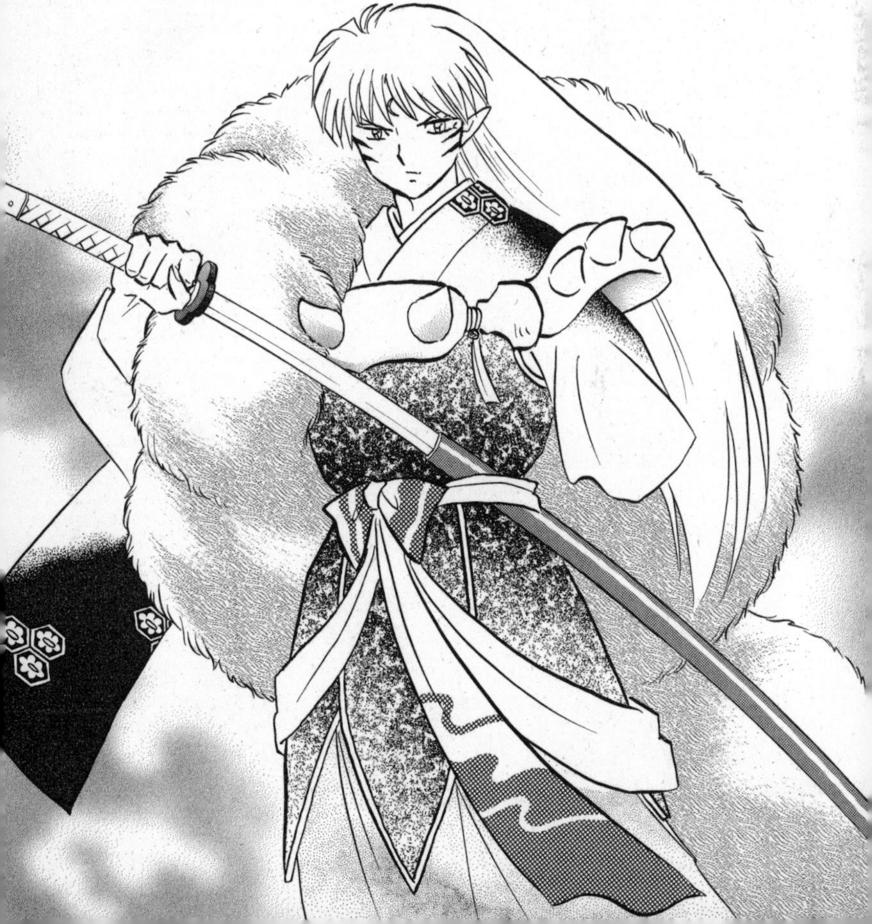

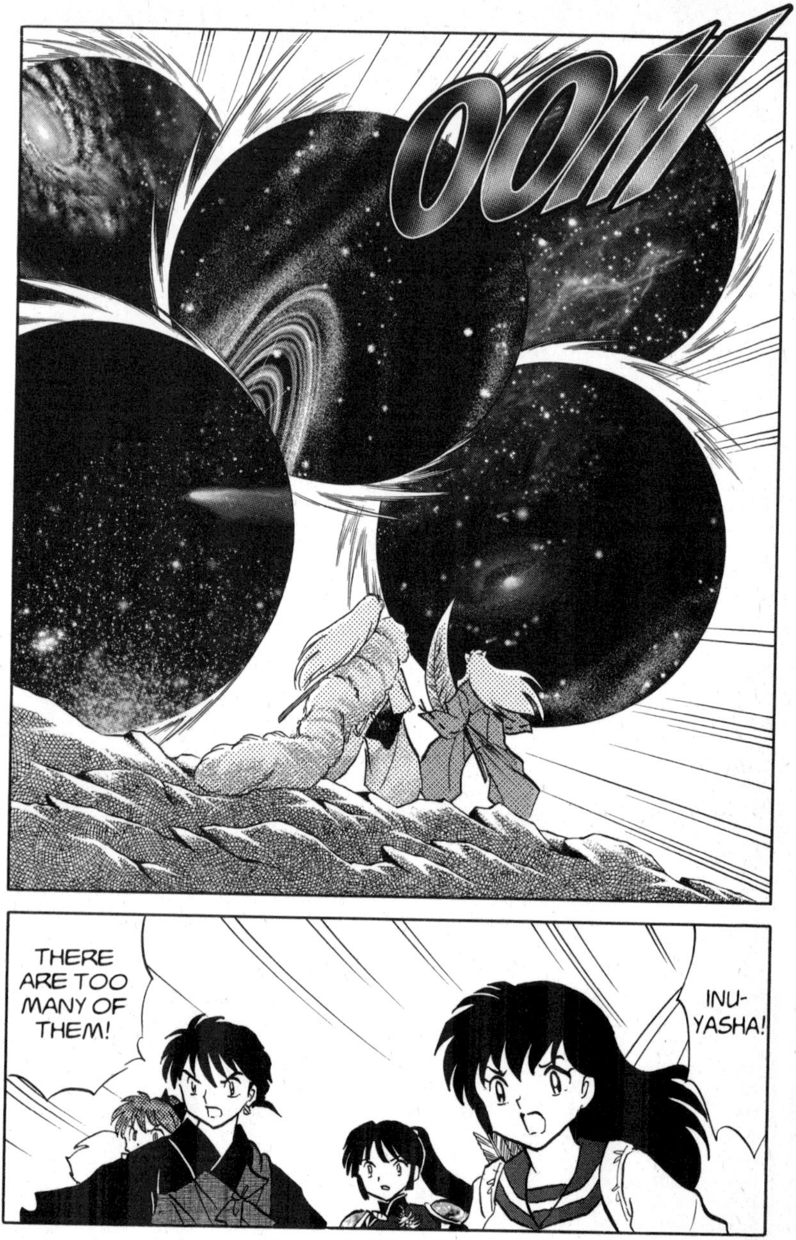
OOM
INU-YASHA!
THERE ARE TOO MANY OF THEM!

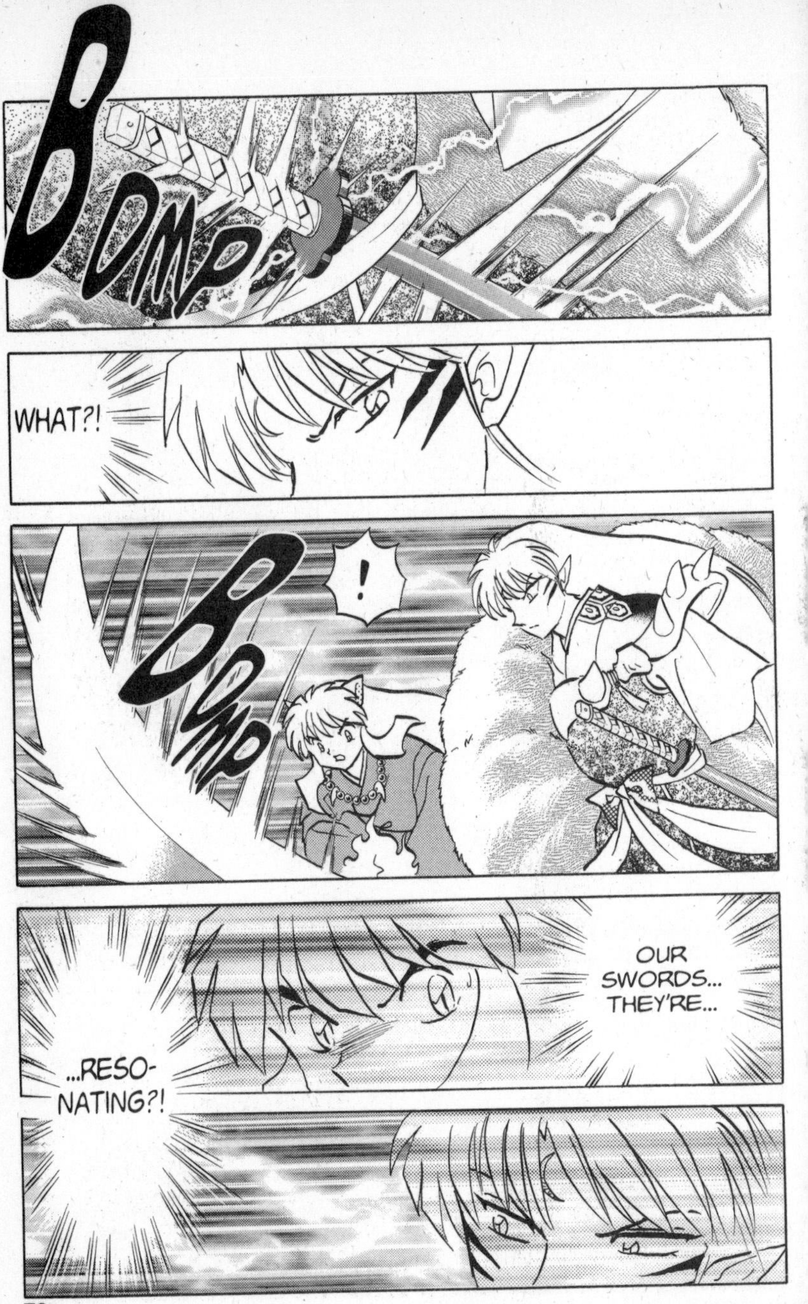
BDMP
WHAT?!
!
BDMP
OUR SWORDS... THEY'RE...
...RESO-NATING?!

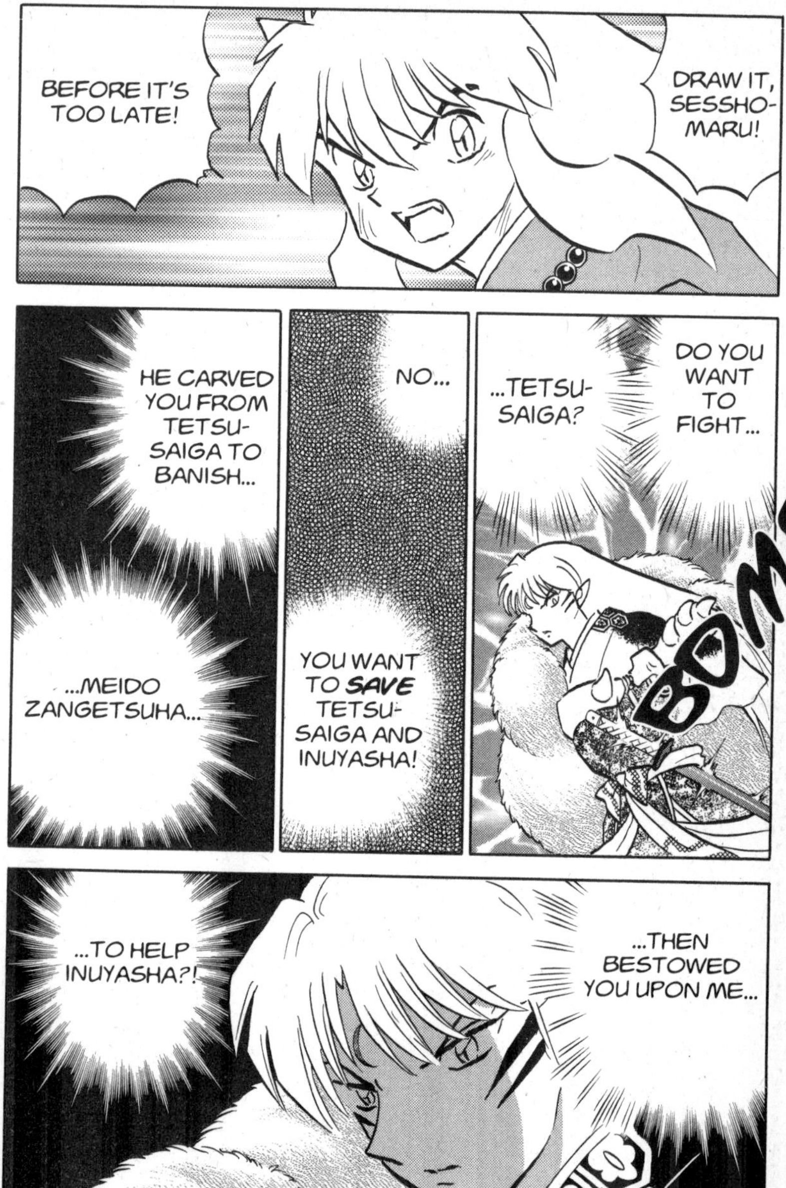
DRAW IT, SESSHO-MARU!
BEFORE IT'S TOO LATE!
DO YOU WANT TO FIGHT...
...TETSU-SAIGA?
BOMP
NO...
YOU WANT TO *SAVE* TETSU-SAIGA AND INUYASHA!
HE CARVED YOU FROM TETSU-SAIGA TO BANISH...
...MEIDO ZANGETSUHA...
...THEN BESTOWED YOU UPON ME...
...TO HELP INUYASHA?!

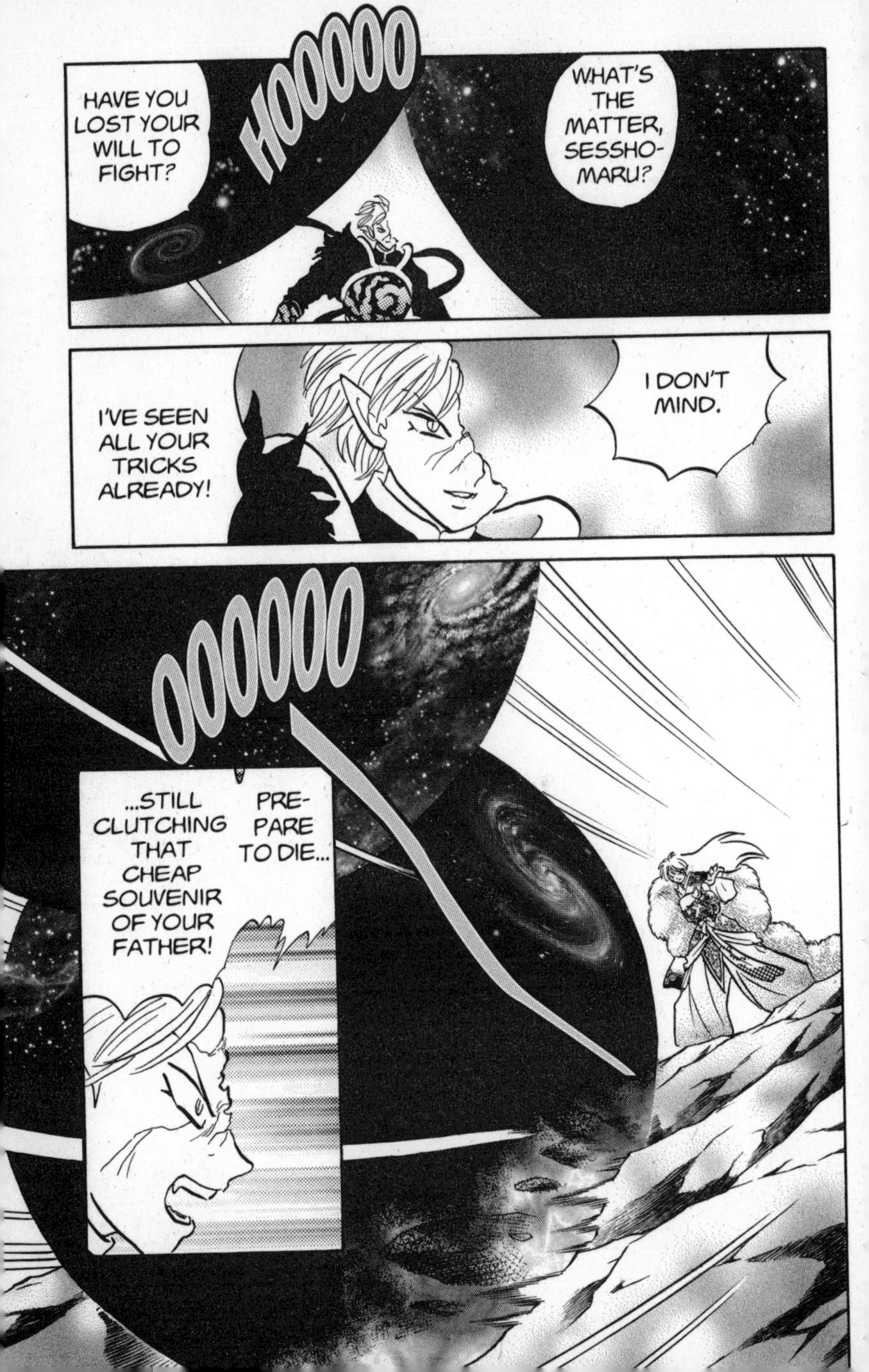
WHAT'S THE MATTER, SESSHO-MARU?
HOOOOO
HAVE YOU LOST YOUR WILL TO FIGHT?
I DON'T MIND.
I'VE SEEN ALL YOUR TRICKS ALREADY!
OOOOOO
PRE-PARE TO DIE...
...STILL CLUTCHING THAT CHEAP SOUVENIR OF YOUR FATHER!

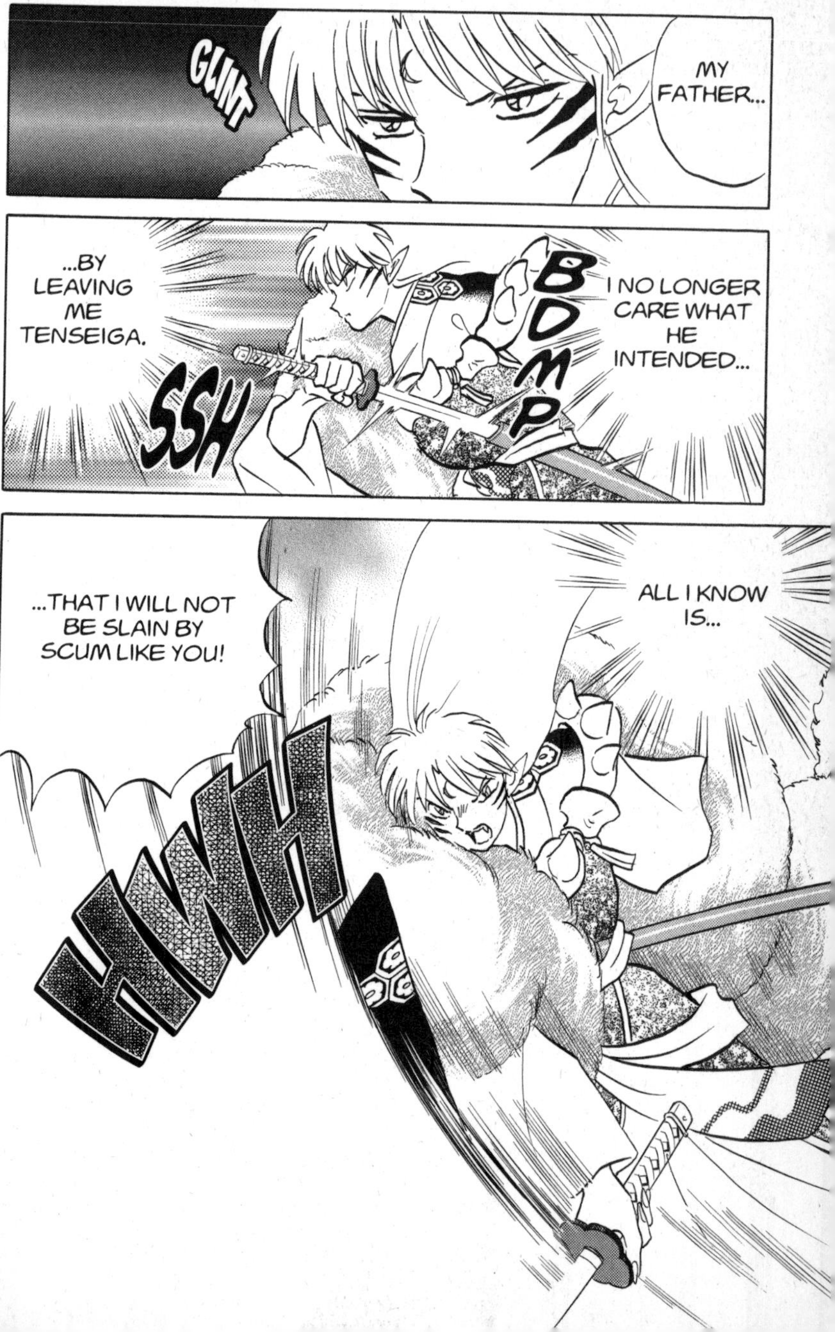

MY FATHER...
GLINT
I NO LONGER CARE WHAT HE INTENDED...
BDOMP
...BY LEAVING ME TENSEIGA.
SSH
ALL I KNOW IS...
...THAT I WILL NOT BE SLAIN BY SCUM LIKE YOU!
HWWH

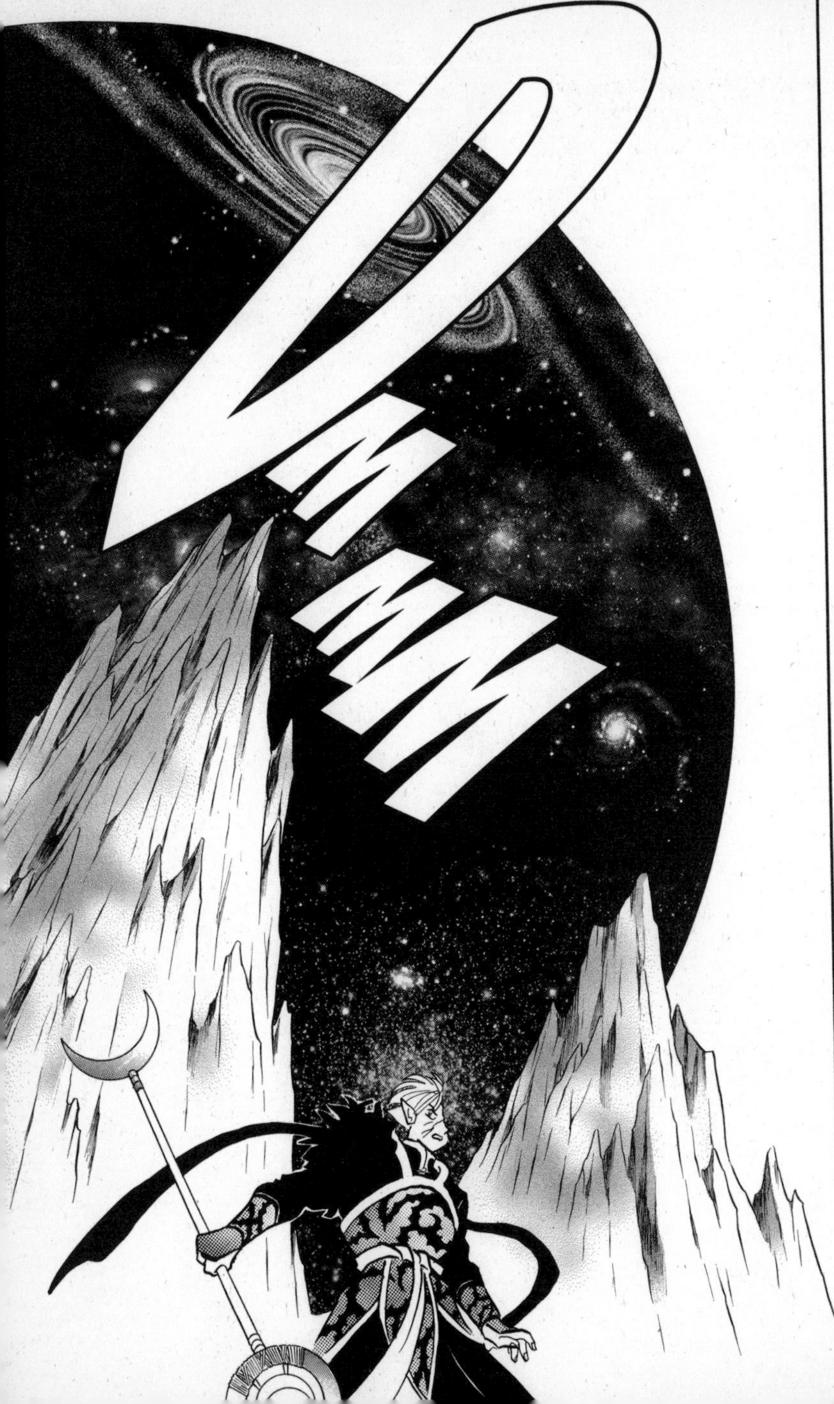

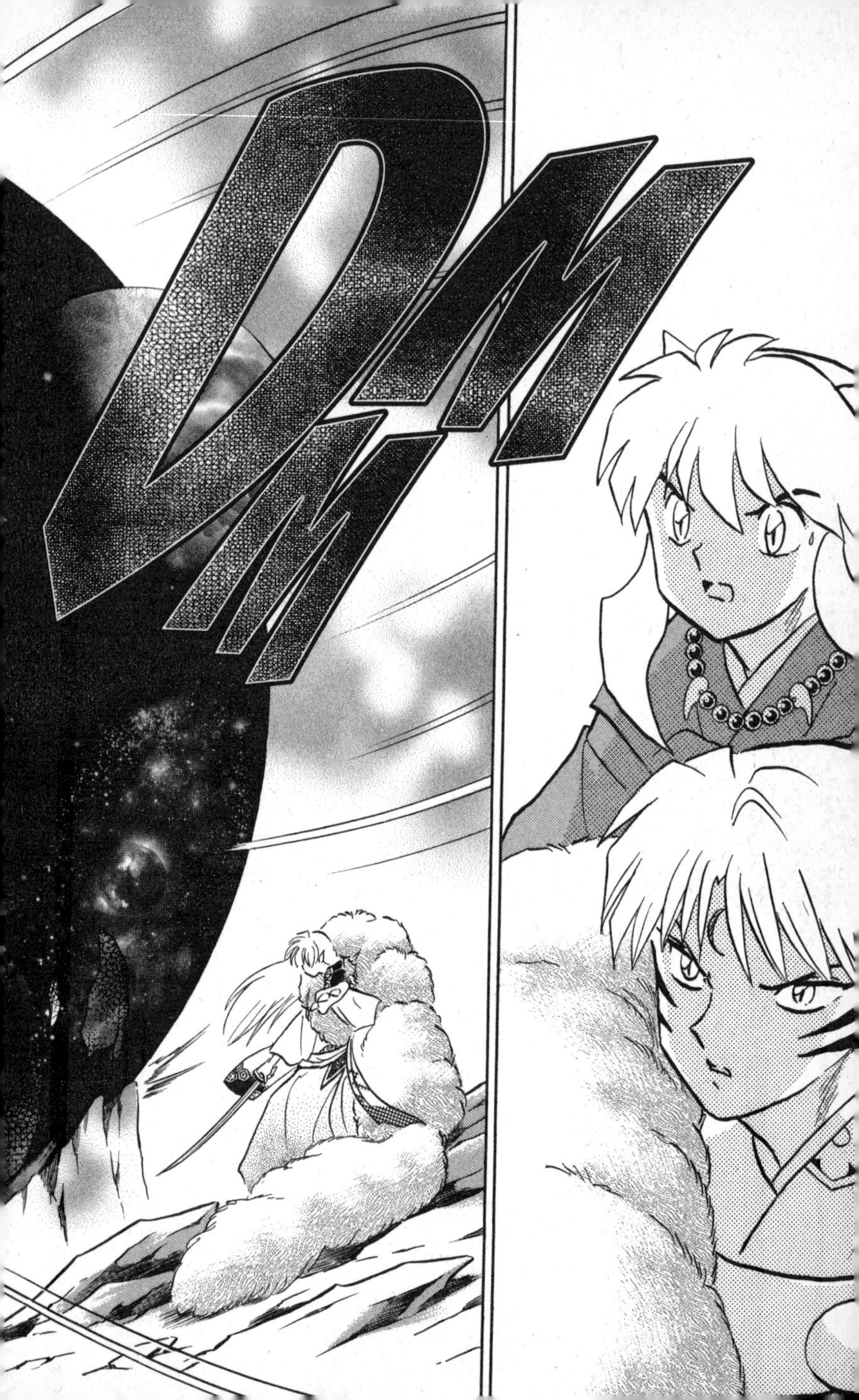
DMM

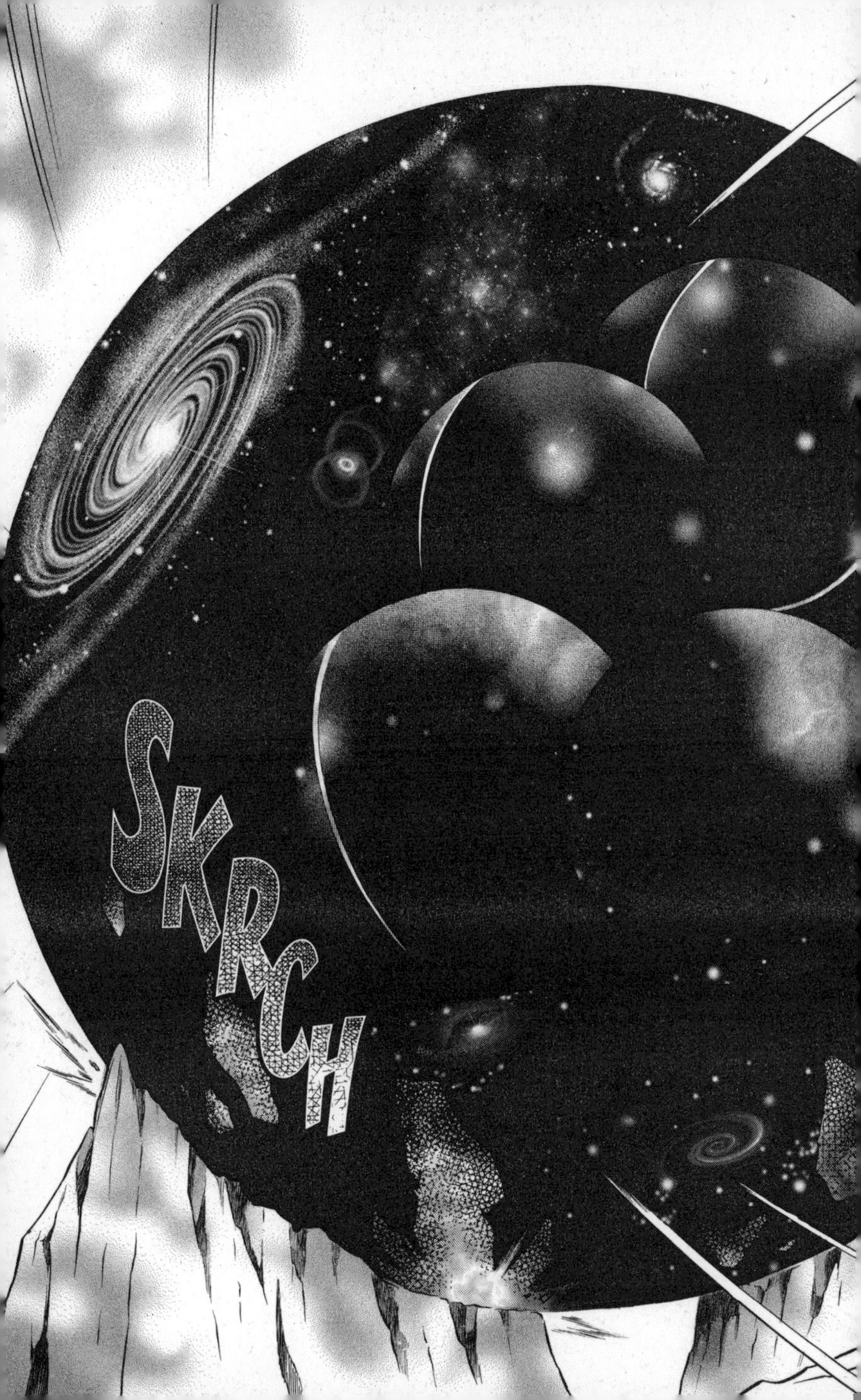
SKRCH

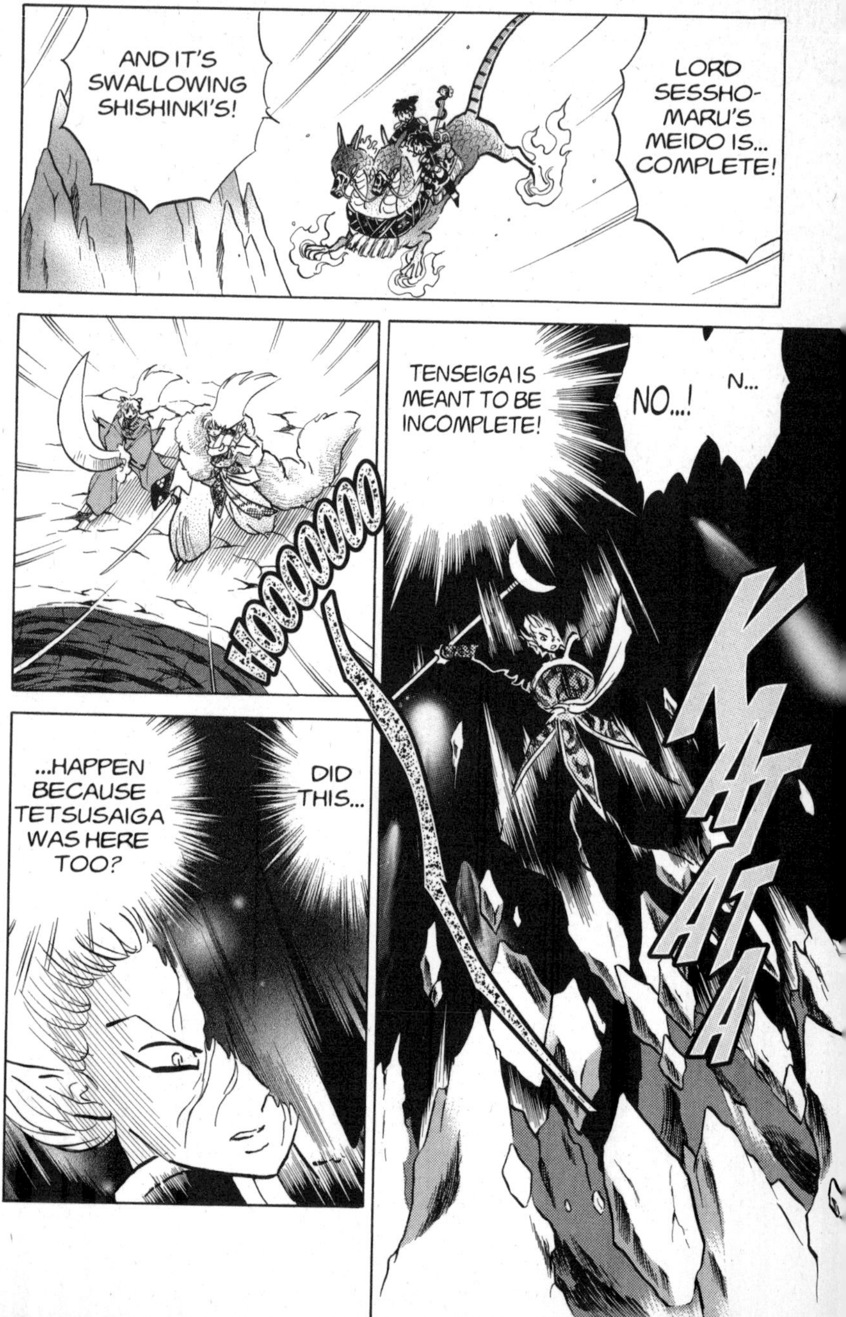
LORD SESSHOMARU'S MEIDO IS... COMPLETE!
AND IT'S SWALLOWING SHISHINKI'S!
N...
NO...!
TENSEIGA IS MEANT TO BE INCOMPLETE!
HOOOOOOOO
DID THIS...
...HAPPEN BECAUSE TETSUSAIGA WAS HERE TOO?

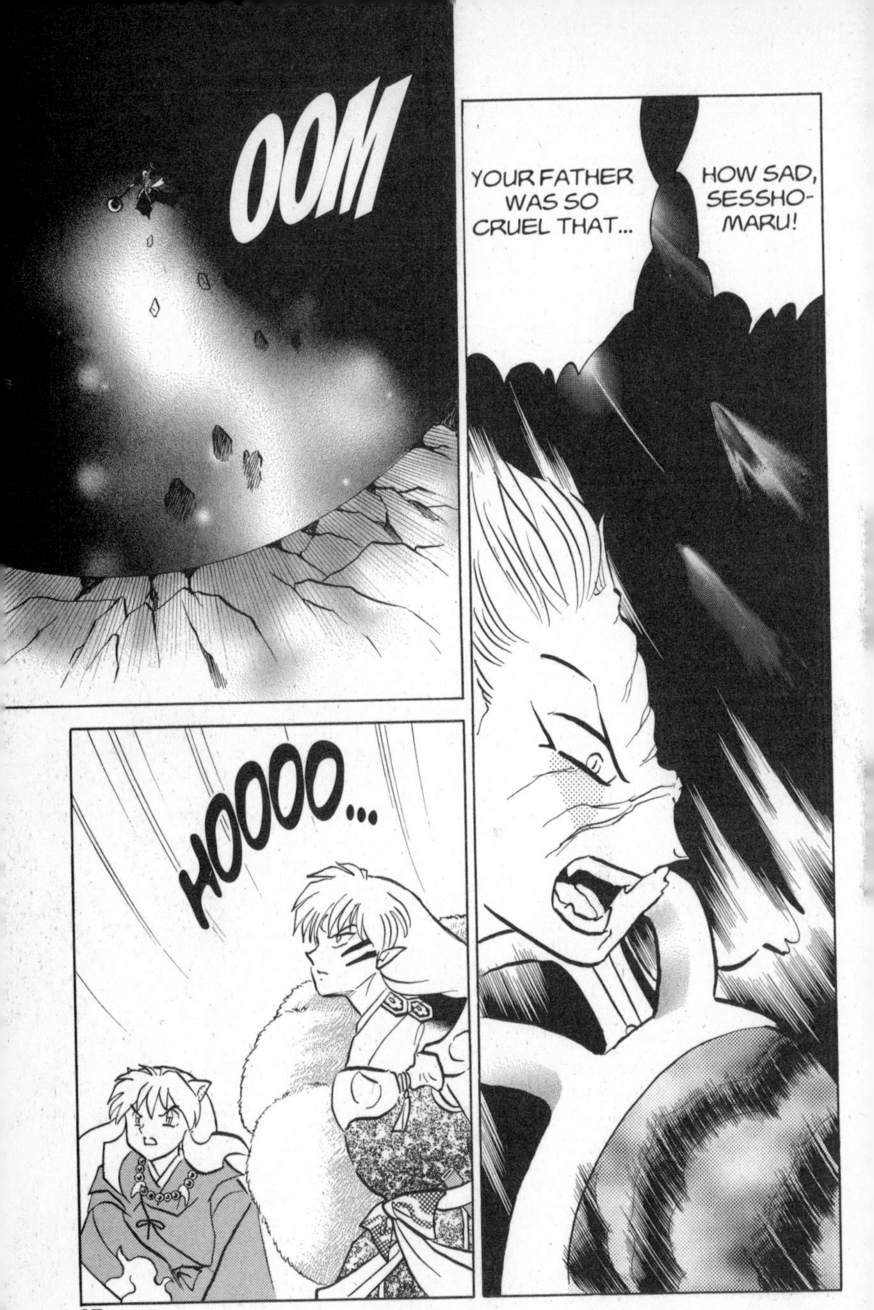
HOW SAD, SESSHO-MARU!
YOUR FATHER WAS SO CRUEL THAT...
OOM
HOOOO...

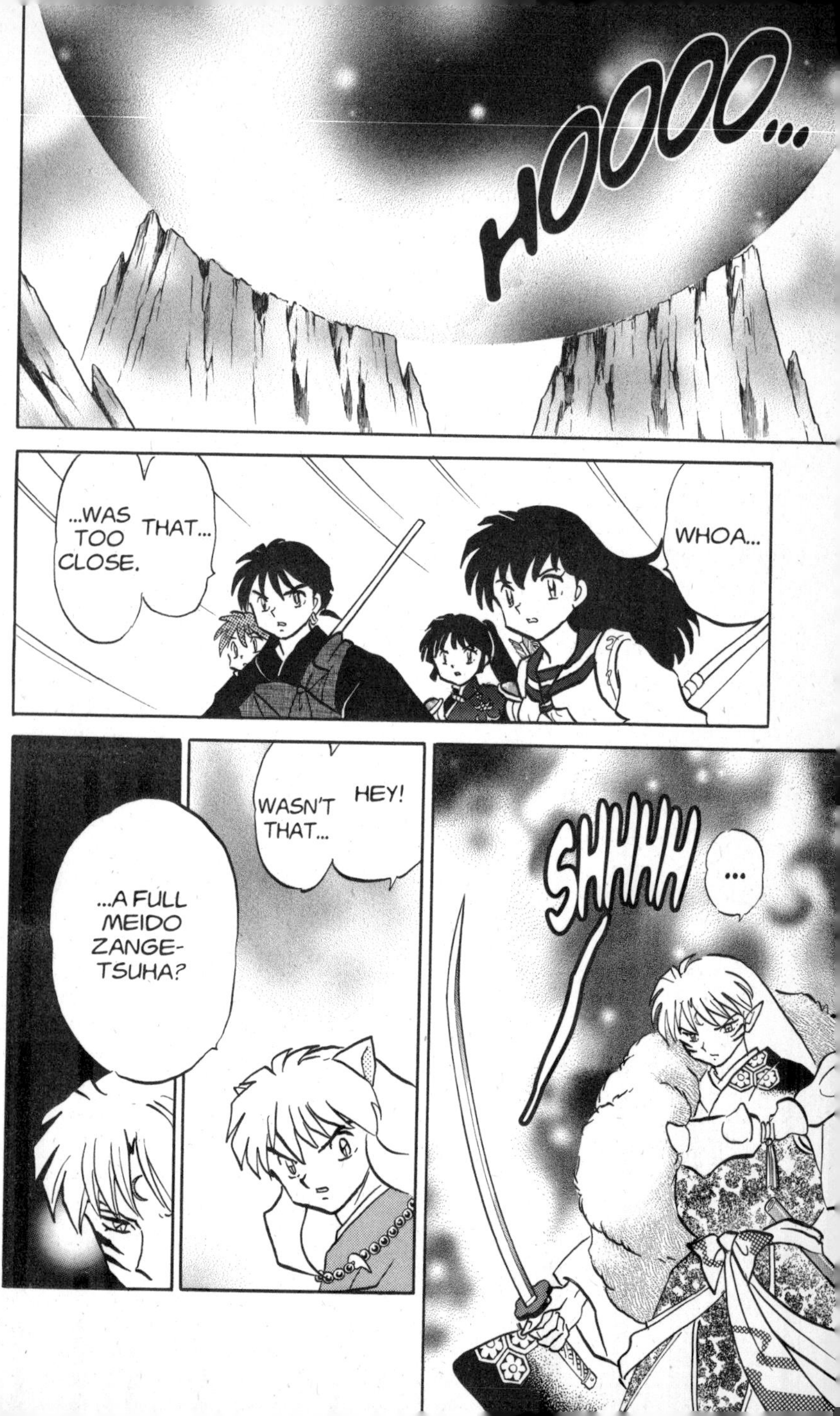
HOOOO...
WHOA...
THAT...
...WAS TOO CLOSE.
SHHHH
...
HEY!
WASN'T THAT...
...A FULL MEIDO ZANGE-TSUHA?

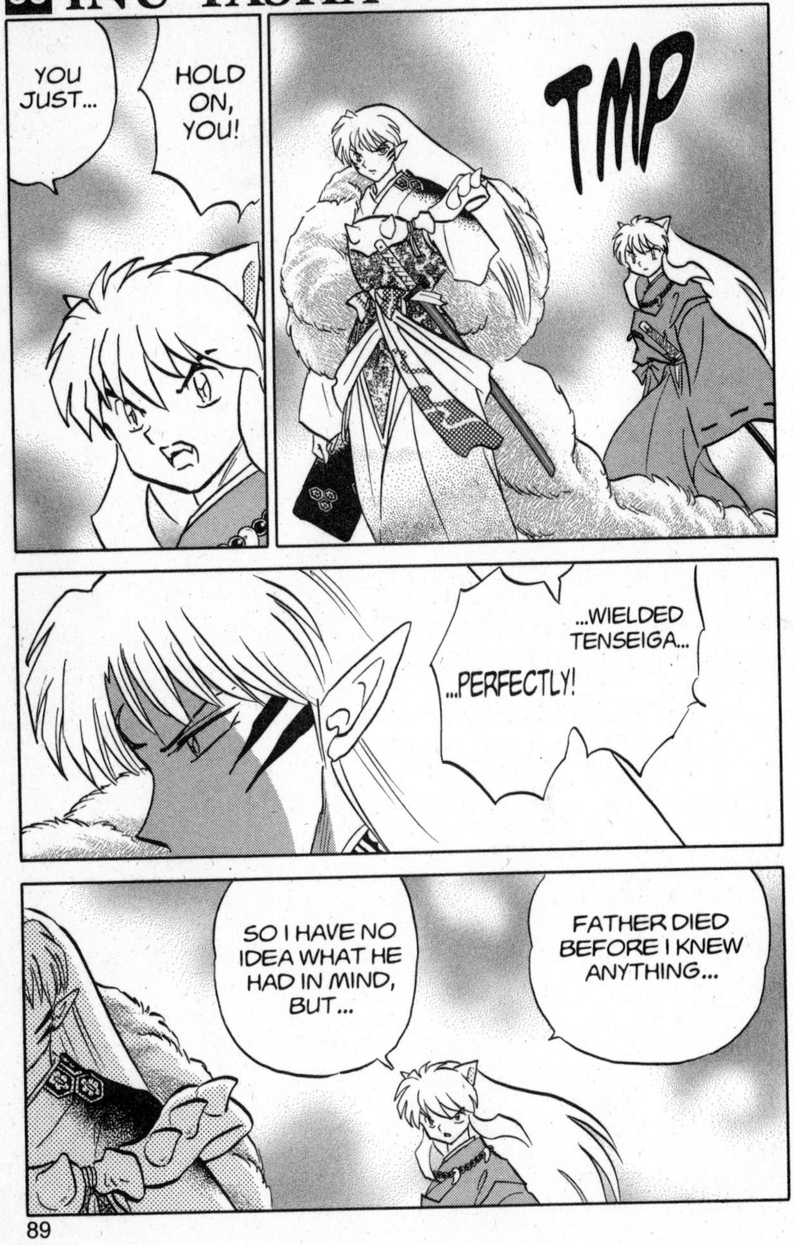
TMP
HOLD ON, YOU!
YOU JUST...
...WIELDED TENSEIGA...
...PERFECTLY!
FATHER DIED BEFORE I KNEW ANYTHING...
SO I HAVE NO IDEA WHAT HE HAD IN MIND, BUT...

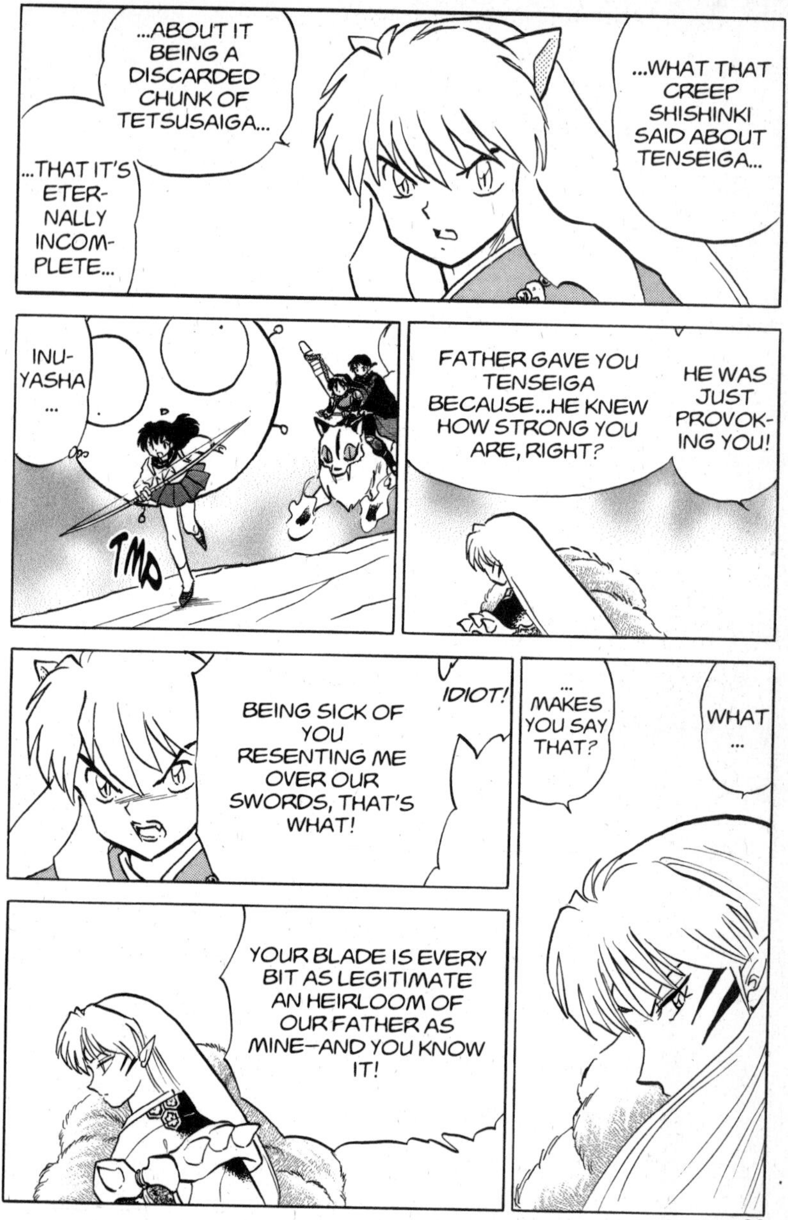
...WHAT THAT CREEP SHISHINKI SAID ABOUT TENSEIGA...
...ABOUT IT BEING A DISCARDED CHUNK OF TETSUSAIGA...
...THAT IT'S ETER-NALLY INCOM-PLETE...
HE WAS JUST PROVOK-ING YOU!
FATHER GAVE YOU TENSEIGA BECAUSE...HE KNEW HOW STRONG YOU ARE, RIGHT?
INU-YASHA ...
TMP
WHAT ...
... MAKES YOU SAY THAT?
IDIOT!
BEING SICK OF YOU RESENTING ME OVER OUR SWORDS, THAT'S WHAT!
YOUR BLADE IS EVERY BIT AS LEGITIMATE AN HEIRLOOM OF OUR FATHER AS MINE—AND YOU KNOW IT!

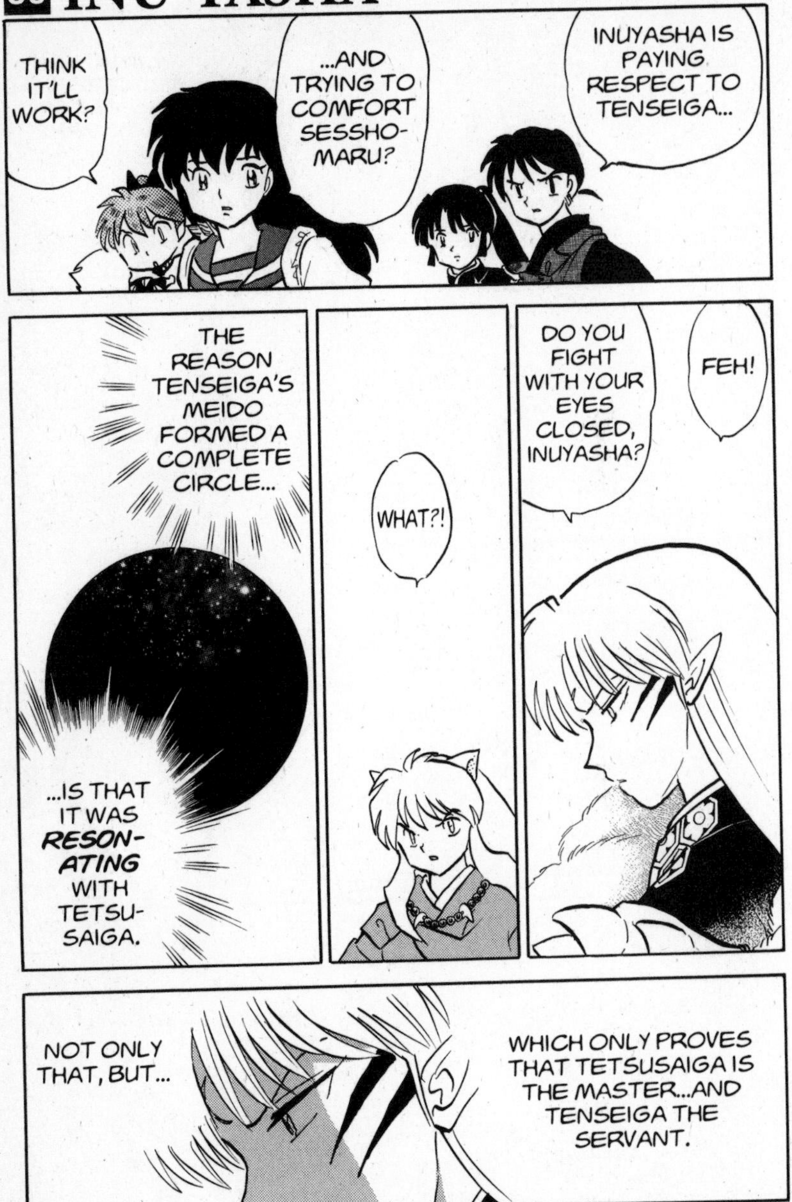
INUYASHA IS PAYING RESPECT TO TENSEIGA...
...AND TRYING TO COMFORT SESSHO-MARU?
THINK IT'LL WORK?
FEH!
DO YOU FIGHT WITH YOUR EYES CLOSED, INUYASHA?
WHAT?!
THE REASON TENSEIGA'S MEIDO FORMED A COMPLETE CIRCLE...
...IS THAT IT WAS RESONATING WITH TETSU-SAIGA.
WHICH ONLY PROVES THAT TETSUSAIGA IS THE MASTER...AND TENSEIGA THE SERVANT.
NOT ONLY THAT, BUT...

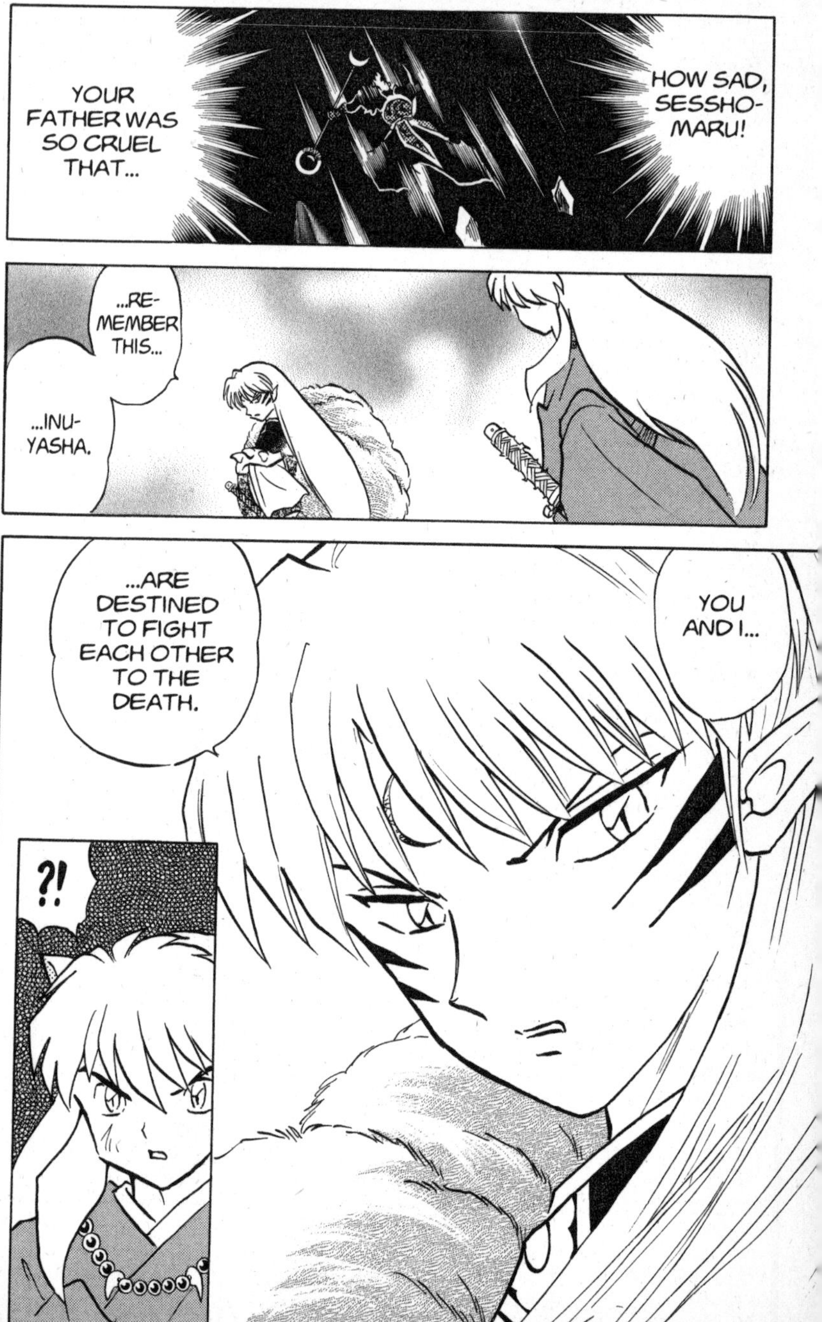
HOW SAD, SESSHOMARU!
YOUR FATHER WAS SO CRUEL THAT...
...REMEMBER THIS...
...INUYASHA.
YOU AND I...
...ARE DESTINED TO FIGHT EACH OTHER TO THE DEATH.
?!

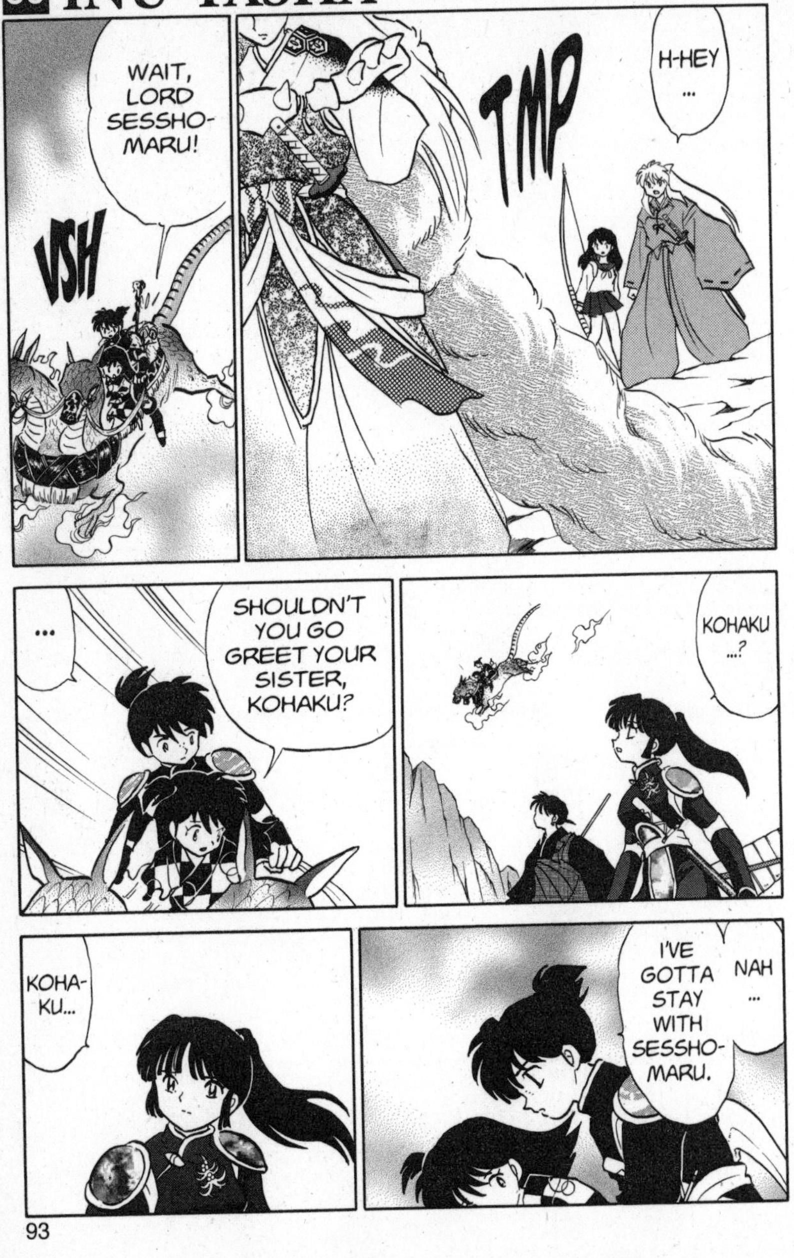
H-HEY ...
TMP
WAIT, LORD SESSHO-MARU!
VSH
KOHAKU ...?
SHOULDN'T YOU GO GREET YOUR SISTER, KOHAKU?
...
NAH ...
I'VE GOTTA STAY WITH SESSHO-MARU.
KOHA-KU...

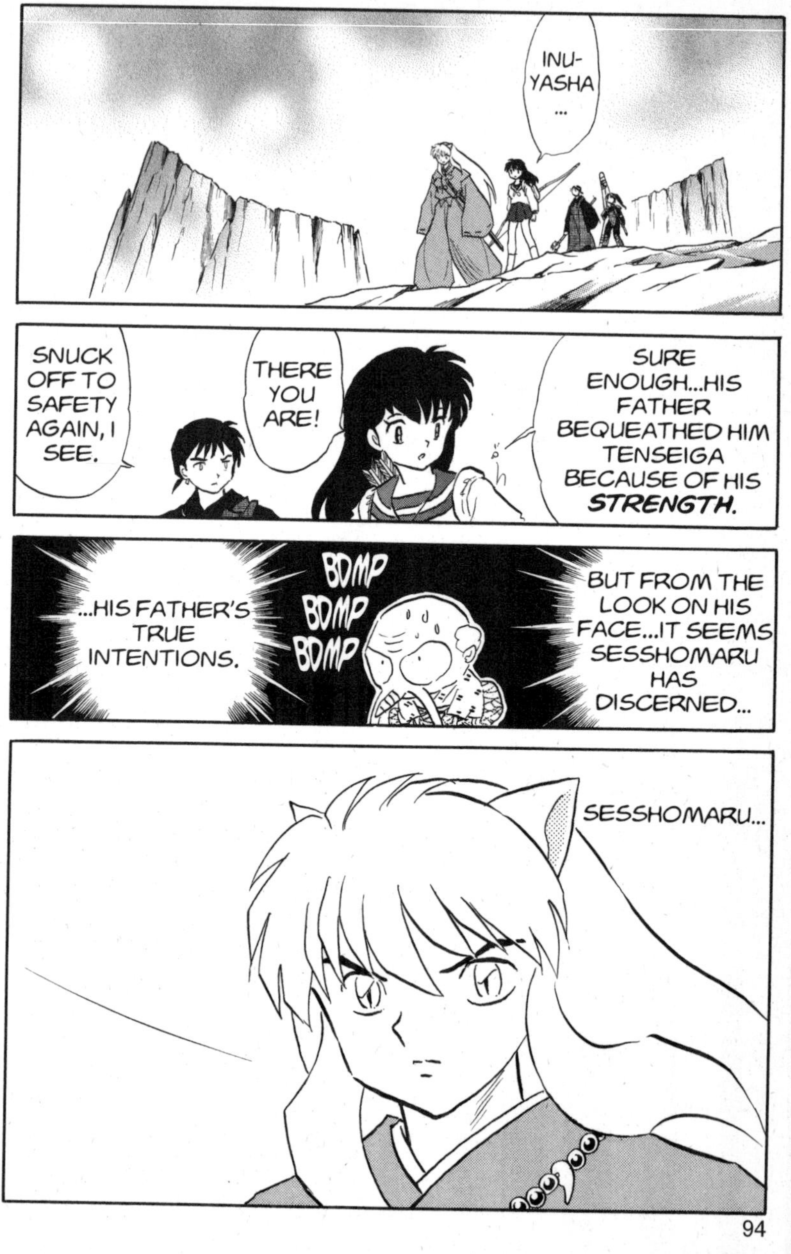
INU-YASHA ...
SURE ENOUGH...HIS FATHER BEQUEATHED HIM TENSEIGA BECAUSE OF HIS STRENGTH.
THERE YOU ARE!
SNUCK OFF TO SAFETY AGAIN, I SEE.
BUT FROM THE LOOK ON HIS FACE...IT SEEMS SESSHOMARU HAS DISCERNED...
BDMP BDMP BDMP
...HIS FATHER'S TRUE INTENTIONS.
SESSHOMARU...

SCROLL 6
TWO WORLDS

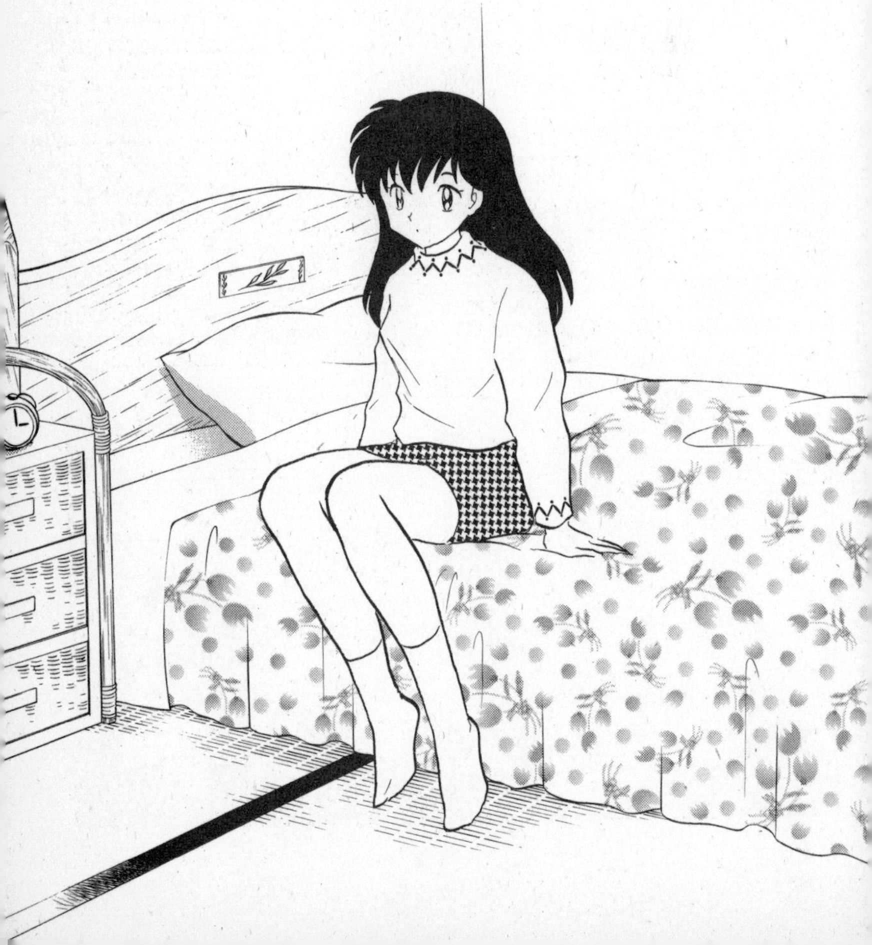

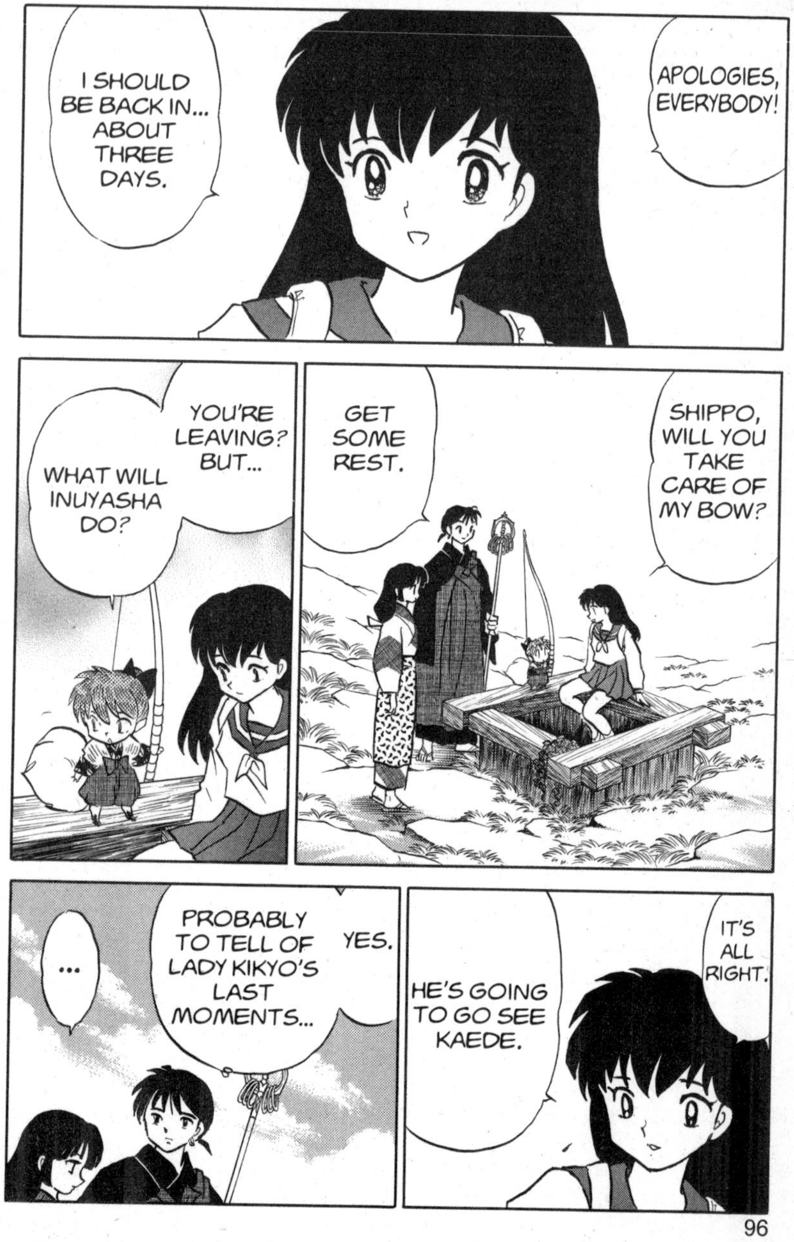
APOLOGIES, EVERYBODY!
I SHOULD BE BACK IN... ABOUT THREE DAYS.
SHIPPO, WILL YOU TAKE CARE OF MY BOW?
GET SOME REST.
YOU'RE LEAVING? BUT...
WHAT WILL INUYASHA DO?
IT'S ALL RIGHT!
HE'S GOING TO GO SEE KAEDE.
YES.
PROBABLY TO TELL OF LADY KIKYO'S LAST MOMENTS...
...

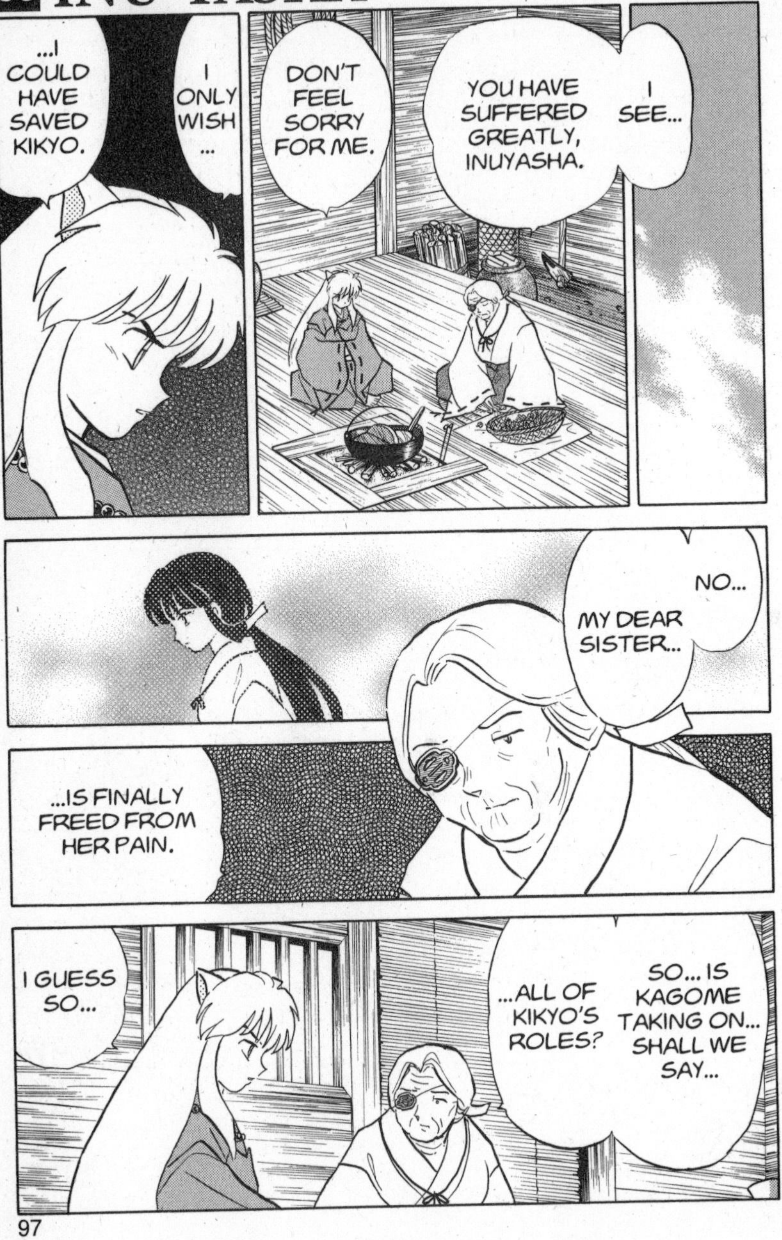
I SEE...
YOU HAVE SUFFERED GREATLY, INUYASHA.
DON'T FEEL SORRY FOR ME.
I ONLY WISH ...
...I COULD HAVE SAVED KIKYO.
NO...
MY DEAR SISTER...
...IS FINALLY FREED FROM HER PAIN.
SO... IS KAGOME TAKING ON... SHALL WE SAY...
...ALL OF KIKYO'S ROLES?
I GUESS SO...

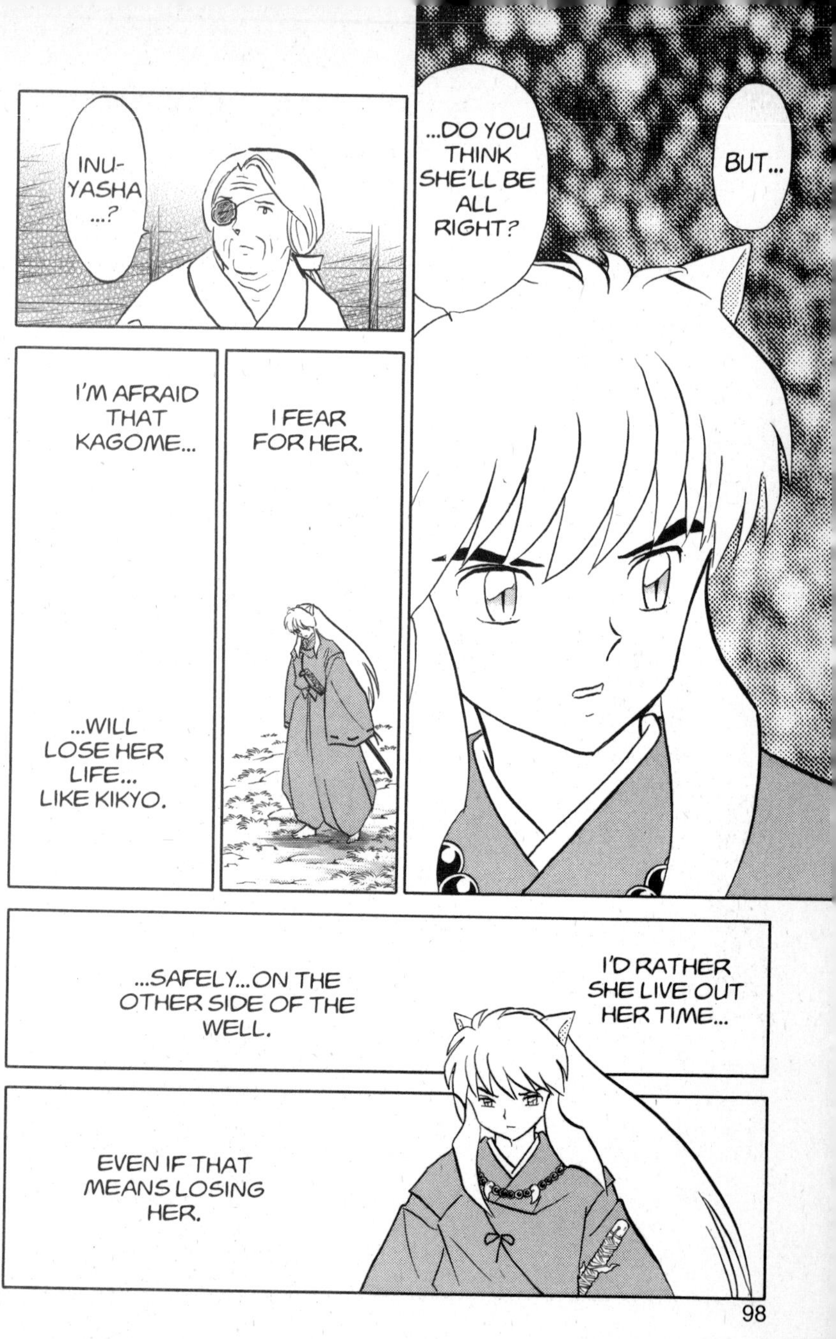
BUT...
...DO YOU THINK SHE'LL BE ALL RIGHT?
INU-YASHA ...?
I FEAR FOR HER.
I'M AFRAID THAT KAGOME...
...WILL LOSE HER LIFE... LIKE KIKYO.
I'D RATHER SHE LIVE OUT HER TIME...
...SAFELY...ON THE OTHER SIDE OF THE WELL.
EVEN IF THAT MEANS LOSING HER.

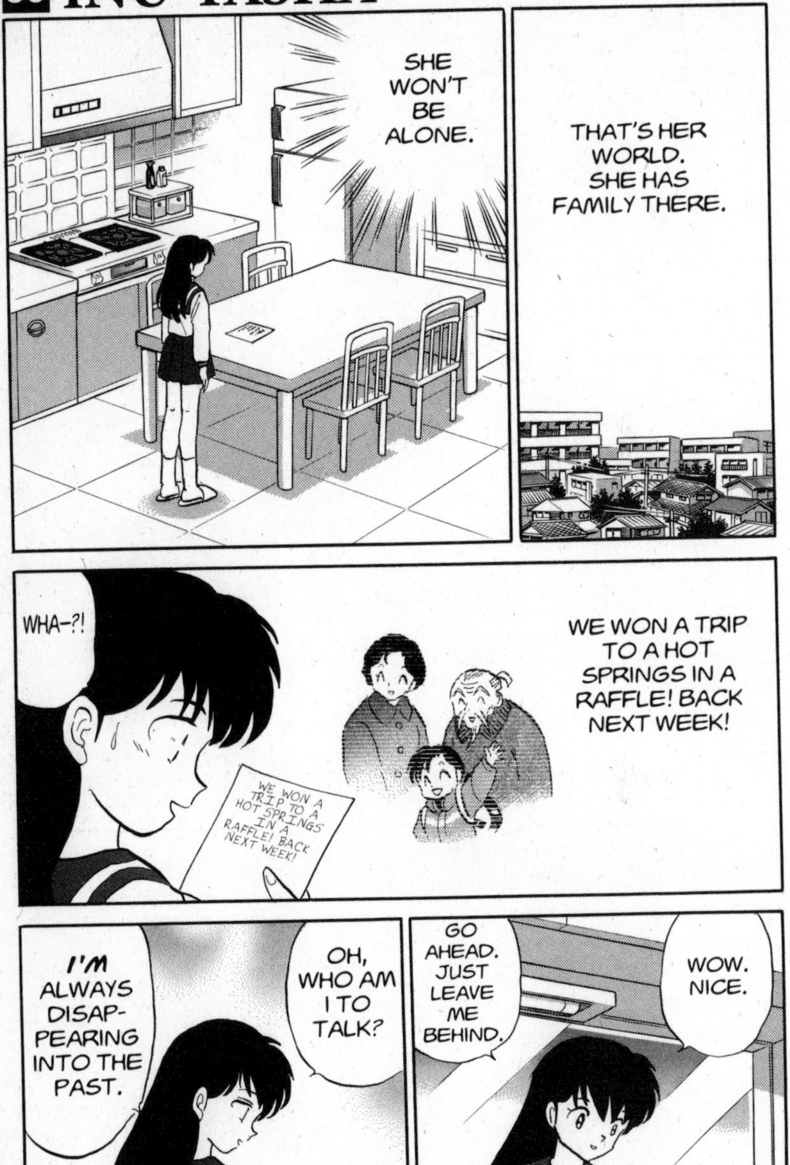
THAT'S HER WORLD. SHE HAS FAMILY THERE.
SHE WON'T BE ALONE.
WE WON A TRIP TO A HOT SPRINGS IN A RAFFLE! BACK NEXT WEEK!
WHA-?!
WE WON A TRIP TO A HOT SPRINGS IN A RAFFLE! BACK NEXT WEEK!
WOW. NICE.
GO AHEAD. JUST LEAVE ME BEHIND.
OH, WHO AM I TO TALK?
I'M ALWAYS DISAP-PEARING INTO THE PAST.

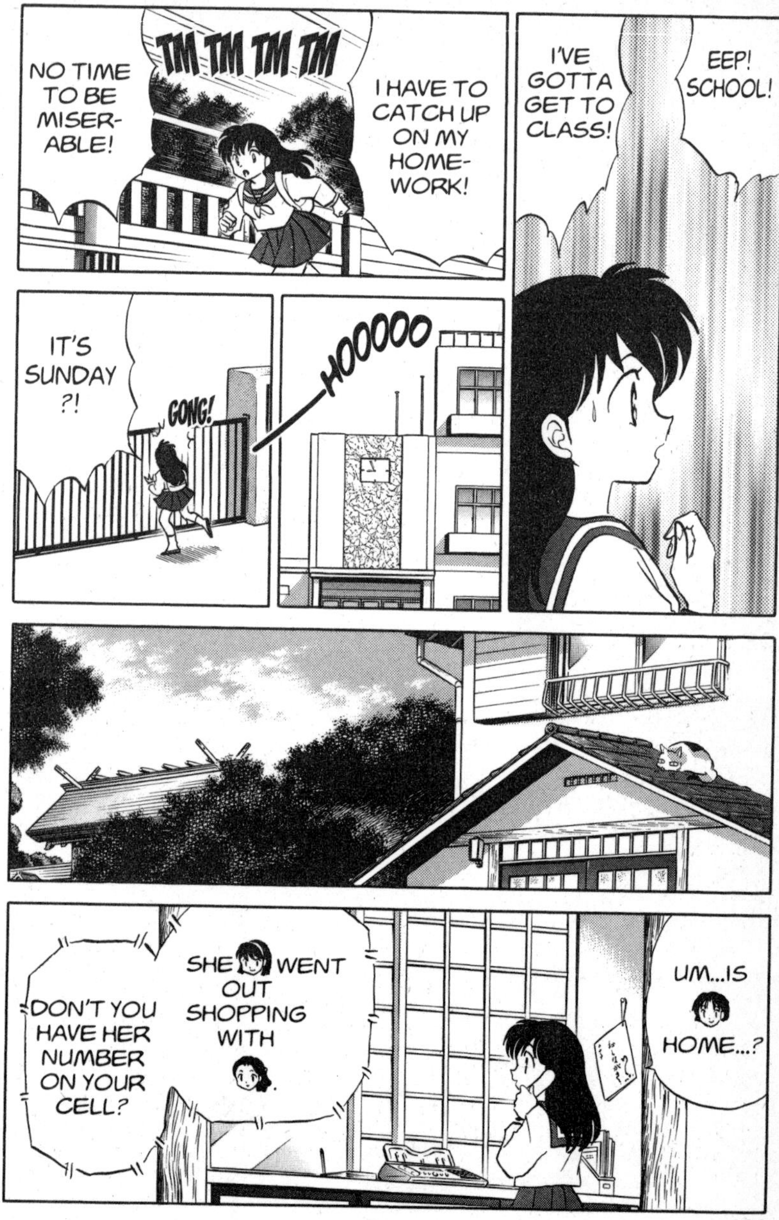
EEP! SCHOOL!
I'VE GOTTA GET TO CLASS!
TM TM TM TM
I HAVE TO CATCH UP ON MY HOME-WORK!
NO TIME TO BE MISER-ABLE!
HOOOOO
GONG!
IT'S SUNDAY ?!
UM...IS HOME...?
SHE WENT OUT SHOPPING WITH .
DON'T YOU HAVE HER NUMBER ON YOUR CELL?

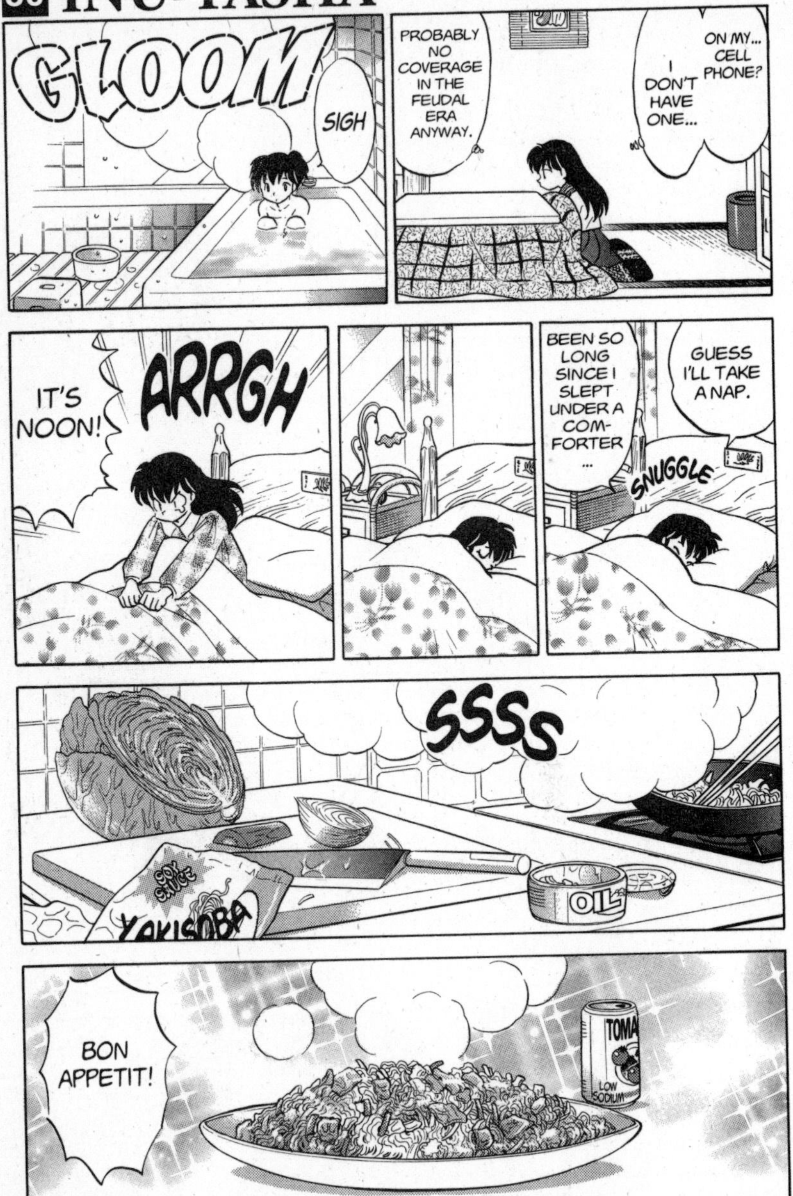
ON MY... CELL PHONE?
I DON'T HAVE ONE...
PROBABLY NO COVERAGE IN THE FEUDAL ERA ANYWAY.
GLOOM
SIGH
GUESS I'LL TAKE A NAP.
BEEN SO LONG SINCE I SLEPT UNDER A COMFORTER...
SNUGGLE
ARRGH
IT'S NOON!
SSSS
SOY SAUCE
YAKISOBA
OIL
BON APPETIT!
TOMA
LOW SODIUM

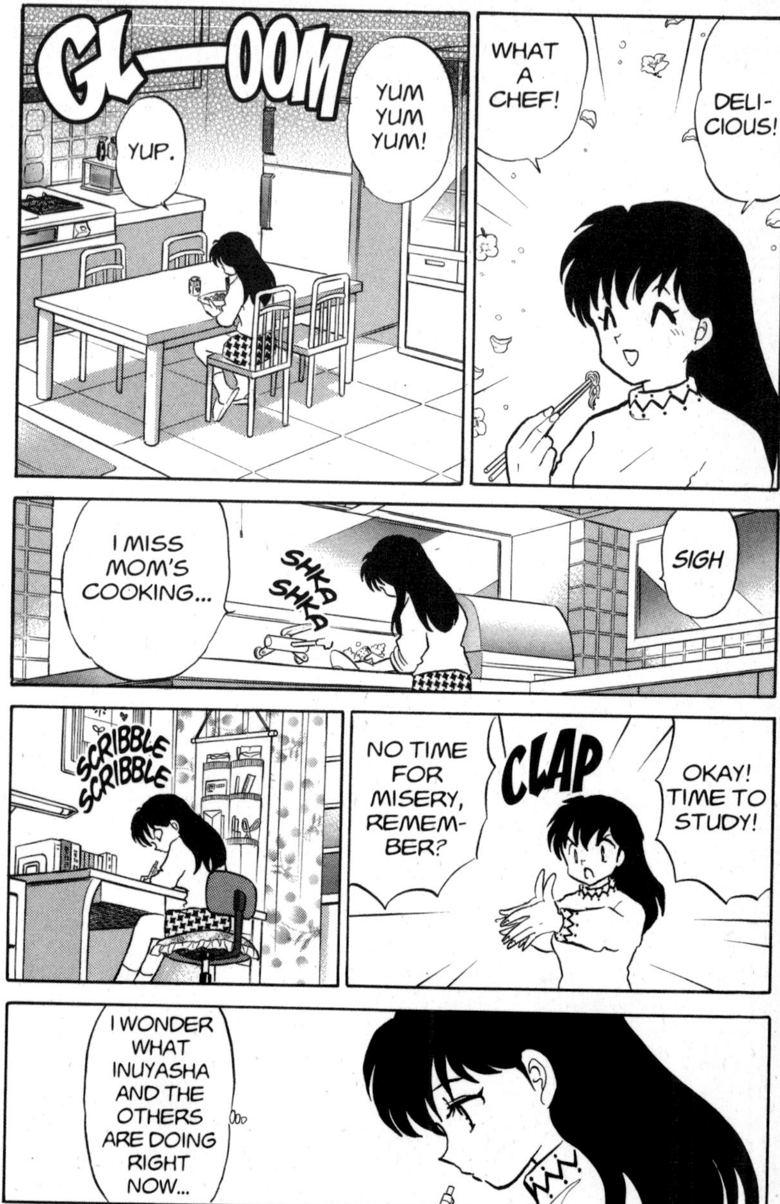
DELI-CIOUS!
WHAT A CHEF!
GL—OOM
YUM YUM YUM!
YUP.
SIGH
SHKA SHKA
I MISS MOM'S COOKING...
OKAY! TIME TO STUDY!
CLAP
NO TIME FOR MISERY, REMEMBER?
SCRIBBLE SCRIBBLE
I WONDER WHAT INUYASHA AND THE OTHERS ARE DOING RIGHT NOW...

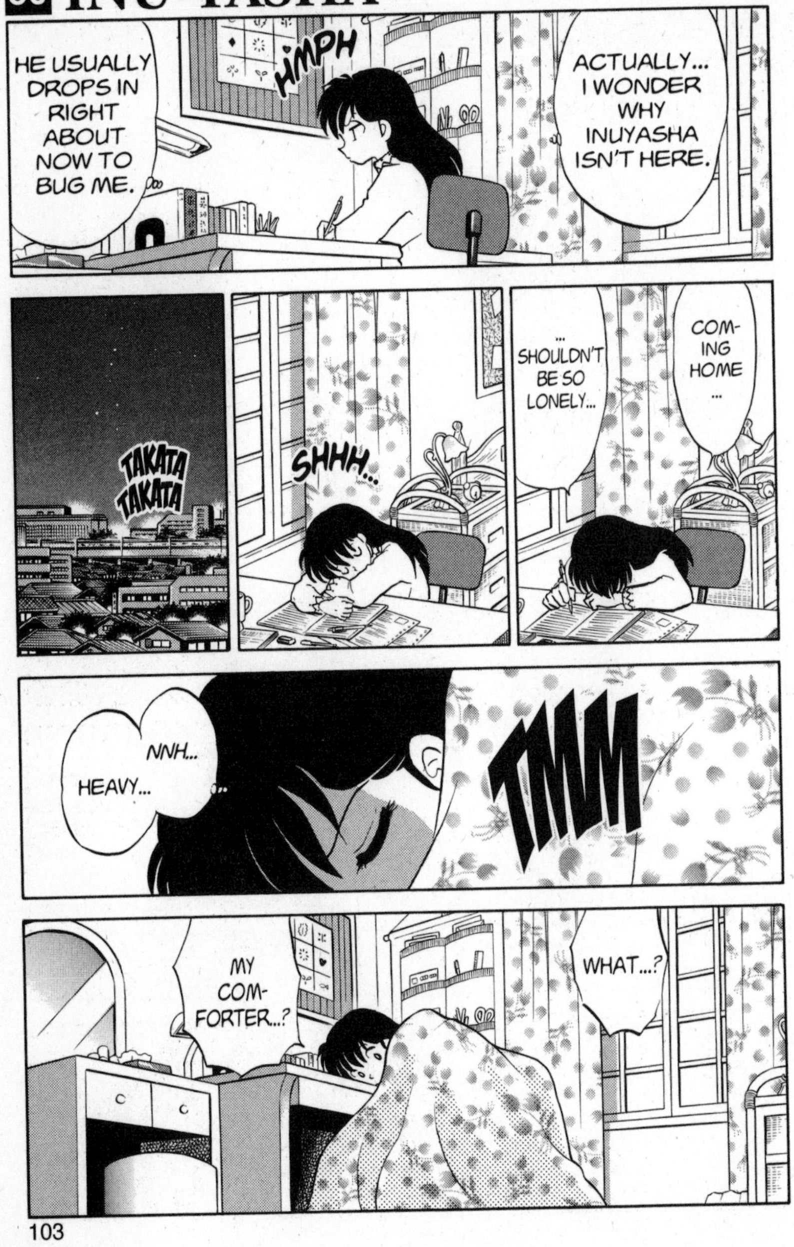
ACTUALLY... I WONDER WHY INUYASHA ISN'T HERE.
HMPH
HE USUALLY DROPS IN RIGHT ABOUT NOW TO BUG ME.
COM-ING HOME ...
... SHOULDN'T BE SO LONELY...
SHHH...
TAKATA TAKATA
TMM
NNH... HEAVY...
WHAT...?
MY COM-FORTER...?

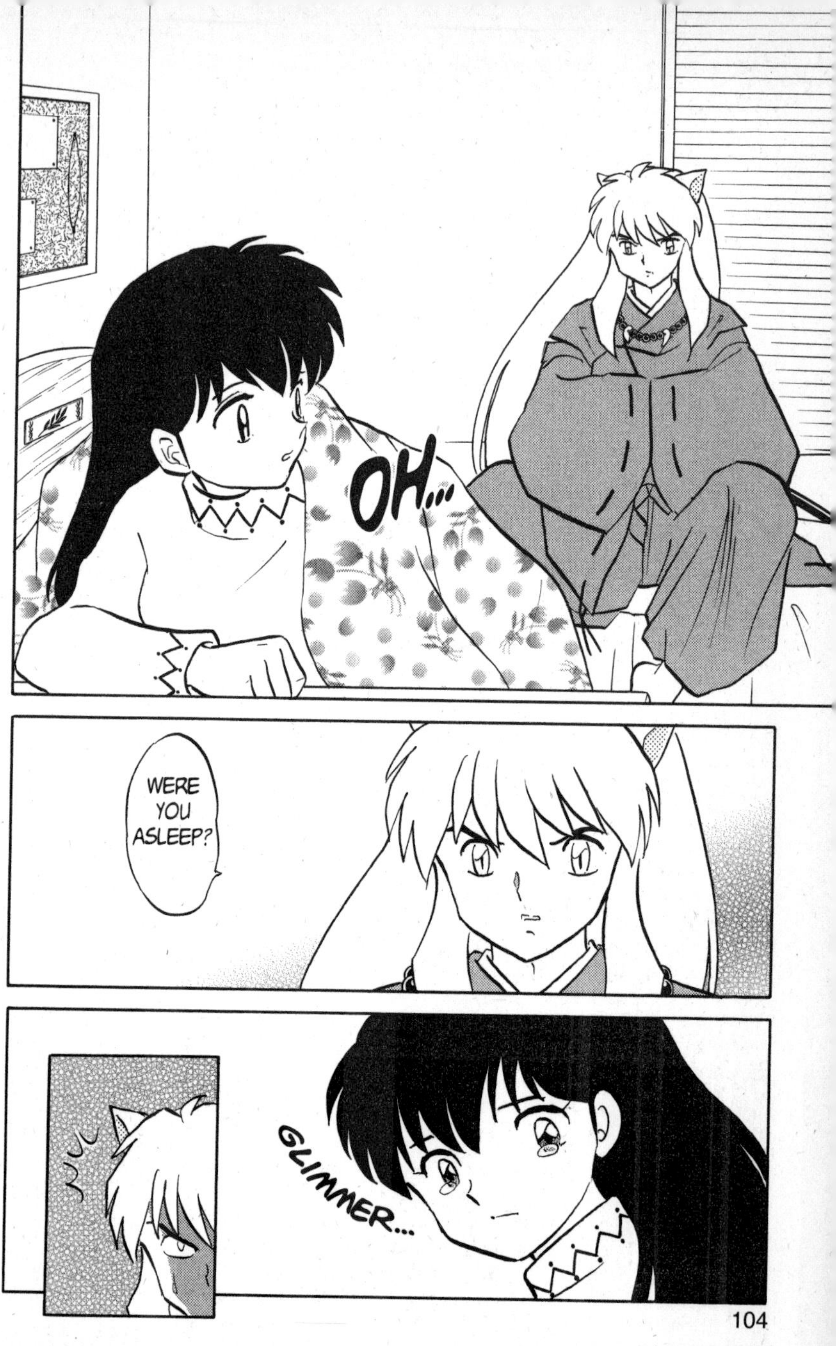
OH...
WERE YOU ASLEEP?
GLIMMER...

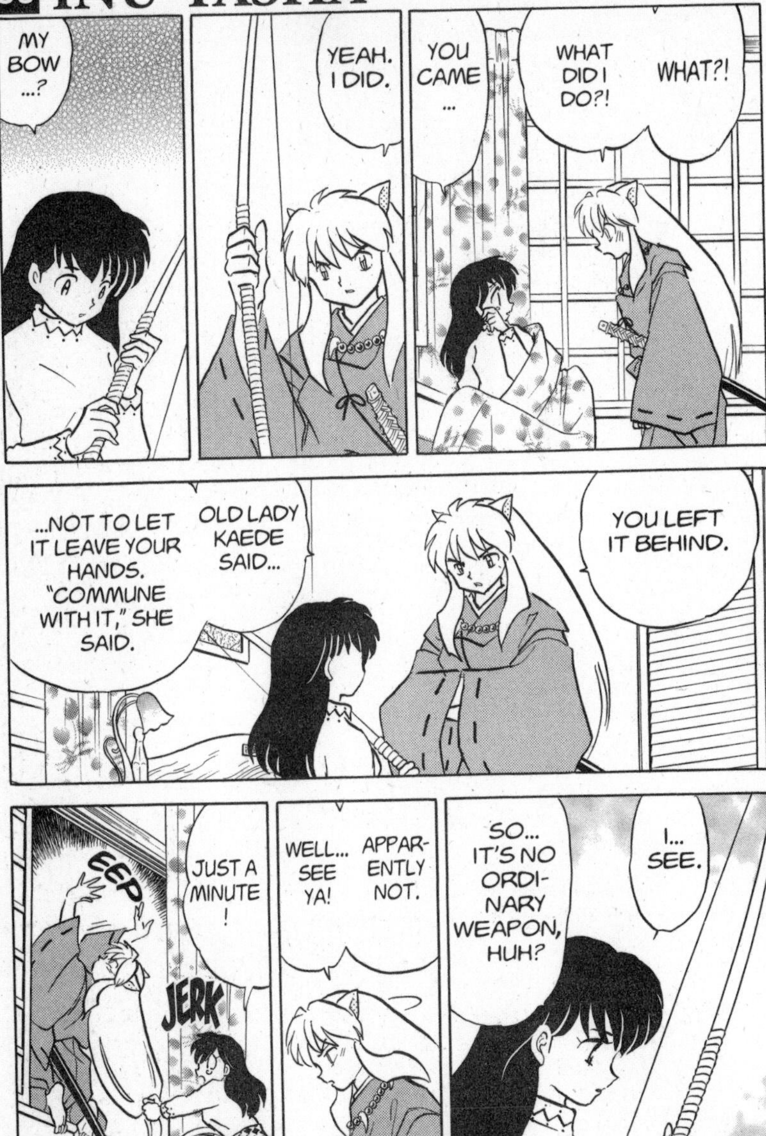
WHAT?!
WHAT DID I DO?!
YOU CAME ...
YEAH. I DID.
MY BOW ...?
YOU LEFT IT BEHIND.
OLD LADY KAEDE SAID...
...NOT TO LET IT LEAVE YOUR HANDS. "COMMUNE WITH IT," SHE SAID.
I... SEE.
SO... IT'S NO ORDINARY WEAPON, HUH?
APPARENTLY NOT.
WELL... SEE YA!
JUST A MINUTE!
EEP
JERK

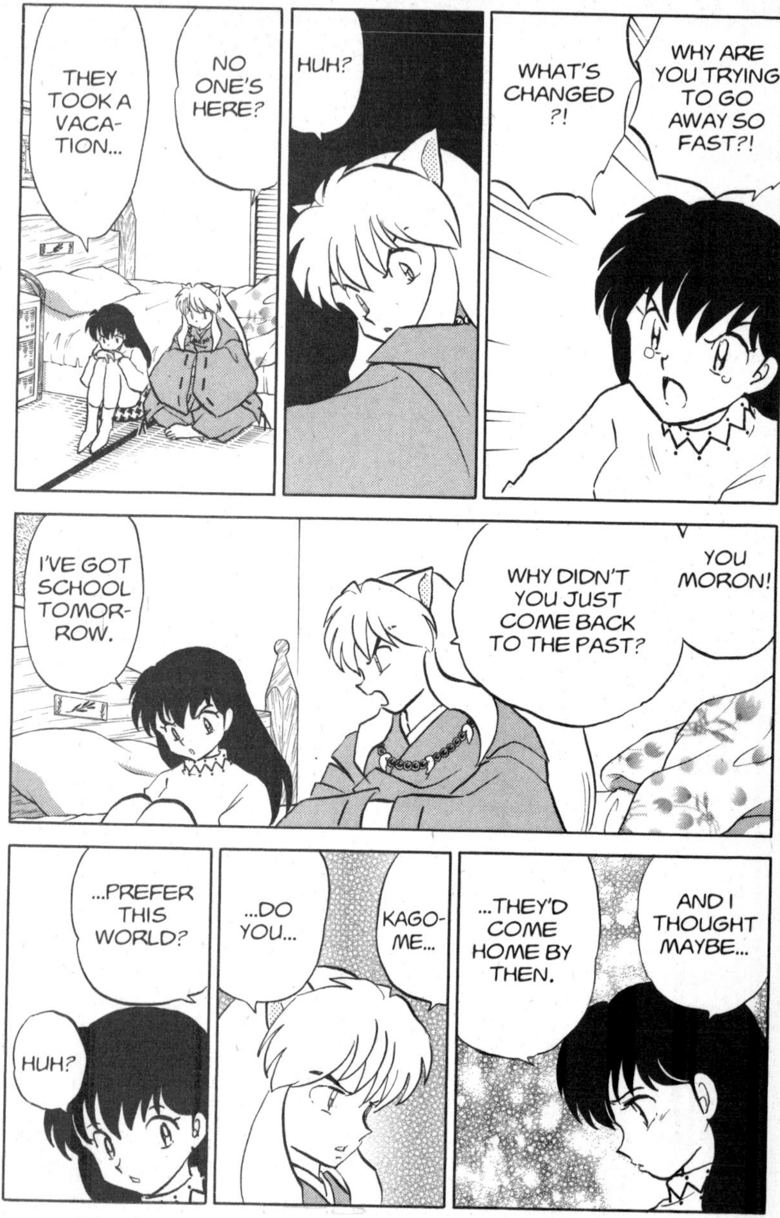
WHY ARE YOU TRYING TO GO AWAY SO FAST?!
WHAT'S CHANGED ?!
HUH?
NO ONE'S HERE?
THEY TOOK A VACA-TION...
YOU MORON!
WHY DIDN'T YOU JUST COME BACK TO THE PAST?
I'VE GOT SCHOOL TOMOR-ROW.
AND I THOUGHT MAYBE...
...THEY'D COME HOME BY THEN.
KAGO-ME...
...DO YOU...
...PREFER THIS WORLD?
HUH?

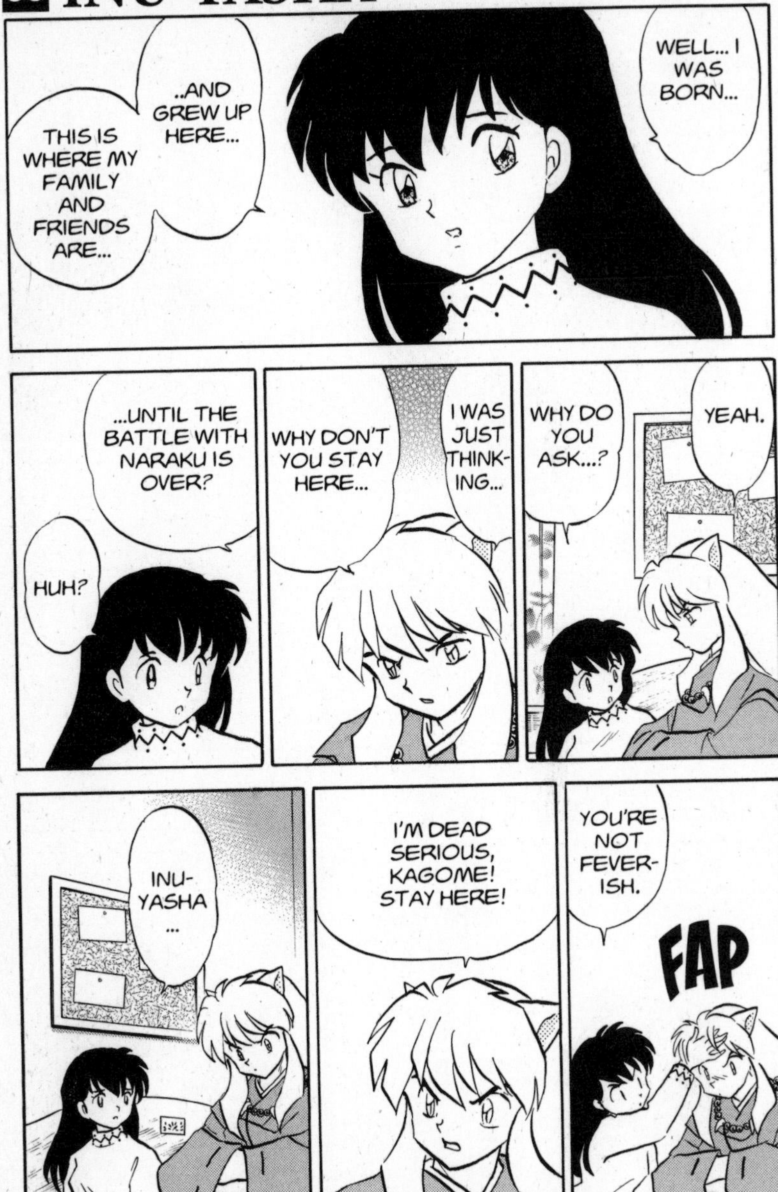
WELL... I WAS BORN...
..AND GREW UP HERE...
THIS IS WHERE MY FAMILY AND FRIENDS ARE...
YEAH.
WHY DO YOU ASK...?
I WAS JUST THINK-ING...
WHY DON'T YOU STAY HERE...
...UNTIL THE BATTLE WITH NARAKU IS OVER?
HUH?
YOU'RE NOT FEVER-ISH.
FAP
I'M DEAD SERIOUS, KAGOME! STAY HERE!
INU-YASHA ...

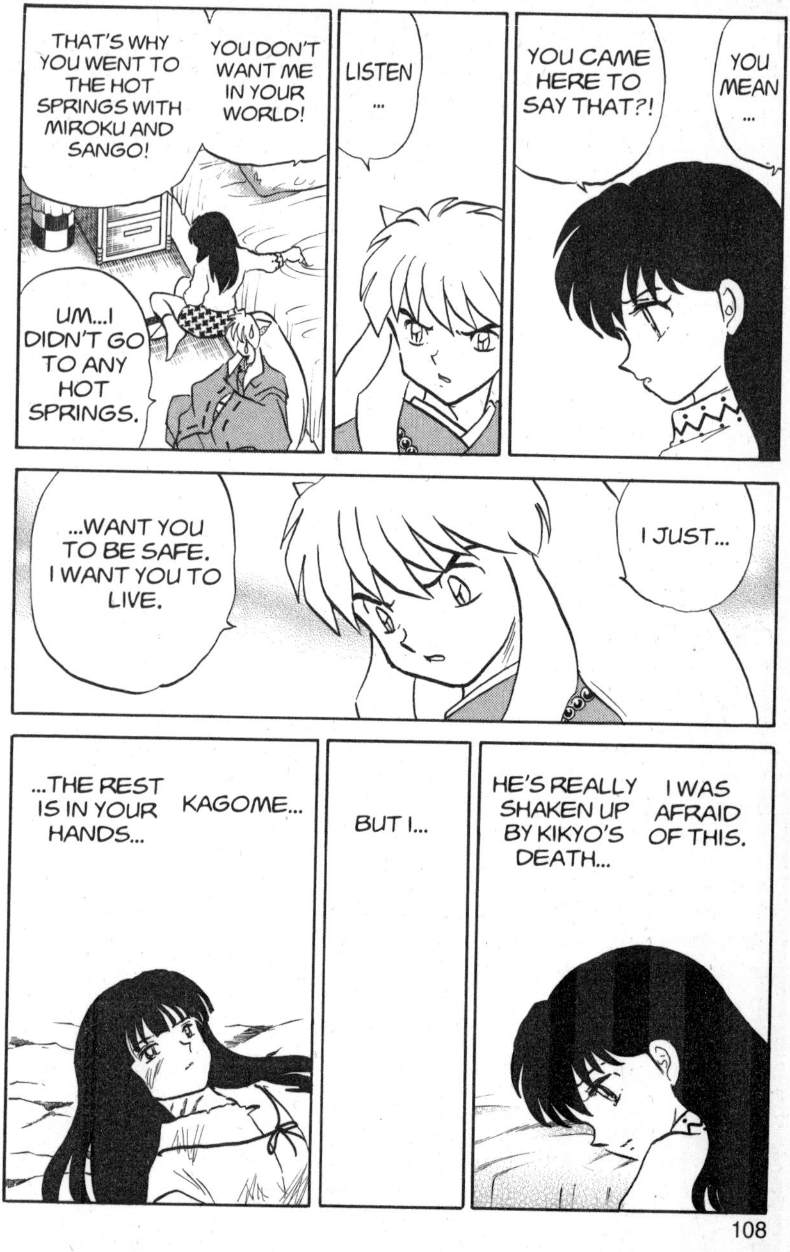
YOU MEAN ...
YOU CAME HERE TO SAY THAT?!
LISTEN ...
YOU DON'T WANT ME IN YOUR WORLD!
THAT'S WHY YOU WENT TO THE HOT SPRINGS WITH MIROKU AND SANGO!
UM...I DIDN'T GO TO ANY HOT SPRINGS.
I JUST...
...WANT YOU TO BE SAFE. I WANT YOU TO LIVE.
I WAS AFRAID OF THIS.
HE'S REALLY SHAKEN UP BY KIKYO'S DEATH...
BUT I...
KAGOME...
...THE REST IS IN YOUR HANDS...

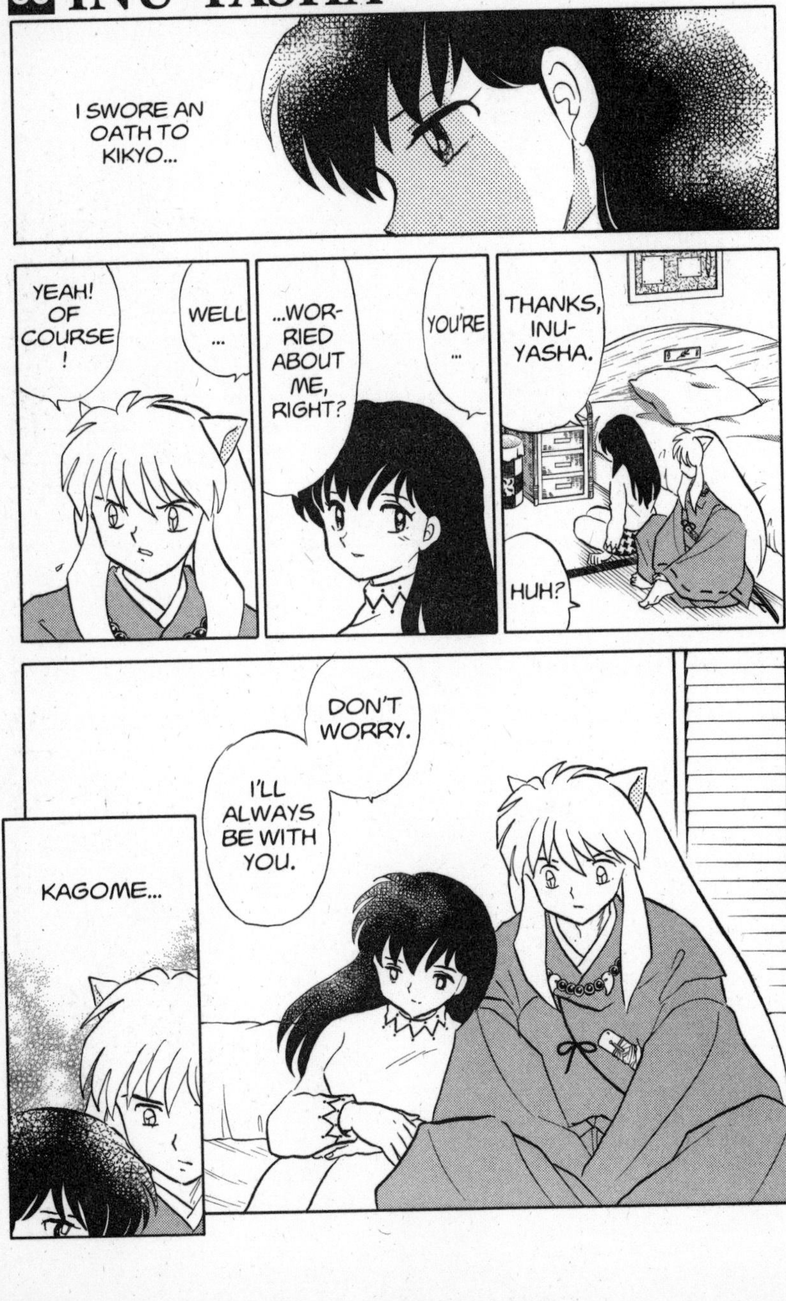
I SWORE AN OATH TO KIKYO...
THANKS, INU-YASHA.
HUH?
YOU'RE ...
...WOR-RIED ABOUT ME, RIGHT?
WELL ...
YEAH! OF COURSE !
DON'T WORRY.
I'LL ALWAYS BE WITH YOU.
KAGOME...

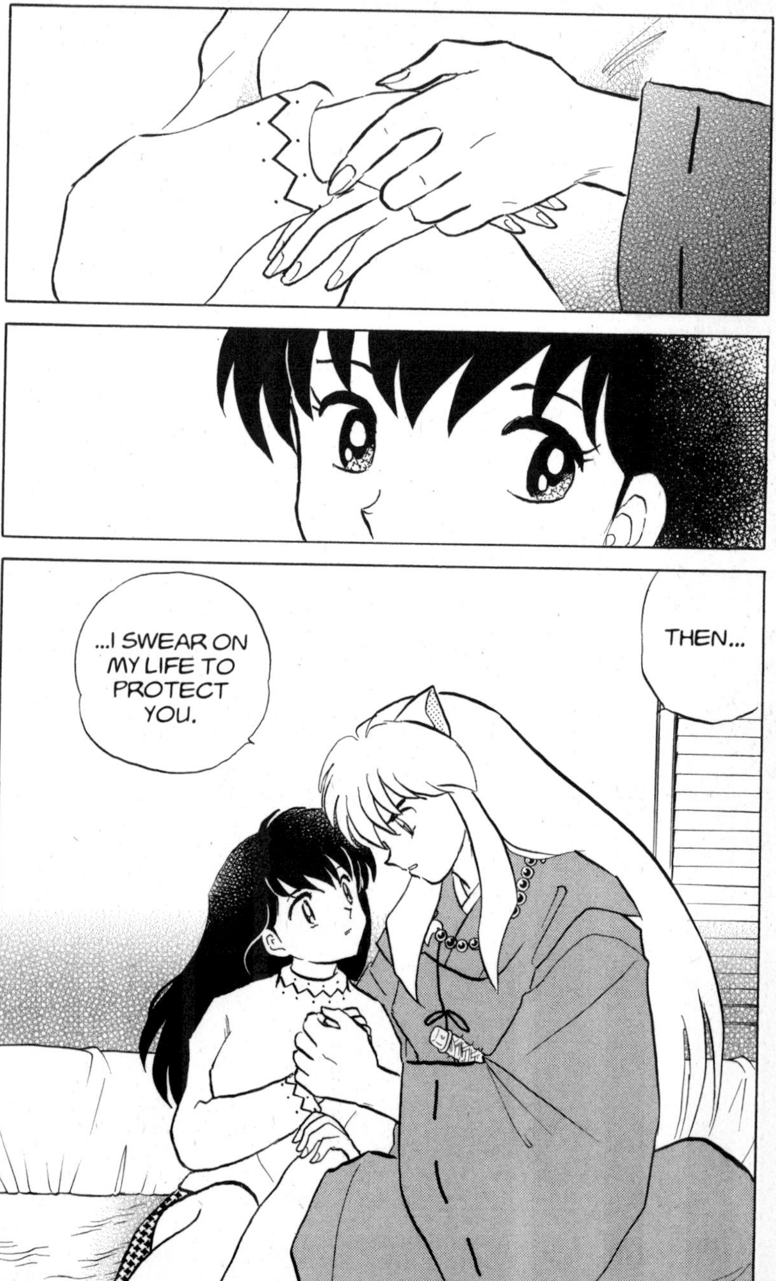
THEN...
...I SWEAR ON MY LIFE TO PROTECT YOU.

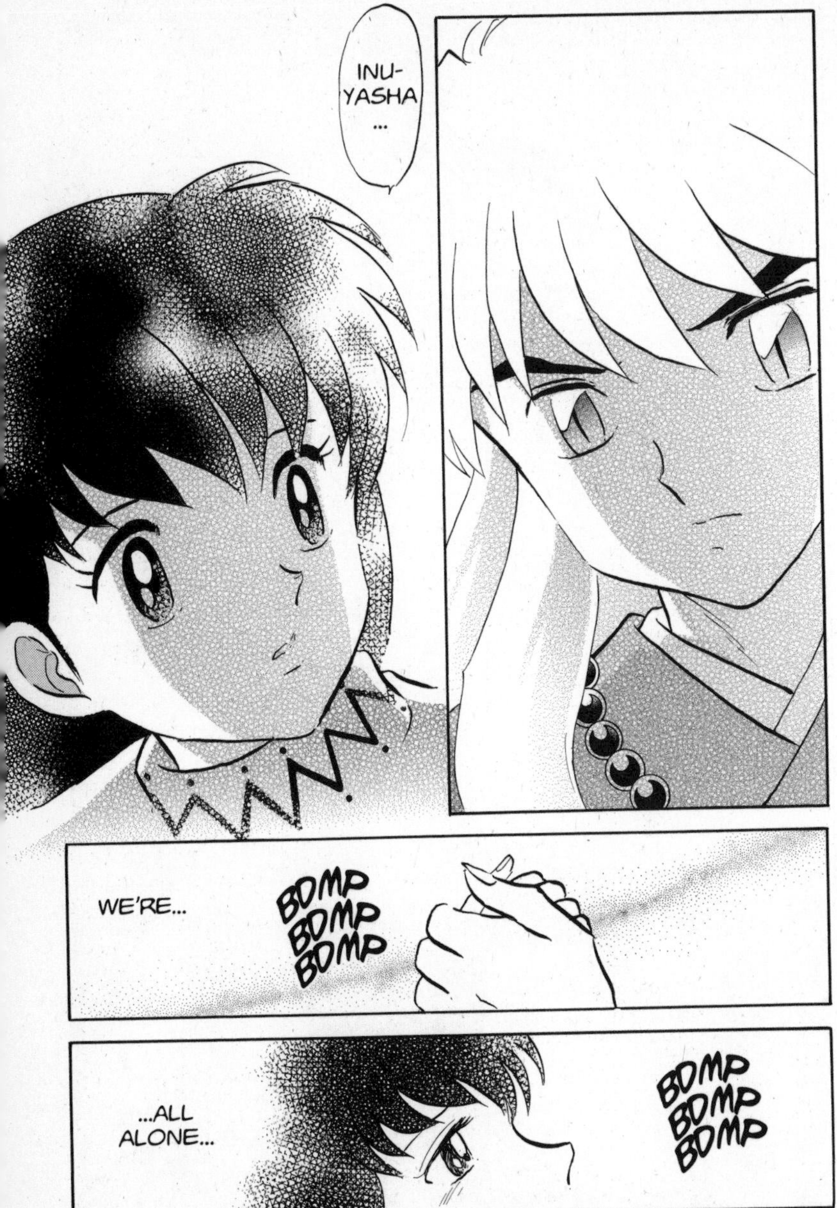
INU-YASHA...
BDMP BDMP BDMP
WE'RE...
BDMP BDMP BDMP
...ALL ALONE...

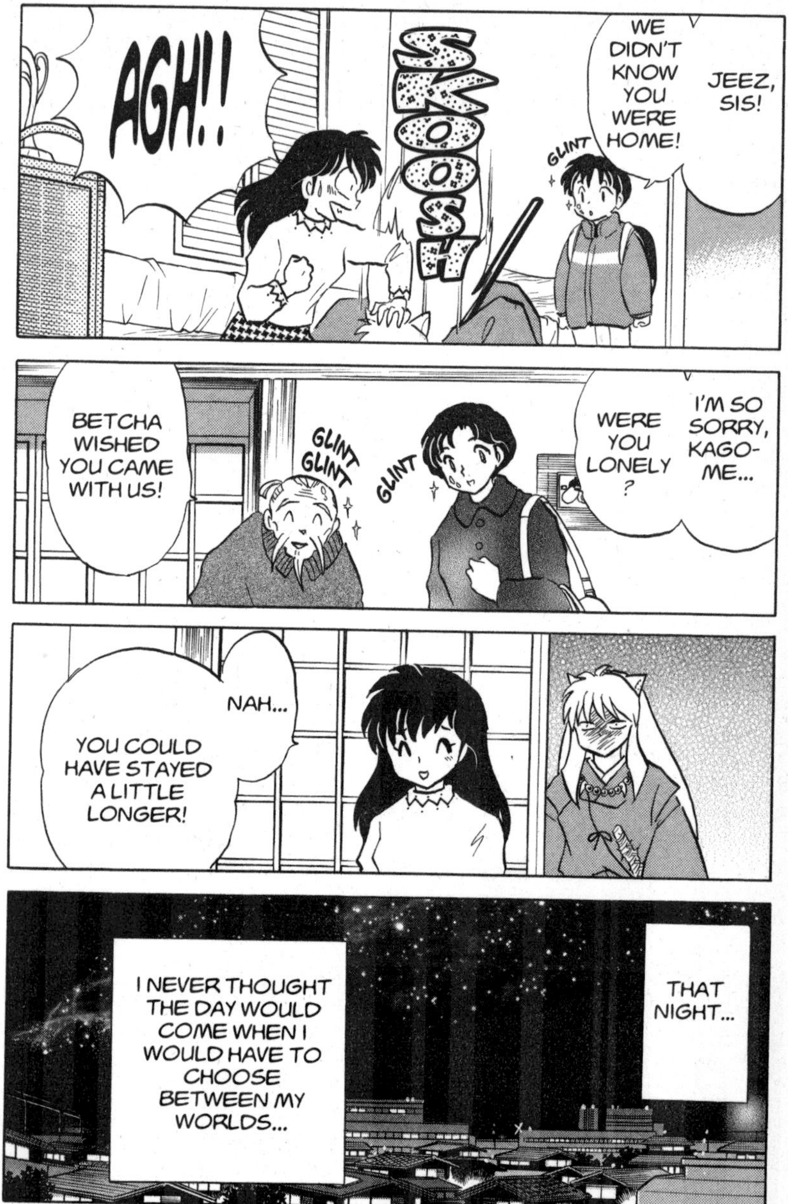
JEEZ, SIS!
WE DIDN'T KNOW YOU WERE HOME!
GLINT
SKWOOSH
AGH!!
I'M SO SORRY, KAGO-ME...
WERE YOU LONELY?
GLINT
GLINT GLINT
BETCHA WISHED YOU CAME WITH US!
NAH...
YOU COULD HAVE STAYED A LITTLE LONGER!
THAT NIGHT...
I NEVER THOUGHT THE DAY WOULD COME WHEN I WOULD HAVE TO CHOOSE BETWEEN MY WORLDS...

SCROLL 7
THE PATH AHEAD

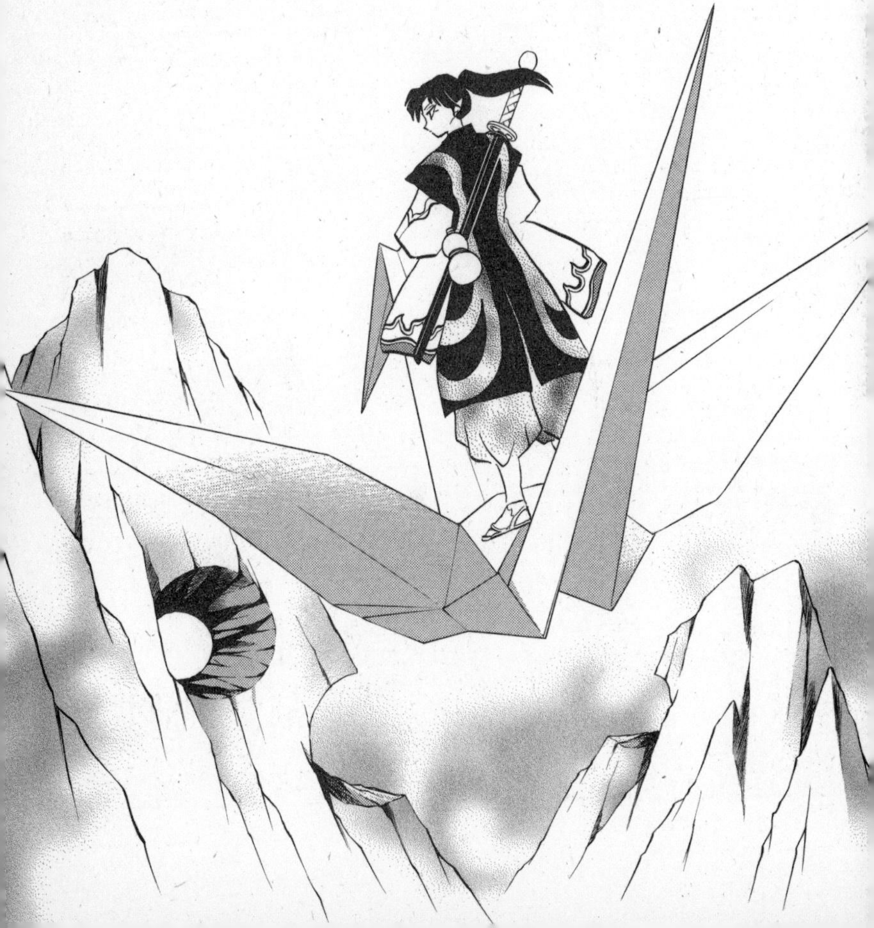

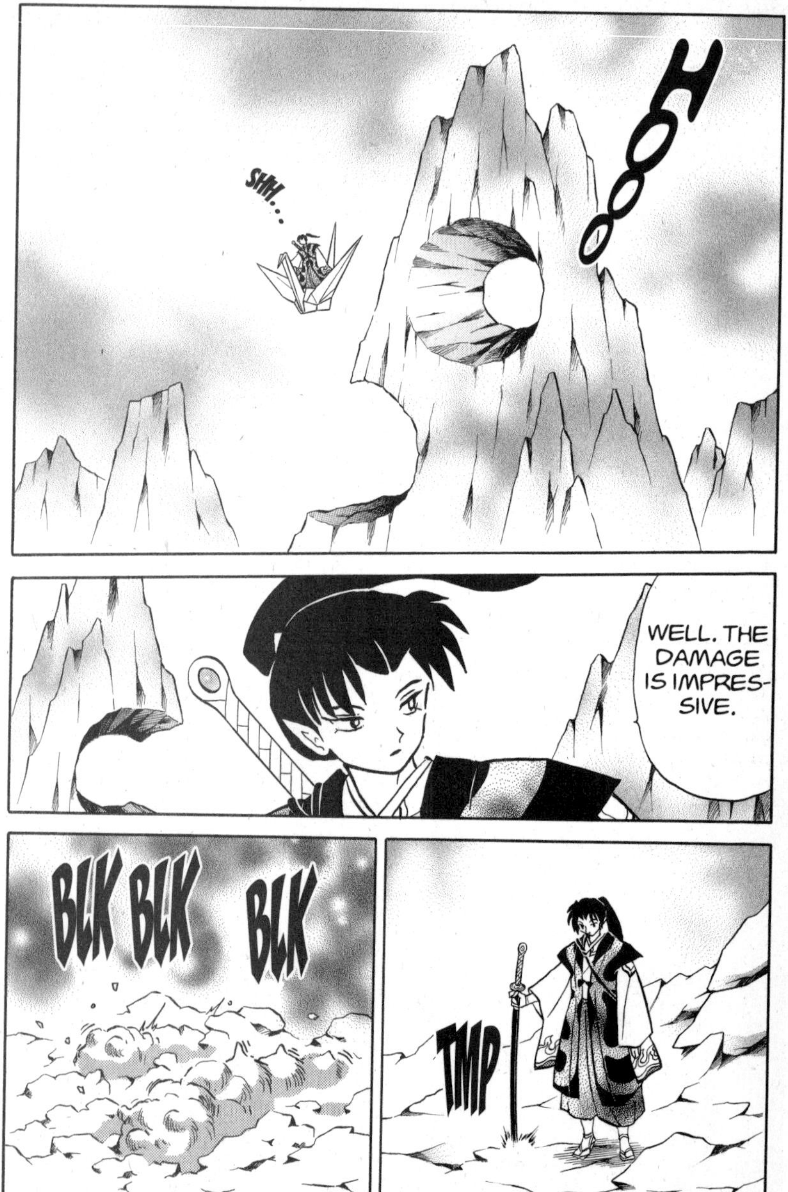
HOOOO
SHH...
WELL. THE DAMAGE IS IMPRES-SIVE.
TMP
BLK BLK BLK

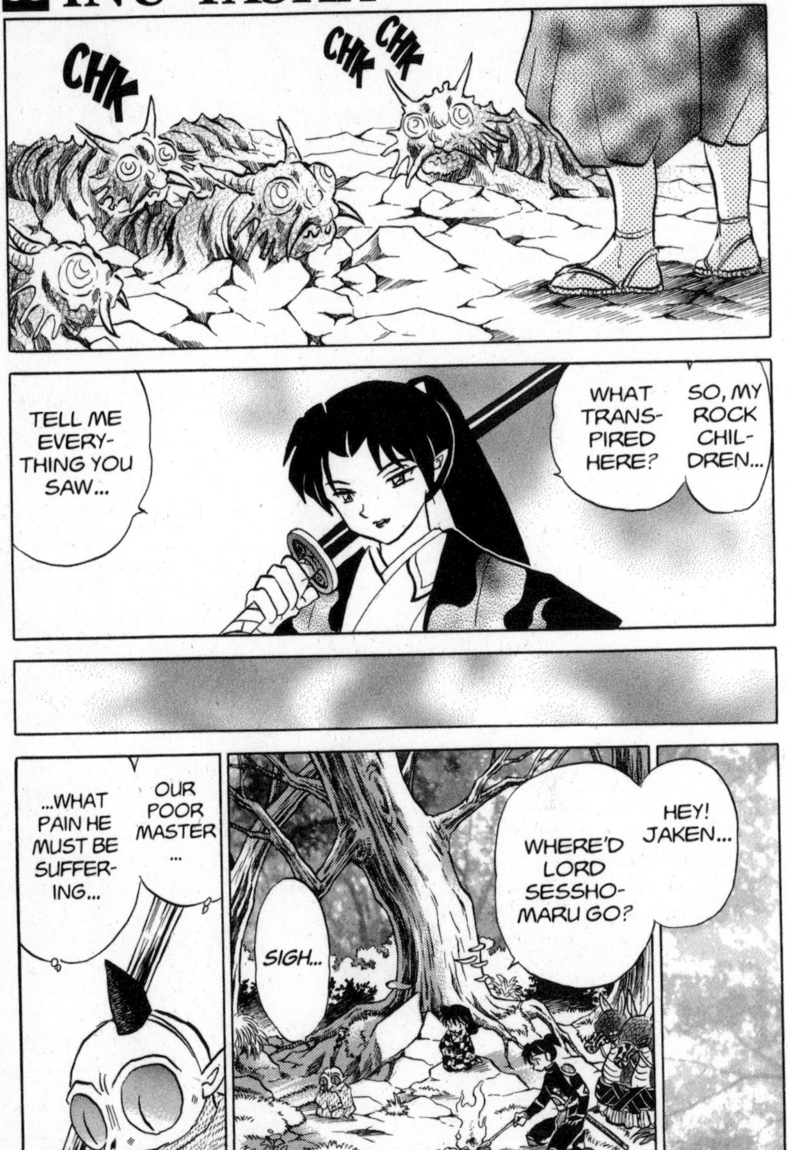
CHK
CHK
CHK
SO, MY ROCK CHILDREN...
WHAT TRANSPIRED HERE?
TELL ME EVERYTHING YOU SAW...
HEY! JAKEN...
WHERE'D LORD SESSHOMARU GO?
SIGH...
OUR POOR MASTER...
...WHAT PAIN HE MUST BE SUFFERING...

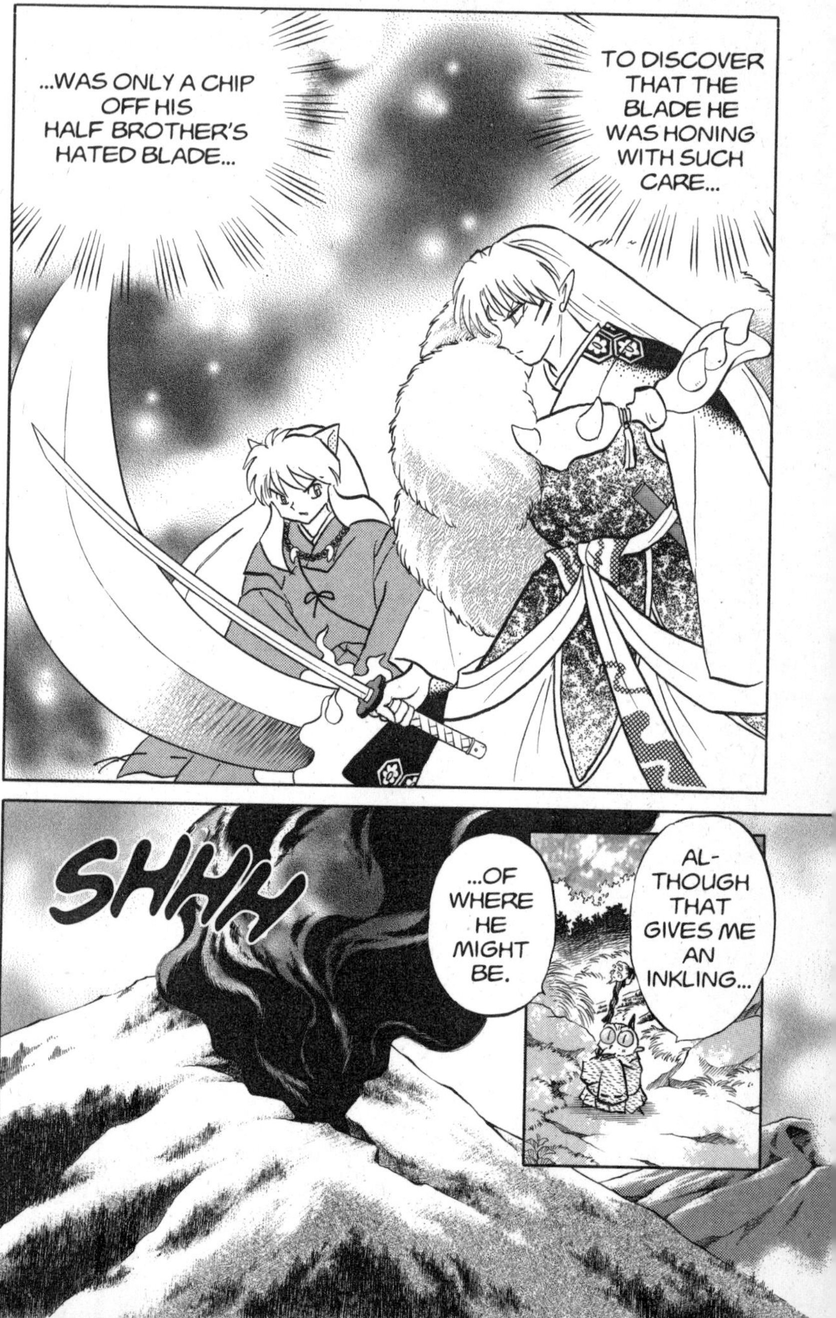
TO DISCOVER THAT THE BLADE HE WAS HONING WITH SUCH CARE...
...WAS ONLY A CHIP OFF HIS HALF BROTHER'S HATED BLADE...
AL-THOUGH THAT GIVES ME AN INKLING...
...OF WHERE HE MIGHT BE.
SHHH

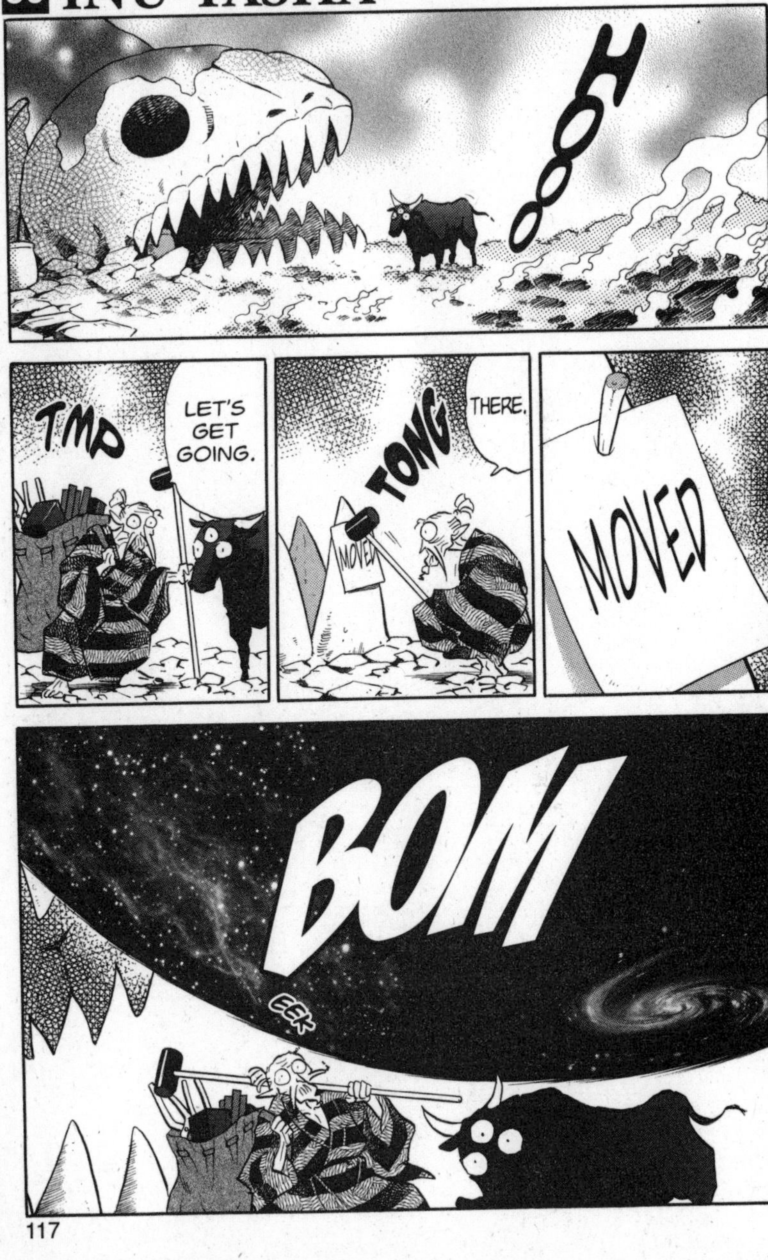
OOOOH
MOVED
THERE.
TONG
MOVED
LET'S GET GOING.
TMP
BOM
EEK

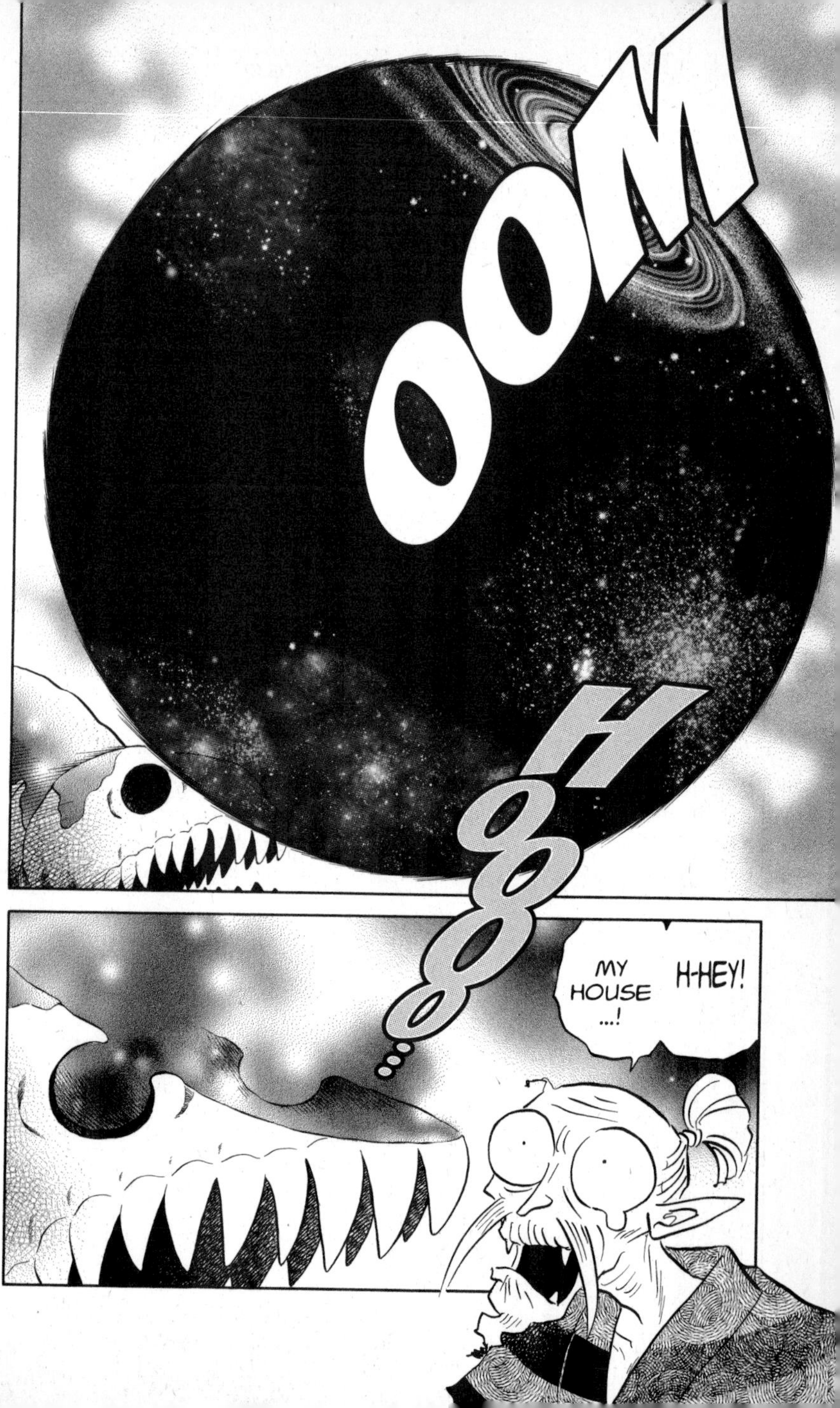
OOM
H
H-HEY!
MY HOUSE ...!

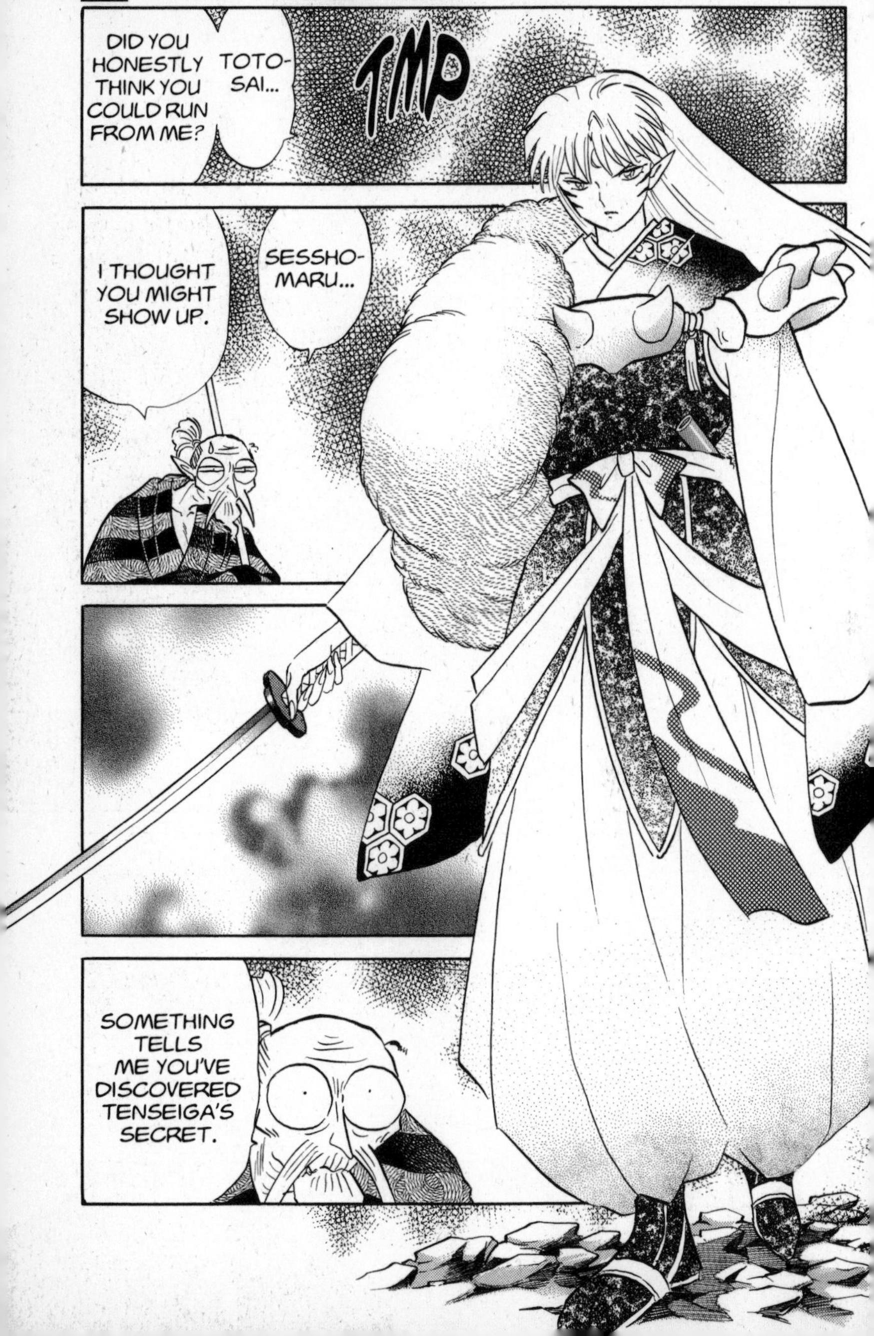
TMP
TOTO-SAI...
DID YOU HONESTLY THINK YOU COULD RUN FROM ME?
SESSHO-MARU...
I THOUGHT YOU MIGHT SHOW UP.
SOMETHING TELLS ME YOU'VE DISCOVERED TENSEIGA'S SECRET.

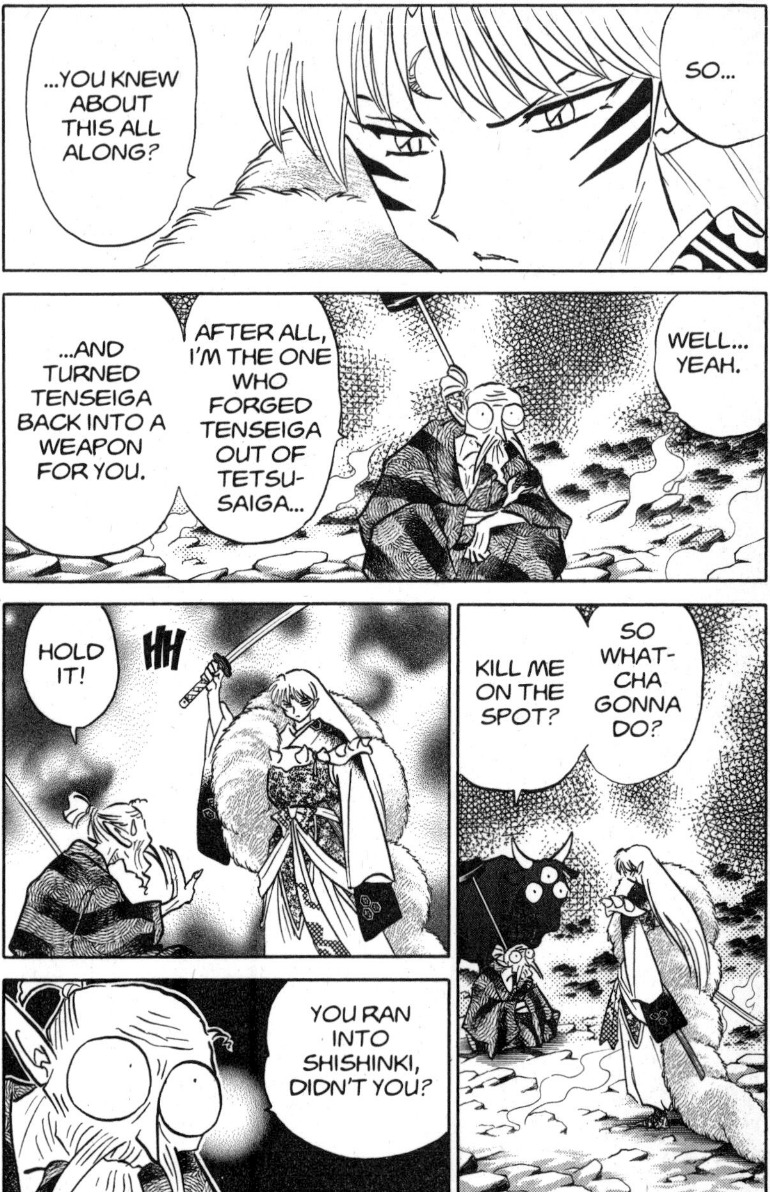
SO...
...YOU KNEW ABOUT THIS ALL ALONG?
WELL... YEAH.
AFTER ALL, I'M THE ONE WHO FORGED TENSEIGA OUT OF TETSU-SAIGA...
...AND TURNED TENSEIGA BACK INTO A WEAPON FOR YOU.
SO WHAT-CHA GONNA DO?
KILL ME ON THE SPOT?
HOLD IT!
HH
YOU RAN INTO SHISHINKI, DIDN'T YOU?

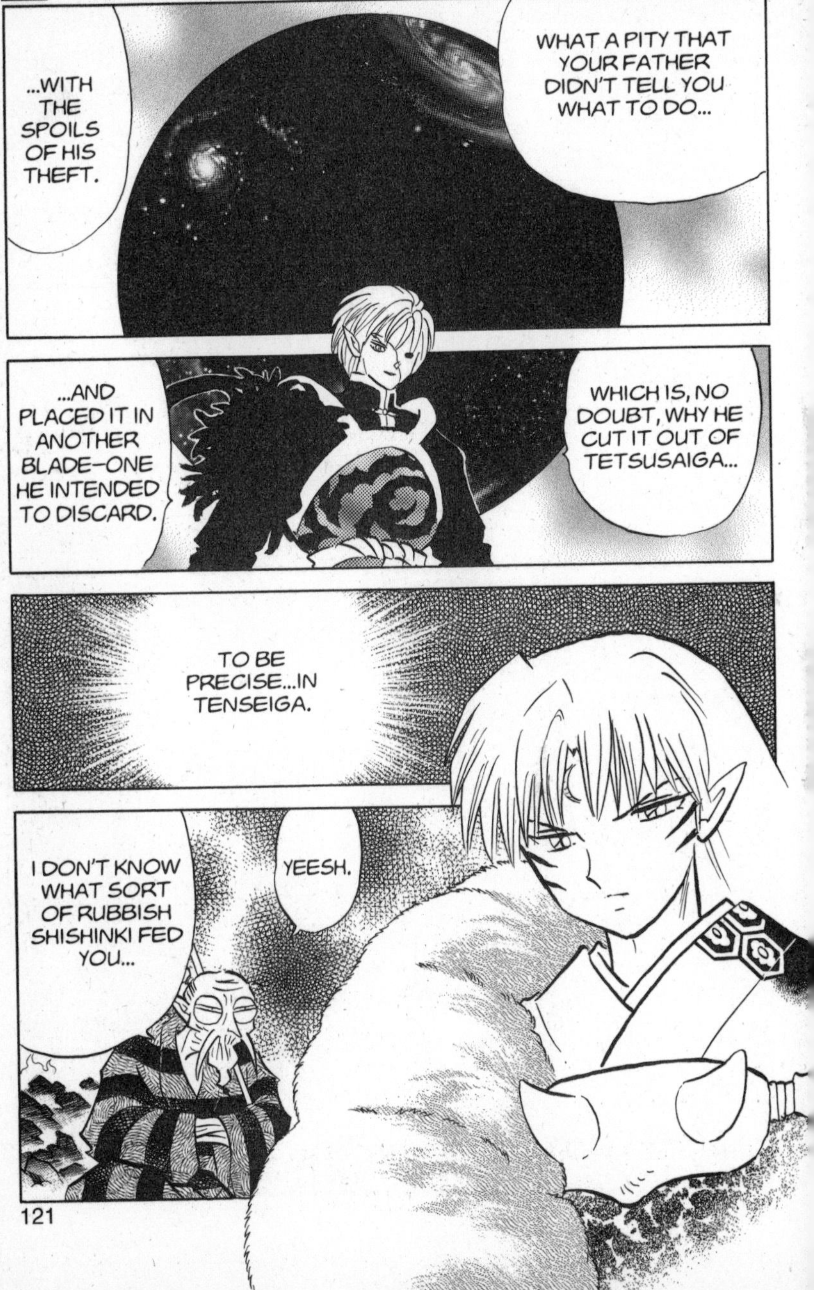
WHAT A PITY THAT YOUR FATHER DIDN'T TELL YOU WHAT TO DO...
...WITH THE SPOILS OF HIS THEFT.
WHICH IS, NO DOUBT, WHY HE CUT IT OUT OF TETSUSAIGA...
...AND PLACED IT IN ANOTHER BLADE–ONE HE INTENDED TO DISCARD.
TO BE PRECISE...IN TENSEIGA.
YEESH.
I DON'T KNOW WHAT SORT OF RUBBISH SHISHINKI FED YOU...

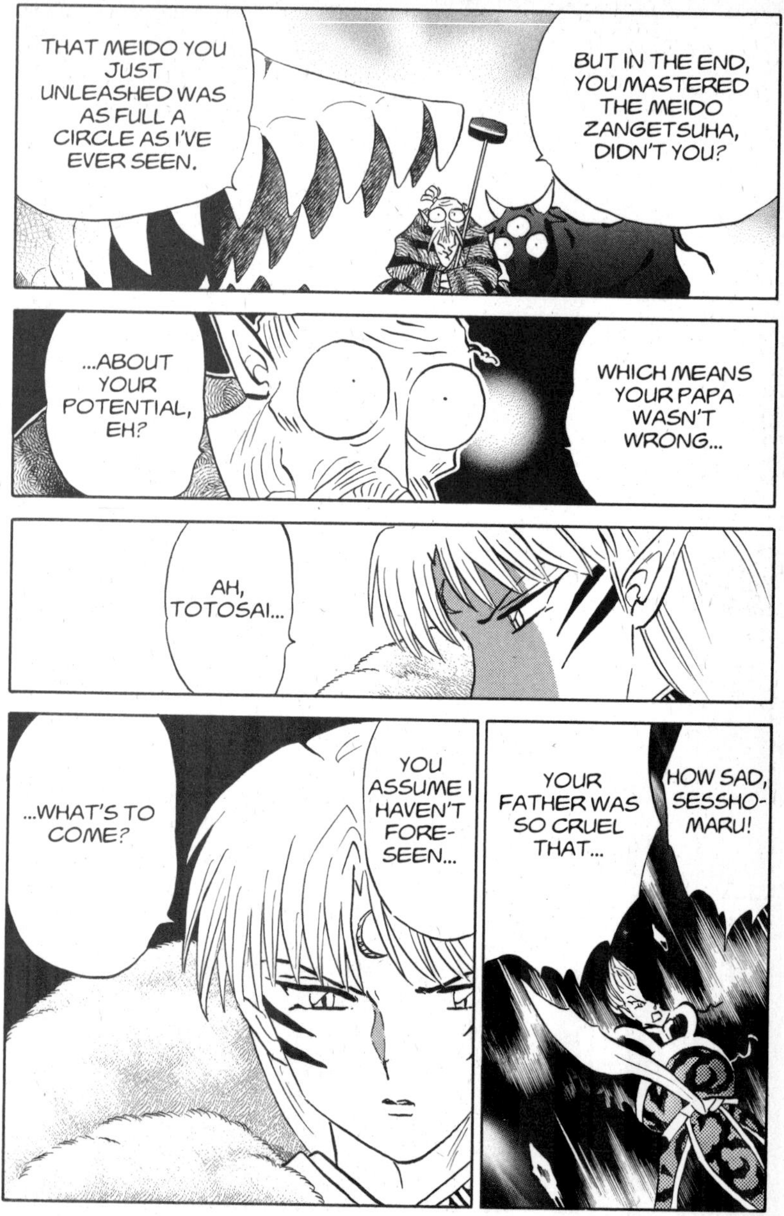
BUT IN THE END, YOU MASTERED THE MEIDO ZANGETSUHA, DIDN'T YOU?
THAT MEIDO YOU JUST UNLEASHED WAS AS FULL A CIRCLE AS I'VE EVER SEEN.
WHICH MEANS YOUR PAPA WASN'T WRONG...
...ABOUT YOUR POTENTIAL, EH?
AH, TOTOSAI...
HOW SAD, SESSHO-MARU!
YOUR FATHER WAS SO CRUEL THAT...
YOU ASSUME I HAVEN'T FORE-SEEN...
...WHAT'S TO COME?

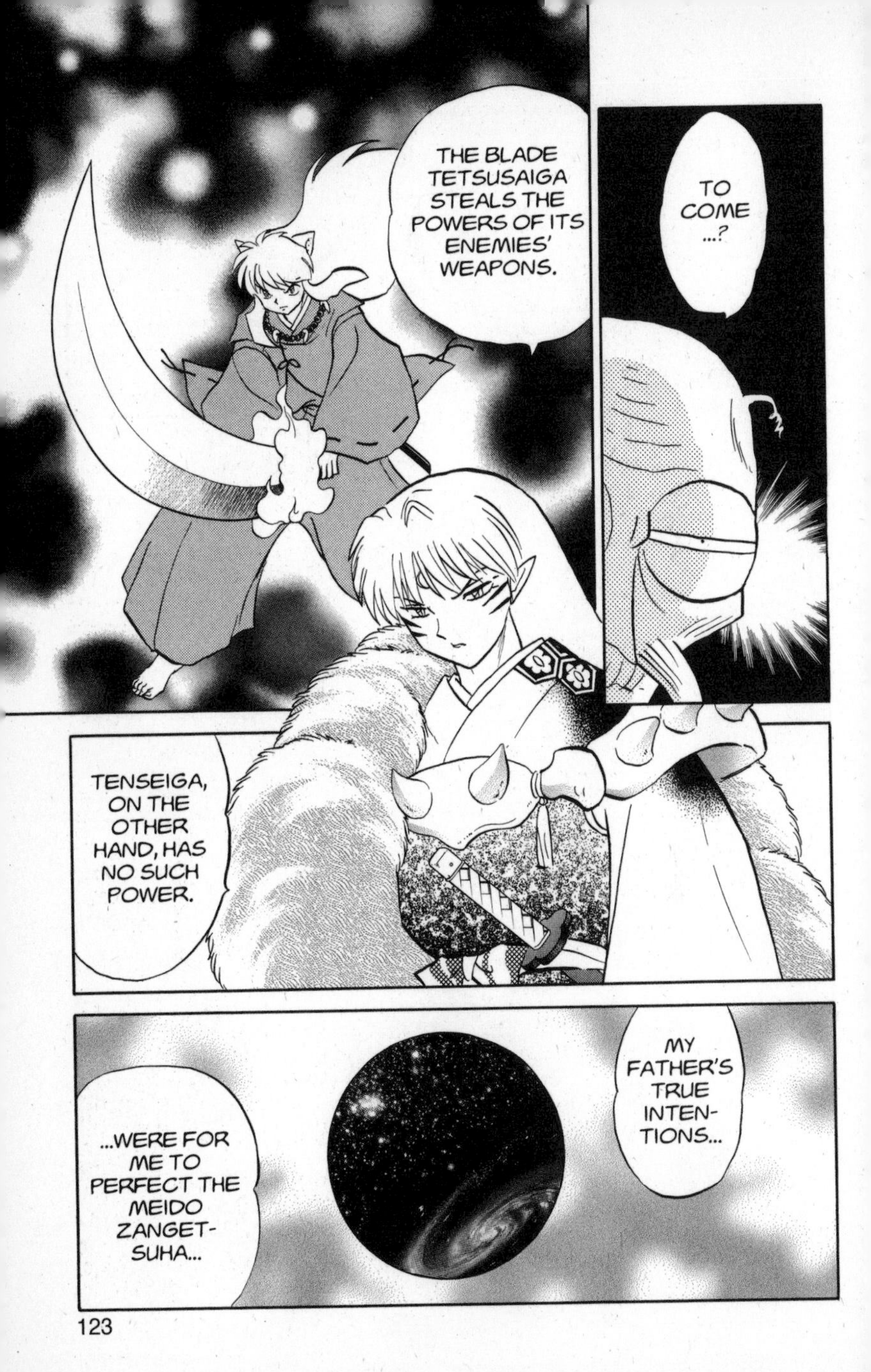
TO COME ...?
THE BLADE TETSUSAIGA STEALS THE POWERS OF ITS ENEMIES' WEAPONS.
TENSEIGA, ON THE OTHER HAND, HAS NO SUCH POWER.
MY FATHER'S TRUE INTEN-TIONS...
...WERE FOR ME TO PERFECT THE MEIDO ZANGET-SUHA...

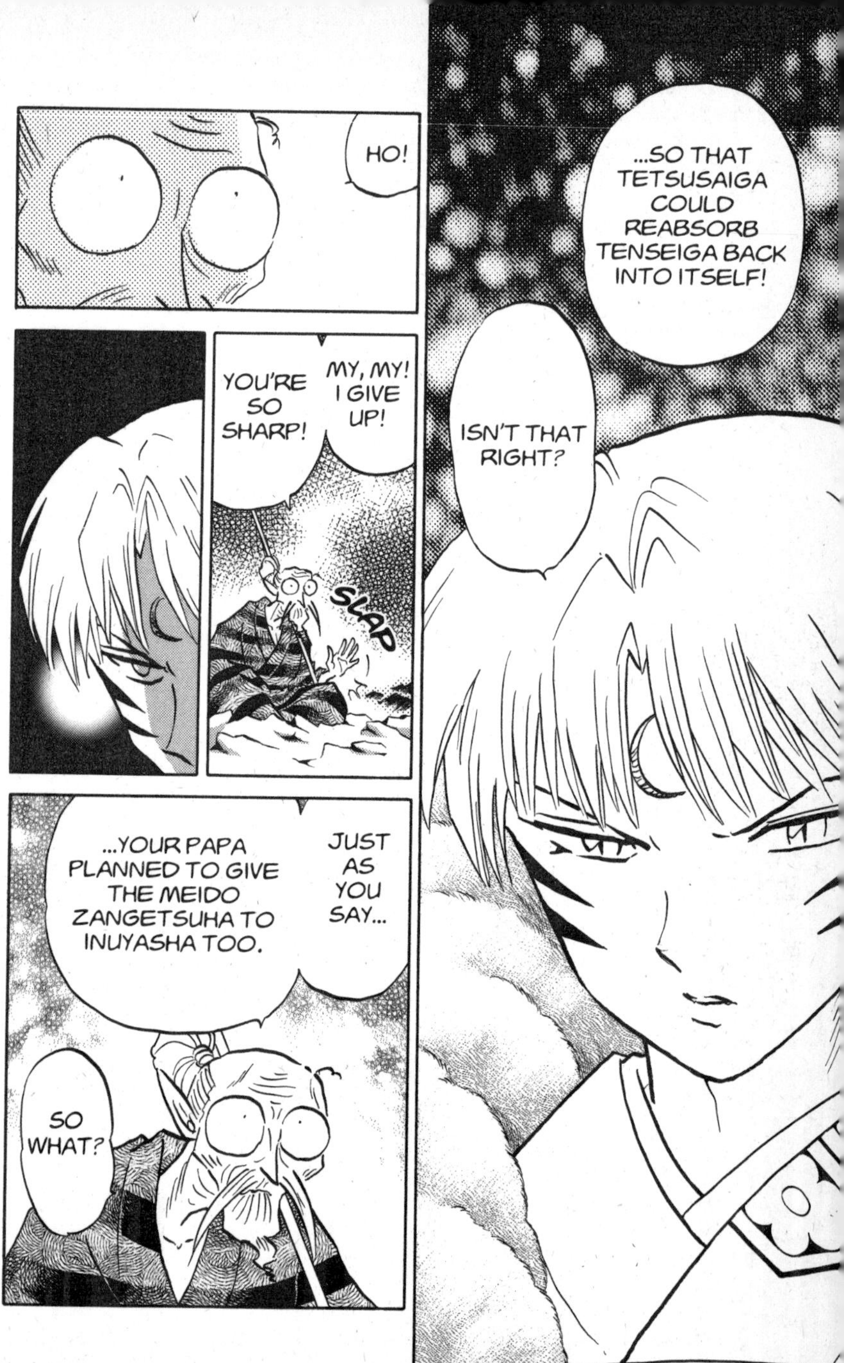
...SO THAT TETSUSAIGA COULD REABSORB TENSEIGA BACK INTO ITSELF!
ISN'T THAT RIGHT?
HO!
MY, MY! I GIVE UP!
YOU'RE SO SHARP!
SLAP
JUST AS YOU SAY...
...YOUR PAPA PLANNED TO GIVE THE MEIDO ZANGETSUHA TO INUYASHA TOO.
SO WHAT?

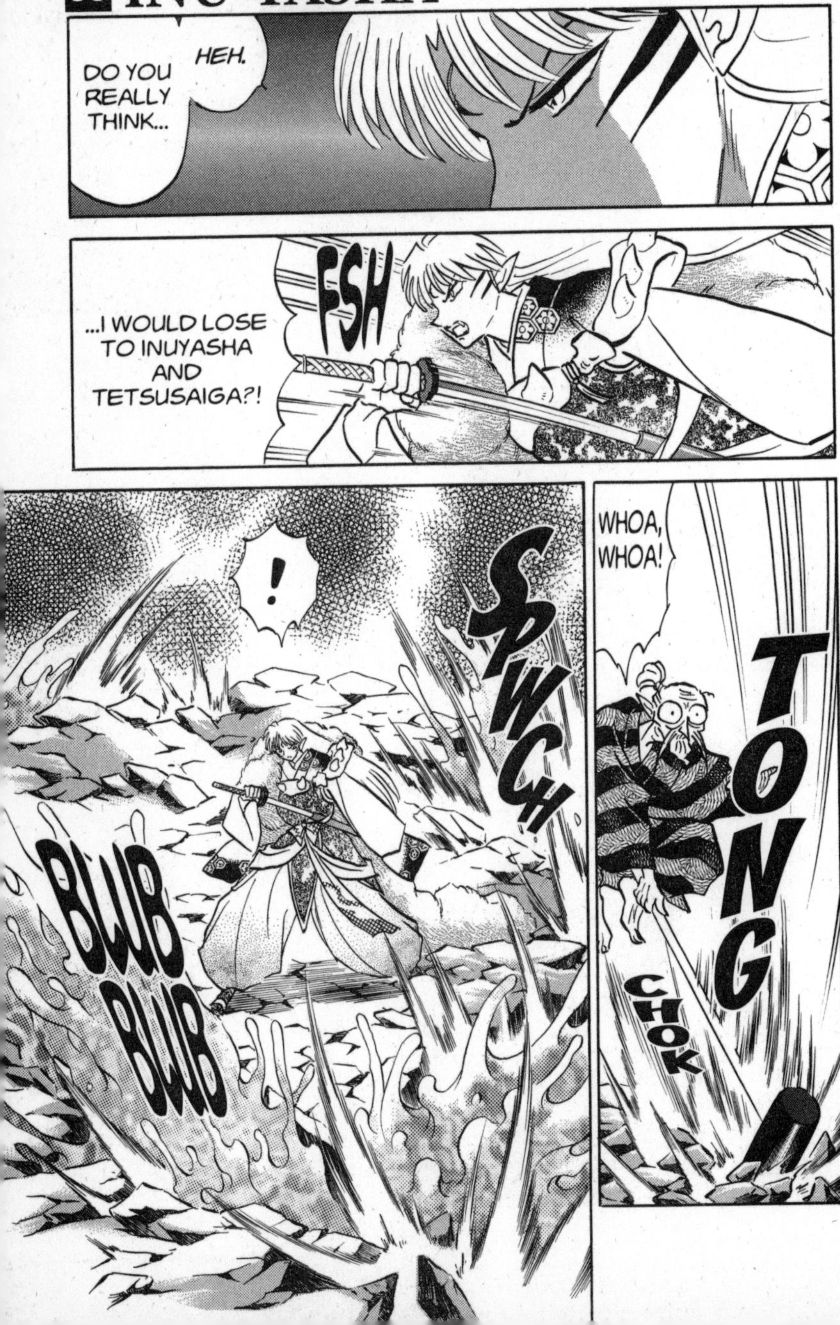
HEH.
DO YOU REALLY THINK...
FSH
...I WOULD LOSE TO INUYASHA AND TETSUSAIGA?!
WHOA, WHOA!
TONG
CHOK
!
SPWCH!
BLUB BLUB

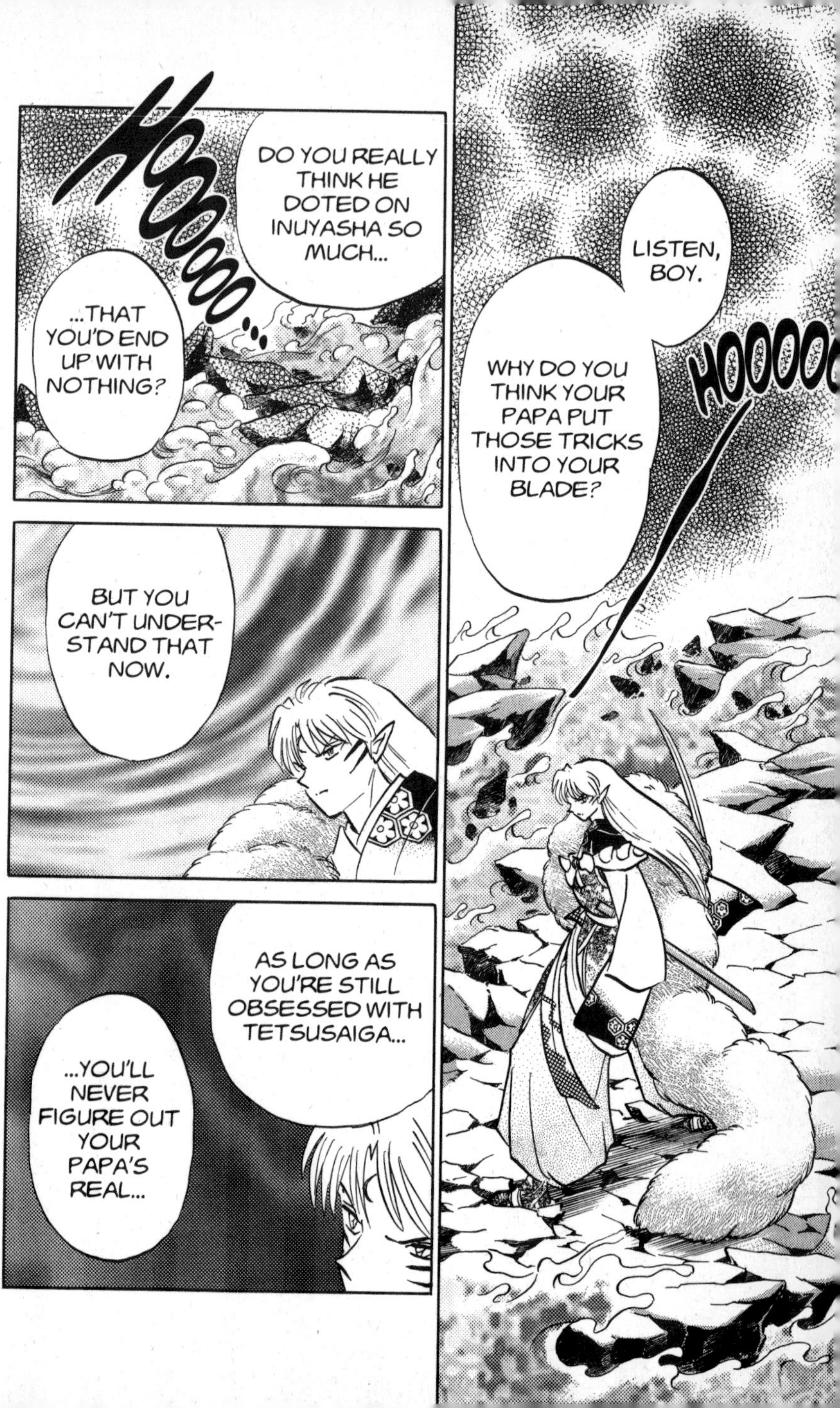
LISTEN, BOY.
WHY DO YOU THINK YOUR PAPA PUT THOSE TRICKS INTO YOUR BLADE?
HOOOOO
HOOOOOO...
DO YOU REALLY THINK HE DOTED ON INUYASHA SO MUCH...
...THAT YOU'D END UP WITH NOTHING?
BUT YOU CAN'T UNDER-STAND THAT NOW.
AS LONG AS YOU'RE STILL OBSESSED WITH TETSUSAIGA...
...YOU'LL NEVER FIGURE OUT YOUR PAPA'S REAL...

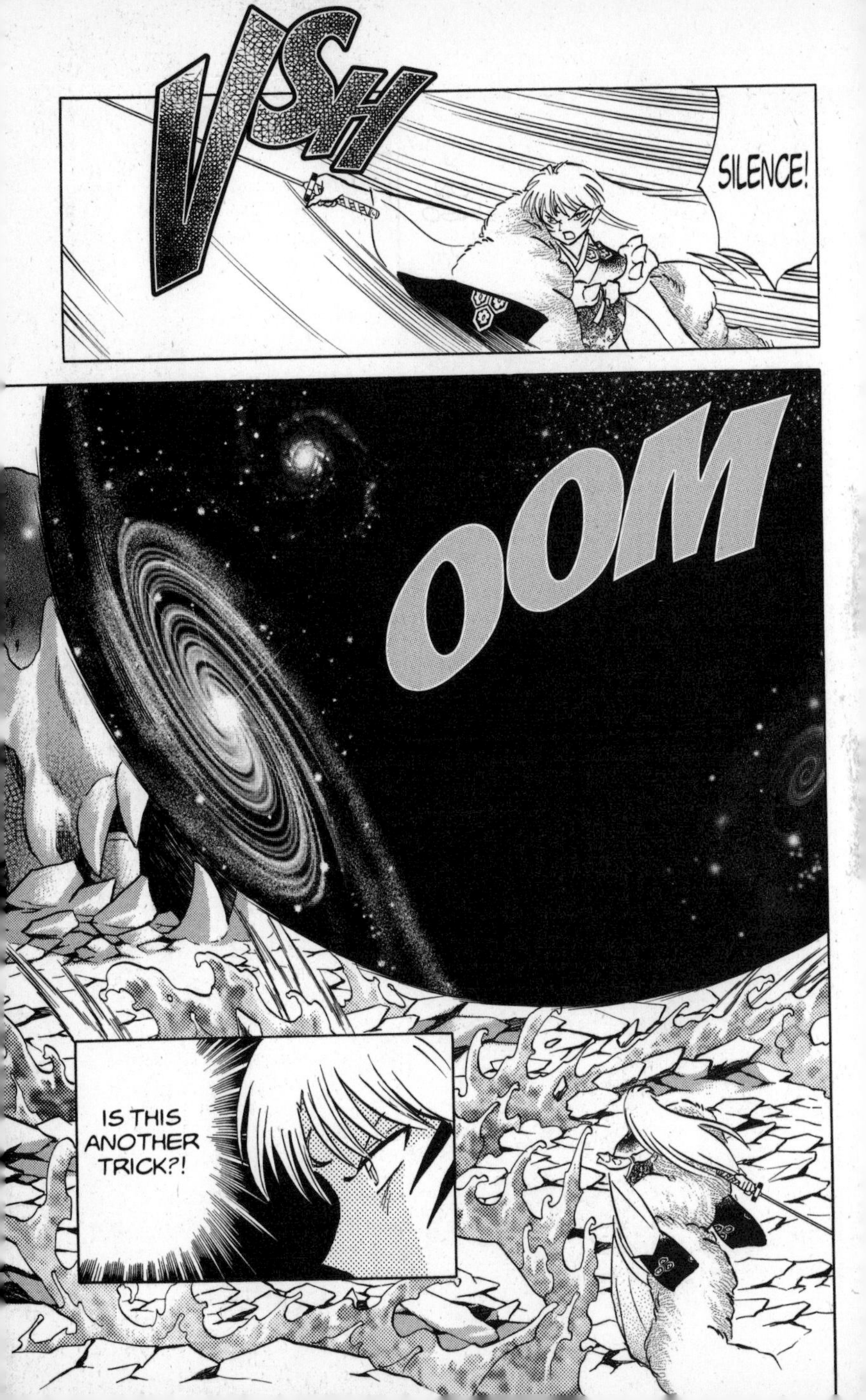
VISH
SILENCE!
OOM
IS THIS ANOTHER TRICK?!

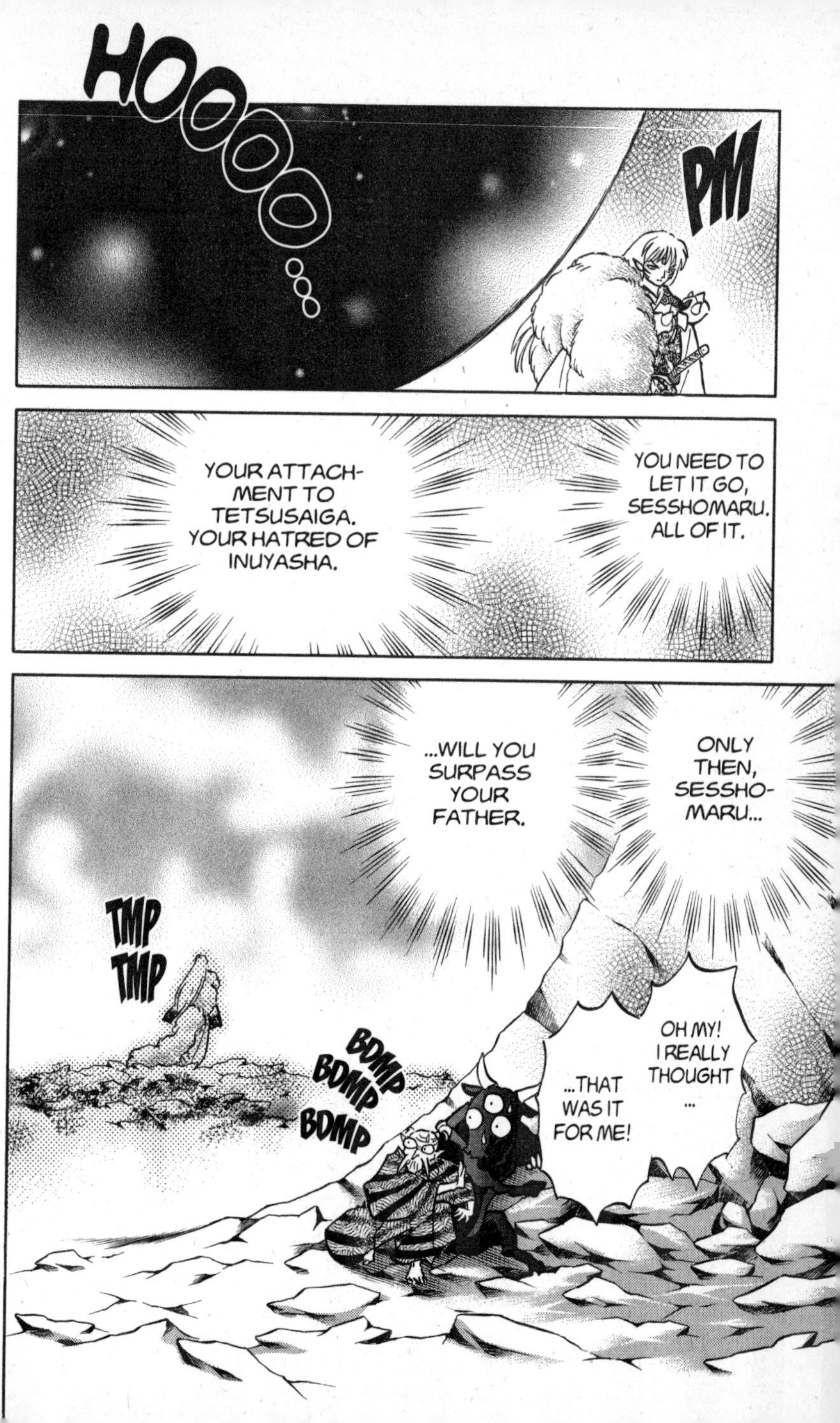
PM
HOOOOOOooo
YOU NEED TO LET IT GO, SESSHOMARU. ALL OF IT.
YOUR ATTACHMENT TO TETSUSAIGA. YOUR HATRED OF INUYASHA.
ONLY THEN, SESSHOMARU...
...WILL YOU SURPASS YOUR FATHER.
OH MY! I REALLY THOUGHT...
...THAT WAS IT FOR ME!
BDMP BDMP BDMP
TMP TMP

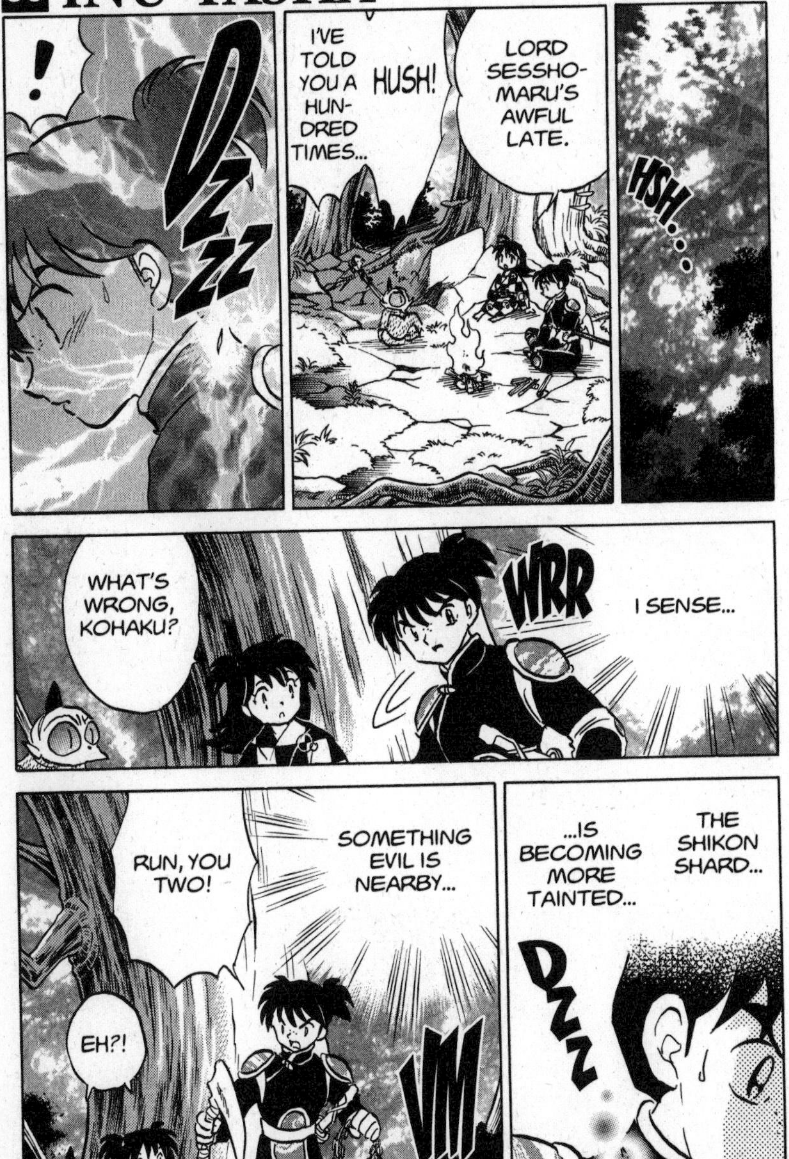
HSH...
LORD SESSHOMARU'S AWFUL LATE.
HUSH!
I'VE TOLD YOU A HUNDRED TIMES...
!
DZZZ
I SENSE...
WRR
WHAT'S WRONG, KOHAKU?
THE SHIKON SHARD...
...IS BECOMING MORE TAINTED...
DZZ
SOMETHING EVIL IS NEARBY...
RUN, YOU TWO!
EH?!
VMM

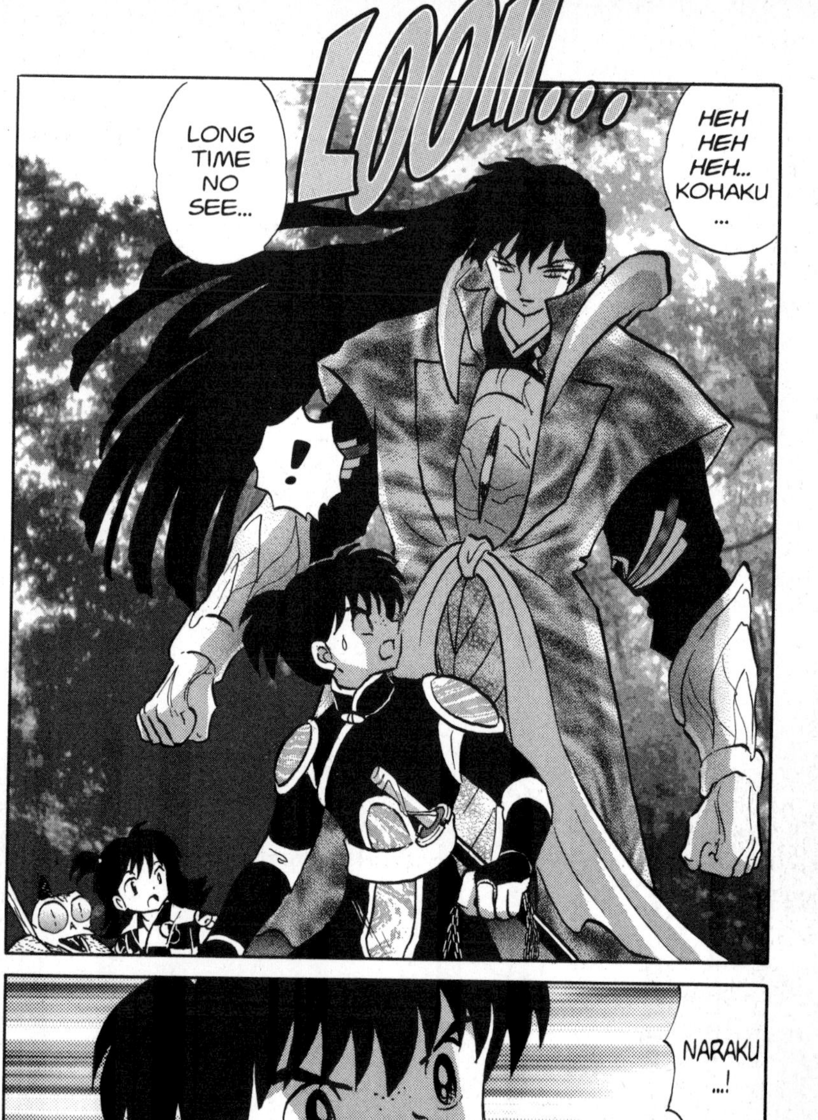
HEH HEH HEH... KOHAKU ...
LOOM...
LONG TIME NO SEE...
!
NARAKU ...!

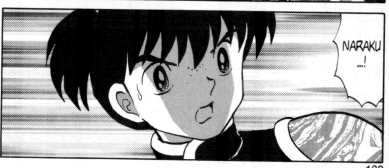

SCROLL 8

TRAP

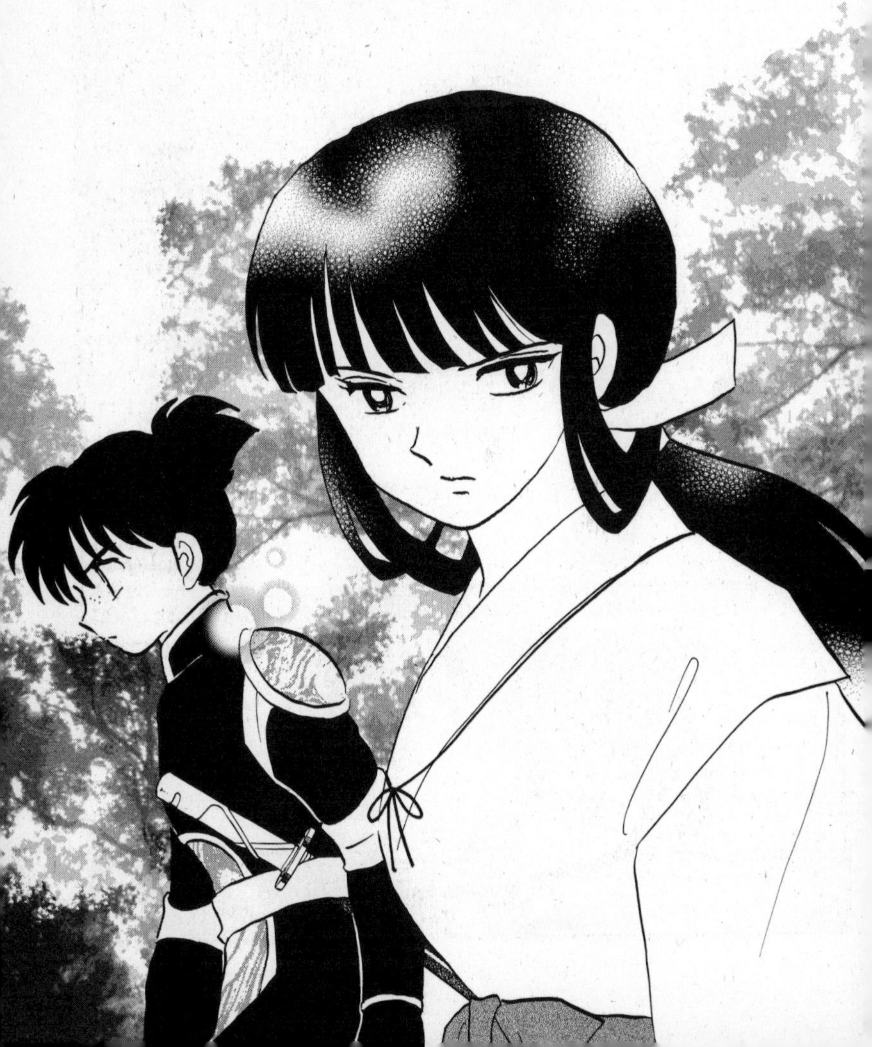

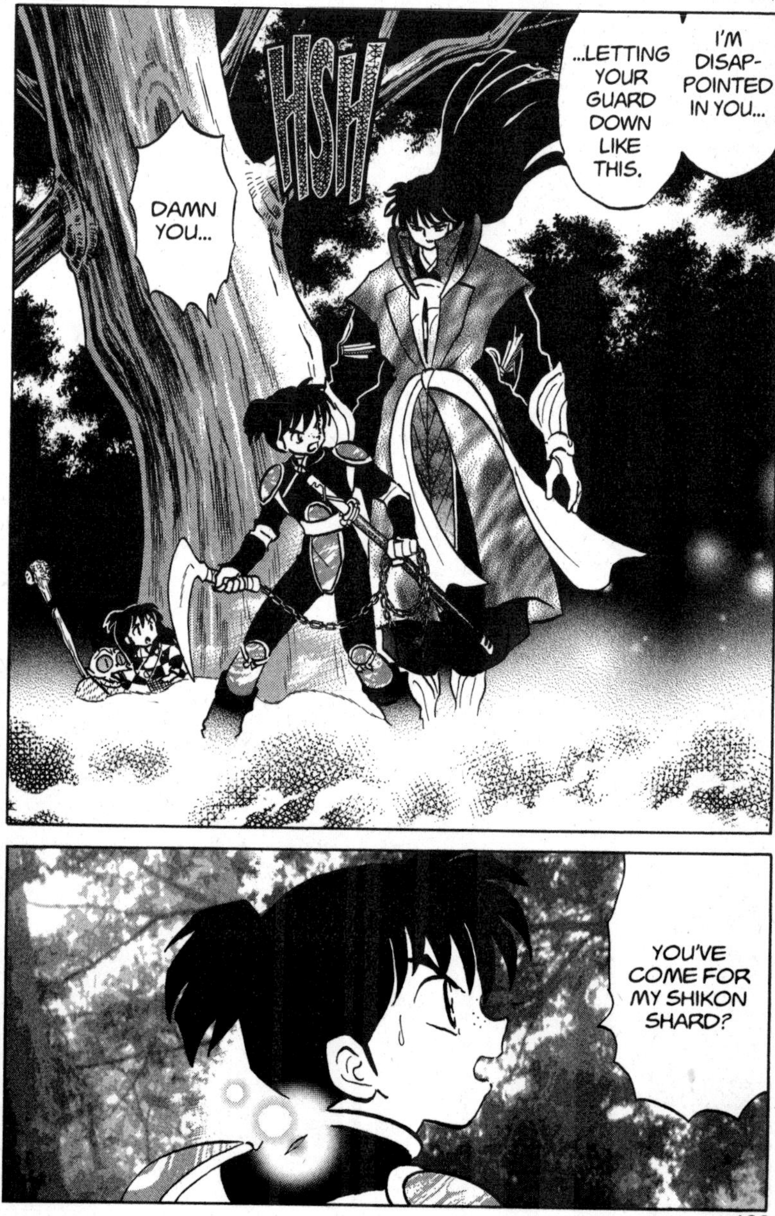
I'M DISAP-POINTED IN YOU...
...LETTING YOUR GUARD DOWN LIKE THIS.
HSH
DAMN YOU...
YOU'VE COME FOR MY SHIKON SHARD?

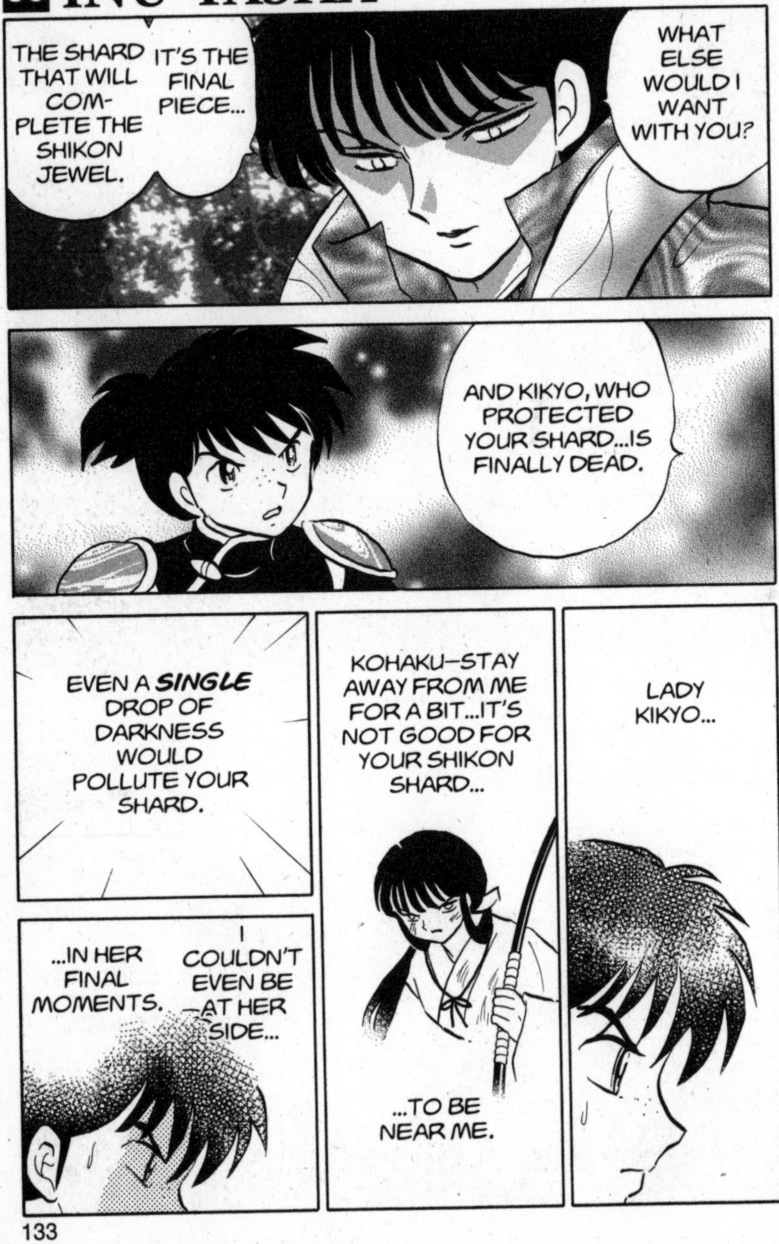
WHAT ELSE WOULD I WANT WITH YOU?
IT'S THE FINAL PIECE...
THE SHARD THAT WILL COM-PLETE THE SHIKON JEWEL.
AND KIKYO, WHO PROTECTED YOUR SHARD...IS FINALLY DEAD.
LADY KIKYO...
KOHAKU—STAY AWAY FROM ME FOR A BIT...IT'S NOT GOOD FOR YOUR SHIKON SHARD...
...TO BE NEAR ME.
EVEN A SINGLE DROP OF DARKNESS WOULD POLLUTE YOUR SHARD.
I COULDN'T EVEN BE AT HER SIDE...
...IN HER FINAL MOMENTS.

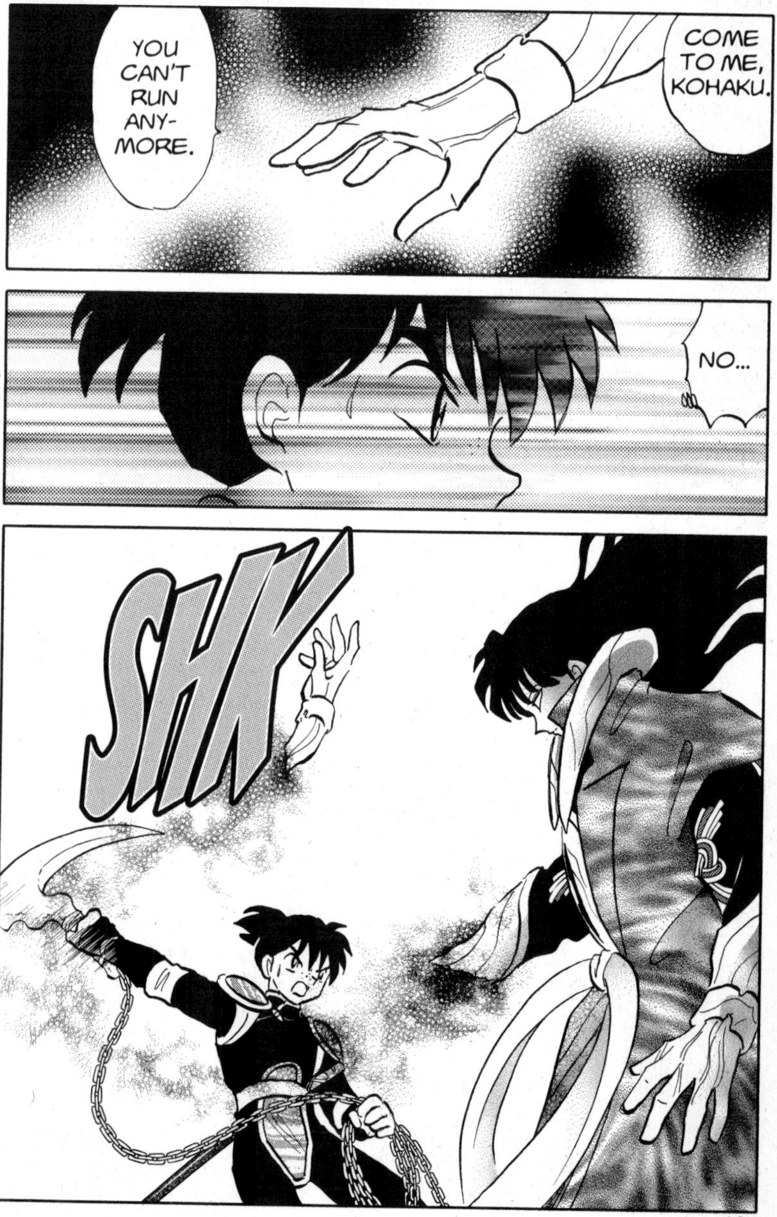
COME TO ME, KOHAKU.
YOU CAN'T RUN ANY-MORE.
NO...
SHK

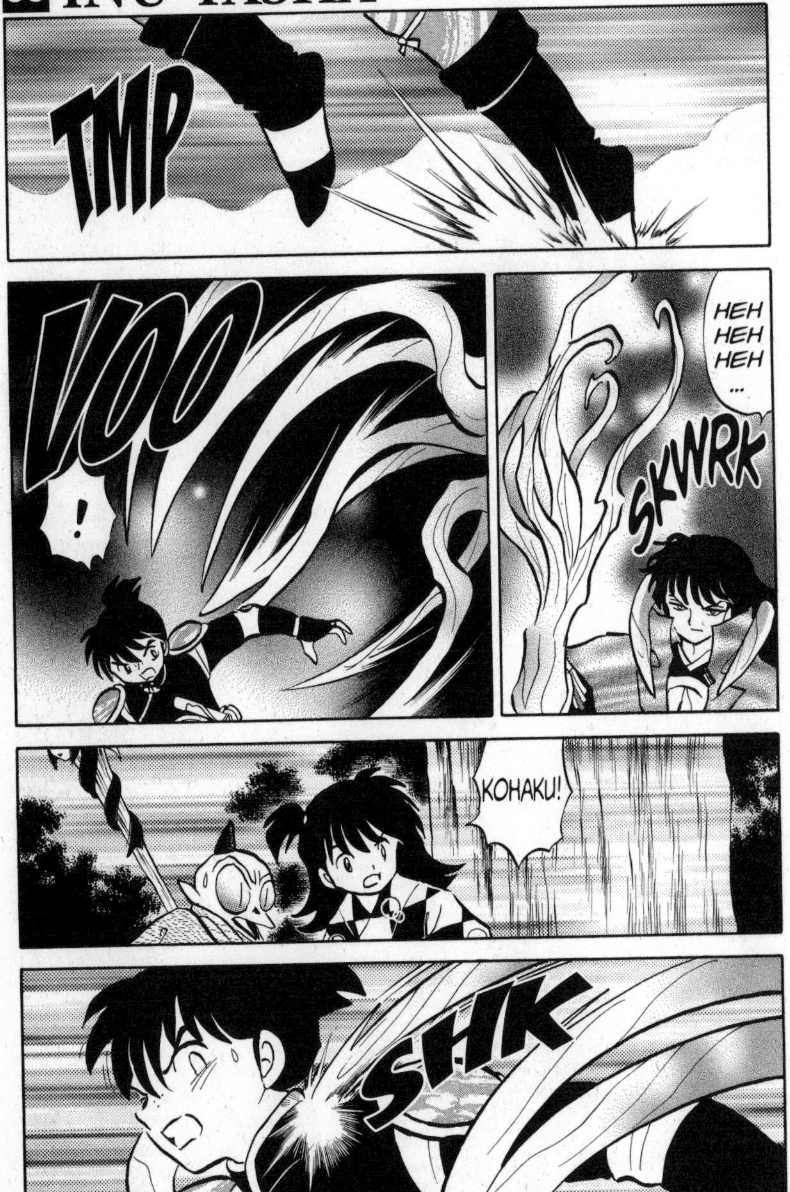
TMP
HEH HEH HEH ...
SKWRK
VOO
!
KOHAKU!
SHK

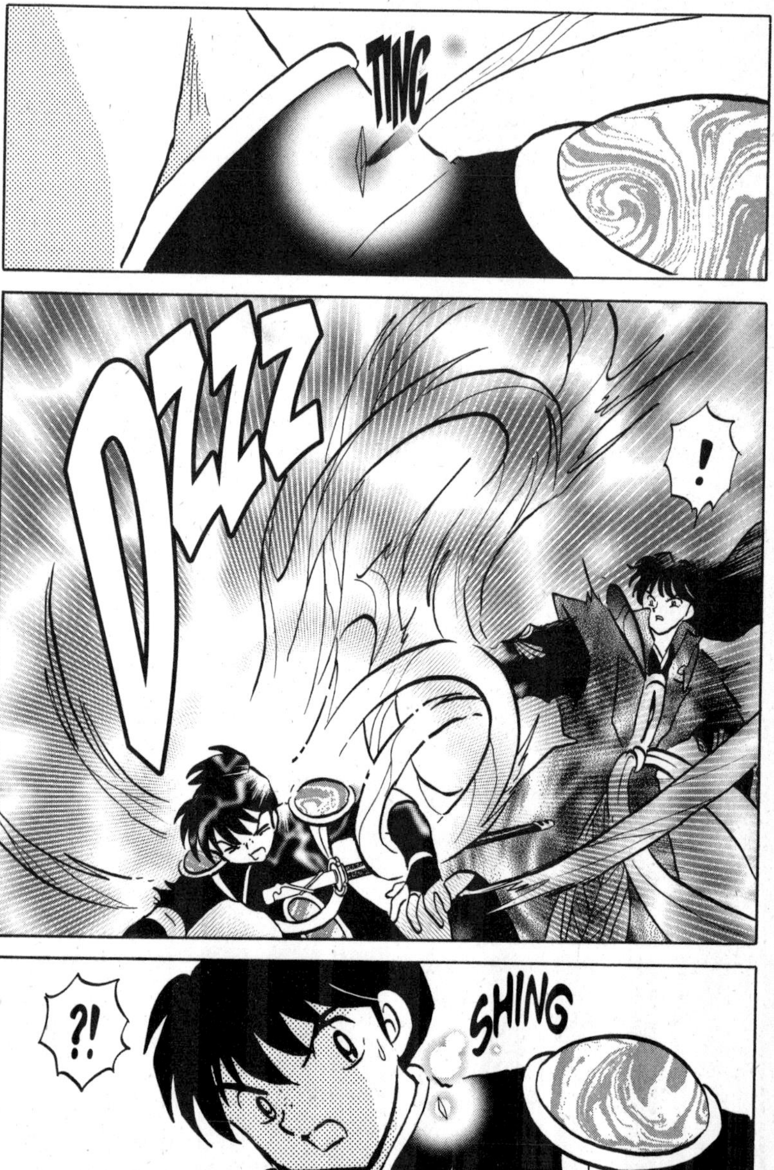
TING
!
DZZZ
SHING
?!

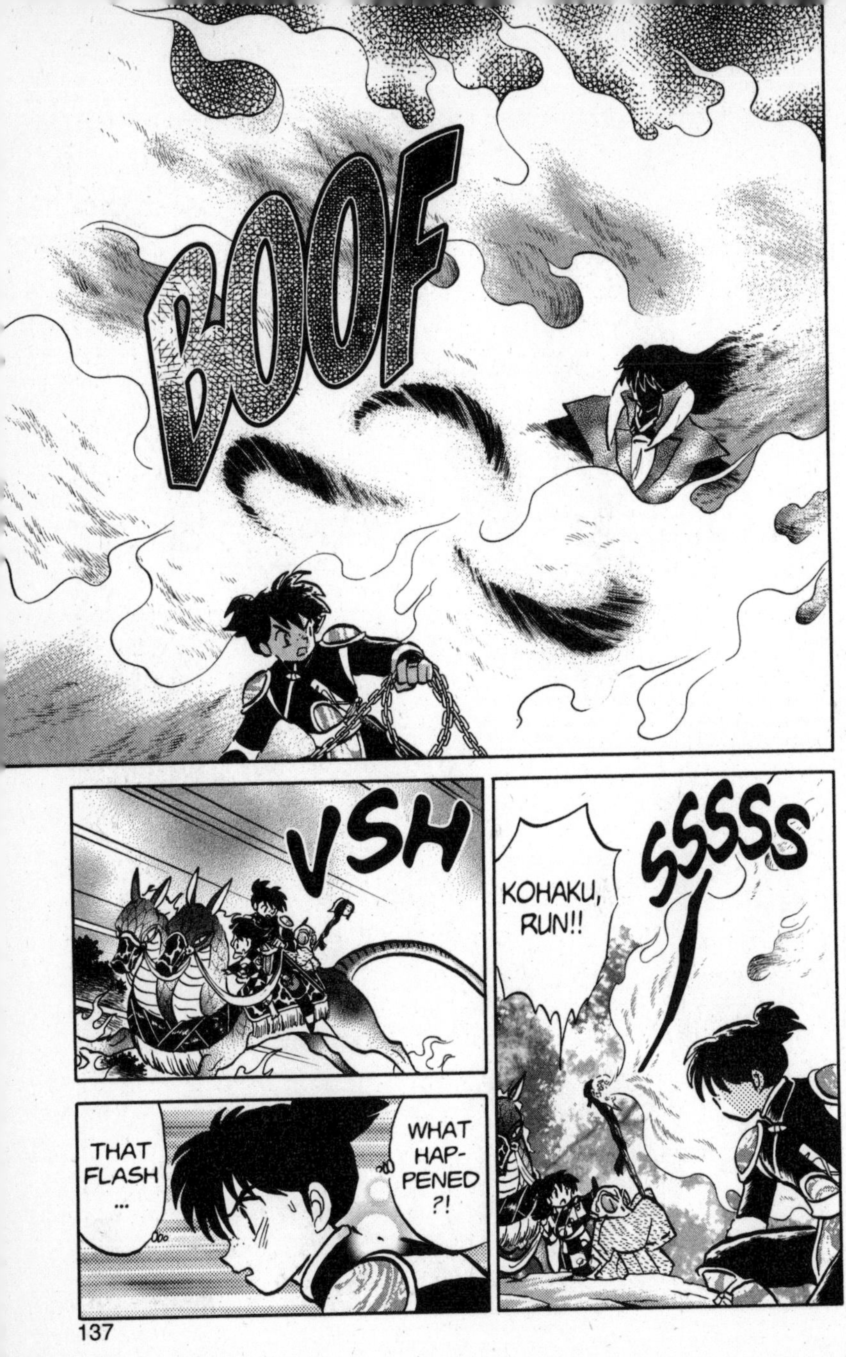
BOOF
KOHAKU, RUN!!
SSSSS
VSH
WHAT HAP-PENED?!
THAT FLASH...

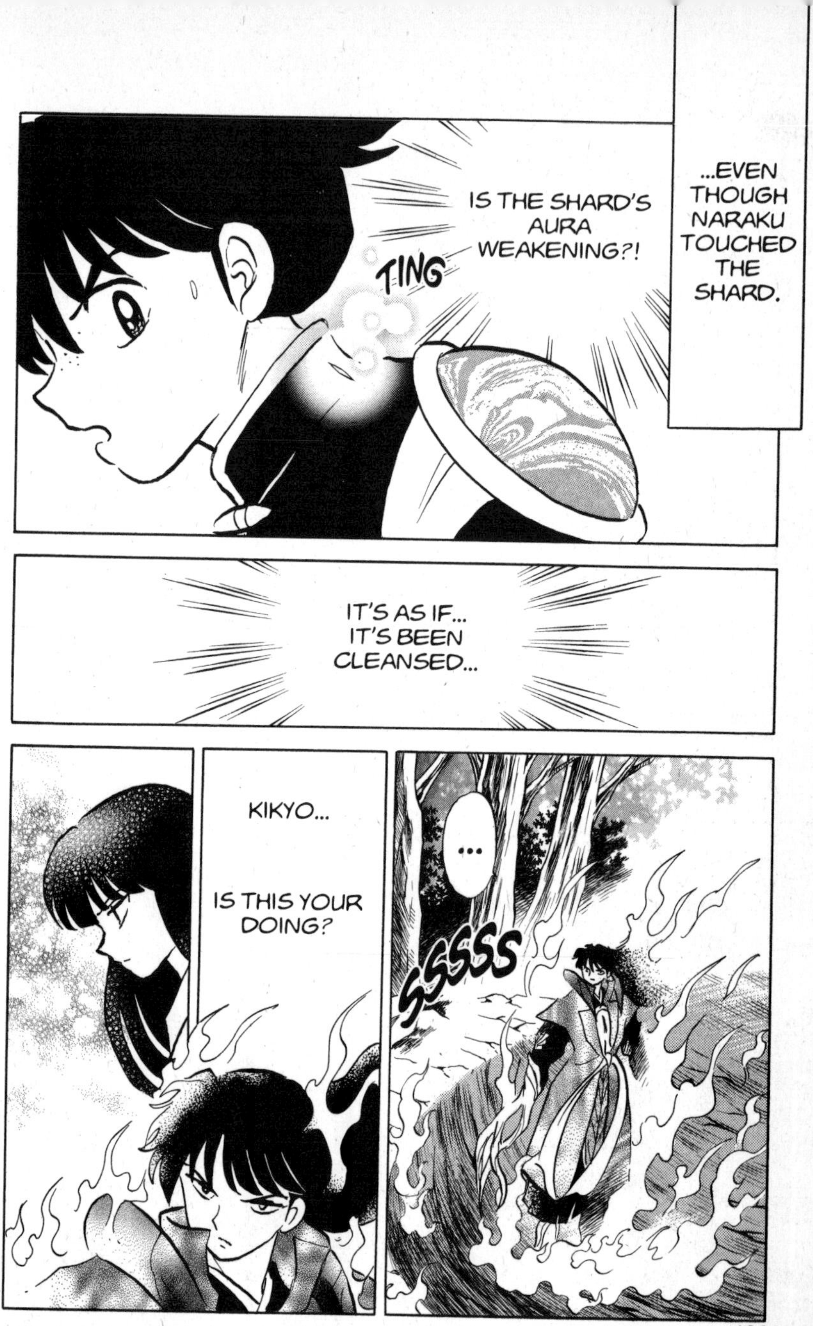
...EVEN THOUGH NARAKU TOUCHED THE SHARD.
IS THE SHARD'S AURA WEAKENING?!
TING
IT'S AS IF... IT'S BEEN CLEANSED...
...
SSSSS
KIKYO...
IS THIS YOUR DOING?

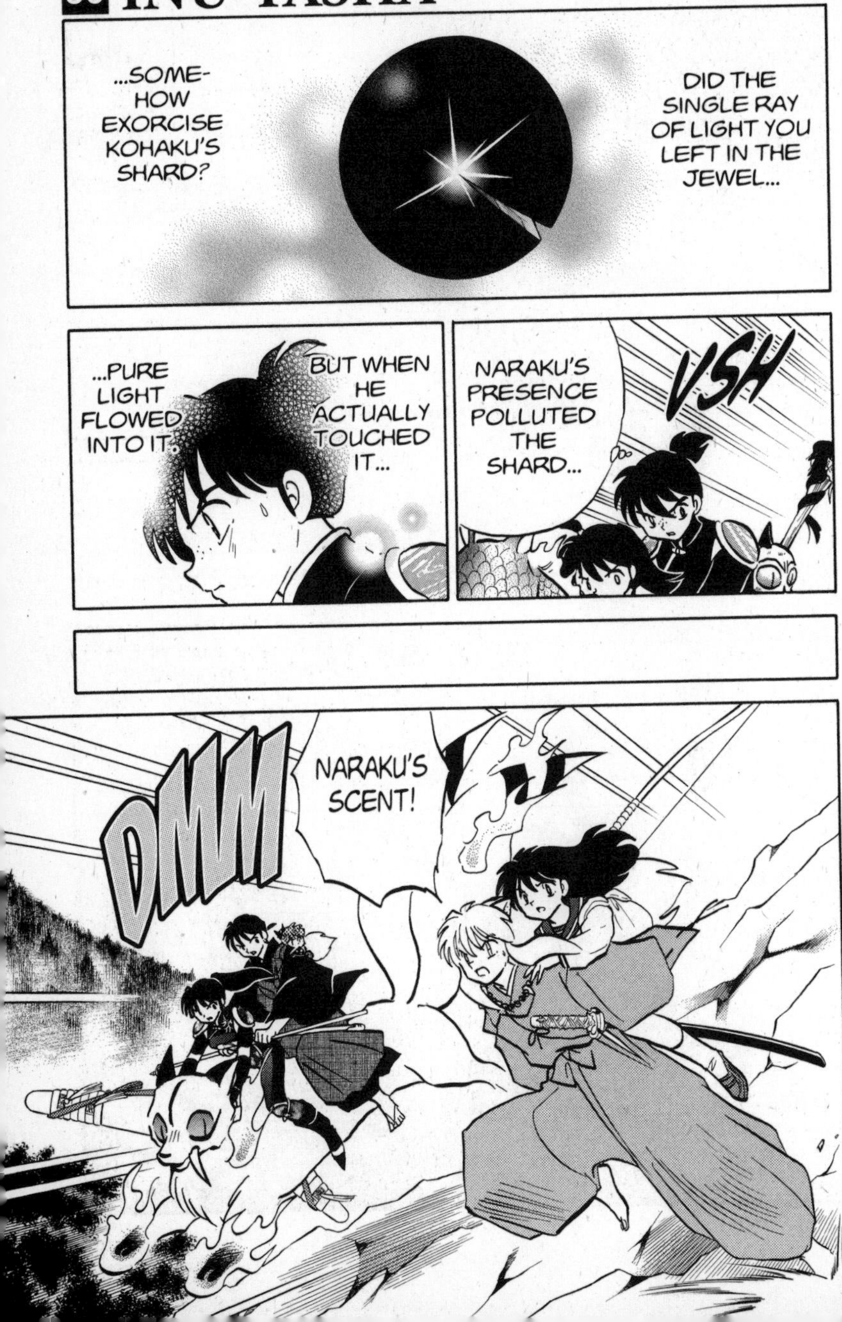
DID THE SINGLE RAY OF LIGHT YOU LEFT IN THE JEWEL...
...SOME-HOW EXORCISE KOHAKU'S SHARD?
VSH
NARAKU'S PRESENCE POLLUTED THE SHARD...
BUT WHEN HE ACTUALLY TOUCHED IT...
...PURE LIGHT FLOWED INTO IT.
NARAKU'S SCENT!
DMM

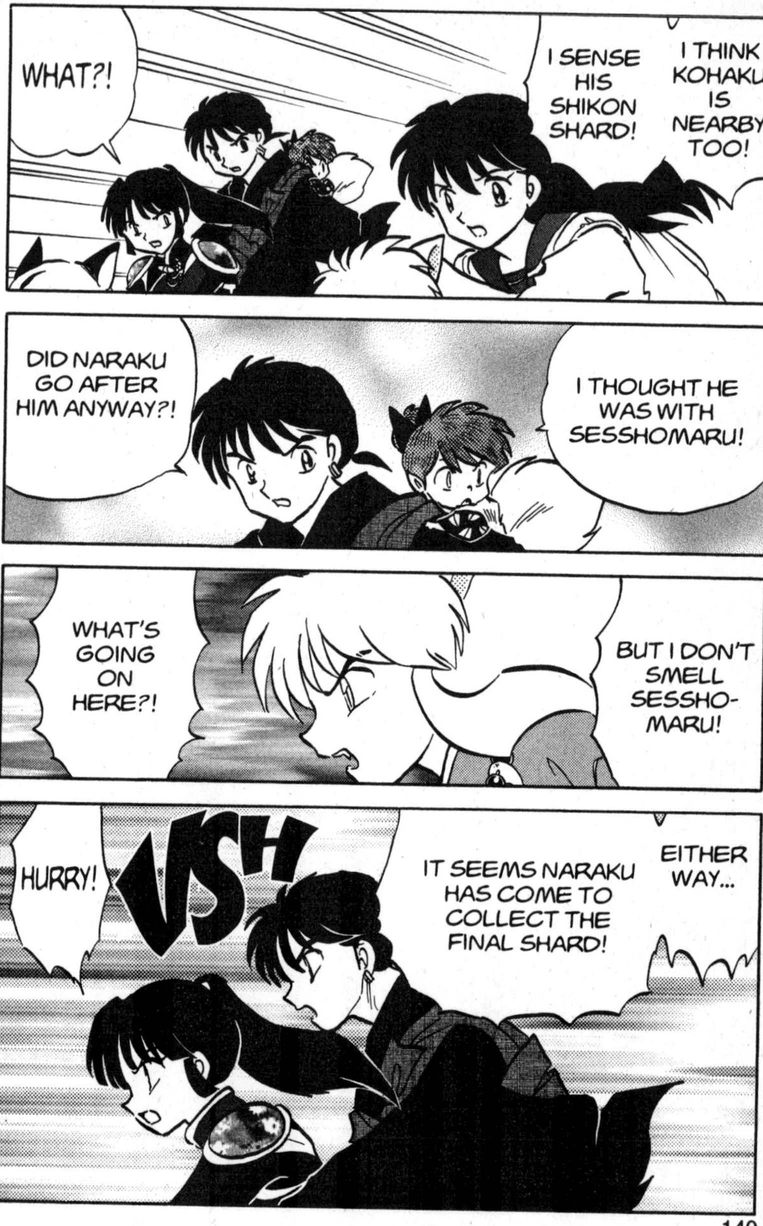
I THINK KOHAKU IS NEARBY TOO!
I SENSE HIS SHIKON SHARD!
WHAT?!
I THOUGHT HE WAS WITH SESSHOMARU!
DID NARAKU GO AFTER HIM ANYWAY?!
BUT I DON'T SMELL SESSHO-MARU!
WHAT'S GOING ON HERE?!
EITHER WAY...
IT SEEMS NARAKU HAS COME TO COLLECT THE FINAL SHARD!
VSH
HURRY!

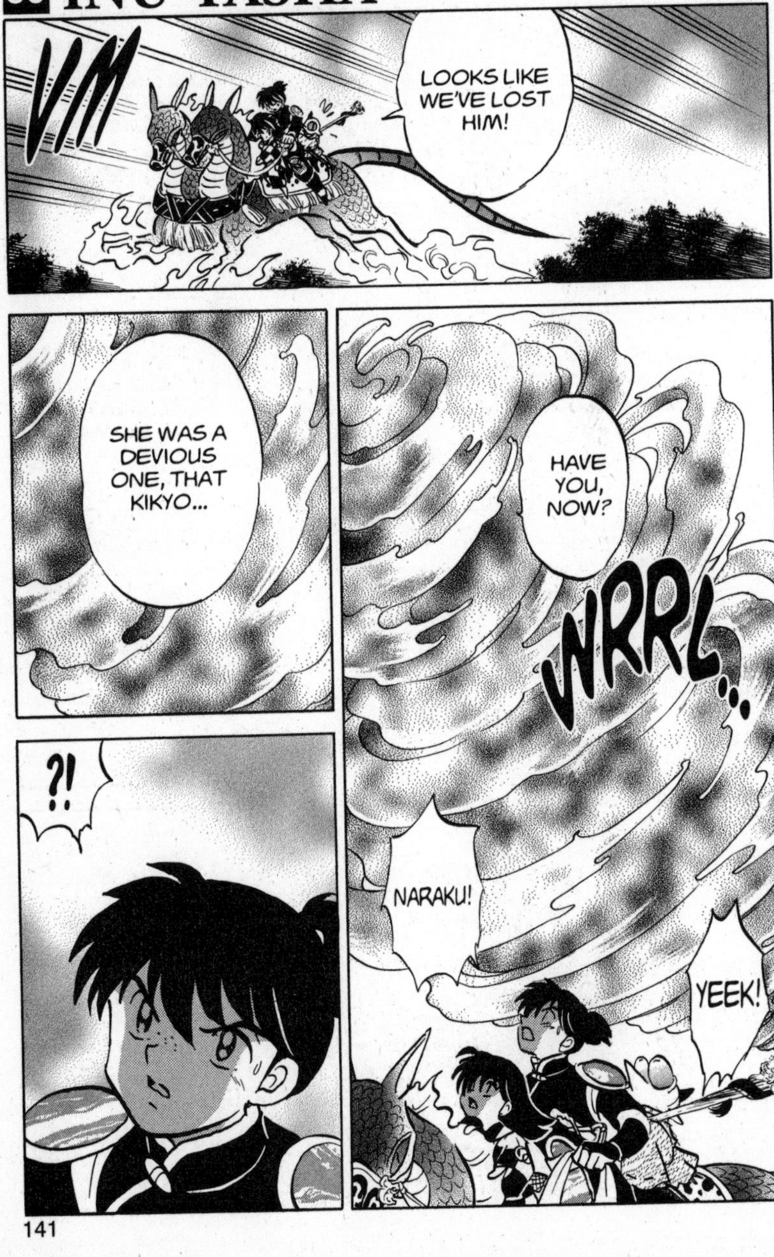
VM
LOOKS LIKE WE'VE LOST HIM!
HAVE YOU, NOW?
WRRL...
NARAKU!
YEEK!
SHE WAS A DEVIOUS ONE, THAT KIKYO...
?!

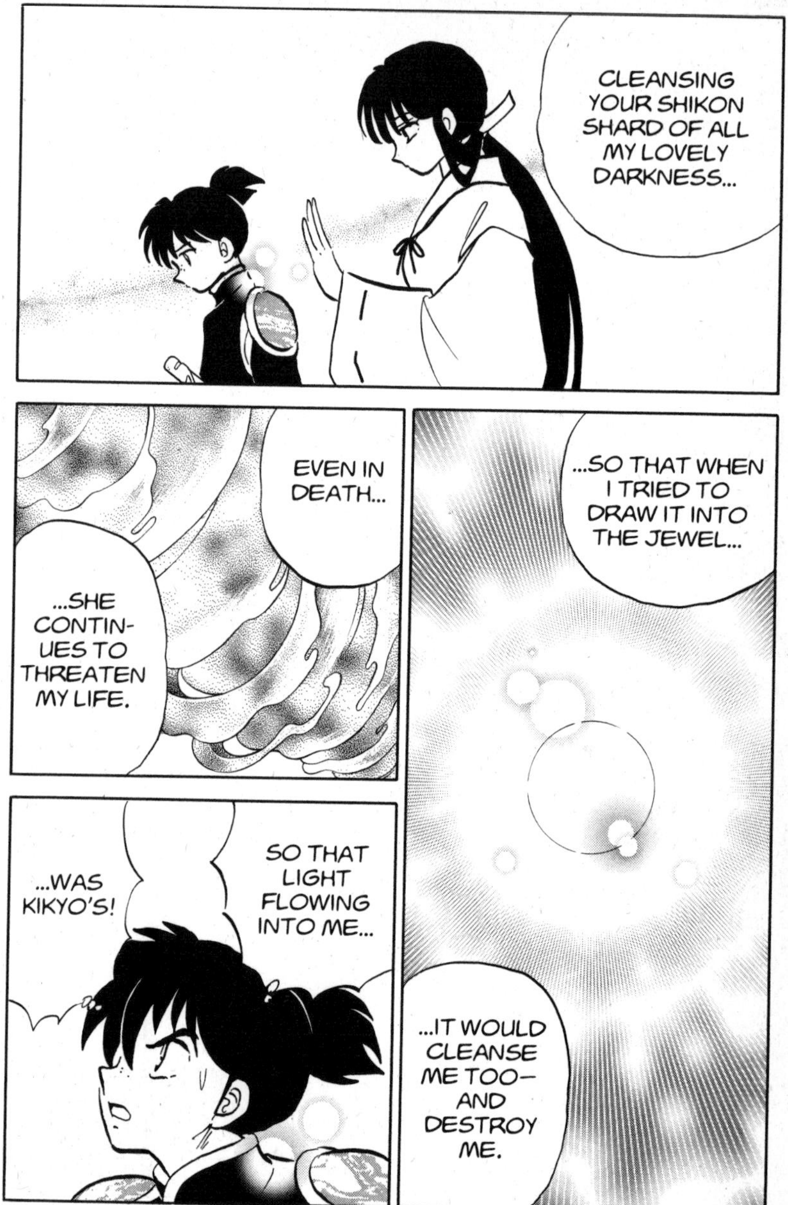
CLEANSING YOUR SHIKON SHARD OF ALL MY LOVELY DARKNESS...
...SO THAT WHEN I TRIED TO DRAW IT INTO THE JEWEL...
...IT WOULD CLEANSE ME TOO— AND DESTROY ME.
EVEN IN DEATH...
...SHE CONTIN-UES TO THREATEN MY LIFE.
SO THAT LIGHT FLOWING INTO ME...
...WAS KIKYO'S!

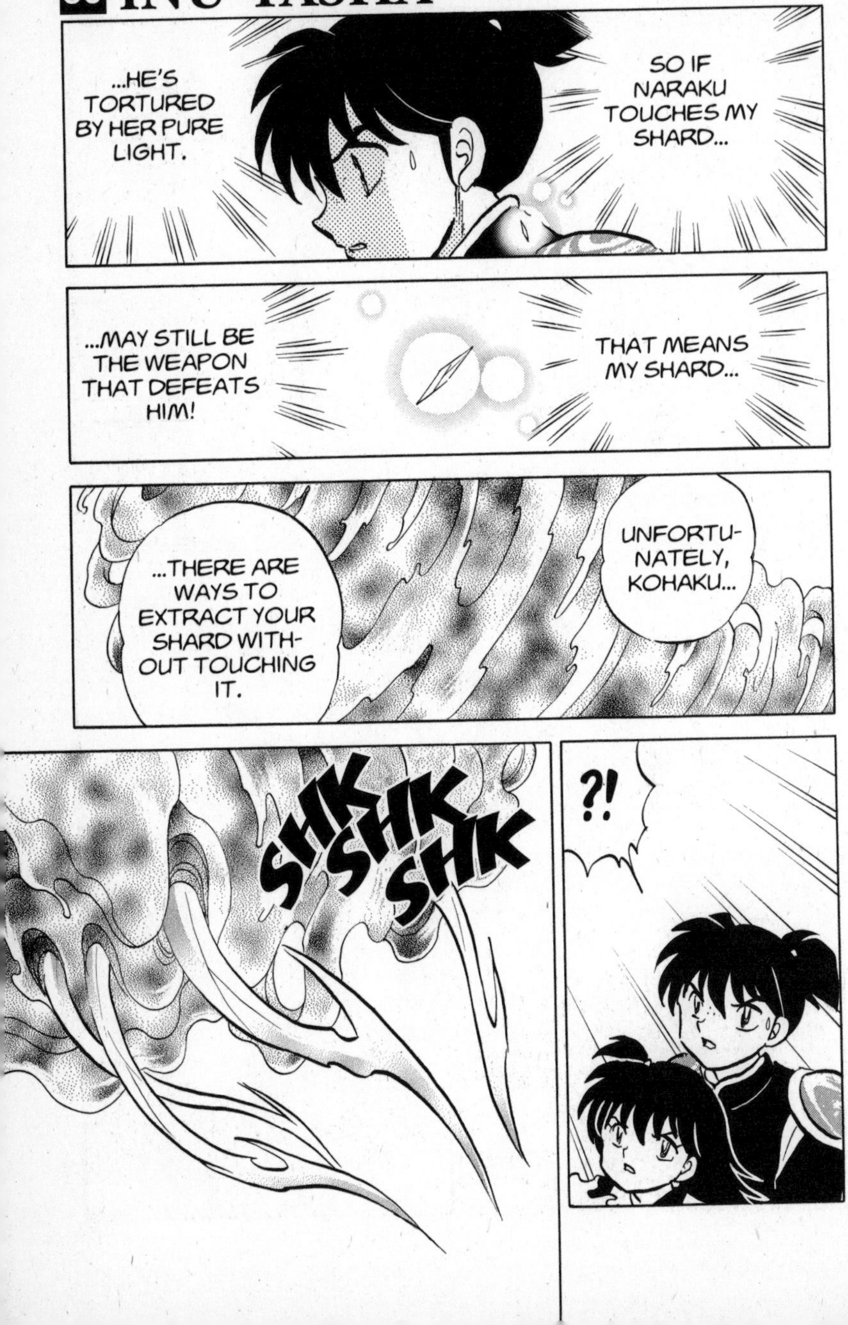
SO IF NARAKU TOUCHES MY SHARD...
...HE'S TORTURED BY HER PURE LIGHT.
THAT MEANS MY SHARD...
...MAY STILL BE THE WEAPON THAT DEFEATS HIM!
UNFORTU-NATELY, KOHAKU...
...THERE ARE WAYS TO EXTRACT YOUR SHARD WITH-OUT TOUCHING IT.
?!
SHK SHK SHK

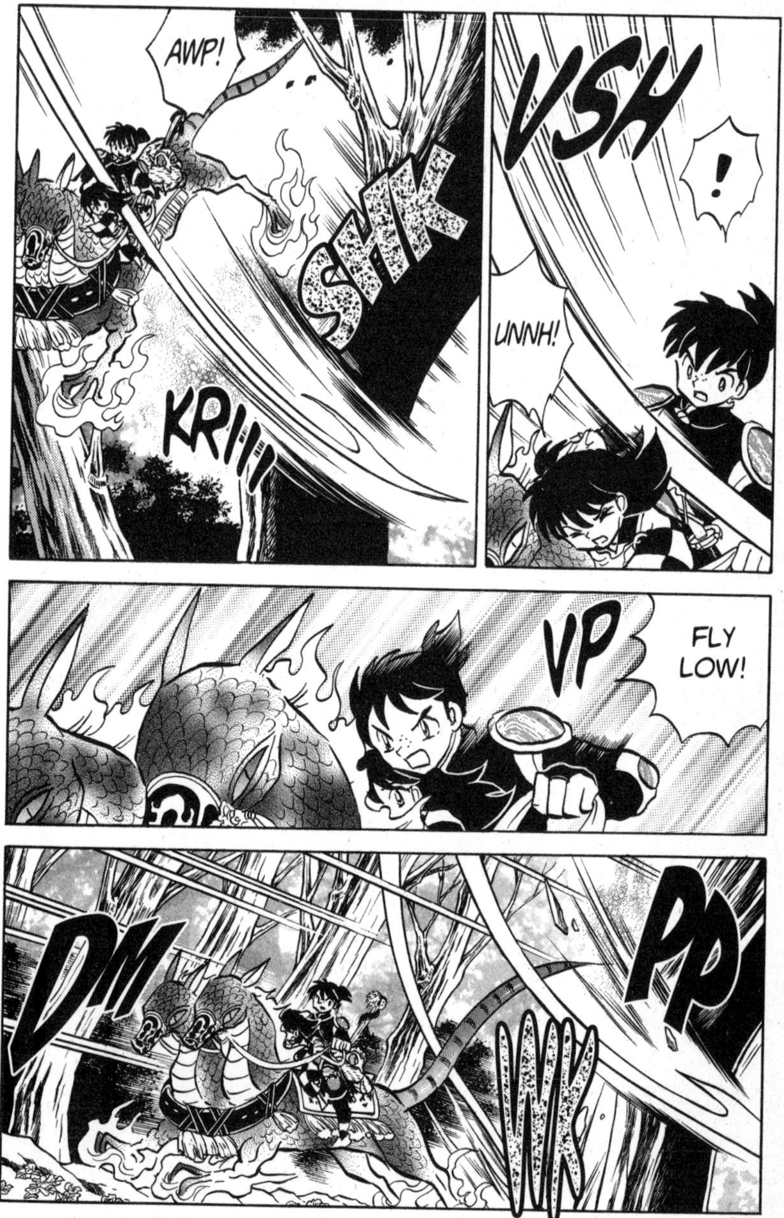
VSH
!
UNNH!
AWP!
SHK
KRIII
FLY LOW!
VP
PP
WK
DM

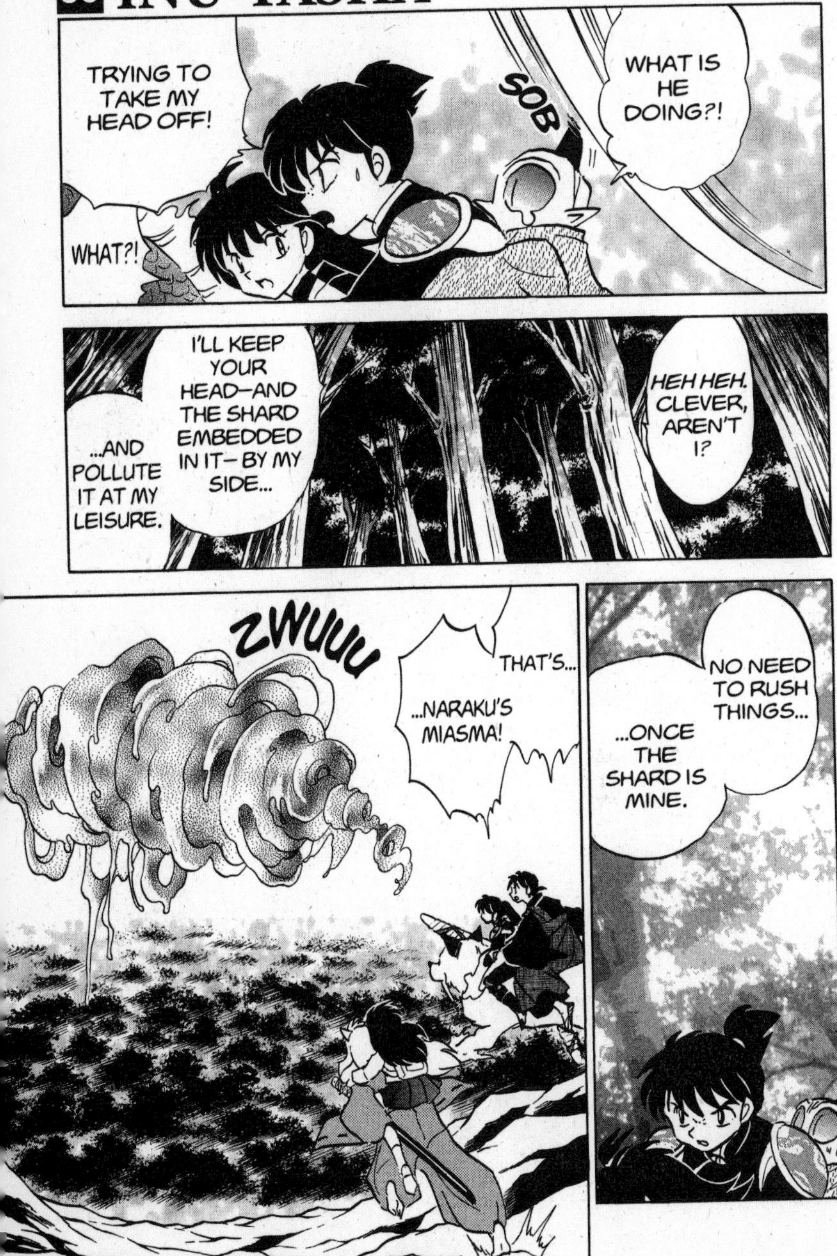
WHAT IS HE DOING?!
SOB
TRYING TO TAKE MY HEAD OFF!
WHAT?!
HEH HEH. CLEVER, AREN'T I?
I'LL KEEP YOUR HEAD—AND THE SHARD EMBEDDED IN IT—BY MY SIDE...
...AND POLLUTE IT AT MY LEISURE.
NO NEED TO RUSH THINGS...
...ONCE THE SHARD IS MINE.
ZWUUU
THAT'S...
...NARAKU'S MIASMA!

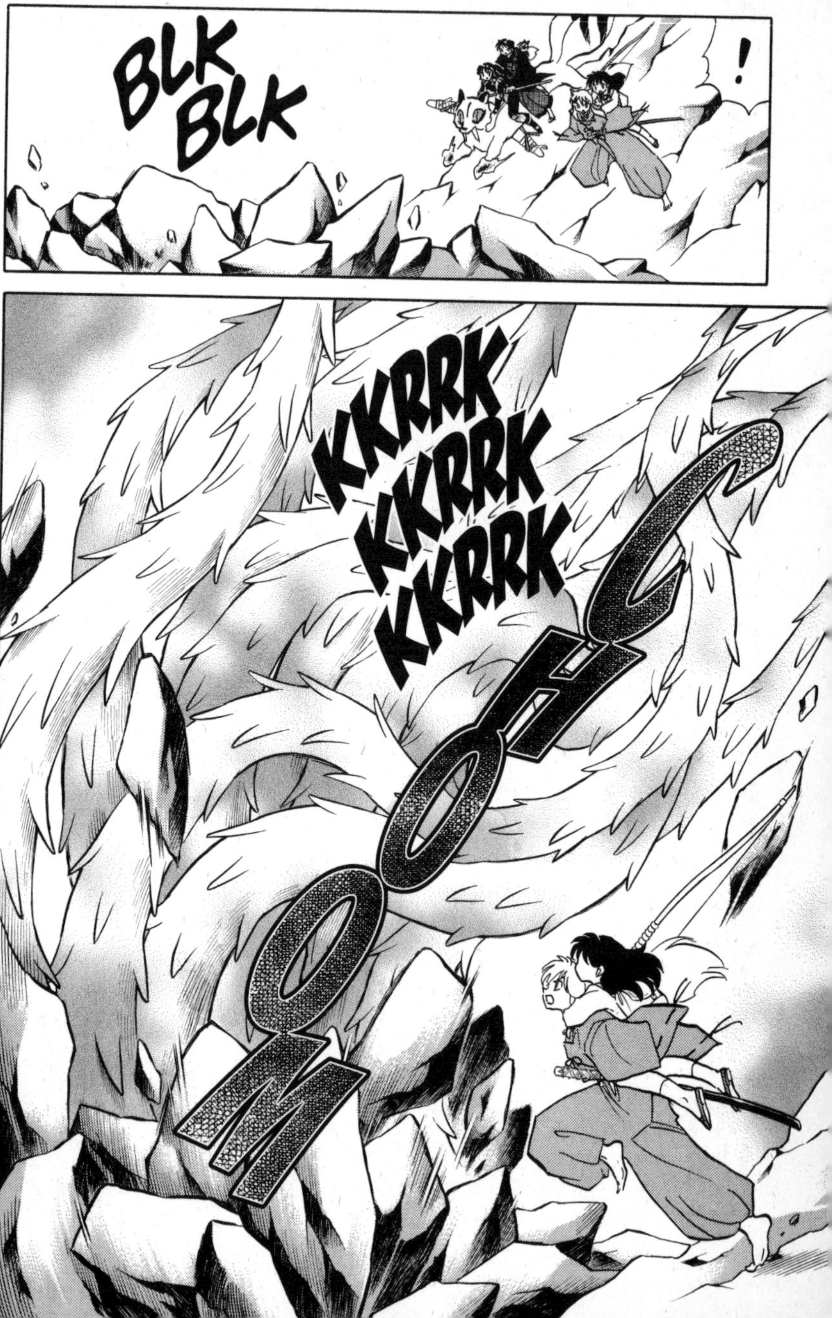
!
BLK BLK
KKRRK KKRRK KKRRK
WOOOH

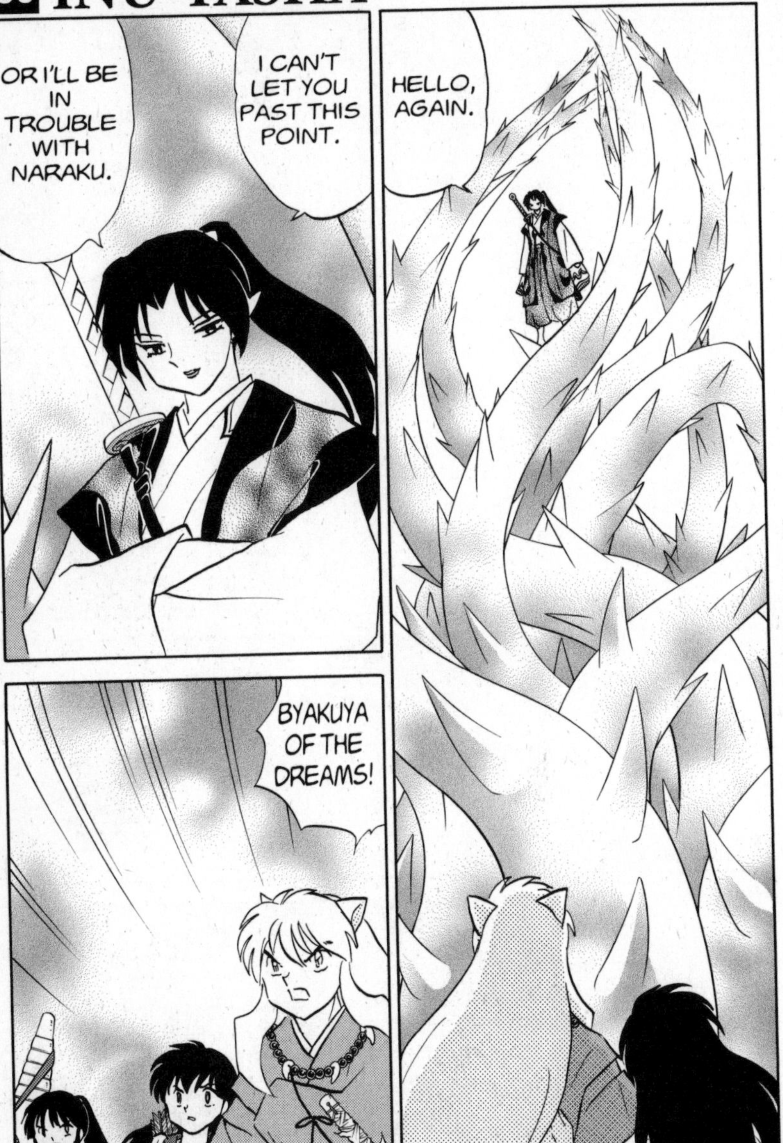
HELLO, AGAIN.
I CAN'T LET YOU PAST THIS POINT.
OR I'LL BE IN TROUBLE WITH NARAKU.
BYAKUYA OF THE DREAMS!

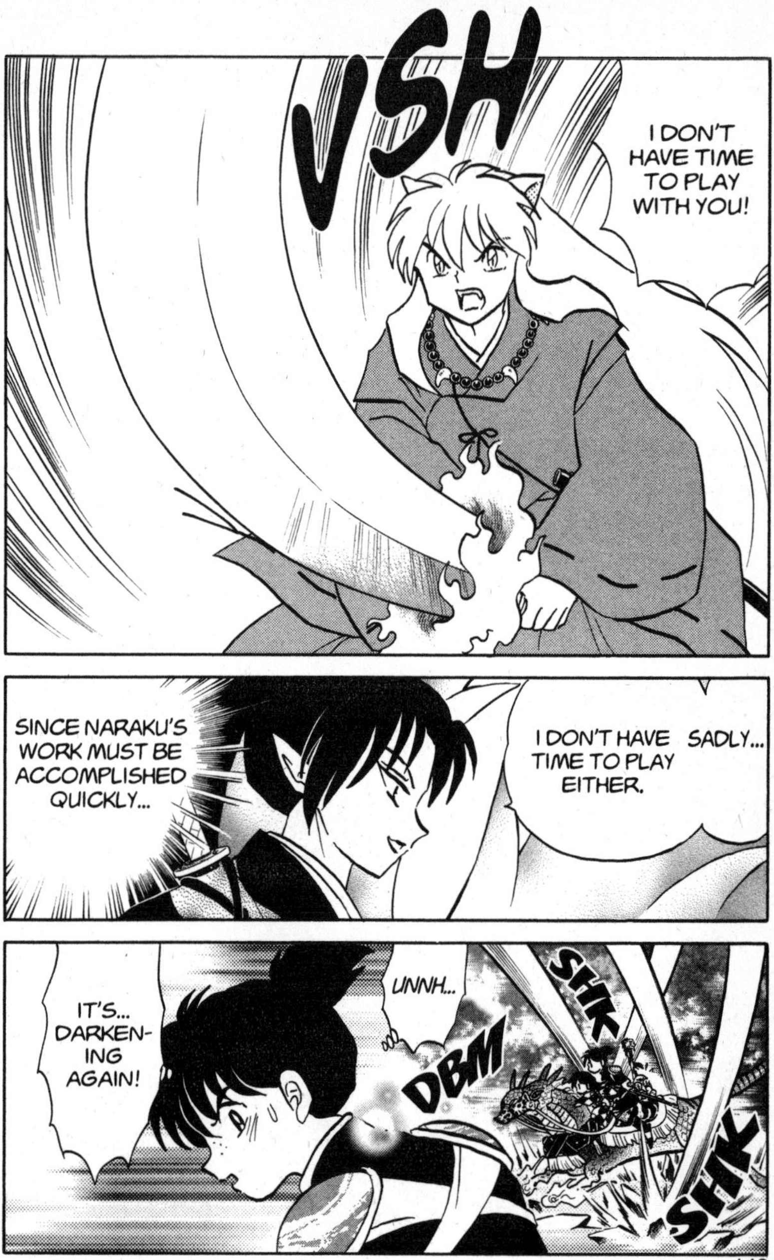
VSH
I DON'T HAVE TIME TO PLAY WITH YOU!
SADLY...
I DON'T HAVE TIME TO PLAY EITHER.
SINCE NARAKU'S WORK MUST BE ACCOMPLISHED QUICKLY...
SHK
SHK
DBM
UNNH...
IT'S... DARKEN-ING AGAIN!

SCROLL 9
KOHAKU'S HEAD

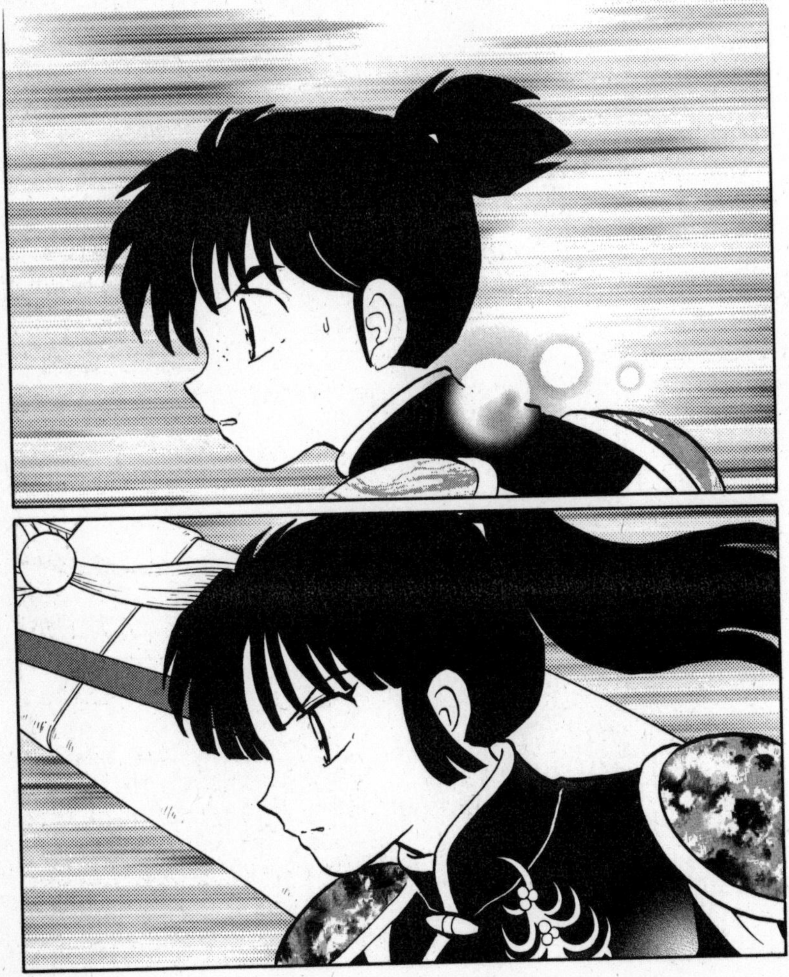

2

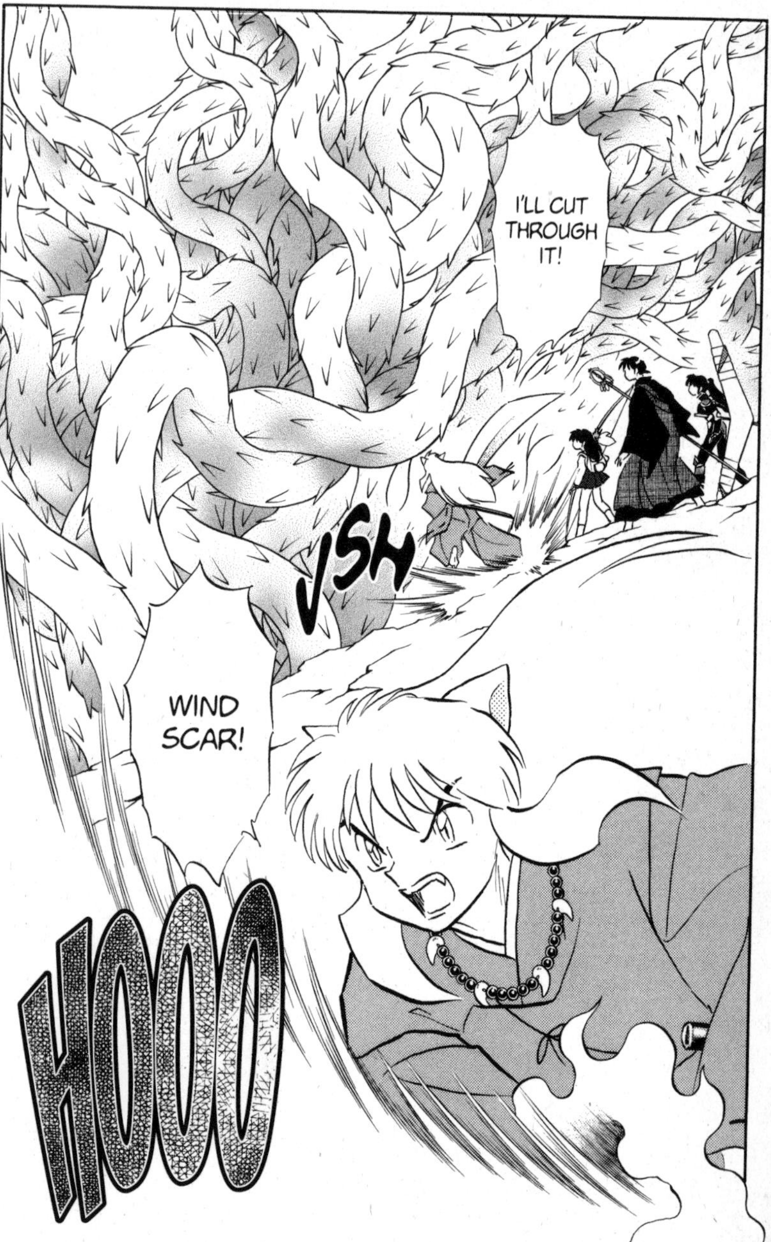
I'LL CUT THROUGH IT!
JSH
WIND SCAR!
HOOO

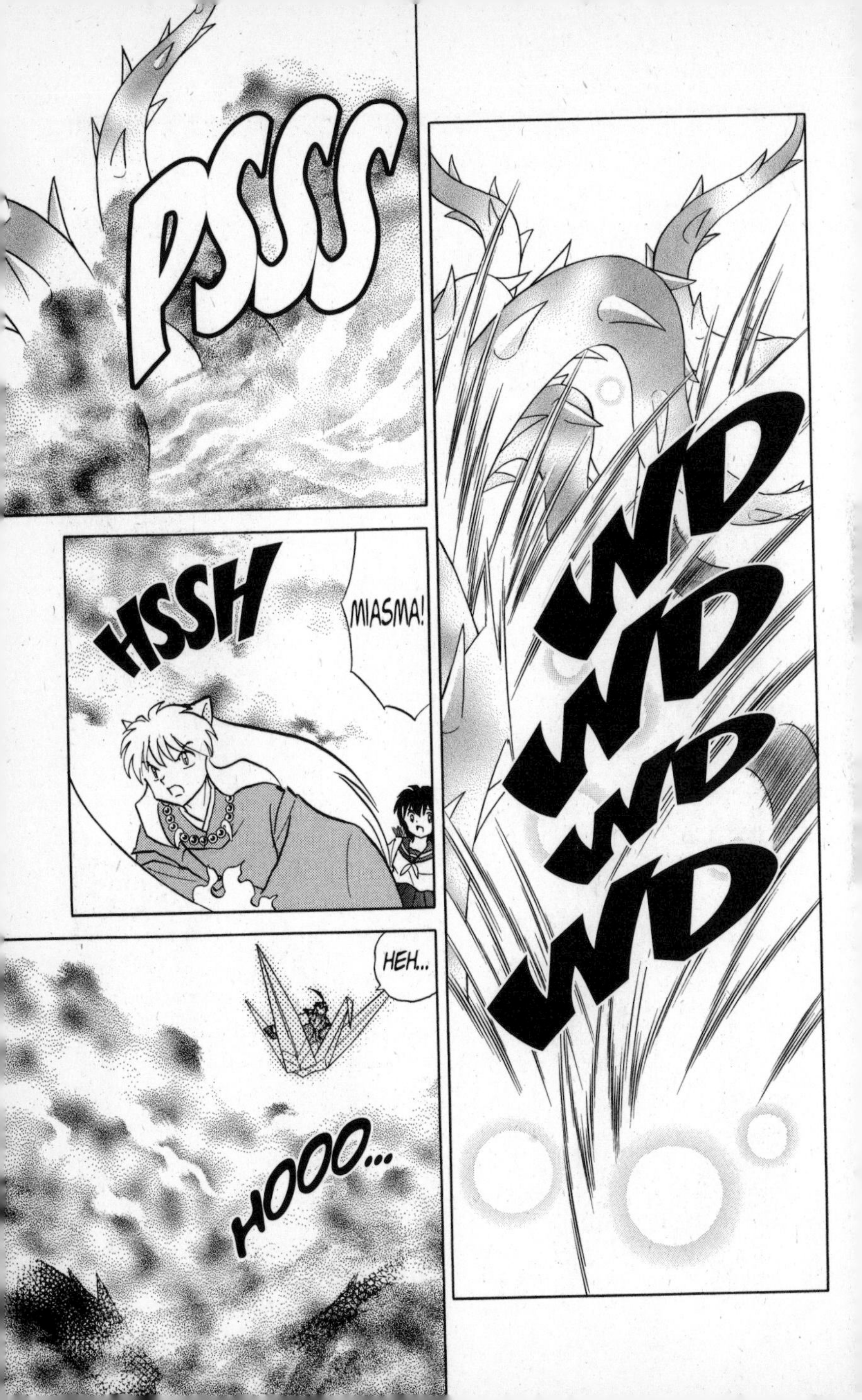
WD
WD
WD
WD
WD
PSSS
HSSH
MIASMA!
HEH...
HOOO...

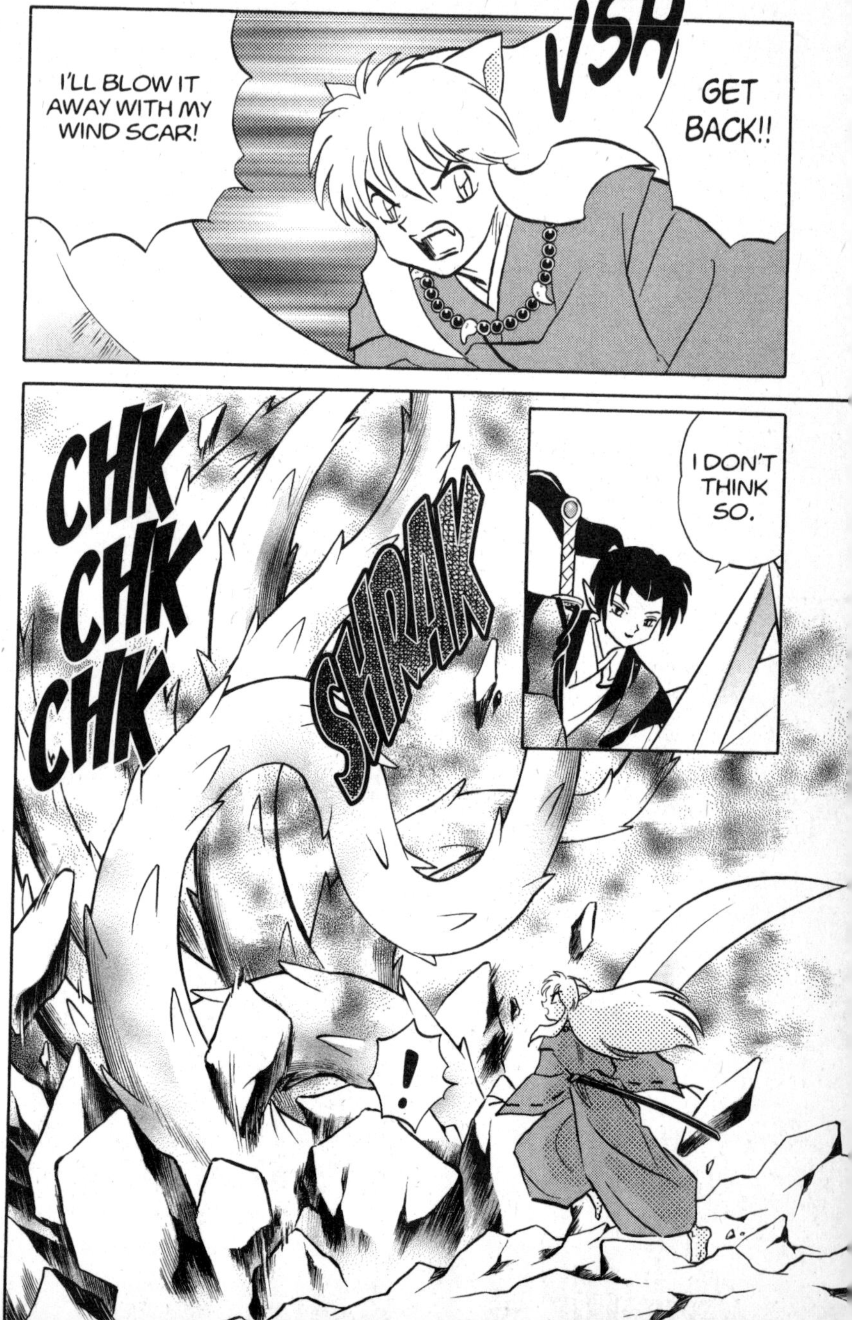
GET BACK!!
VSH
I'LL BLOW IT AWAY WITH MY WIND SCAR!
I DON'T THINK SO.
SHRAK
CHK CHK CHK
!

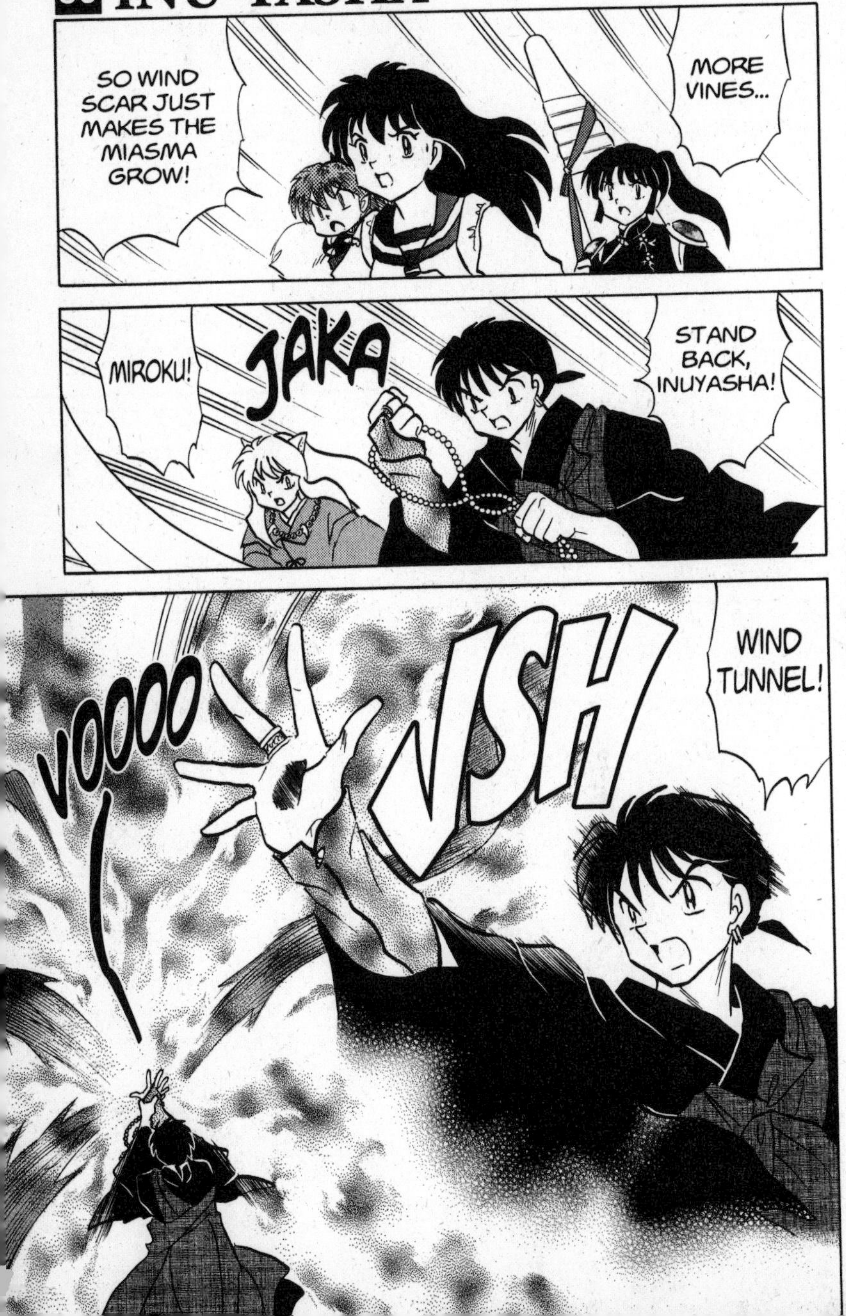
MORE VINES...
SO WIND SCAR JUST MAKES THE MIASMA GROW!
STAND BACK, INUYASHA!
JAKA
MIROKU!
WIND TUNNEL!
VOOOO
VSH

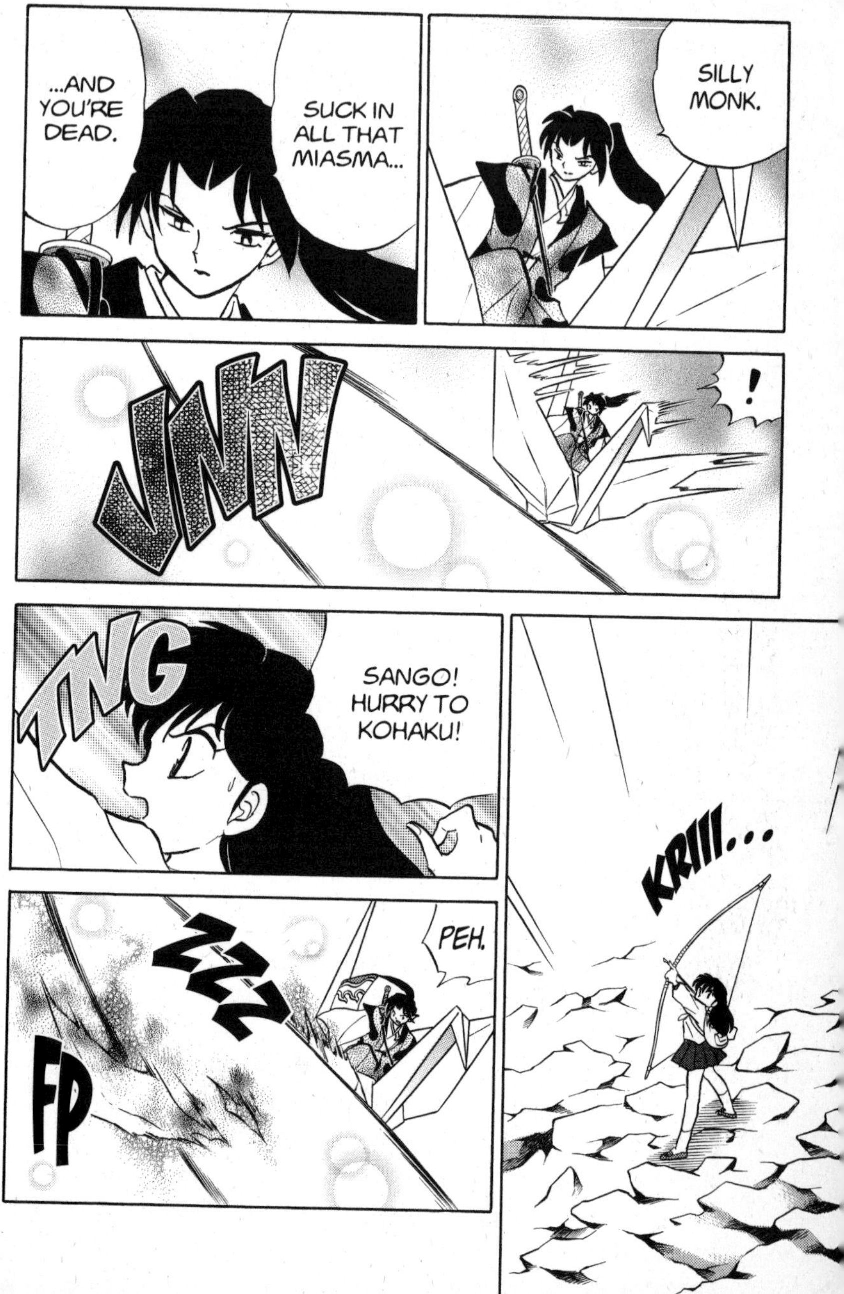
SILLY MONK.
SUCK IN ALL THAT MIASMA...
...AND YOU'RE DEAD.
!
JINNN
KRIIII...
SANGO! HURRY TO KOHAKU!
TNG
PEH.
ZZZ
FP

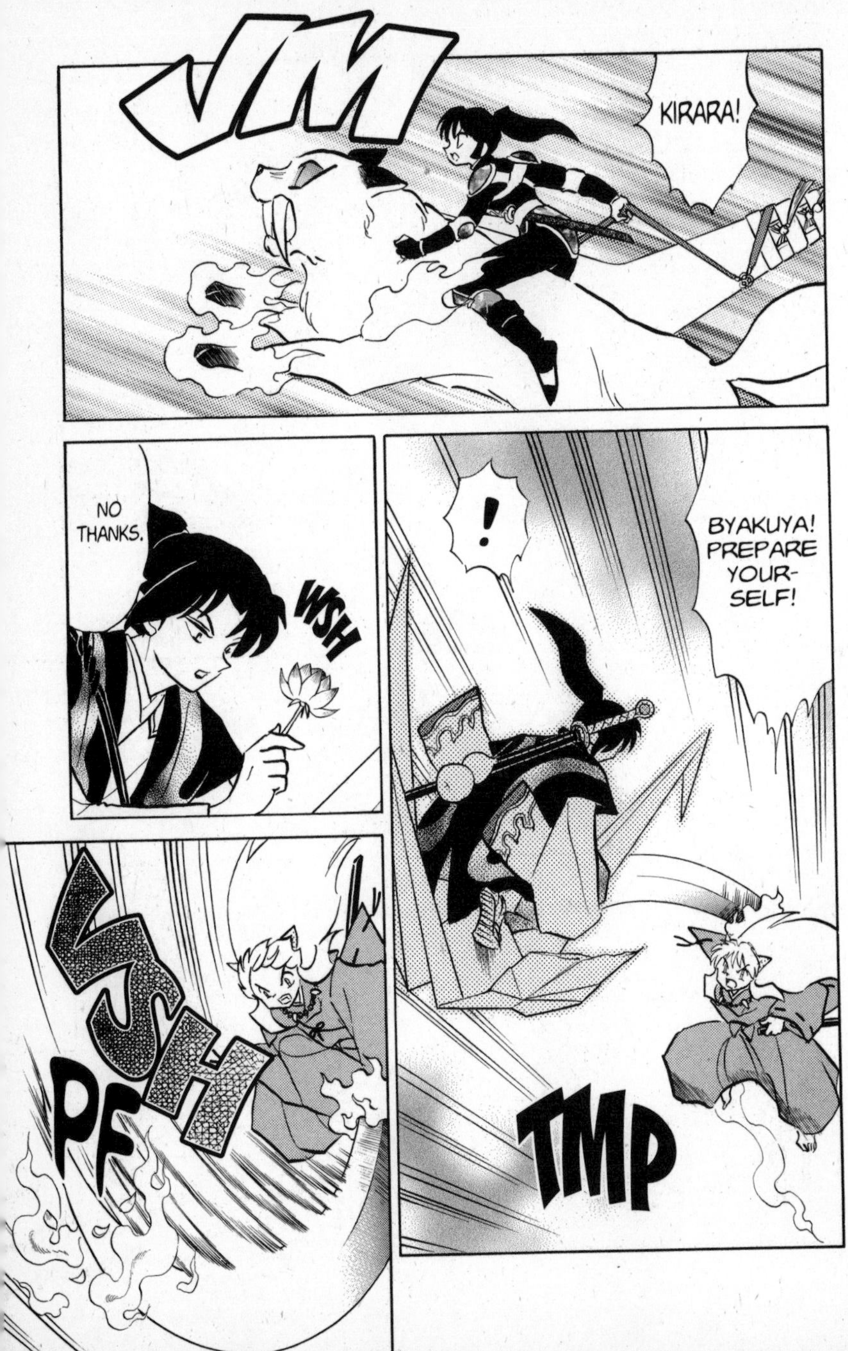
KIRARA!
JM
BYAKUYA! PREPARE YOUR-SELF!
!
TMP
NO THANKS.
WSH
VSH
PF

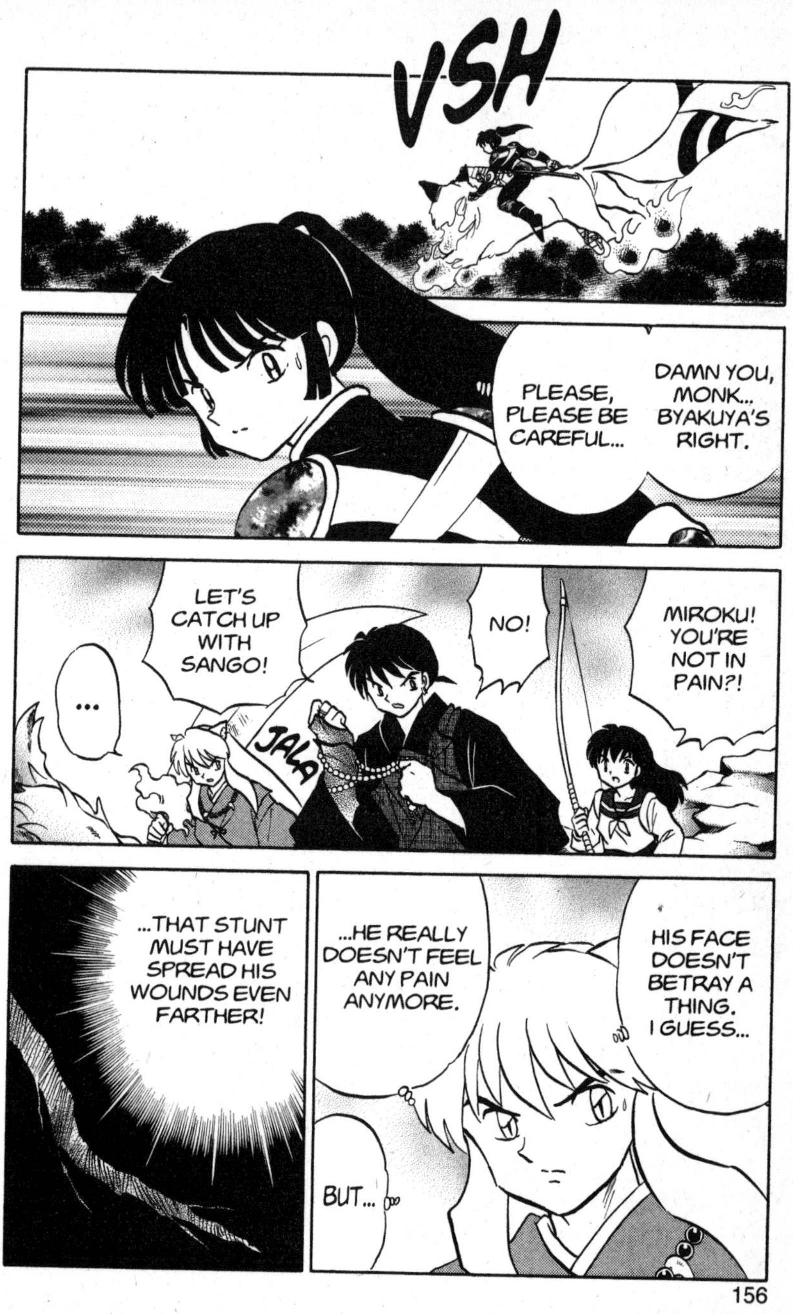
VSH
DAMN YOU, MONK... BYAKUYA'S RIGHT.
PLEASE, PLEASE BE CAREFUL...
MIROKU! YOU'RE NOT IN PAIN?!
NO!
LET'S CATCH UP WITH SANGO!
JALA
...
HIS FACE DOESN'T BETRAY A THING. I GUESS...
...HE REALLY DOESN'T FEEL ANY PAIN ANYMORE.
BUT...
...THAT STUNT MUST HAVE SPREAD HIS WOUNDS EVEN FARTHER!

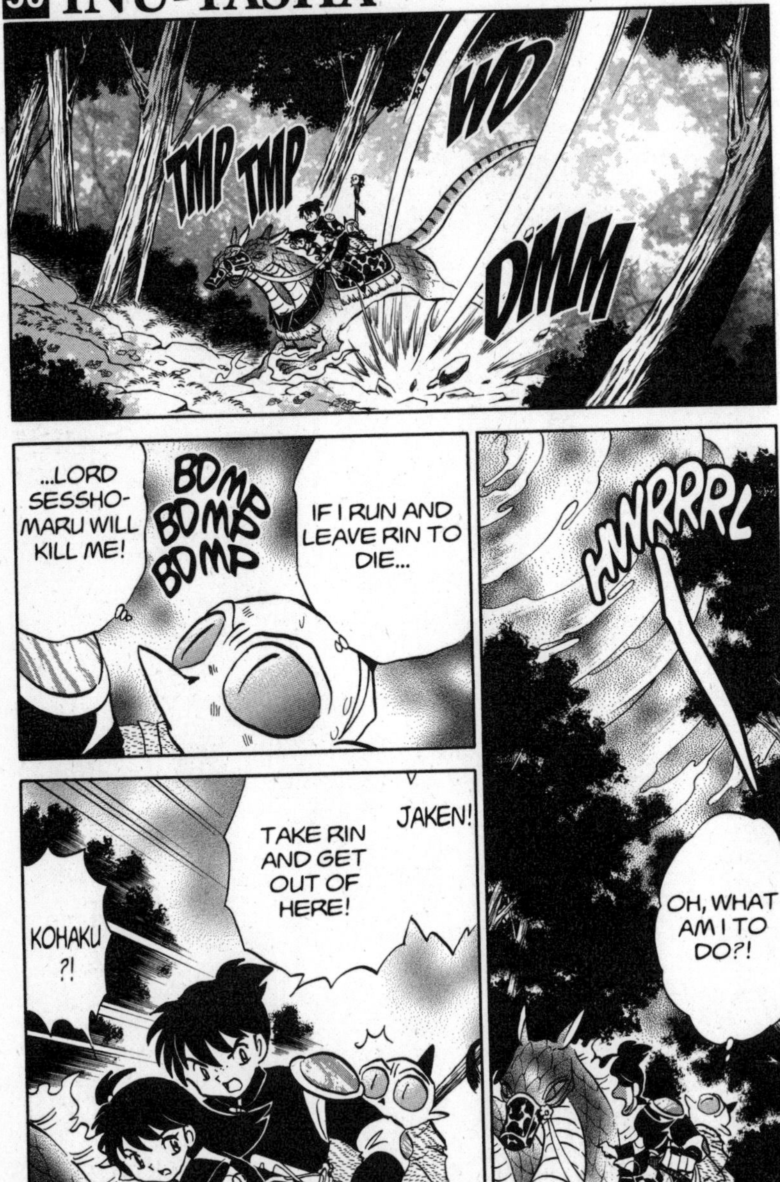
WD
DMM
TMP TMP
HNRRRL
OH, WHAT AM I TO DO?!
IF I RUN AND LEAVE RIN TO DIE...
BDMP BDMP BDMP
...LORD SESSHOMARU WILL KILL ME!
JAKEN!
TAKE RIN AND GET OUT OF HERE!
KOHAKU?!

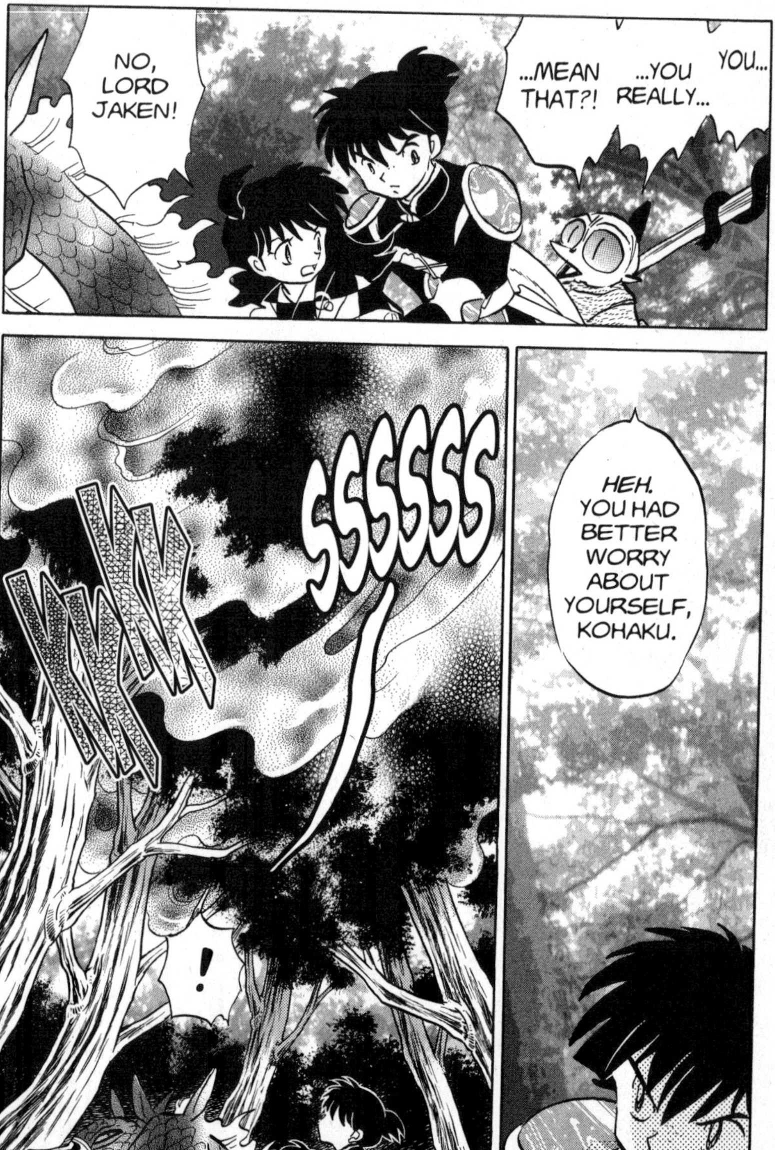
YOU...
...YOU REALLY...
...MEAN THAT?!
NO, LORD JAKEN!
HEH. YOU HAD BETTER WORRY ABOUT YOURSELF, KOHAKU.
SSSSSS
!

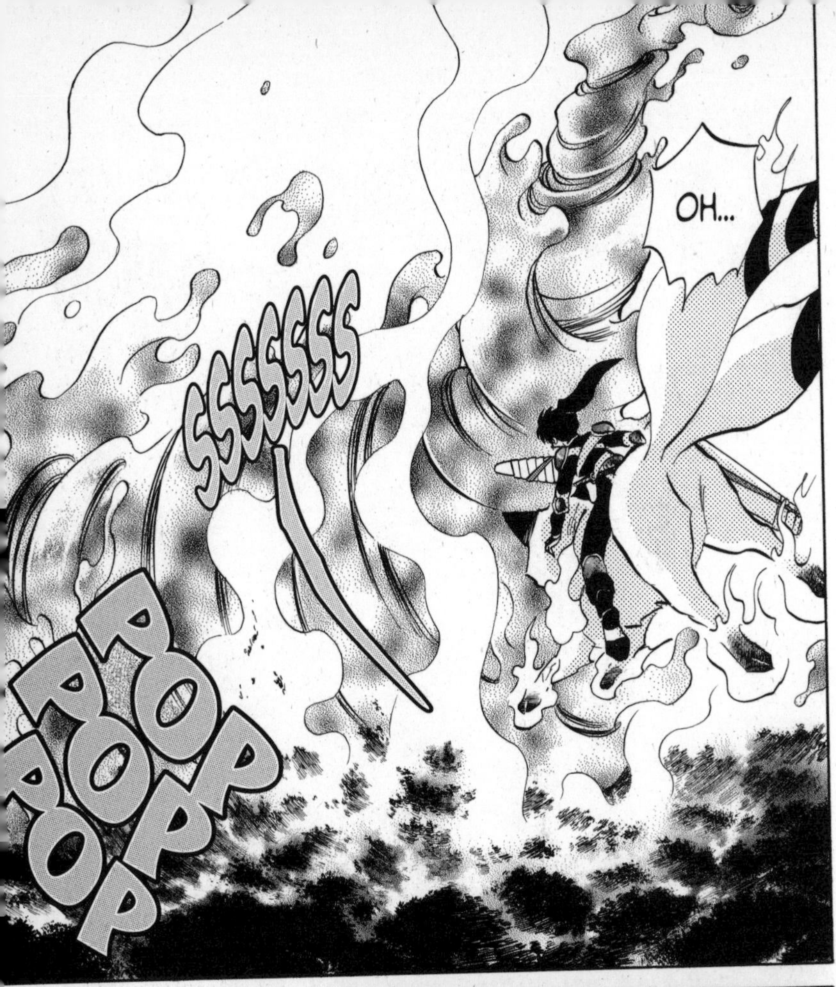
OH...
SSSSSSS
POP POP POP
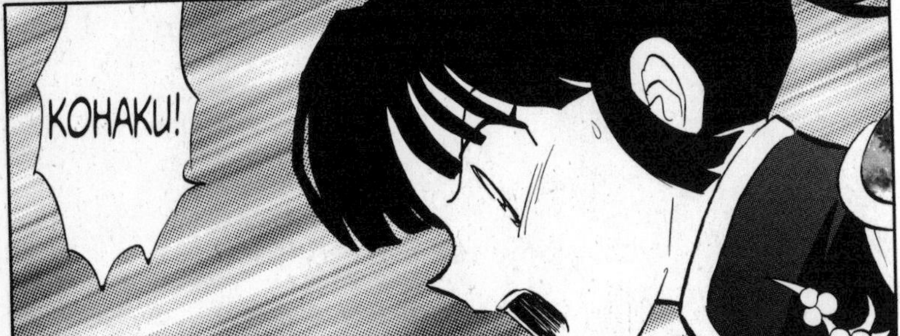
KOHAKU!

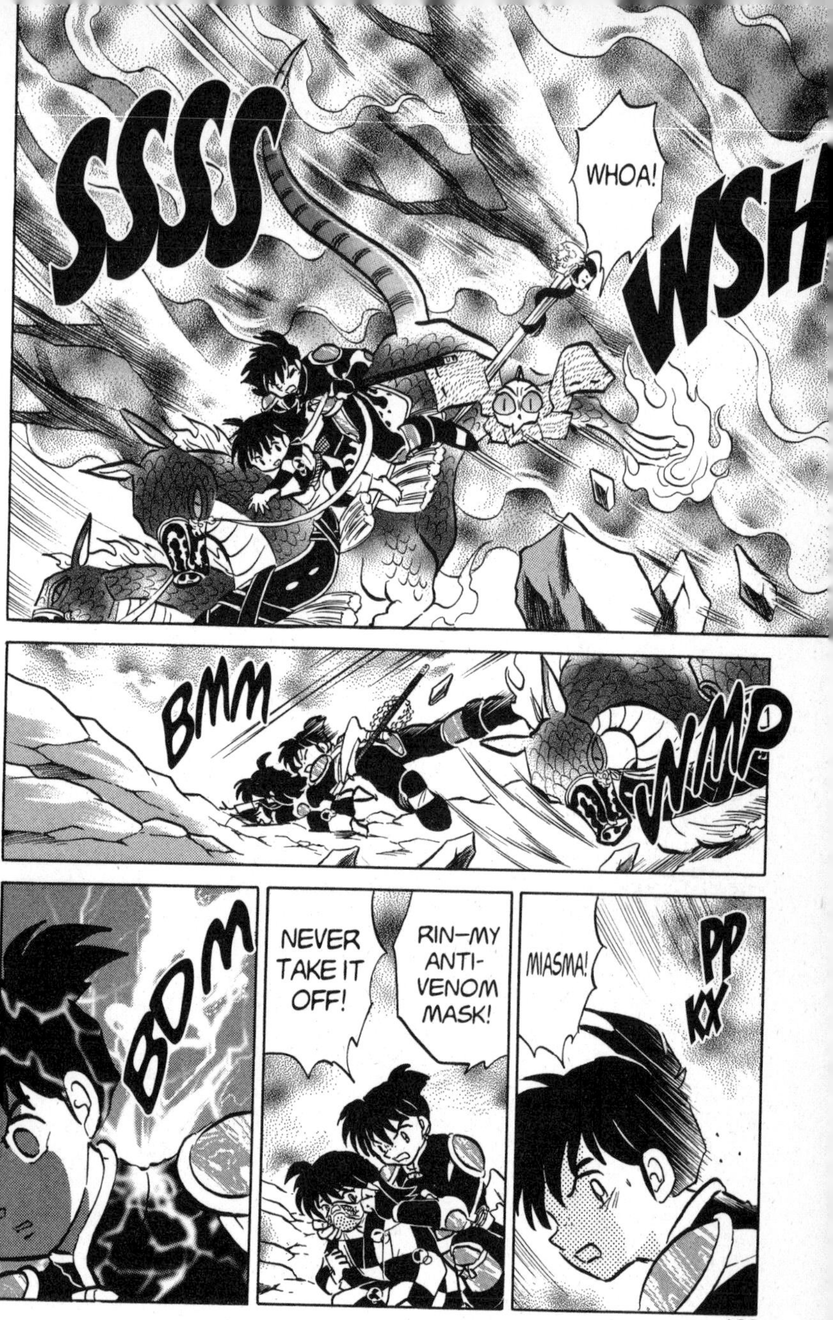
WHOA!
WSH
SSSS
WMP
BMM
MIASMA!
PP
KX
RIN—MY ANTI-VENOM MASK!
NEVER TAKE IT OFF!
BOM

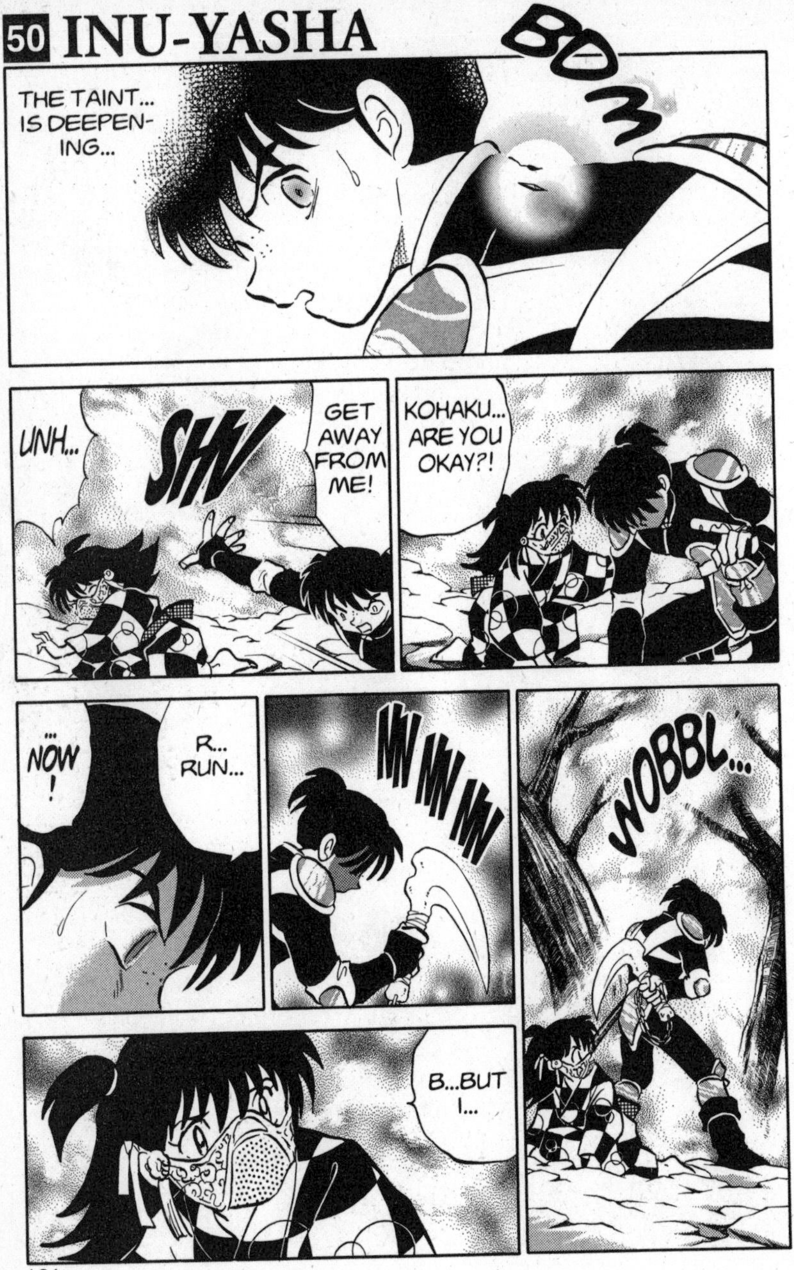
BOOM
THE TAINT... IS DEEPEN-ING...
KOHAKU... ARE YOU OKAY?!
GET AWAY FROM ME!
SHW
UNH...
WOBBL...
R... RUN...
... NOW!
B...BUT I...

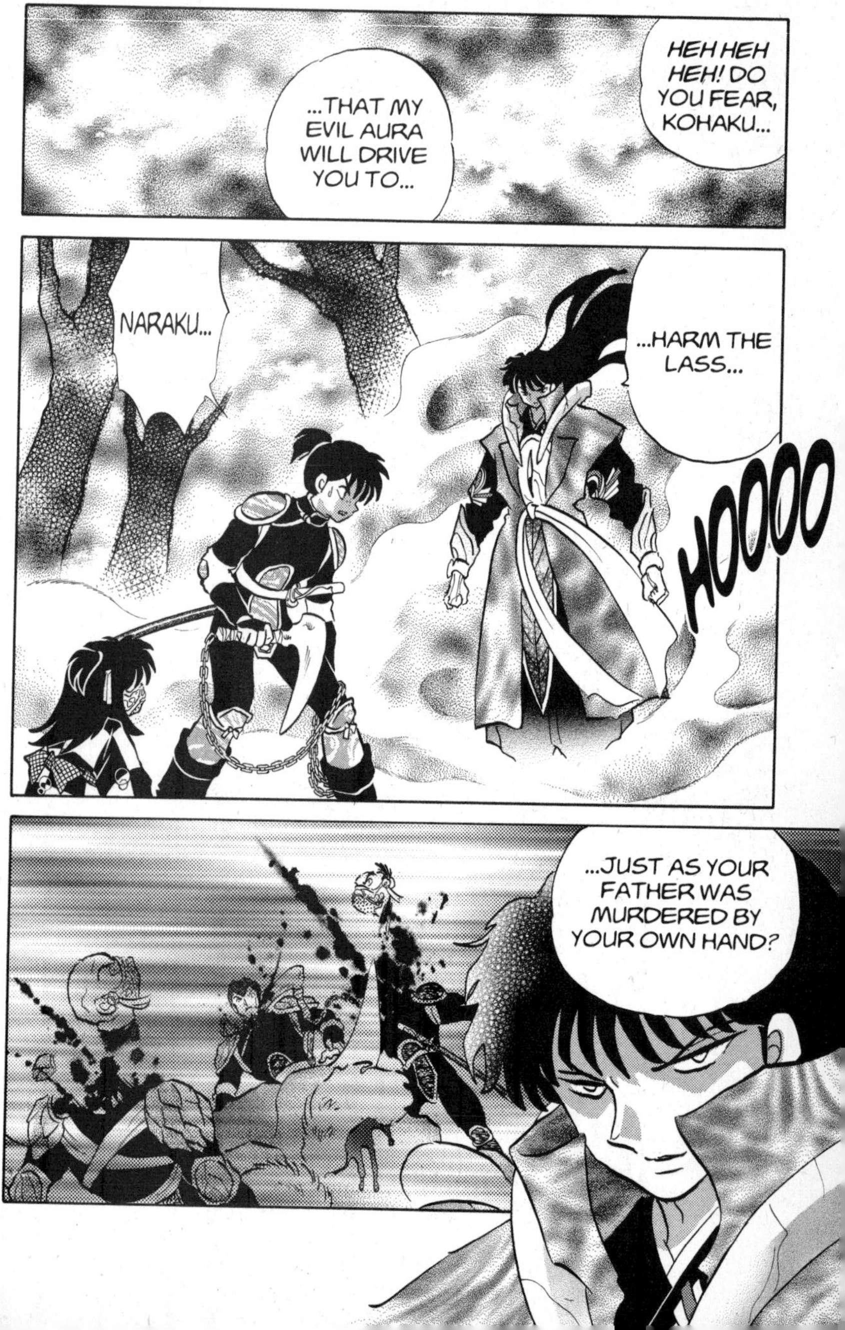
HEH HEH HEH! DO YOU FEAR, KOHAKU...
...THAT MY EVIL AURA WILL DRIVE YOU TO...
...HARM THE LASS...
HOOOO
NARAKU...
...JUST AS YOUR FATHER WAS MURDERED BY YOUR OWN HAND?

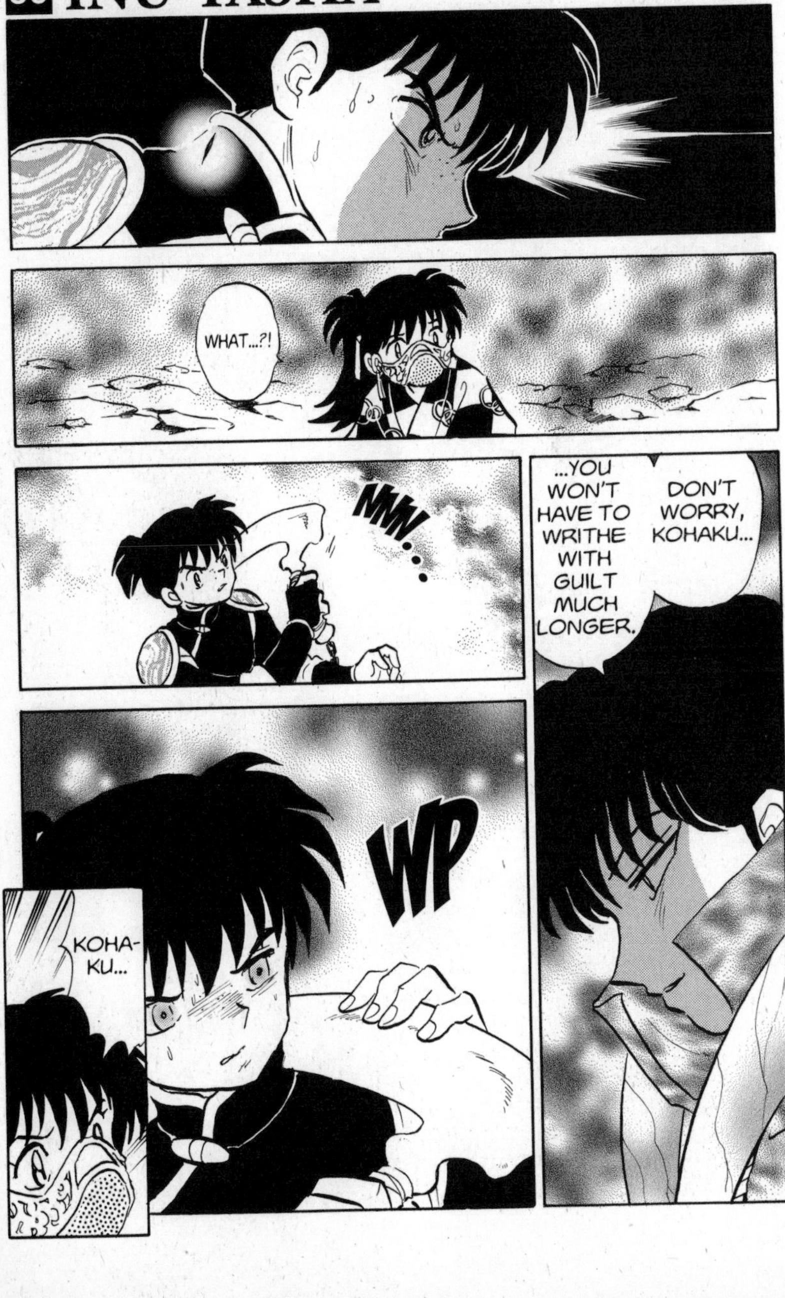
WHAT...?!
DON'T WORRY, KOHAKU...
...YOU WON'T HAVE TO WRITHE WITH GUILT MUCH LONGER.
NNN...
WP
KOHA-KU...

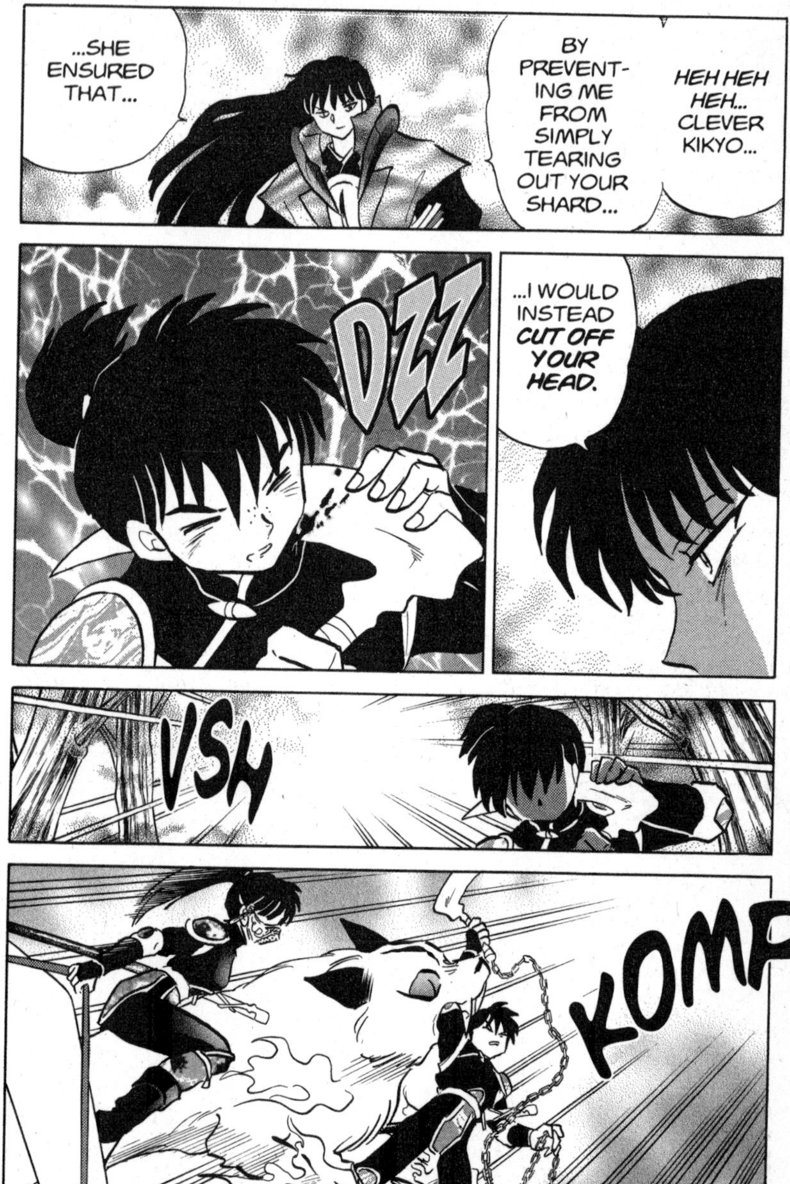
HEH HEH HEH... CLEVER KIKYO...
BY PREVENT-ING ME FROM SIMPLY TEARING OUT YOUR SHARD...
...SHE ENSURED THAT...
...I WOULD INSTEAD *CUT OFF YOUR HEAD.*
DZZ
VSH
KOMP

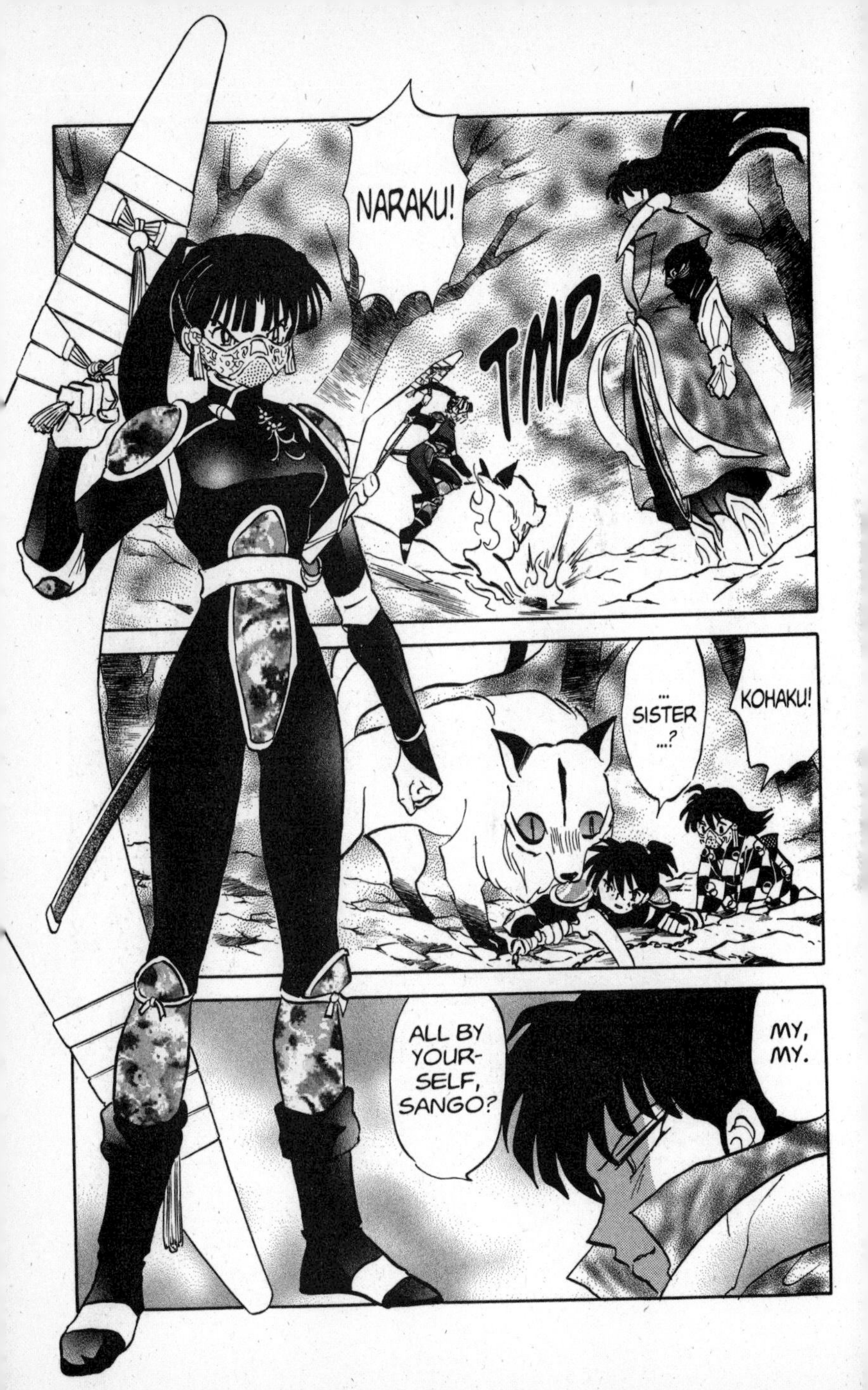
NARAKU!
TMP
KOHAKU!
... SISTER ...?
MY, MY.
ALL BY YOURSELF, SANGO?

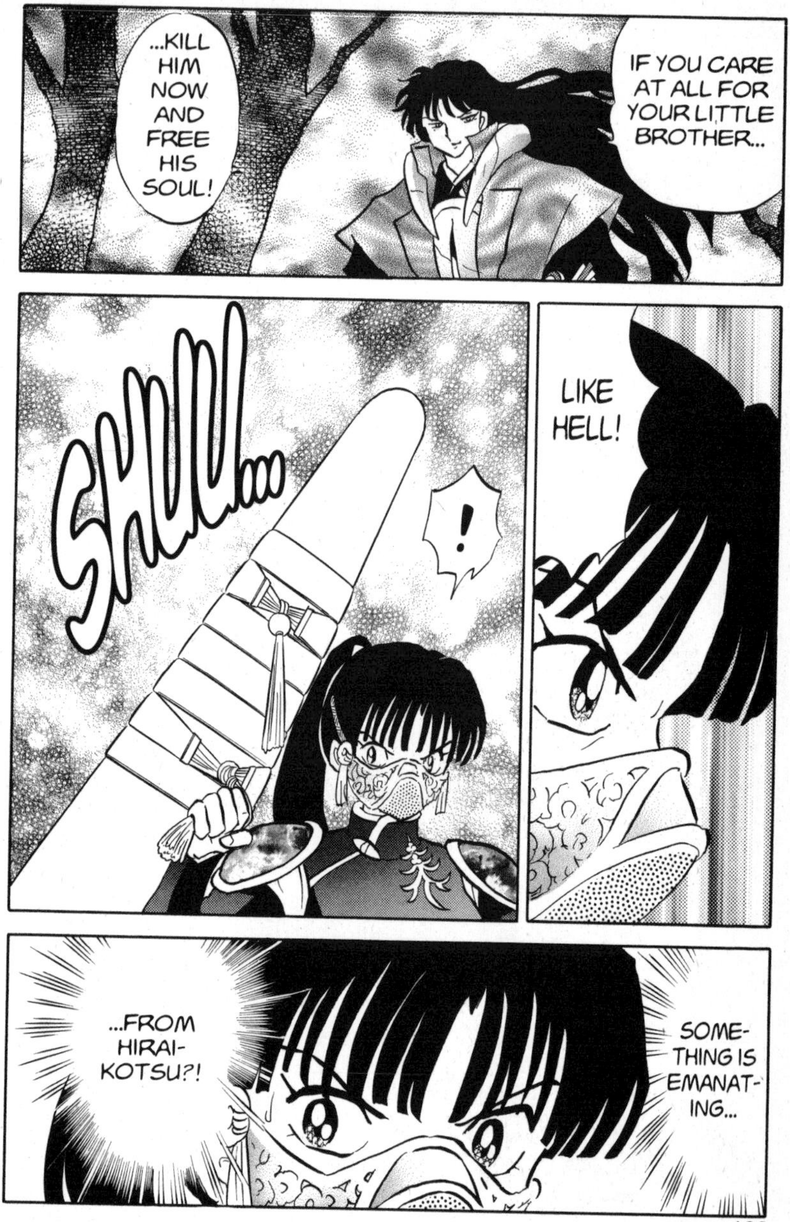
IF YOU CARE AT ALL FOR YOUR LITTLE BROTHER...
...KILL HIM NOW AND FREE HIS SOUL!
LIKE HELL!
!
SHUU...
SOME-THING IS EMANAT-ING...
...FROM HIRAI-KOTSU?!

SCROLL 10

THE NEW HIRAIKOTSU

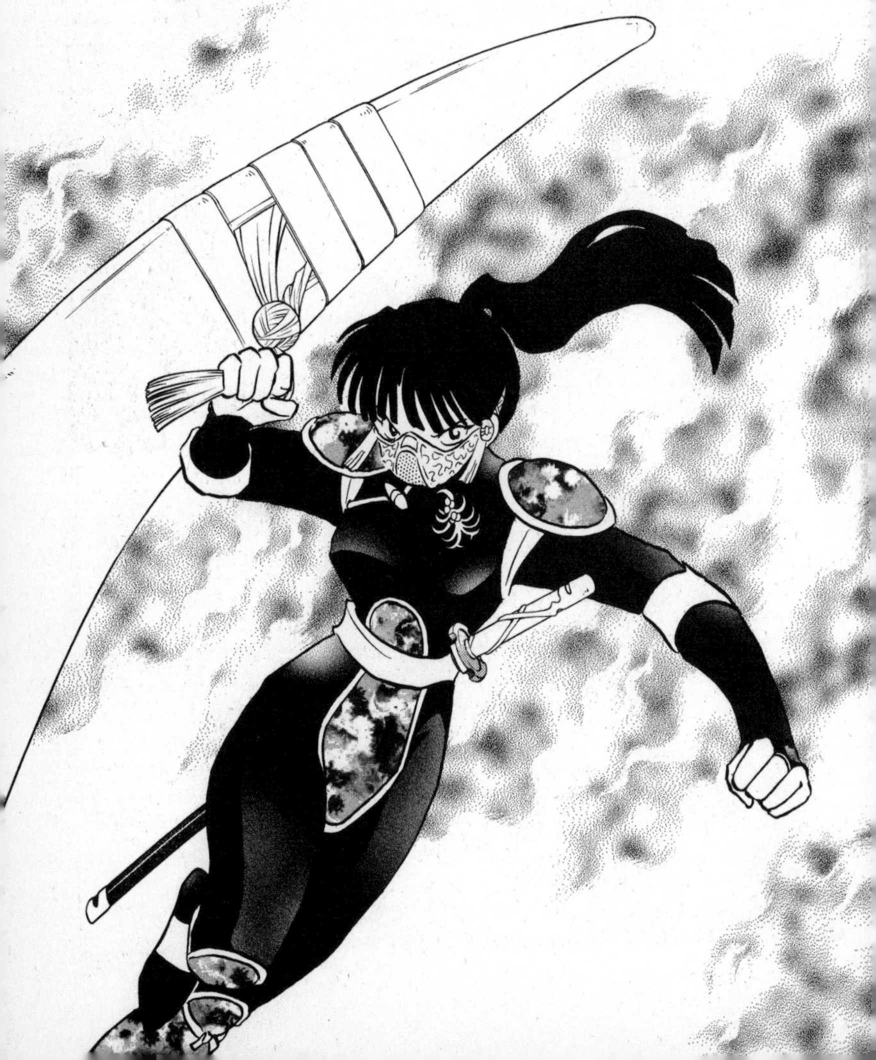

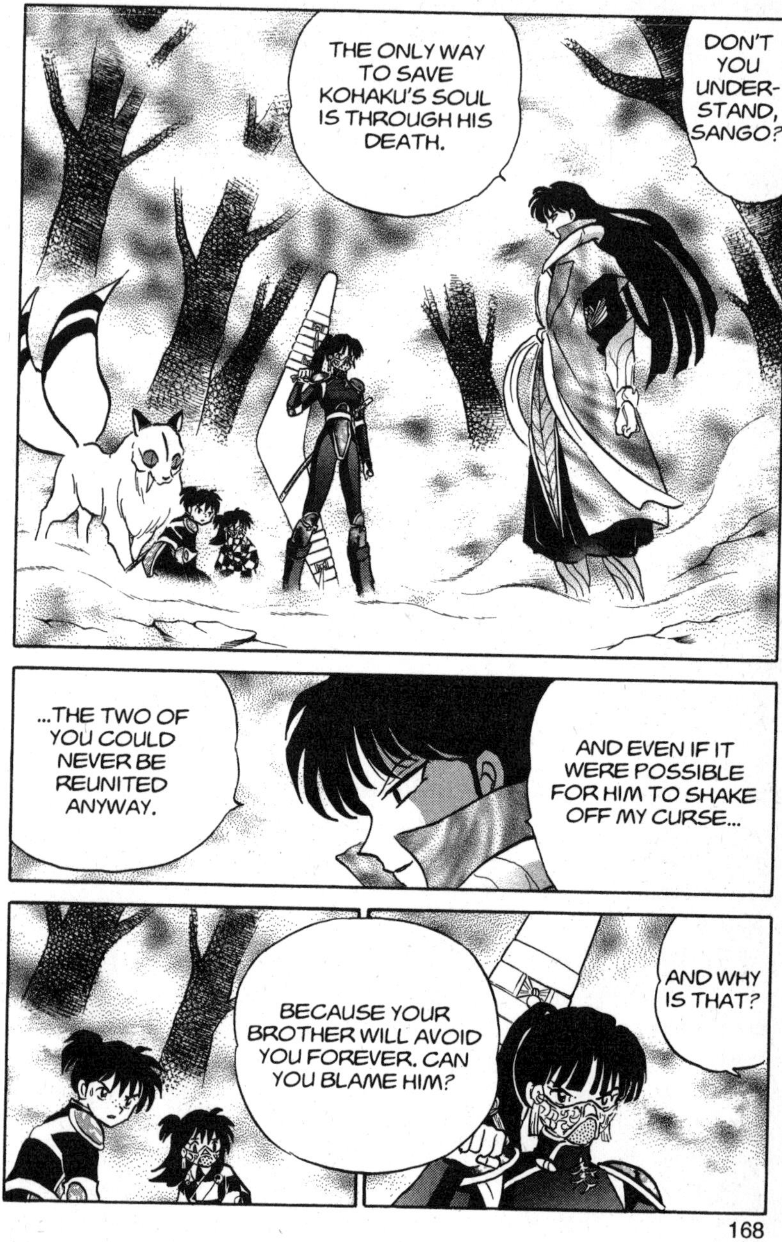
DON'T YOU UNDER-STAND, SANGO?
THE ONLY WAY TO SAVE KOHAKU'S SOUL IS THROUGH HIS DEATH.
AND EVEN IF IT WERE POSSIBLE FOR HIM TO SHAKE OFF MY CURSE...
...THE TWO OF YOU COULD NEVER BE REUNITED ANYWAY.
AND WHY IS THAT?
BECAUSE YOUR BROTHER WILL AVOID YOU FOREVER. CAN YOU BLAME HIM?

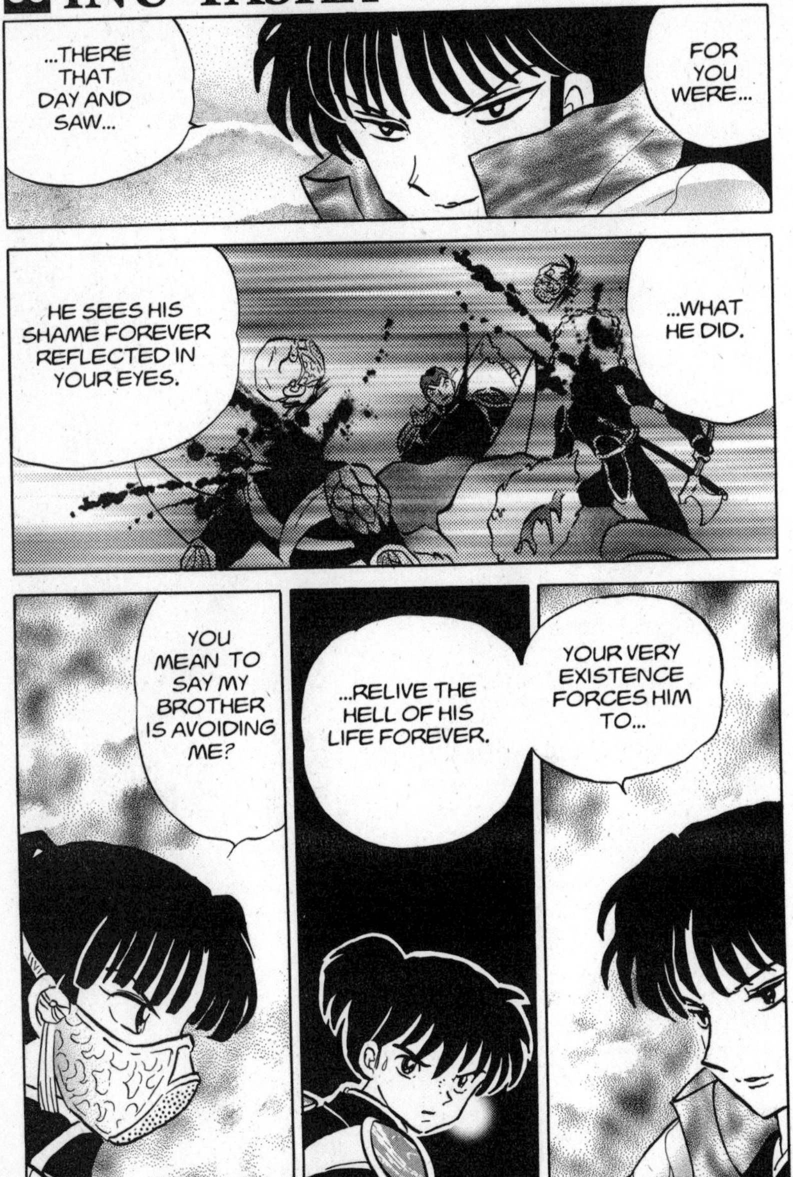
FOR YOU WERE...
...THERE THAT DAY AND SAW...
...WHAT HE DID.
HE SEES HIS SHAME FOREVER REFLECTED IN YOUR EYES.
YOUR VERY EXISTENCE FORCES HIM TO...
...RELIVE THE HELL OF HIS LIFE FOREVER.
YOU MEAN TO SAY MY BROTHER IS AVOIDING ME?

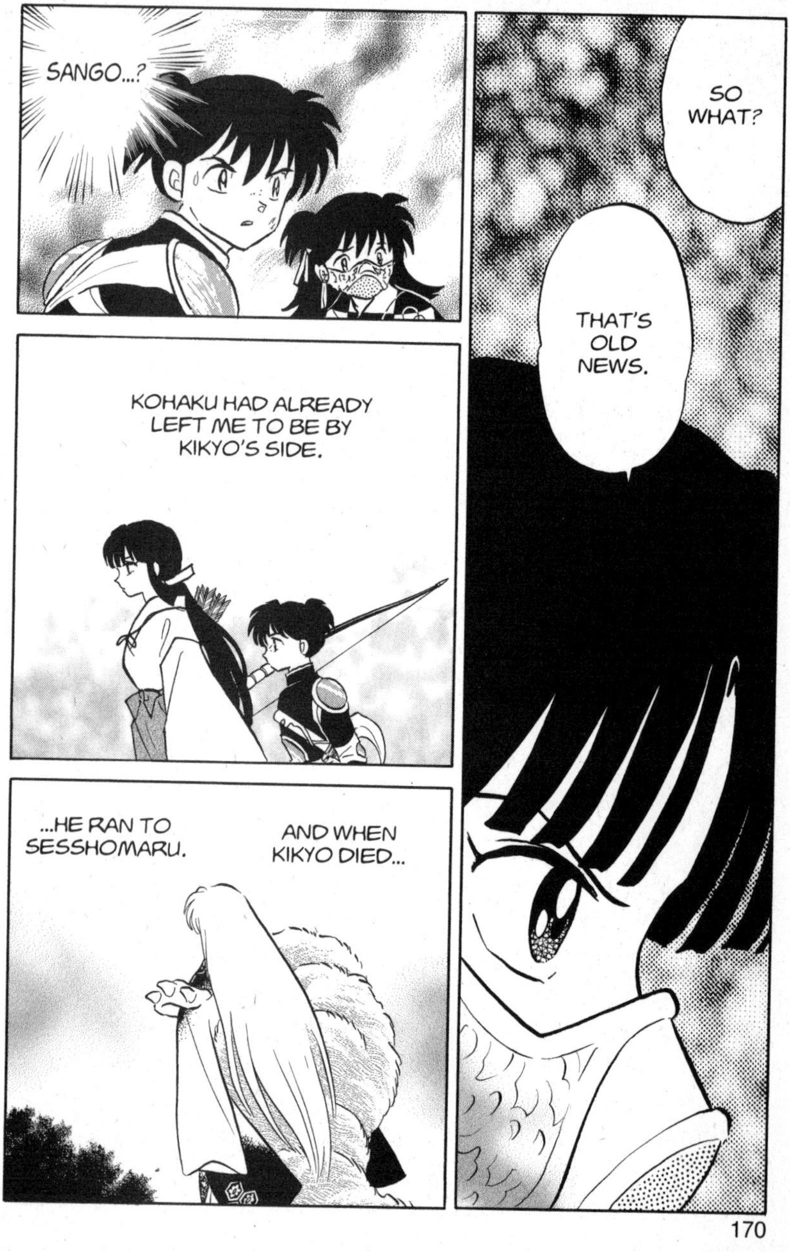
SO WHAT?
THAT'S OLD NEWS.
SANGO...?
KOHAKU HAD ALREADY LEFT ME TO BE BY KIKYO'S SIDE.
AND WHEN KIKYO DIED...
...HE RAN TO SESSHOMARU.

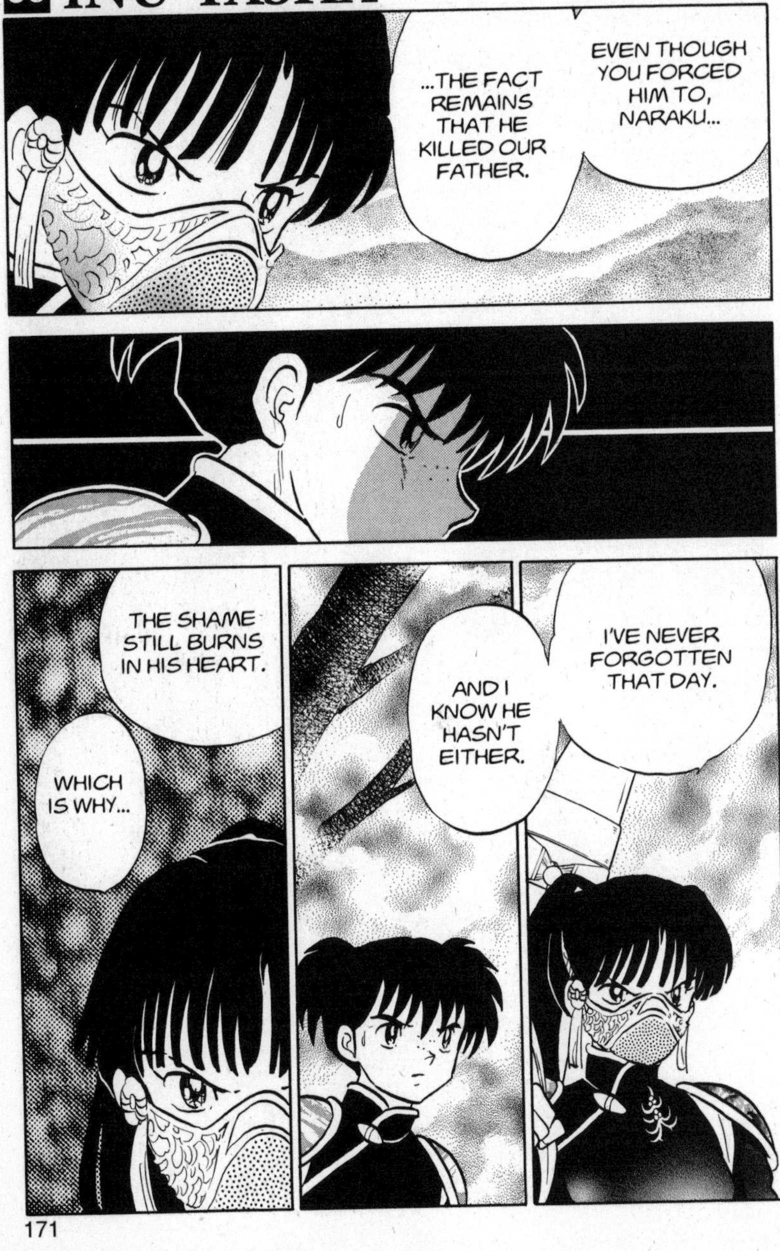
EVEN THOUGH YOU FORCED HIM TO, NARAKU...
...THE FACT REMAINS THAT HE KILLED OUR FATHER.
I'VE NEVER FORGOTTEN THAT DAY.
AND I KNOW HE HASN'T EITHER.
THE SHAME STILL BURNS IN HIS HEART.
WHICH IS WHY...

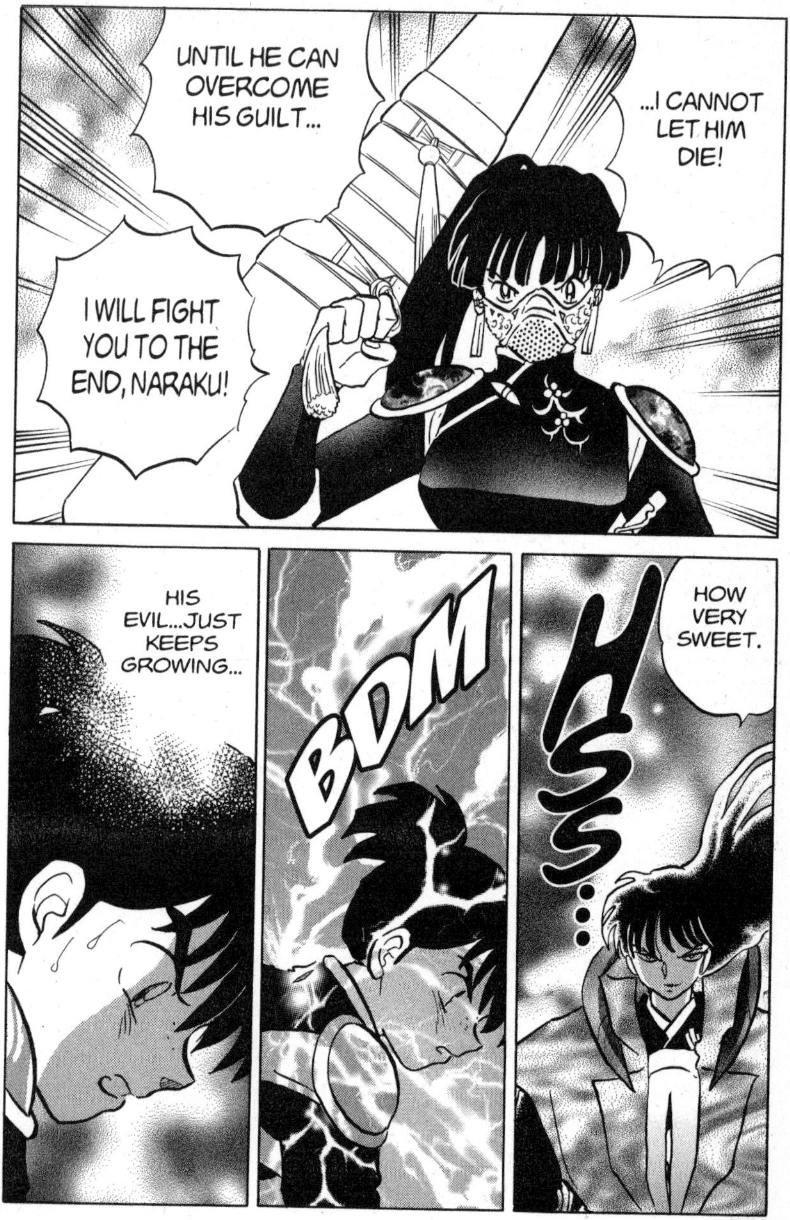
UNTIL HE CAN OVERCOME HIS GUILT...
...I CANNOT LET HIM DIE!
I WILL FIGHT YOU TO THE END, NARAKU!
HOW VERY SWEET.
HSS...
BDM
HIS EVIL...JUST KEEPS GROWING...

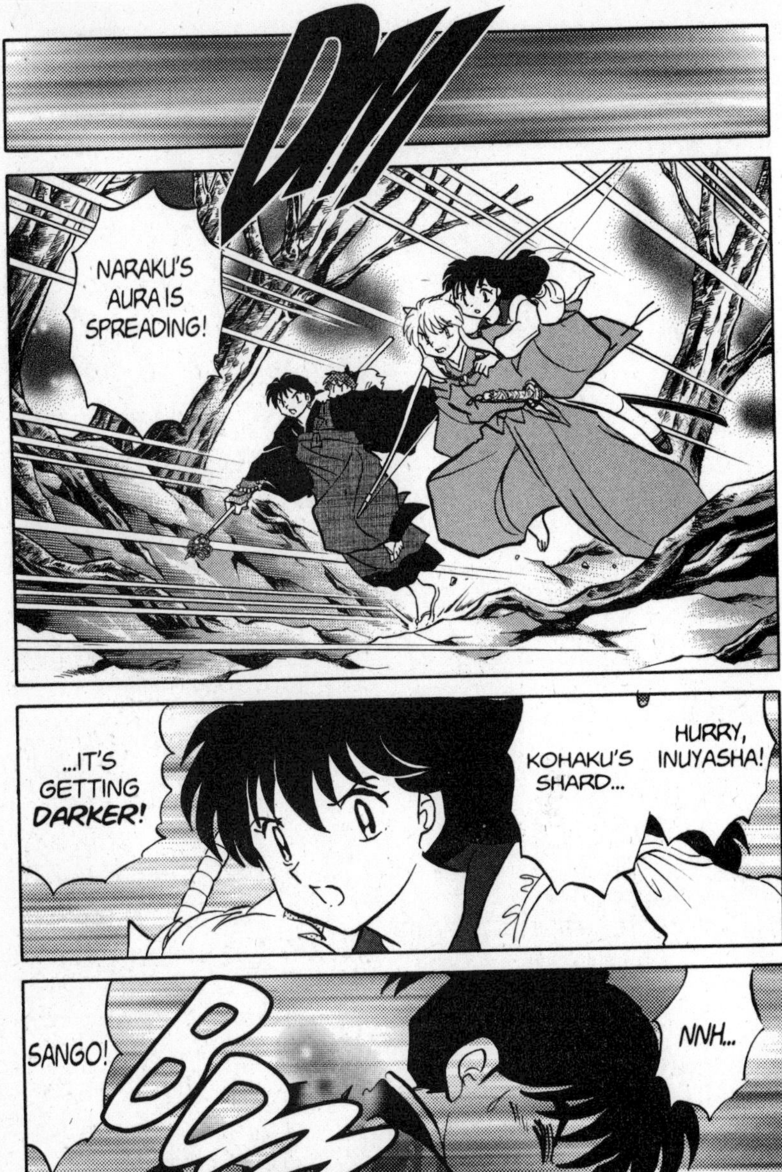
DN
NARAKU'S AURA IS SPREADING!
HURRY, INUYASHA!
KOHAKU'S SHARD...
...IT'S GETTING DARKER!
NNH...
BOOM
SANGO!

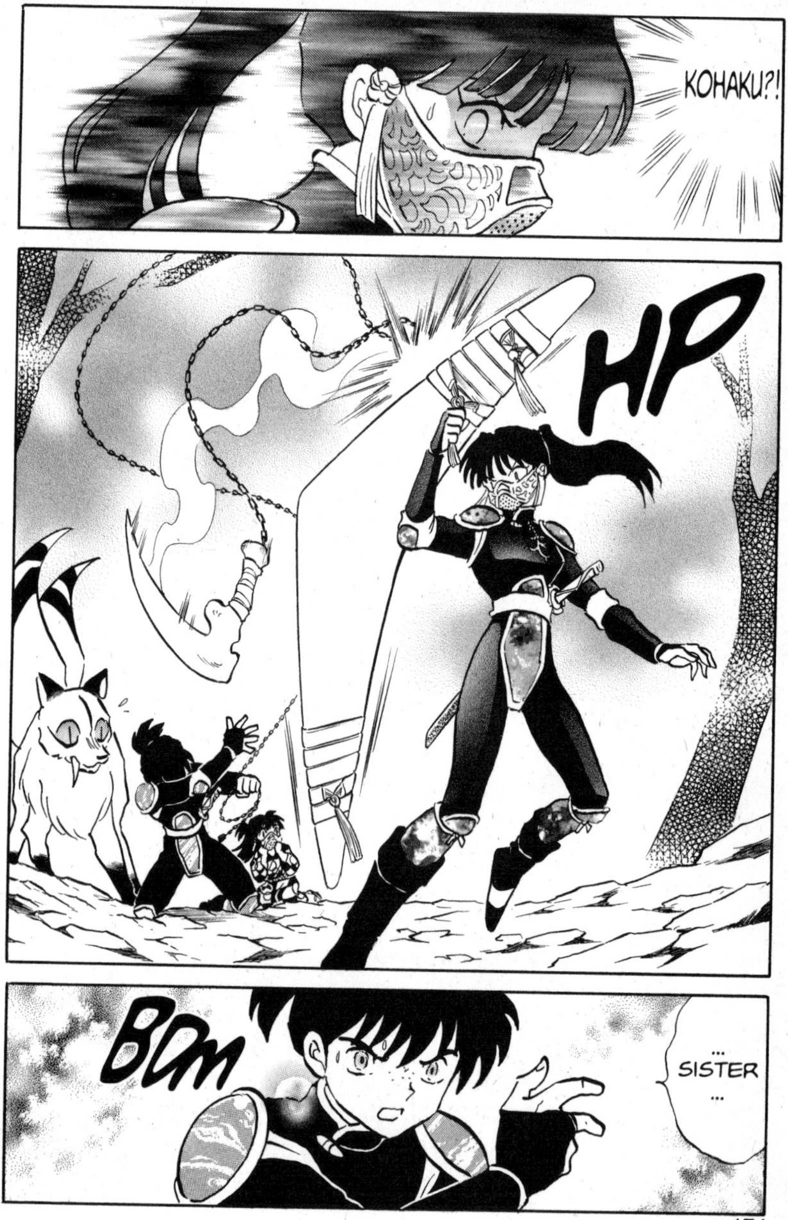
KOHAKU?!
HP
... SISTER ...
BOM

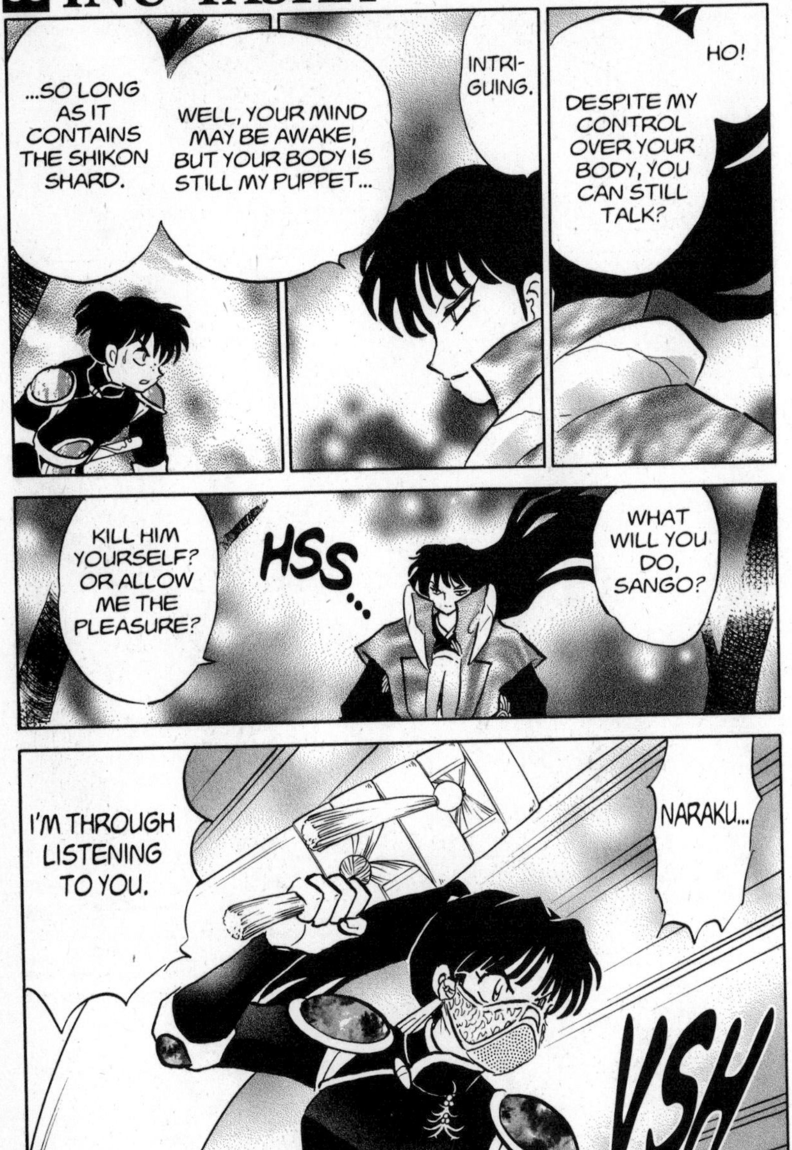
HO!
DESPITE MY CONTROL OVER YOUR BODY, YOU CAN STILL TALK?
INTRI-GUING.
WELL, YOUR MIND MAY BE AWAKE, BUT YOUR BODY IS STILL MY PUPPET...
...SO LONG AS IT CONTAINS THE SHIKON SHARD.
WHAT WILL YOU DO, SANGO?
HSS...
KILL HIM YOURSELF? OR ALLOW ME THE PLEASURE?
NARAKU...
VSH
I'M THROUGH LISTENING TO YOU.

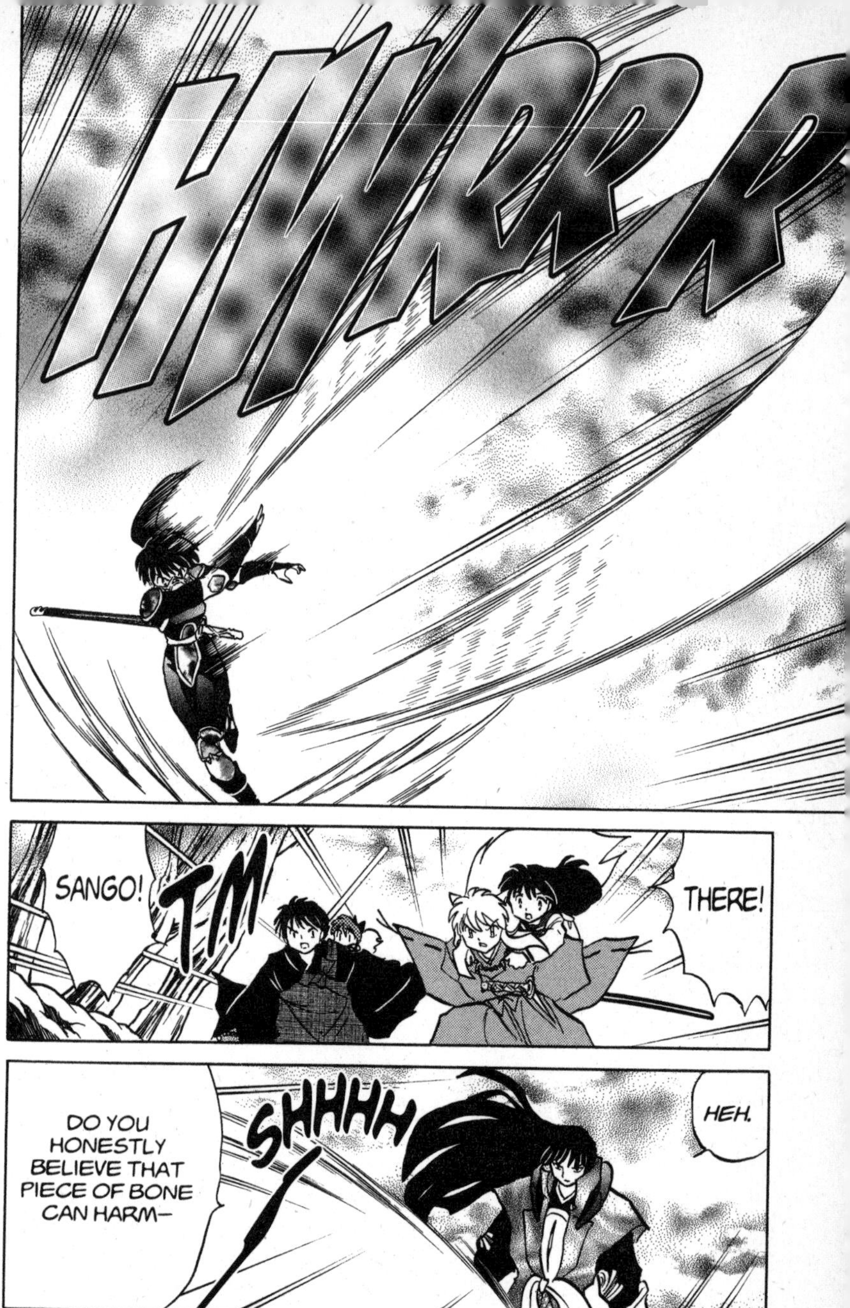
THERE!
TM
SANGO!
HEH.
SHHHH
DO YOU HONESTLY BELIEVE THAT PIECE OF BONE CAN HARM–

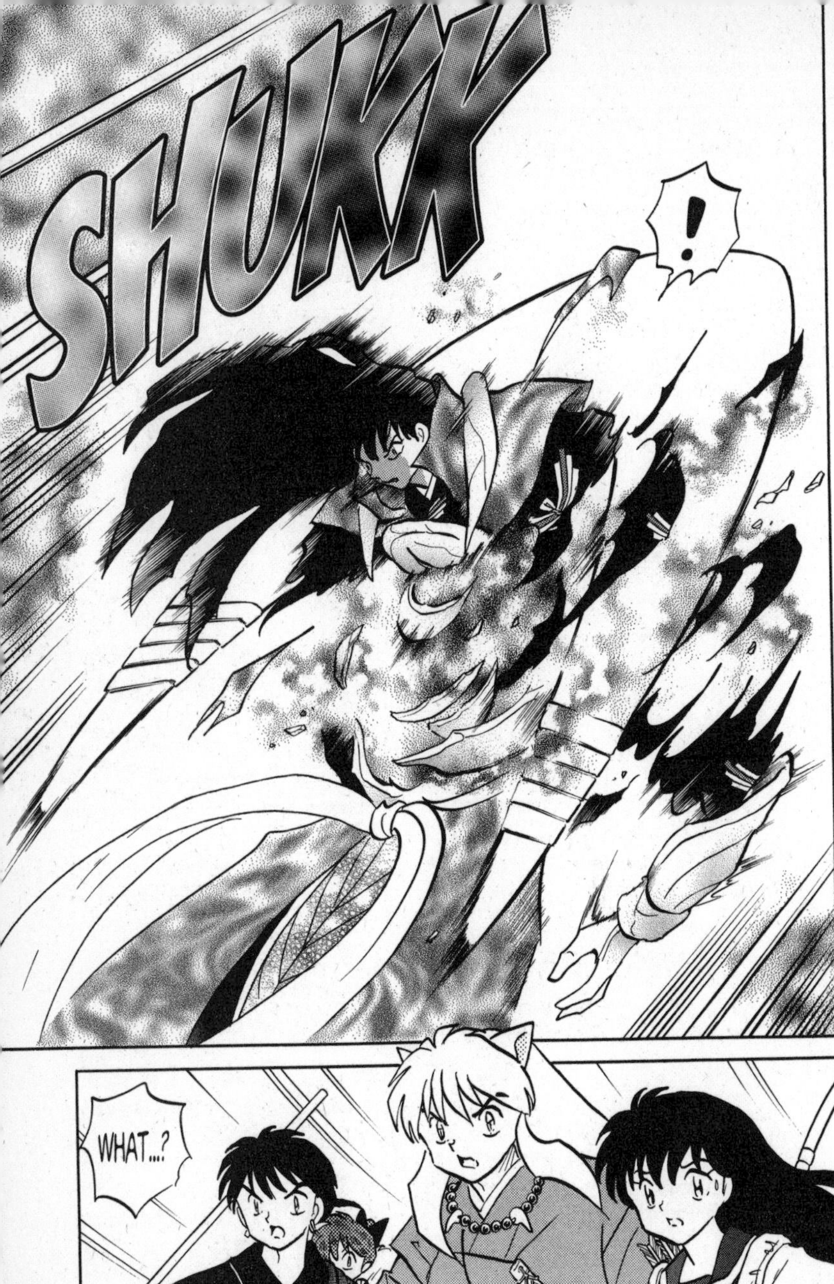
SHUKK
!
WHAT...?

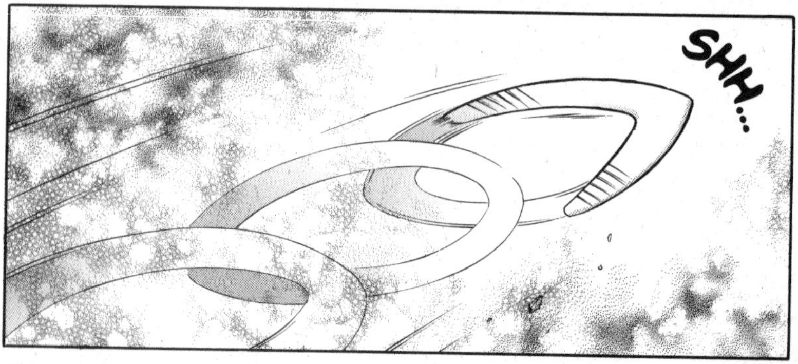
SHH...

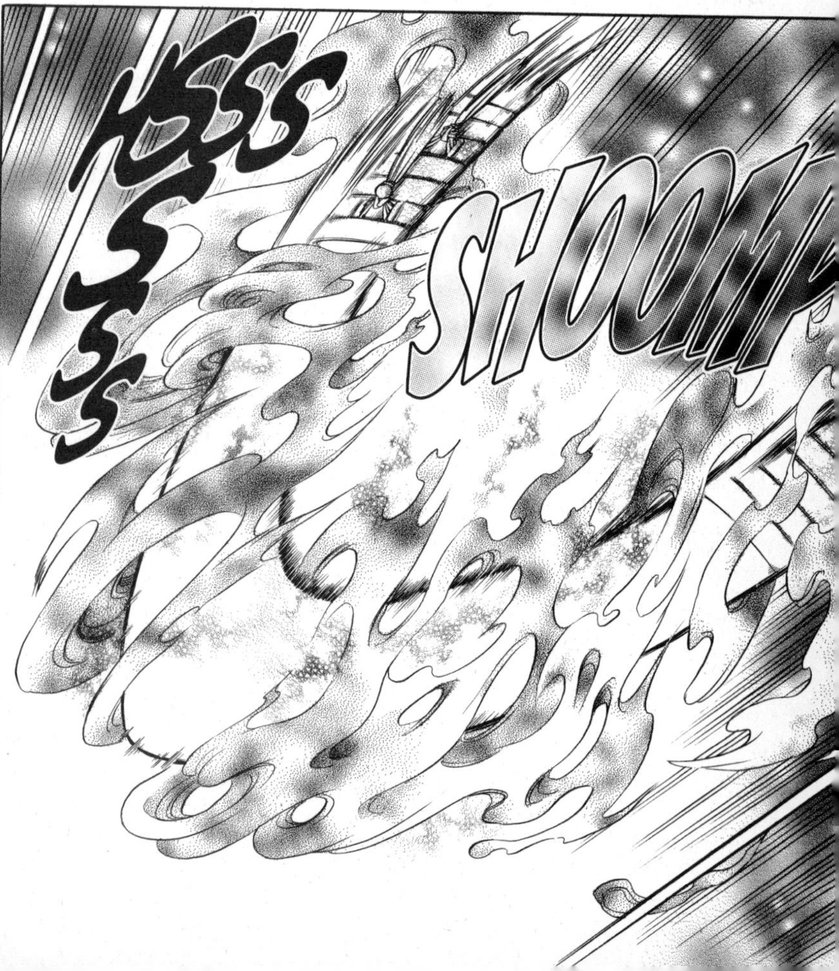
HSSSSSSS
SHOOM

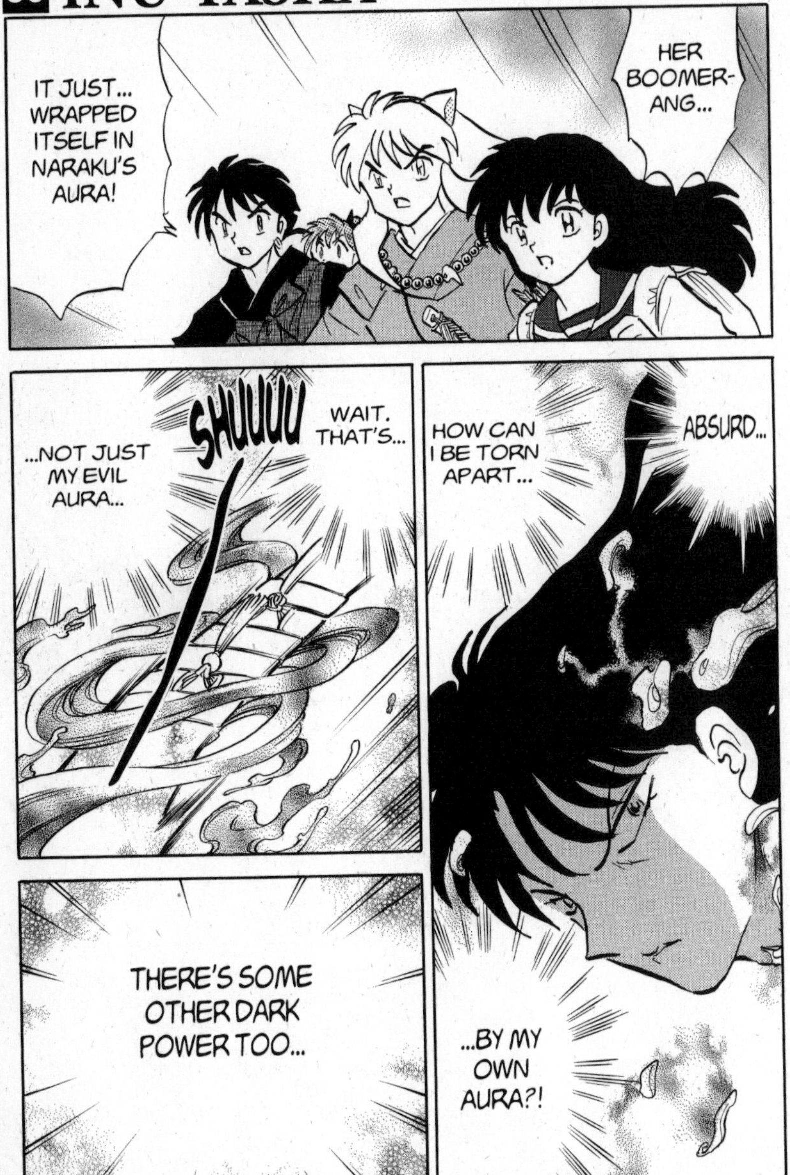
HER BOOMER-ANG...
IT JUST... WRAPPED ITSELF IN NARAKU'S AURA!
ABSURD...
HOW CAN I BE TORN APART...
...BY MY OWN AURA?!
WAIT. THAT'S...
SHUUUU
...NOT JUST MY EVIL AURA...
THERE'S SOME OTHER DARK POWER TOO...

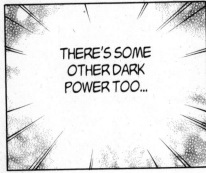

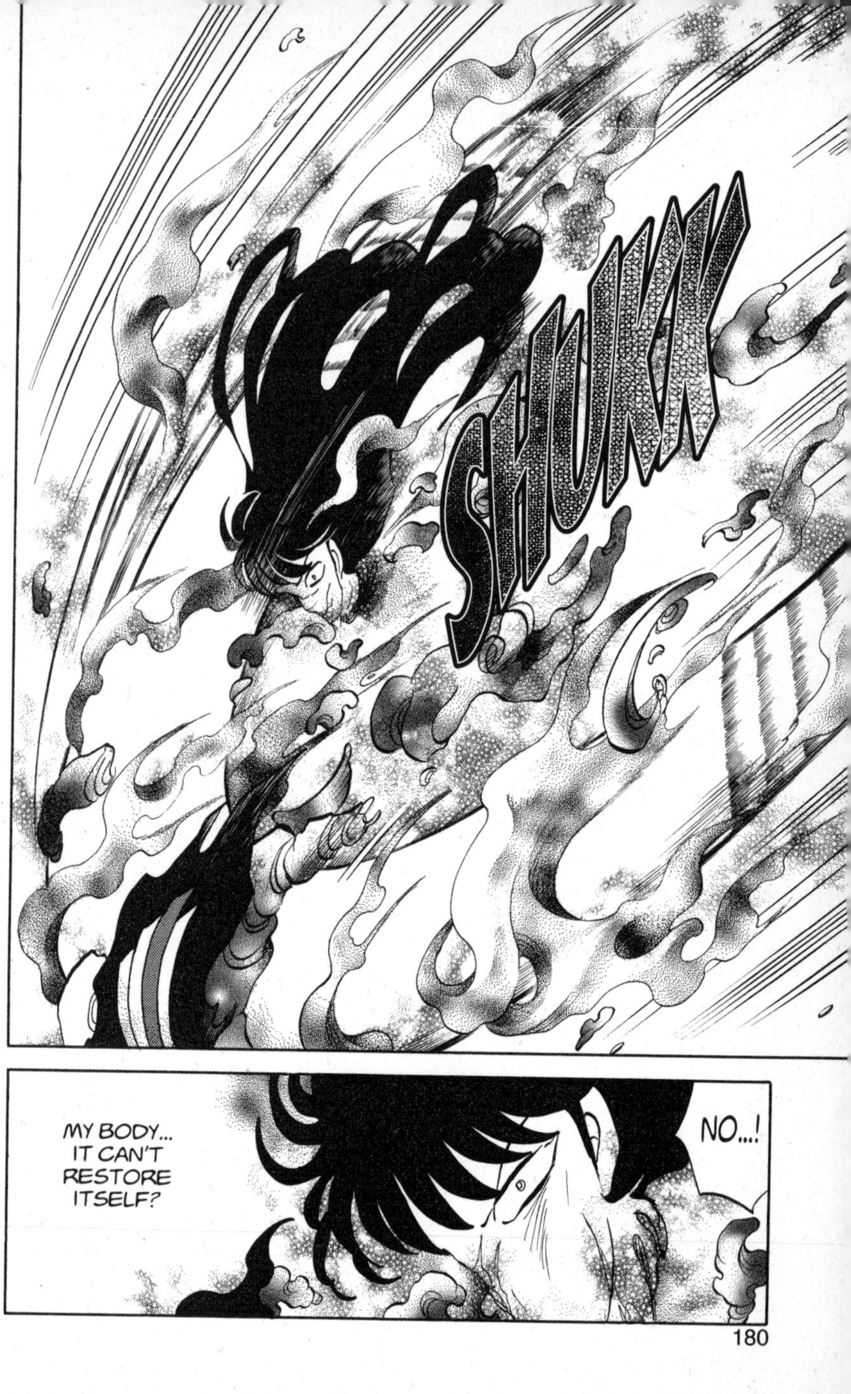
SHUKK
NO...!
MY BODY... IT CAN'T RESTORE ITSELF?

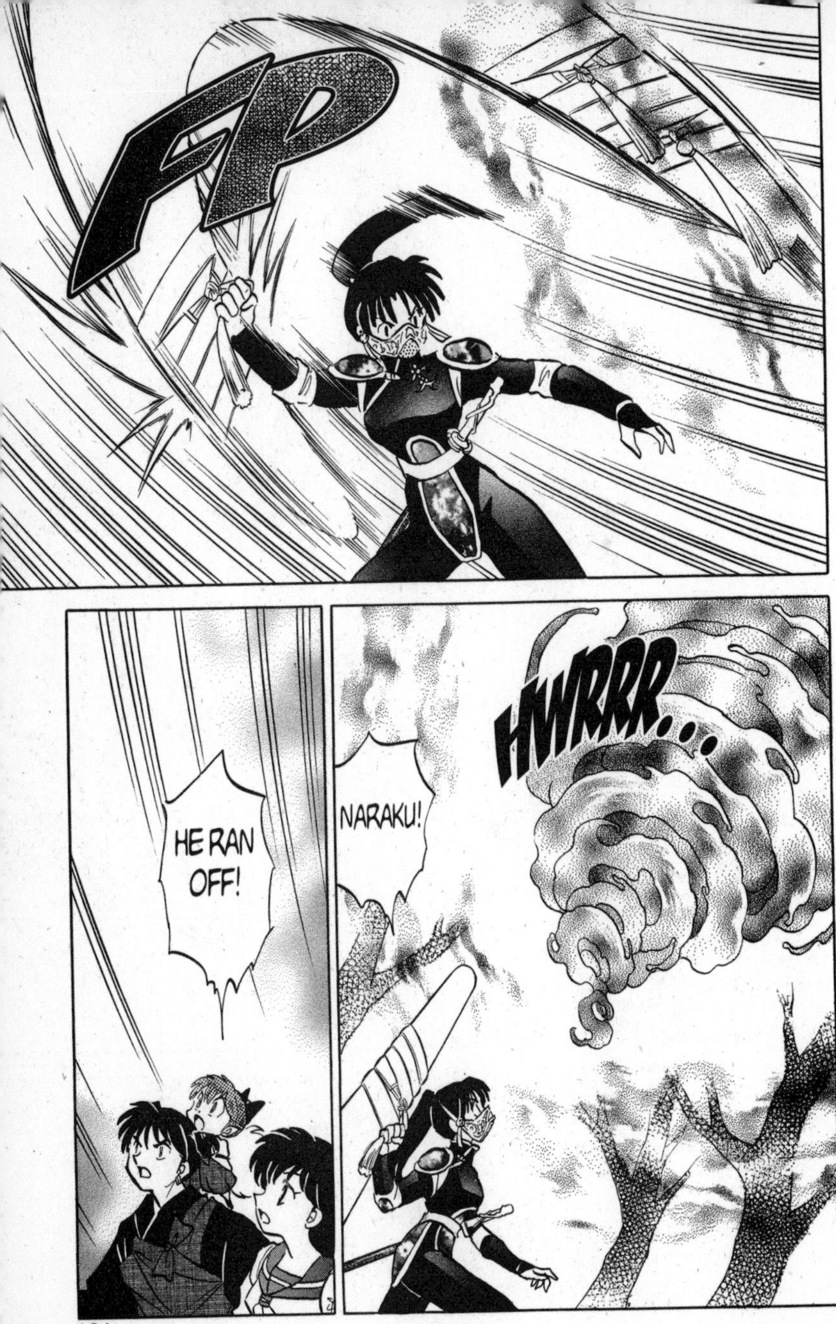
FP
HWRRR...
NARAKU!
HE RAN OFF!

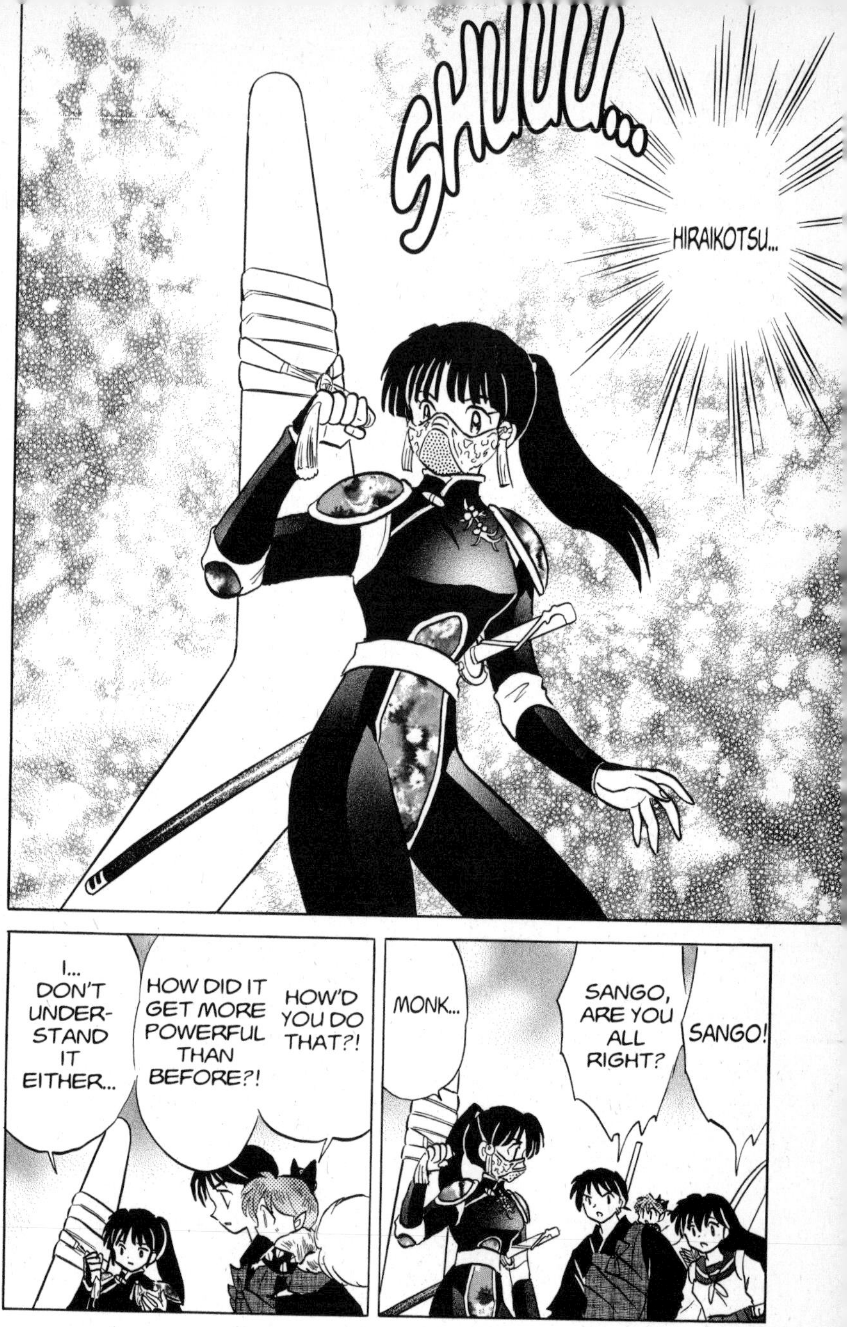
SHUUU...
HIRAIKOTSU...
SANGO!
SANGO, ARE YOU ALL RIGHT?
MONK...
HOW'D YOU DO THAT?!
HOW DID IT GET MORE POWERFUL THAN BEFORE?!
I... DON'T UNDER-STAND IT EITHER...

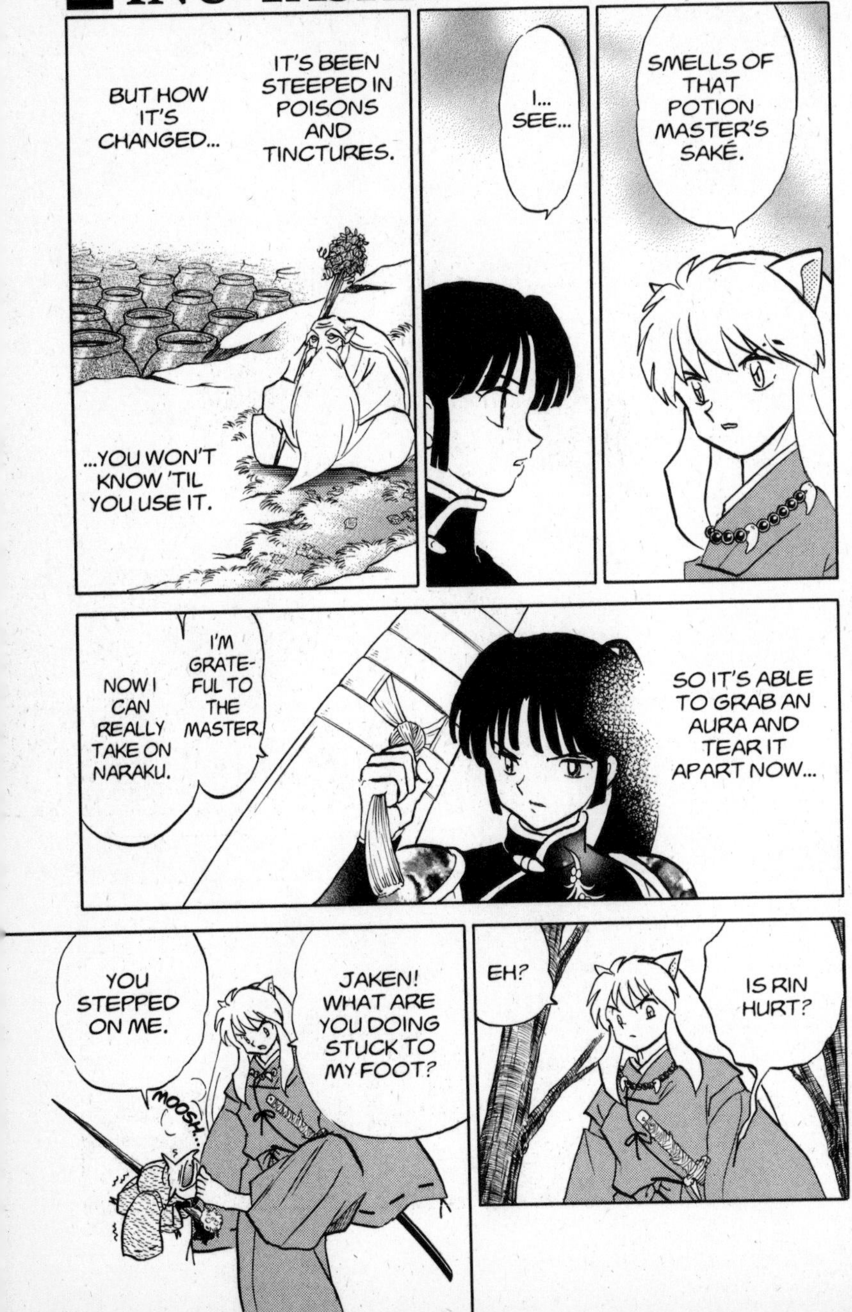
SMELLS OF THAT POTION MASTER'S SAKÉ.
I... SEE...
IT'S BEEN STEEPED IN POISONS AND TINCTURES.
BUT HOW IT'S CHANGED...
...YOU WON'T KNOW 'TIL YOU USE IT.
SO IT'S ABLE TO GRAB AN AURA AND TEAR IT APART NOW...
I'M GRATE-FUL TO THE MASTER.
NOW I CAN REALLY TAKE ON NARAKU.
IS RIN HURT?
EH?
JAKEN! WHAT ARE YOU DOING STUCK TO MY FOOT?
YOU STEPPED ON ME.
MOOSH...

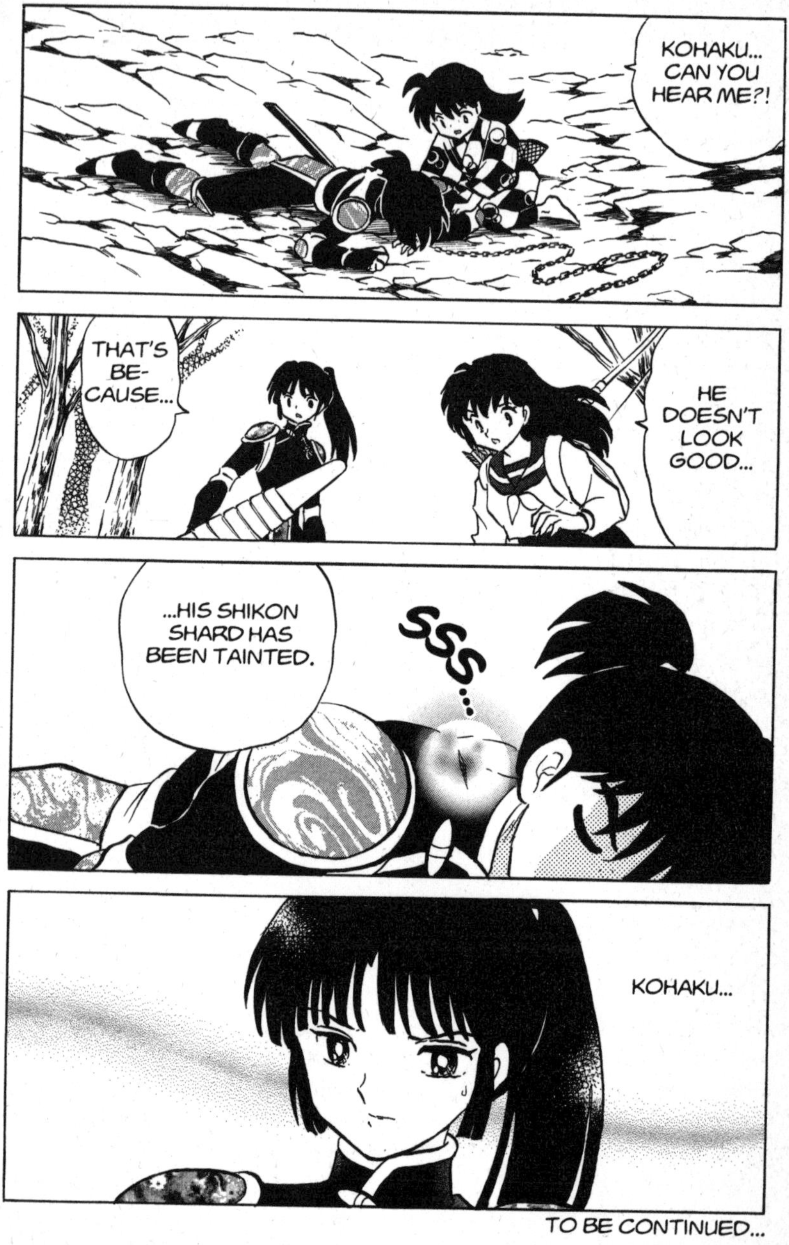
KOHAKU... CAN YOU HEAR ME?!
HE DOESN'T LOOK GOOD...
THAT'S BE-CAUSE...
...HIS SHIKON SHARD HAS BEEN TAINTED.
SSS...
KOHAKU...

TO BE CONTINUED...

INUYASHA

VOL. 50

Shonen Sunday Edition

Story and Art by
RUMIKO TAKAHASHI

© 1997 Rumiko TAKAHASHI/Shogakukan
All rights reserved.
Original Japanese edition "INUYASHA"
published by SHOGAKUKAN Inc.

English Adaptation by Gerard Jones

Translation/Mari Morimoto
Touch-up Art & Lettering/Bill Schuch
Cover & Interior Graphic Design/Yuki Ameda
Editor/Annette Roman

VP, Production/Alvin Lu
VP, Sales & Product Marketing/Gonzalo Ferreyra
VP, Creative/Linda Espinosa
Publisher/Hyoe Narita

Printed in the U.S.A.

Published by VIZ Media, LLC
P.O. Box 77010
San Francisco, CA 94107

10 9 8 7 6 5 4 3 2 1
First printing, July 2010

www.viz.com   WWW.SHONENSUNDAY.COM

TV SERIES & MOVIES ON DVD!

See more of the action in *Inuyasha* full-length movies

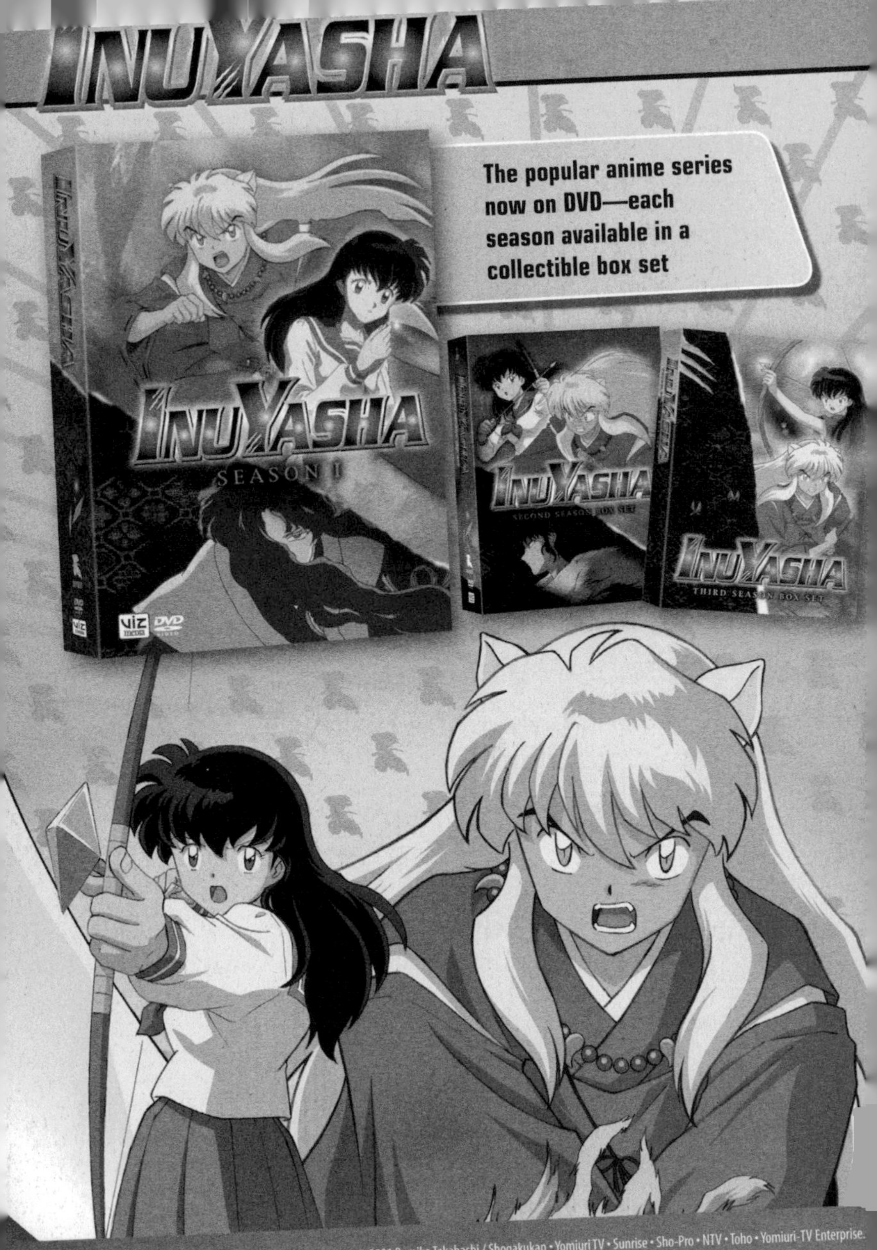
INUYASHA
The popular anime series now on DVD—each season available in a collectible box set
INUYASHA
SEASON 1
INUYASHA
SECOND SEASON BOX SET
INUYASHA
THIRD SEASON BOX SET

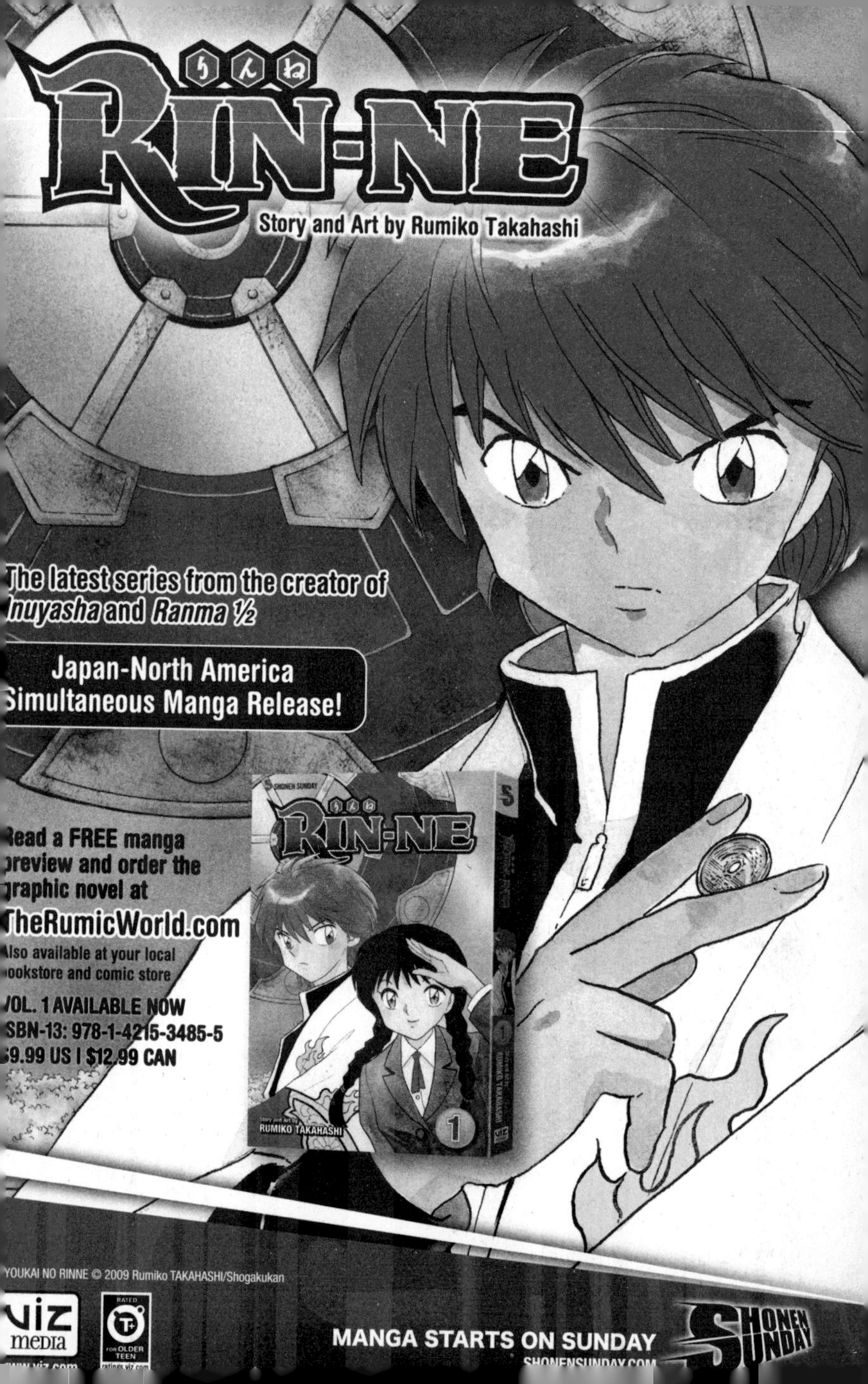
りんね
RIN-NE
Story and Art by Rumiko Takahashi
The latest series from the creator of Inuyasha and Ranma ½
Japan-North America Simultaneous Manga Release!
SHONEN SUNDAY
RIN-NE
Story and Art by RUMIKO TAKAHASHI
1
Read a FREE manga preview and order the graphic novel at
TheRumicWorld.com
Also available at your local bookstore and comic store
VOL. 1 AVAILABLE NOW
ISBN-13: 978-1-4215-3485-5
$9.99 US | $12.99 CAN
YOUKAI NO RINNE © 2009 Rumiko TAKAHASHI/Shogakukan
viz media
RATED T+ FOR OLDER TEEN
ratings.viz.com
MANGA STARTS ON SUNDAY
SHONENSUNDAY.COM
SHONEN SUNDAY

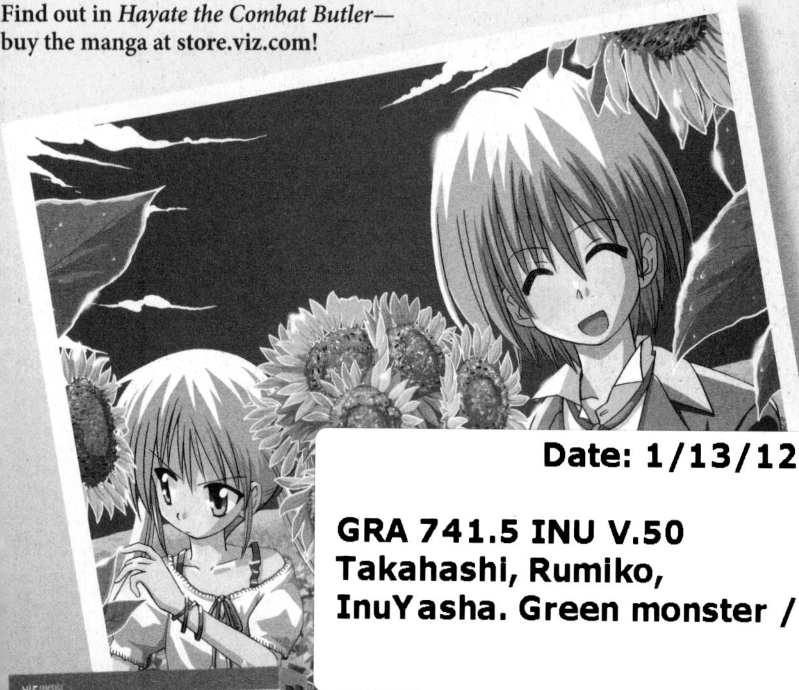

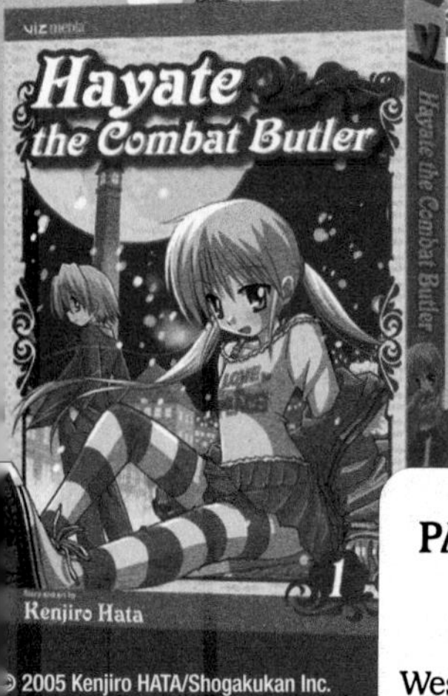
Hayate the Combat Butler
Hayate the Combat Butler
1
Kenjiro Hata

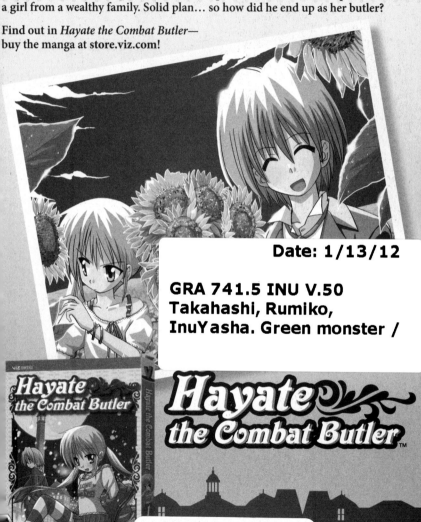

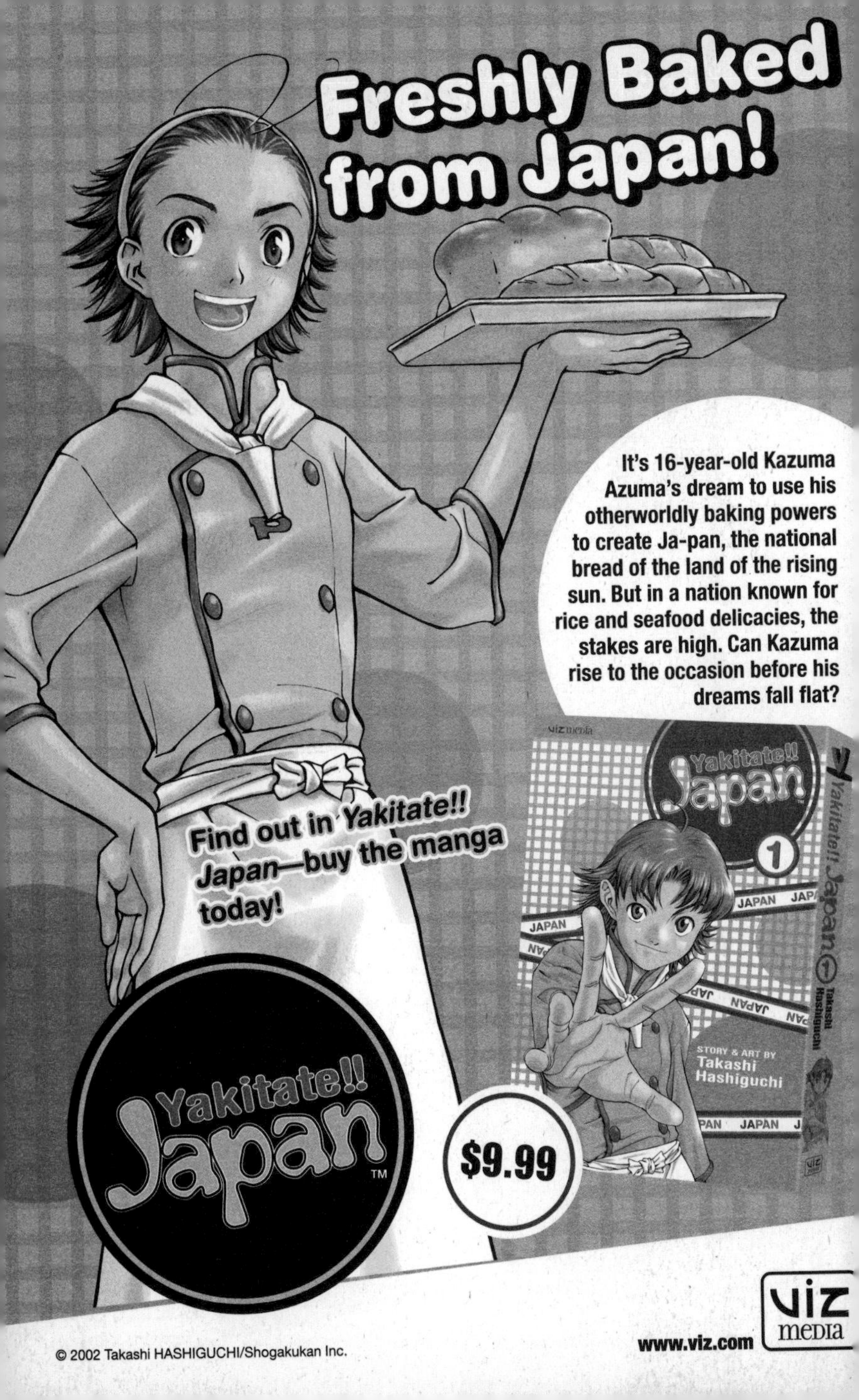
Freshly Baked from Japan!
It's 16-year-old Kazuma Azuma's dream to use his otherworldly baking powers to create Ja-pan, the national bread of the land of the rising sun. But in a nation known for rice and seafood delicacies, the stakes are high. Can Kazuma rise to the occasion before his dreams fall flat?
Find out in Yakitate!! Japan—buy the manga today!
Yakitate!! Japan™
$9.99
Yakitate!! Japan 1
STORY & ART BY Takashi Hashiguchi
www.viz.com
VIZ MEDIA
© 2002 Takashi HASHIGUCHI/Shogakukan Inc.